iPhone Programming
THE BIG NERD RANCH GUIDE

JOE CONWAY & AARON HILLEGASS

BiG
nerd
ranch

iPhone Programming: The Big Nerd Ranch Guide

by Joe Conway and Aaron Hillegass

Big Nerd Ranch, Inc.
1963 Hosea L. Williams Drive SE
Suite 209
Atlanta, GA 30317
(404) 478-9005
http://www.bignerdranch.com/
book-comments@bignerdranch.com

The 10-gallon hat with propeller logo is a trademark of Big Nerd Ranch, Inc.

Exclusive worldwide distribution of the English edition of this book by

Pearson Technology Group
800 East 96th Street
Indianapolis, IN 46240 USA
http://www.informit.com

ISBN-13 978-0321706249
ISBN-10 0321706242

Library of Congress Control Number: 2010903421

Second printing, August 2010

Acknowledgements

While our names appear on the cover, many people helped make this book a reality. We would like to take this chance to thank them.

- The other instructors who teach the iPhone Bootcamp fed us with a never-ending stream of suggestions and corrections. They are Scott Ritchie, Brian Hardy, and Alex von Below.

- Our tireless editor, Susan Loper, took our distracted mumblings and made them into readable prose.

- Several technical reviewers helped us find and fix flaws. They are Bill Monk, Mark Miller, Alex Silverman, Jonathan Saggau, and Mikey Ward.

- Ellie Volckhausen designed the cover. (The photo is of the bottom bracket of a bicycle frame.)

- The amazing team at Pearson Technology Group patiently guided us through the business end of book publishing.

The final and most important thanks goes to our students whose questions inspired us to write this book and whose frustrations inspired us to make it clear and comprehensible.

Table of Contents

Introduction

An aspiring iPhone developer faces three basic hurdles:

- *You must learn the Objective-C language.* Objective-C is a small and simple extension to the C language. After the first four chapters of this book, you will have a working knowledge of Objective-C.

- *You must master the big ideas.* These include things like memory management techniques, delegation, archiving, and the proper use of view controllers. The big ideas take a few days to understand. When you reach the halfway point of this book, you will understand these big ideas.

- *You must master the frameworks.* The eventual goal is to know how to use every method of every class in every framework on the iPhone. This is a project for a lifetime: there are over 3000 methods and more than 200 classes available for the iPhone. To make things even worse, Apple adds new classes and new methods with every release of the iPhone OS. In this book, you will be introduced to each of the subsystems that make up the iPhone SDK, but we will not study each one deeply. Instead, our goal is get you to the point where you can search and understand Apple's reference documentation.

We have used this material many times at our iPhone Development Bootcamp at Big Nerd Ranch. It is well-tested and has helped hundreds of people become iPhone application developers. We sincerely hope that it proves useful to you.

Prerequisites

This book assumes that you are already motivated to learn to write iPhone apps. We won't spend any time convincing you that the iPhone is a compelling piece of technology.

We also assume that you know the C programming language and something about object-oriented programming. If this is not true, you should probably start with an introductory book on C and Objective-C. We recommend Kochan's *Programming in Objective-C*.

Our Teaching Philosophy

This book is based on our iPhone Development Bootcamp course. It will teach you the essential concepts of iPhone programming. At the same time, you'll type in a lot of code and build a bunch of applications. By the end of the book, you'll have knowledge *and* experience. However, all the knowledge shouldn't (and, in this book, won't) come first. That's sort of the traditional way we've all come to know and hate. Instead, we take a learn-while-doing approach. Development concepts and actual coding go together.

Here's what we've learned over the years of teaching iPhone programming:

- We've learned what ideas people must have to get started programming, and we focus on that subset.

- We've learned that people learn best when these concepts are introduced *as they are needed*.

- We've learned that programming knowledge and experience grow best when they grow together.

- We've learned that "going through the motions" is much more important than it sounds. Many times we'll ask you to start typing in code before you understand it. We get that you may feel like a trained monkey typing in a bunch of code that you don't fully grasp. But the best way to learn coding is to find and fix your typos. Far from being a drag, this basic debugging is where you really learn the ins and outs of the code. That's why we encourage you to type in the code yourself. You could just download it, but copying and pasting is not programming. We want better for you and your skills.

What does this mean for you, the reader? To learn this way takes some trust. And we appreciate yours. It also takes patience. As we lead you through these chapters, we will try to keep you comfortable and tell you what's happening. However, there will be times when you'll have to take our word for it. (If you think this will bug you, keep reading — we've got some ideas that might help.) Don't get discouraged if you run across a concept that you don't understand right away. Remember that we're intentionally *not* providing all the knowledge you will ever need all at once. If a concept seems unclear, we will likely discuss it in more detail later when it becomes necessary. And some things that aren't clear at the beginning will suddenly make sense when you implement them the first (or the twelfth) time.

People learn differently. It's possible that you will love how we hand out concepts on an as-needed basis. It's also possible that you'll find it frustrating. In case of the latter, here are some options:

- Take a deep breath and wait it out. We'll get there, and so will you.

- Check the index. We'll let it slide if you look ahead and read through a more advanced discussion that occurs later in the book.

- Check the online Apple documentation. This is an essential developer tool, and you'll want plenty of practice using it. Consult it early and often.

- If it's Objective-C or object-oriented programming concepts that are giving you a hard time (or if you think they will), try Kochan's *Programming in Objective-C*. It's a great book that presents these concepts in a more traditional way.

How To Use This Book

This book is based on the class we teach at Big Nerd Ranch. As such, it was designed to be consumed in a certain manner.

Set yourself a reasonable goal, like "I will do one chapter every day." When you sit down to attack a chapter, find a quiet place where you won't be interrupted for at least an hour. Shut down your email, your Twitter client, and your chat program. This is not a time for multi-tasking; you will need to concentrate.

Do the actual programming. You can read through a chapter first, if you'd like. But the real learning comes when you sit down and code as you go. You will not really understand the idea until you have written a program that uses it and, perhaps more importantly, debugged that program.

A couple of the exercises require supporting files. For example, the SQLite exercise is a lot more fun if you have some data to browse. Thus, we have made a script that inserts data into a SQLite file. You can download these resources and solutions to the exercises from `http://www.bignerdranch.com/solutions/iPhoneProgramming.zip`.

There are two types of learning. When you learn about the Civil War, you are simply adding details to a scaffolding of ideas that you already understand. This is what we will call "Easy Learning". Yes, learning about the Civil War can take a long time, but you are seldom flummoxed by it. Learning iPhone programming, on the other hand, is "Hard Learning," and you may find yourself quite baffled at times, especially in the first few days. In writing this book, we have tried to create an experience that will ease you over the bumps in the learning curve. Here are two things you can do to make the journey easier:

- Find someone who already knows iPhone programming and will answer your questions. In particular, getting your application onto the device the first time is usually very frustrating if you are doing it without the help of an experienced developer.

- Get enough sleep. Sleepy people don't remember what they have learned.

How This Book Is Organized

In this book, each chapter addresses one or more ideas of iPhone development followed by hands-on practice. For more coding practice, we issue challenges towards the end of each chapter. We encourage you to take on at least some of these. They are excellent for firming up the concepts introduced in the chapter and making you a more confident iPhone programmer. Finally, most chapters conclude with one or two "For the More Curious" sections that explain certain consequences of the concepts that were introduced earlier.

Chapter 1 introduces you to iPhone programming as you build and deploy a tiny application. You'll get your feet wet with Xcode, Interface Builder, and the iPhone simulator along with all the steps for creating projects and files. The chapter includes a discussion of Model-View-Controller and how it relates to iPhone development.

Chapters 2 and 3 provide an overview of Objective-C and memory management. Although you won't create an iPhone application in these two chapters, you will build and debug a tool called RandomPossessions to ground you in these concepts. (You will reuse this tool and its related class in the Homepwner application introduced in Chapter 10.)

In Chapters 4 and 5, you will learn about the Core Location and MapKit frameworks and create a mapping application called Whereami. You will also get plenty of experience with the important design pattern of delegation and working with protocols, frameworks, and object diagrams.

Chapters 6 and 7 focus on the iPhone user interface with the Hypnosister and HypnoTime applications. You will get lots of practice working with views and view controllers as well as implementing scrolling, zooming, paging, and navigating between screens.

Chapter 8 covers the iPhone's accelerometer. You will learn how to obtain, filter, and use the data from the accelerometer to handle motion events, including shakes. You will use accelerometer data to add a new feature to the HypnoTime application.

In Chapter 9, you will create a smaller application named HeavyRotation while learning about **UIDevice** notifications and how to implement autorotation in an application.

Chapter 10 introduces the largest application in the book — Homepwner. (By the way, "Homepwner" is not a typo; you can find the definition of "pwn" at www.urbandictionary.com.) This application keeps a record of your possessions in case of fire or another catastrophe. Homepwner will take nine chapters total to complete.

In Chapters 10, 11, and 16, you will build experience developing tables on the iPhone. You will learn about table views, their view controllers, and their data sources. You will learn how to display data in a table, how to allow the user to edit the table, and how to improve the interface.

Chapter 12 builds on the navigation experience gained in Chapter 7. You will learn how to use **UINavigationController**, and you will give Homepwner a drill-down interface and a navigation bar.

In Chapter 13, you'll learn how to take pictures with the iPhone's camera and how to display and store images in Homepwner. You'll use **NSDictionary** and **UIImagePickerController**. You'll also learn about **UIPopoverController** for the iPad.

Chapter 14 delves into ways to save and load data. In particular, you will archive data in the Homepwner application using the NSCoding protocol. The chapter also shows you how to work with multitasking and transistions between application states, such as active, background, and suspended.

Chapter 15 teaches you how to prepare for low-memory warnings and leads you through handling low-memory warnings in Homepwner.

In Chapter 17, you'll take a break from Homepwner and create a drawing application named TouchTracker. You'll learn how to add multi-touch capability and more about touch events. You'll also get experience with the first responder and responder chain concepts and more practice with **NSDictionary**. In addition, you'll learn about the Instruments application while debugging performance and memory issues in TouchTracker.

Chapters 18 and 19 introduce layers and the Core Animation framework with a brief return to the HypnoTime application to implement animations. You will learn about implicit and explicit animations and animation objects, like **CABasicAnimation** and **CAKeyFrameAnimation**.

Chapter 20 will teach you how to play audio and video as you build an application called MediaPlayer. You will learn about playing audio and video on the iPhone, where to keep these resources, streaming limits, and the low-level audio API. You will also enable MediaPlayer to play music while in the background state and learn guidelines and other uses for background execution.

Chapter 21 ventures into the wide world of web services. You will fetch and parse XML data from the iTunes server in an application you create named TopSongs. You'll use **NSURLConnection** and **NSXMLParser** along the way.

In Chapter 22, you'll return to Homepwner to learn about the iPhone's Address Book functions and the People Picker as you update Homepwner to allow the user to assign people to inherit possessions.

Chapter 23 introduces the concepts and techniques of internationalization and localization. You will learn about **NSLocale**, strings tables, and **NSBundle** as you localize Homepwner.

Chapter 24 teaches you how to publish a service on the peer-to-peer network Bonjour. You will start a new application named Nayberz that advertises itself on the network.

Chapter 25 explores how to get an application to work with the iPhone's Settings application to create application settings and preferences that the user can customize. You will use **NSUserDefaults** and give Nayberz a pane in Settings.

Chapter 26 introduces the SQLite library for storing and fetching data on the iPhone. You get a chance to practice with a small data application named Nayshunz.

Chapter 27 gives you a good grounding in using Core Data to store and access data in an iPhone application. In this chapter, you will build a complex and business-like application named Inventory.

Chapter 28 introduces the iPad and some of its features, like **UIGestureRecognizer** and Core Text. You will turn the Whereami application into a universal application, enabling it to run natively on the iPad and the iPhone.

It is important to note something that is not covered in this book: OpenGL ES. We actually wrote a chapter. And then we rewrote it. And rewrote it. And rewrote it. It got longer with every pass. Thus, we've decided to take that chapter and expand it into a separate book.

Style Choices

This book contains a lot of code. We have attempted to make that code and the designs behind it exemplary. We have done our best to follow the idioms of the community, but at times we have wandered from what you might see in Apple's sample code or code you might find in other books. You may not understand these points now, but it is best that we spell them out before you commit to reading this book:

- There is an alternative syntax for calling accessor methods known as *dot-notation*. In this book, we will explain dot-notation, but we will not use it. For us and most beginners, dot-notation tends to obfuscate what is really happening.

- In our subclasses of **UIViewController**, we always change the designated initializer to **init**. It is our opinion that the creator of the instance should not need to know the name of the NIB file that the view controller uses, or even if it has a NIB file at all.

- We will always create view controllers programmatically. Some programmers will instantiate view controllers inside XIB files. We've found this practice leads to projects that are difficult to comprehend and debug.

- We will nearly always start a project with the simplest template project: the window-based application. The boilerplate code in the other template projects doesn't follow the rules that precede this one, so we think they make a poor basis upon which to build.

We believe that following these rules makes our code easier to understand and easier to maintain. After you have worked through this book (where you *will* do it our way), you should try breaking the rules to see if we're wrong.

Typographical Conventions

To make this book easier to read, certain items appear in certain fonts. Class names, method names, and function names appear in a bold, fixed-width font. Class names start with capital letters, and method names start with lowercase letters. In this book, method and function names will be formatted the same for simplicity's sake. For example, "In the **loadView** method of the **RexViewController** class, use the **NSLog** function to print the value to the console."

Variables, constants, and types appear in a fixed-width font but are not bold. So you'll see, "The variable `fido` will be of type `float`. Initialize it to `M_PI`."

Applications and menu choices appear in the Mac system font. For example, "Open XCode and select New Project... from the File menu."

All code blocks will be in a fixed-width font. Code that you need to type in is always bold. For example, in the following code, you would type in everything but the first and last lines. (Those lines are already in the code and appear here to let you know where to add the new stuff.)

```
@interface QuizAppDelegate : NSObject <UIApplicationDelegate> {
    int currentQuestionIndex;

    // The model objects
    NSMutableArray *questions;
    NSMutableArray *answers;

    // The view objects
    IBOutlet UILabel *questionField;
    IBOutlet UILabel *answerField;
    UIWindow *window;
}
```

Hardware, Software, and Deployment

To develop iPhone applications, you will need an Intel Mac running Mac OS X Leopard (or above). You will also need to download the iPhone SDK (Software Development Kit). The SDK includes Xcode (Apple's Integrated Development Environment), the iPhone simulator, and other development tools. To download the iPhone SDK, you only need to register as an iPhone Developer, which is free. As a "Registered iPhone Developer," you will be able to access the iPhone Dev Center (including the Development docs). Go to `http://developer.apple.com/iphone/program/download.html` to register. Make sure you have the USB cable that connects the device to the computer.

You can do a lot with just the simulator, but for more complete and realistic testing, you'll want to install your applications on a real device — an iPhone, iPad, or iPod touch. (Nearly everything in this book will apply to all three devices, but we will usually refer to the "iPhone." The iPad runs the same OS as the iPhone, and writing iPad applications uses the same techiniques with a few additions discussed in the final chapter. The iPod touch is nearly the same as the iPhone except for the telephone.) To install applications on your iPhone or to distribute them on the App Store, you have to join the "iPhone Developer Program," which costs $99/year. Go to `http://developer.apple.com/` to join.

Excited yet? Good. Let's get started.

1

A Simple iPhone Application

In this chapter, you are going to write your first iPhone application. You probably won't understand everything that you are doing, and you may feel stupid just going through the motions. But going through the motions is enough for now. Mimicry is a powerful form of learning; it is how you learned to speak, and it is how you will start to do iPhone programming. As you become more capable, you can experiment and challenge yourself to do creative things on the platform. For now, just do what we show you. The details will be explained in later chapters.

When you are writing an iPhone application, you must answer two basic questions:

- How do I get my objects created and configured properly? (Example: "I want a button here entitled Show Estimate.")

- How do I deal with user interaction? (Example: "When the user presses the button, I want this piece of code to be executed.")

Most of this book is dedicated to answering these questions.

When an iPhone application starts, it puts a *window* on the screen. You can think of the window as the canvas on which everything else appears: buttons, labels, etc. Anything that can appear on the window is a *view*.

The iPhone SDK is an object-oriented library, and the window and views are represented by objects. The window is an instance of the class **UIWindow**. Each view is an instance of one of several subclasses of **UIView**. For example, a button is an instance of **UIButton**, which inherits from **UIView**.

Views can be placed on a window in two different ways:

- by creating views and controls programmatically and adding them to the **UIWindow**

- by using Interface Builder to visually lay out views

In this chapter, you will use Interface Builder to visually lay out the views and build the user interface for your first iPhone application, Quiz (Figure 1.1).

Figure 1.1   Your first application

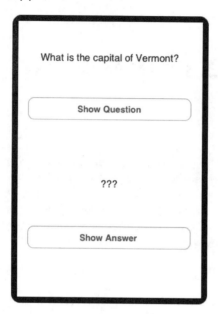

Creating an Xcode Project

Open Xcode and select New Project... from the File menu. A window will appear giving you several application templates to choose from. Create a barebones Cocoa Touch application by selecting the Window-Based Application icon (Figure 1.2). Click the Choose... button. A sheet will drop down and ask you to name this new project. Save it as "Quiz."

Figure 1.2   Creating a new project

Once the project is created, the project window will appear on your screen (Figure 1.3). Take a look at the contents of the Groups and Files table on the lefthand side of the project window. Overall, there are two kinds of files used to create an application: code and resources. Code is written in Objective-C, C, or C++, and the code files are listed in the Classes and Other Sources groups. Resources are things like images and sounds that are used by the application at runtime. The groups in the project window are purely for the organization of files. You can rename them whatever you want.

Figure 1.3   Xcode project window

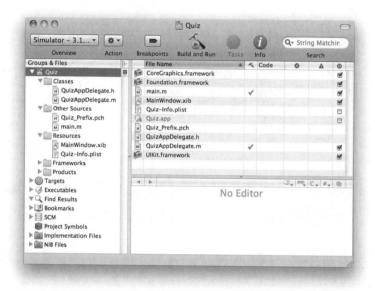

Inside the Resources group, you'll find two files: MainWindow.xib and Quiz-Info.plist. The Info property list (Quiz-Info.plist) contains a list of key-value pairs. The values in this list specify things like the icon to display on the home screen, whether the application needs a persistent Wi-Fi connection, and the default language of the application.

The MainWindow.xib file contains the interface for your application. Double-click on MainWindow.xib to open it in Interface Builder.

Using Interface Builder

At the simplest level, Interface Builder is a GUI builder. Most GUI builders let the developer describe what they want the application to look like. Then the developer presses a button, and the builder generates reams upon reams of code. Interface Builder, however, is an object editor: the developer creates and configures objects and then saves them into an archive. This archive is a XIB (pronounced "zib") or a NIB file. A XIB file is an XML representation of your objects and their instance variables, and it is compiled into a NIB file when your application is built. The XIB file is easier to work with, but the NIB file is smaller and easier to parse, which is why the file that actually ships with your application is a NIB.

When you build your application, the NIB file is copied into the application's bundle. (An iPhone application is really a directory containing the executable and any resources the executable uses. We refer to this directory as a *bundle*.) When your application reads in the NIB file, all of the objects in the archive are brought back to life. This particular application has only one NIB file created from MainWindow.xib, but a complex application can have many NIB files that are read in as they are needed.

Once Interface Builder starts up, you will see several windows, as shown in Figure 1.4.

Figure 1.4 Windows in Interface Builder

In Figure 1.4, find the window with the title bar that reads MainWindow.xib. We call this window the "doc window," and it represents the open XIB file. The doc window contains four objects:

File's Owner	An instance of **UIApplication**. The event queue for your application is managed by this object.
First Responder	This object doesn't have much of a use on the iPhone right now; it is more of a relic from Desktop Cocoa. You can ignore it.
QuizAppDelegate	An instance of **QuizAppDelegate**, a subclass of **NSObject** that was created by Xcode specifically for this project. You will be editing the source code for this class.
Window	An instance of **UIWindow** that represents this application's only window. (All iPhone applications have only one window.)

The Library and the Inspector are two tools you will use all the time, so leave those windows open. (If these windows are not visible, select them from the Tools menu.) You drag objects from the Library to create new instances in your XIB file. You use the Inspector to "inspect" and edit the configuration of objects in the XIB file. The Inspector has four panels: Attributes, Connections, Size, and Info represented by the icons at the top of the frame. You'll be using the Attributes and the Connections panels in this chapter.

In the doc window, double-click on the **UIWindow** object to make it appear full-sized. (Feel free to close and re-open that window. Sometimes beginners close the window and fear that they have deleted it.)

From the Library, drag two instances of **UILabel** onto the window. Make the labels nearly as wide as the window (Figure 1.5). Then, drag two instances of **UIButton** onto the window. You can change the text an object displays by double-clicking it. Set the text for one button to Show Question and the other to Show Answer.

Figure 1.5   Adding buttons and labels to the window

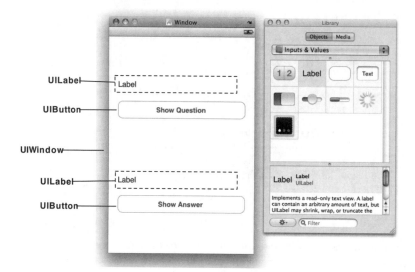

Objects have instance variables, and many of these can be set in the Inspector. As an example, you are going to center the text in the **UILabel** objects. Select a **UILabel**. In the Attributes panel of the Inspector, you will see the options for Alignment. Select the option that centers the text, as shown in Figure 1.6.

Figure 1.6   Centering the label text

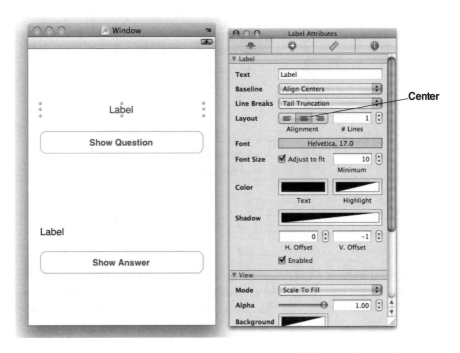

Now center the text in the other label.

Model-View-Controller

You will hear iPhone programmers speak of the "Model-View-Controller pattern." What that means is every object you create will be exactly one of the following: a model object, a view object, or a controller object.

View objects are visible to the user; the button, the label, and the window are all view objects. The views are often standard `UIView` subclasses (`UIButton`, `UISlider`), but you will sometimes write custom view classes. These typically have names like `DangerMeterView` or `IncomeGraphView`.

Model objects hold data and should know nothing about the user interface. In this application, the model objects will be two arrays of strings: the questions array and the answers array. Figure 1.7 displays the object diagram of the Quiz app's model objects.

Figure 1.7   Diagram of model objects in Quiz

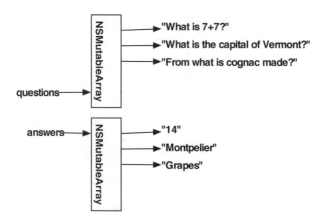

Model objects typically use standard collection classes (**NSArray**, **NSDictionary**, **NSSet**) and standard value types (**NSString**, **NSDate**, **NSNumber**). But there can be custom classes, which typically have names that sound like data-bearing objects like **InsurancePolicy** or **PlayerHistory**.

Controller objects keep the view and model objects in sync, control the "flow" of the application, and save the model objects out to the filesystem. Controllers are the least reusable classes that you will write, and they tend to have names like **ScheduleController** and **ScoreViewController**. When you create a new iPhone project from a template, as you did at the beginning of this chapter, the template will automatically give you a controller object called **BlahAppDelegate**, where Blah is the name of your application.

The controller for your application is the instance of **QuizAppDelegate**. Pressing one of the application's buttons will trigger a method in that object. The instance of **QuizAppDelegate** will have pointers to the questions and answers arrays. It will use those model objects to update the button label. These interactions are laid out in the object diagram for Quiz (Figure 1.8).

Figure 1.8   Object diagram for Quiz

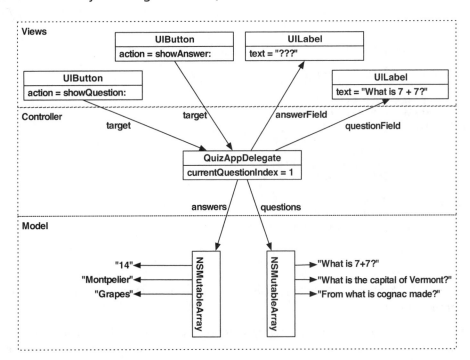

Declarations

To pull all this off, **QuizAppDelegate** will need five instance variables and two methods. In this section, you will declare them in the header file QuizAppDelegate.h

Declaring instance variables

Here are the five instance variables **QuizAppDelegate** needs:

questions	a pointer to an **NSMutableArray** containing instances of **NSString**
answers	a pointer to another **NSMutableArray** containing instances of **NSString**
currentQuestionIndex	an int that holds the index of the current question in the questions array
questionField	a pointer to the **UILabel** object where the current question will be displayed
answerField	a pointer to the **UILabel** object where the current answer will be displayed

Back in Xcode, take a look at the header file `QuizAppDelegate.h`. Inside the curly braces, add declarations for five instance variables. (Notice the bold type? In this book, code that you need to type in is always bold; the code that's not bold is there to tell you where to type in the new stuff.)

```
@interface QuizAppDelegate : NSObject <UIApplicationDelegate>
{
    int currentQuestionIndex;

    // The model objects
    NSMutableArray *questions;
    NSMutableArray *answers;

    // The view objects
    IBOutlet UILabel *questionField;
    IBOutlet UILabel *answerField;

    UIWindow *window;
}
@property (nonatomic, retain) IBOutlet UIWindow *window;

@end
```

(Scary syntax? Feelings of dismay? Don't worry: you will learn the Objective-C language in the next chapter. For now, just keep going.)

In Interface Builder, you will see items referred to as "Outlets." An outlet is a pointer that you can set in Interface Builder. (We'll see how in just a moment.) In this header file, we used the macro `IBOutlet`, which is predefined in the Cocoa Touch frameworks, to explicitly mark these pointers as outlets that can be set in Interface Builder.

Declaring methods

Each of the buttons needs to trigger a method. A method is a lot like a function – a list of instructions to be executed. Declare two methods in `QuizAppDelegate.h` after the closing curly brace and the line containing `@property`. (We will talk about `@property` later in the book; you can ignore it for now.)

```
@interface QuizAppDelegate : NSObject <UIApplicationDelegate>
{
    int currentQuestionIndex;

    // The model objects
    NSMutableArray *questions;
    NSMutableArray *answers;

    // The view objects
    IBOutlet UILabel *questionField;
    IBOutlet UILabel *answerField;
    UIWindow *window;
}
```

```
@property (nonatomic, retain) IBOutlet UIWindow *window;

- (IBAction)showQuestion:(id)sender;
- (IBAction)showAnswer:(id)sender;

@end
```

In Objective-C, instance variables are declared inside the curly braces, and methods are declared after the closing curly brace. Save QuizAppDelegate.h.

Making Connections

The views and the controller object that your application needs have been created, but they know nothing about each other. Now you need to introduce them to each other by making these connections:

- The controller object has two pointers that need to point to the **UILabel** objects.

- The **UIButton** objects need to be wired up to trigger the appropriate methods in the controller object.

Setting pointers

The instance of **QuizAppDelegate** has a pointer called questionField. Let's start by setting that to point to the instance of **UILabel** that is closest to the top of the window. In Interface Builder, Control-click or right-click on the **QuizAppDelegate** to bring up the connections panel (Figure 1.9). Then drag from the circle beside questionField to the **UILabel**.

Figure 1.9   Setting questionField

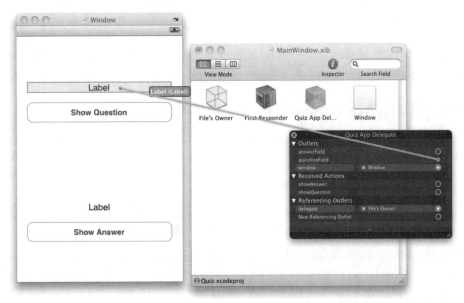

(If you do not see questionField here, double check your QuizAppDelegate.h file. Did you end each line with a semicolon? Has the file saved since you added questionField?)

When the NIB file is read in, the **QuizAppDelegate**'s questionField pointer will now automatically point to the instance of **UILabel**.

Now drag from the circle beside answerField to the other **UILabel** (Figure 1.10).

Figure 1.10   Setting answerField

Notice that you drag *from* the object with the pointer and *to* the object that you want that pointer to point at.

Setting targets and actions

UIButton is a subclass of **UIControl** (which is a subclass of **UIView**). A control sends a message to another object when it is activated. So the control needs answers to two questions: what's the action and who's the target? An *action* is the name of the method that is triggered by a control. The *target* is the object that is sent the message.

In the case of the Show Question button, the button is activated when the user touches it. The action the touch triggers is **showQuestion:**, and the target is **QuizAppDelegate**.

In Interface Builder, you set an object's target and action by Control-dragging from the control to its target. At that point, a pop-up menu appears that lets you choose an action. Control-drag (or right-drag) from the Show Question button to the **QuizAppDelegate**. Release the mouse button and choose **showQuestion:** from the pop-up menu as shown in Figure 1.11.

Figure 1.11   Setting Show Question target/action

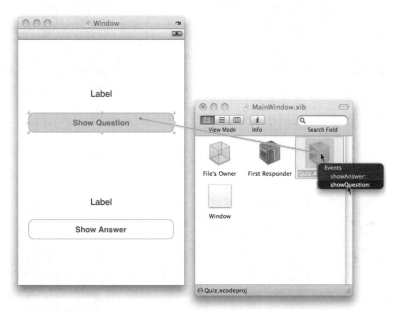

Now set the target and action of the Show Answer button. Control-drag from the button to the **QuizAppDelegate**. Choose **showAnswer:** from the pop-up menu (Figure 1.12). Notice that the choices in this menu are the actions you added to the header file.

Figure 1.12   Setting Show Answer target/action

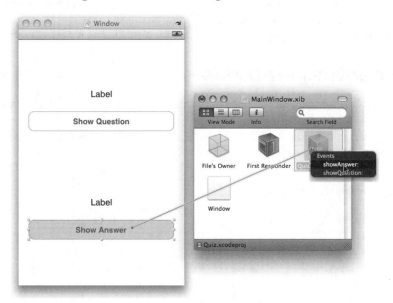

Summary of connections

There are now six connections between your **QuizAppDelegate** and other objects. You've set its pointers answerField and questionField. That's two. The **QuizAppDelegate** is the target for both buttons. That's four. And the template project had two additional connections. First, the **UIApplication** object (File's Owner in this XIB file) has a pointer called delegate which points at the **QuizAppDelegate**. Second, the window pointer of your **QuizAppDelegate** was set to the instance of **UIWindow**. That makes six. You can check all of these connections in the Connections panel of the Inspector shown in Figure 1.13.

Figure 1.13   Checking connections in the Inspector

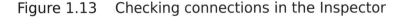

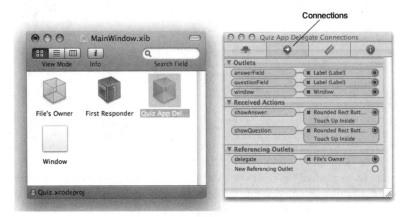

Your XIB file is complete. The view objects and the one controller object have been created. The views have been configured to look and act the way you wish. All the necessary connections have been made. Now it's time to write the methods. Save your XIB file and return to Xcode.

Implementing Methods

Methods and instance variables are declared in the header file (in this case, QuizAppDelegate.h), but the actual code for the methods is placed in the implementation file (in this case, QuizAppDelegate.m). In Xcode, open QuizAppDelegate.m. First, add an **init** method that creates the two arrays and fills them with some questions and answers.

```
@implementation QuizAppDelegate

@synthesize window;

- (id)init
{
    // Call the init method implemented by the superclass
    [super init];

    // Create two arrays and make the pointers point to them
```

```
    questions = [[NSMutableArray alloc] init];
    answers = [[NSMutableArray alloc] init];

    // Add questions and answers to the arrays
    [questions addObject:@"What is 7 + 7?"];
    [answers addObject:@"14"];

    [questions addObject:@"What is the capital of Vermont?"];
    [answers addObject:@"Montpelier"];

    [questions addObject:@"From what is cognac made?"];
    [answers addObject:@"Grapes"];

    // Return the address of the new object
    return self;
}
```

When an Objective-C object is created and memory is allocated for the object to live in, all its instance variables are zeroed. The **init** method is where the instance variables are given useable initial values.

After the **init** method, add the two action methods.

```
- (IBAction)showQuestion:(id)sender
{
    // Step to the next question - just to keep things simple
    // to focus on the iOS elements of the programming,
    // we will start with the "second" question in the list.
    currentQuestionIndex++;

    // Am I past the last question?
    if (currentQuestionIndex == [questions count]) {

        // Go back to the first question
        currentQuestionIndex = 0;
    }

    // Get the string at that index in the questions array
    NSString *question = [questions objectAtIndex:currentQuestionIndex];

    // Log the string to the console
    NSLog(@"displaying question: %@", question);

    // Display the string in the question field
    [questionField setText:question];

    // Clear the answer field
    [answerField setText:@"???"];
}

- (IBAction)showAnswer:(id)sender
{
    // What is the answer to the current question?
    NSString *answer = [answers objectAtIndex:currentQuestionIndex];

    // Display it in the answer field
    [answerField setText:answer];
}
```

You will use the default implementations for **dealloc** and **application:didFinishLaunchingWithOptions:**, so leave those alone.

Build and Run on the Simulator

Now you are ready to build the application and run it in the debugger. Use the Xcode keyboard shortcut for Build and Debug – Command-Y. If there are any errors or warnings, a Build Results window with a list of problems will open. Find and fix any problems (i.e., code typos!) and build and debug again. Repeat this process until your application compiles. (If you close the Build Results window, press Command-Shift-B or click on the Failed icon in the bottom right of the project window to get it back.) Once your application has compiled, it will launch in the iPhone simulator, and you will be able to test it. Note that the output from the log statements will appear in the debugger console window. To open this window, select Console from the Run menu. (Or hit Command-Shift-R.)

Event-driven Programming

When the application launches, it enters a loop as shown in Figure 1.14.

Figure 1.14   iPhone application event loop

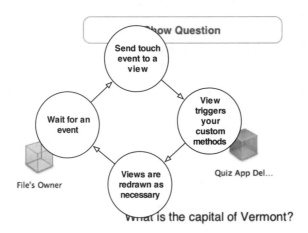

The **UIApplication** object waits around for an event. When the user touches the screen, the touch event is forwarded by the **UIApplication** object to the view that was touched. This is often a control (like a button) that then sends its action message to a controller. This triggers your custom code. Your code changes the state of a view, which redraws itself to reflect the new state.

In iPhone programming, the event loop drives everything. If you are used to a programming environment where you drive the application from a main function that calls other functions, the event loop may seem confusing. We will discuss the event loop in more detail in later chapters.

Deploying an Application

Now that you have finished writing the code for your first iPhone application and have run it on the simulator, it's time to deploy it to a device.

To install an application on your development device, you need a developer certificate from Apple. Developer certificates are issued to registered iPhone Developers who have paid the developer fee. This certificate grants you the ability to sign your code, allowing it to run on a device. Without a valid certificate, devices will not allow your application to run.

Apple's Developer Program Portal (`http://developer.apple.com/iphone/`) contains all the instructions and resources to get a valid certificate. The interface for the set-up process is continually being updated by Apple, so it would be fruitless to describe it in detail. However, a step-by-step guide, the Development Provisioning Assistant, is available on the program portal.

Work through the Development Provisioning Assistant, *paying careful attention to each screen*. At the end, you will have added the required certificates to Keychain Access and the mobile provision file to Xcode. You might be curious as to what exactly is going on here. In the provisioning process, there are four important items:

Developer Certificate
: This certificate file is added to your Mac's keychain using Keychain Access. It is used to digitally sign your code.

App ID
: The application identifier is a string that uniquely identifies your application on the App Store. Application identifiers typically look like this: `com.bignerdranch.AwesomeApp`, where the name of the application follows the name of your company. The App ID in your provisioning profile must match the *bundle identifier* of your application. A development profile, like you just created, can have a wildcard character for its App ID and therefore will match any Bundle Identifier. To see the bundle identifier for an application, open the `AppName-Info.plist` file in the Resources group of the project window.

Device ID (UDID)
: This identifier is unique for each iPhone OS device.

Provisioning Profile
: This is a file that lives on your development device and on your computer. It references a Developer Certificate, a single App ID, and a list of the device IDs for the devices that the application can be installed on. This file is suffixed with `mobileprovision`.

When an application is deployed to a device, Xcode uses a provisioning profile on your computer to access the appropriate certificate. This certificate is used to sign the application binary. Then, the development device's UDID is matched to one of the UDIDs contained within the provisioning profile, and the App ID is matched to the bundle identifier. This signed binary is then sent to your development device where it is confirmed by the provisioning profile on the device and launched.

Open Xcode and plug your development device (iPhone, iPod touch, or iPad) into your computer. This will automatically open the Organizer window, which can be re-opened by selecting Organizer from the Window menu. This window is useful for all things device-related.

To run the Quiz application on your device, you must tell Xcode that it should deploy to the device instead of the simulator. From the Project menu, mouse over the Set Active SDK menu item and select Device - iPhone OS 3.0 (Project Setting). Build and run your application (Command-Y), and it will appear on your device!

Application Icons

When the quiz application installs on your development device, its icon is a plain white tile. But don't worry – you're going to give Quiz a better icon.

For any iPhone application, the icon image must be a 57x57 pixel PNG file. You can download Icon.png (along with resources for other chapters) from http://www.bignerdranch.com/ solutions/iPhoneProgramming.zip to use as Quiz's icon. If you open this image, you'll notice that it isn't glossy and doesn't have rounded corners like other application icons; these effects are applied for you. Drag this file into the Resources group in the project window.

There are a couple of options for the application icon that can be set in Quiz-Info.plist, also located in the Resources group. If you want to use an icon filename other than the default Icon.png, you can set the value of the Icon file key within this file. Also, if you don't want the glossy effect added to the application icon, you can disable it here by adding the key UIPrerenderedIcon and setting its value to true. To add this key to the property list, select a row within the property list and click the plus button that appears on the righthand side. A new row will appear, and you can type UIPrerenderedIcon in the Key column or select Icon already includes gloss and bevel effects from the pop-up list.

In addition to the 57x57 pixel icon that appears on the home screen, you can also add a 512x512 pixel JPEG or PNG image to the Resources group named iTunesArtwork. This image will be shown to iTunes shoppers when viewing your application in iTunes. (You should create a richer and more detailed version of your icon for display in the iTunes Store. Users typically won't be impressed by a scaled-up, pixellated version of your home screen icon.)

Figure 1.15 The Info Property List

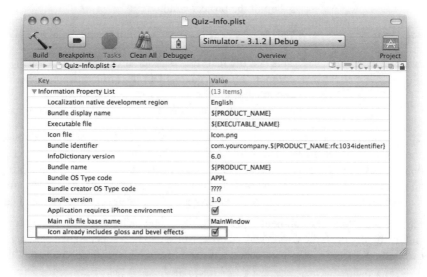

Build and run your application again. The Big Nerd Ranch logo will appear as the icon for Quiz.

Default Images

When launching an application, the code and resources (like MainWindow.xib) need to be loaded into memory. This takes time, and in the meantime all the user sees is a black screen. The iPhone is intended to create an interface that feels like a real object instead of a computer screen, and a delay while loading ruins this effect.

You can fix this problem by using a *default image*. A default image appears as the application is loading, and the name Default.png is reserved for it.

Typically, the default image is a screenshot of your application's user interface as it appears in its freshly opened state. This gives the user the illusion that the application loaded instantly. By the time the user touches the screen, your application will have seamlessly replaced the default image with the actual user interface. (Note that this screenshot is not typically a splash screen. A splash screen draws attention to the loading delay whereas a dummy image of the actual interface minimizes the user's experience of the delay.)

Xcode makes the process of creating and using a default image very easy. Open the Organizer window and select the Screenshots tab while your application is running on your connected device (Figure 1.16).

Figure 1.16   Setting Default.png in the Organizer

Press the Capture button. Xcode will save the image currently displayed on your development device's screen to the view on the left. Select that image and click Save as Default Image.... When you're prompted to add it to an application, add it to Quiz. The selected image is renamed Default.png and added to your project's resources. Run your application again, and the interface will pop up as soon as you touch the application icon.

Congratulations! You have written your first application and installed it on your device. Now it is time to dive into the big ideas that make it work.

2

Objective-C

iPhone applications are written in the Objective-C language, a simple extension of the C language. This book doesn't have enough pages to cover the entire C language. Instead, this book will assume you know some C and understand the ideas of object-oriented programming. If C or object-oriented programming makes you feel uneasy, Kochan's *Programming in Objective-C* is a worthwhile read.

In this chapter, you will learn the basics of Objective-C and create RandomPossessions, a command-line tool that you will reuse in an iPhone application later in the book. (So even if you're familiar with Objective-C, you'll still want to go through this chapter in order to create RandomPossessions.)

Objects

Let's say you need a way to represent a car. That car has a few attributes that are unique to it, like a model name, four wheels, a steering wheel, and whatever other fancy stuff they put on automobiles since the old Model T. The car can also perform actions, like accelerating and turning left.

In C, you would define a structure to hold the data that describes a car. The structure would have data members, one for each of these attributes. Each data member would have a name and a type.

To create an individual car, you would use the function **malloc** to allocate a chunk of memory large enough to hold the structure. You would write C functions to set the value of its attributes and have it perform actions.

In Objective-C, instead of using a structure to represent a car, you would use a *class*. Following the car analogy, think of this class as a car factory. When you write the **Car** class, you build a factory that knows how to create cars.

When you ask the **Car** class to make you a car, you get back a car *object*. This object, like all objects, is a chunk of data allocated from the heap. The car object is an *instance* of the **Car** class, and it stores the values for its attributes in *instance variables* (Figure 2.1).

Figure 2.1   A class and its instances

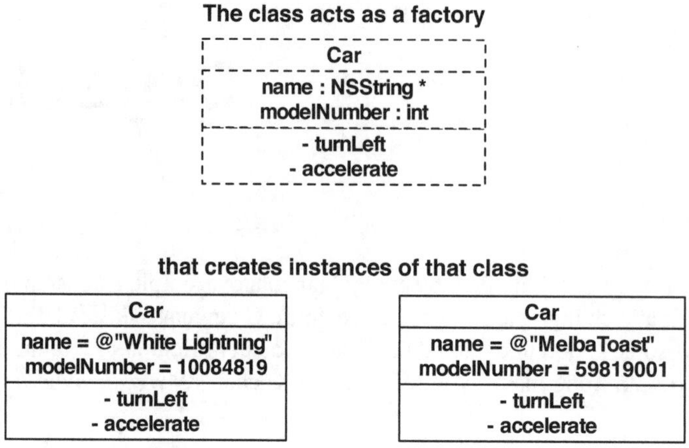

The class acts as a factory

Car
name : NSString * modelNumber : int
- turnLeft - accelerate

that creates instances of that class

Car
name = @"White Lightning" modelNumber = 10084819
- turnLeft - accelerate

Car
name = @"MelbaToast" modelNumber = 59819001
- turnLeft - accelerate

A C structure is a chunk of memory, and so is an object. A C structure has data members, each with a name and a type. Similarly, an object has instance variables, each with a name and type.

But there is an important difference between a structure in C and a class in Objective-C: a class has *methods*. A method is similar to a function: it has a name, a return type, and a list of parameters that it expects. A method also has access to an object's instance variables. If you want an object to run the code in one of its methods, you send that object a *message*.

Using Instances

An instance of a class (an object) has a life span: it is created, sent messages, and then destroyed when it is no longer needed.

To create an object, you send an **alloc** message to a class. In response, that class creates an object in memory and gives you a pointer to it. In code, creating an object looks like this:

```
NSMutableArray *arrayInstance = [NSMutableArray alloc];
```

Here an instance of type **NSMutableArray** is created, and you are returned a pointer to it in the variable arrayInstance. When you have a pointer to an instance, you can send messages to it. The first message you *always* send to a newly allocated instance is an initialization message.

```
[arrayInstance init];
```

Although sending the **alloc** message to a class creates an instance, the object isn't valid until it has been initialized. Since an object must be allocated and initialized before it can be used, we always combine these two messages in one line.

```
NSMutableArray *arrayInstance = [[NSMutableArray alloc] init];
```

This line of code says, "Create an instance of **NSMutableArray** and send it the message **init**." Both **alloc** and **init** return a pointer to the newly created object so that you have a reference to it. Typically, you will use the assignment operator (=) to store that pointer in a variable, as in the previous line of code.

Combining two messages in a single line of code is called a *nested message send*. The innermost brackets are evaluated first, so the message **alloc** is sent to the class **NSMutableArray** first. This returns a new, uninitialized instance of **NSMutableArray** that is then sent the message **init**.

Methods come in two flavors: instance methods and class methods. *Instance methods* (like **init**) are sent to instances of the class, and *class methods* (like **alloc**) are sent to the class itself. Class methods typically either create new instances of the class or retrieve some global property of the class. (We will talk more about class and instance methods later.)

What do you do with an instance that has been initialized? You send it more messages. Messages have three parts:

receiver   a pointer to the object being asked to execute a method

selector   the name of the method to be executed

arguments   the values to be supplied as the parameters to the method

One such message you can send an **NSMutableArray** instance is **addObject:**

```
[arrayInstance addObject:anotherObject];
```

(How do you know you can send this message? **addObject:** is a method of **NSMutableArray**. Sending the **addObject:** message to an instance of **NSMutableArray** will trigger the **addObject:** method.)

The **addObject:** message is an example of a message with one argument. Objective-C methods can take a number of arguments or none at all. The message **init**, for instance, has no arguments. On the other hand, you can also send the message **replaceObjectsInRange:withObjectsFromArray:range:**, which takes three arguments (Figure 2.2).

Figure 2.2   Anatomy of a message

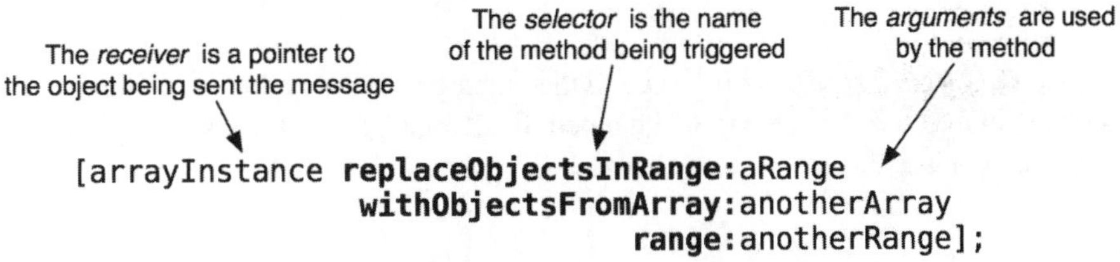

The *receiver* is a pointer to the object being sent the message

The *selector* is the name of the method being triggered

The *arguments* are used by the method

```
[arrayInstance replaceObjectsInRange:aRange
                withObjectsFromArray:anotherArray
                               range:anotherRange];
```

Each argument has a label, and each label ends with a colon. One thing that confuses Objective-C beginners is that the name of the message is all of the labels in a selector. For example, **addObject:** has one label (**addObject:**) for its one argument. The message **replaceObjectsInRange:withObjectsFromArray:range:** has three arguments, so it has three labels.

In C++ or Java, this method would look like this:

```
arrayInstance.replaceObjectsInRangeWithObjectsFromArrayRange(aRange,
                                        anotherArray,
                                        anotherRange);
```

In these languages, it isn't completely obvious what each of the arguments sent to this function are. In Objective-C, however, each argument is paired with the appropriate label:

```
[arrayInstance replaceObjectsInRange:aRange
              withObjectsFromArray:anotherArray
                        range:anotherRange];
```

Objective-C developers learn to appreciate the clarity of having a label for each argument even though it requires a little more typing. For example, you can have two methods **replaceObjectsInRange:withObjectsFromArray:range:** and **replaceObjectsInRange:**. These methods do not have to be related; they are two distinct messages that you can send to an instance of **NSMutableArray**.

To destroy an object, you send it the message **release**.

```
[arrayInstance release];
```

This line of code destroys the object pointed to by the arrayInstance variable. (It's actually a bit more complicated than that, and you'll learn about the details of memory management in the next chapter.) It is important to note that although you destroyed the object, the variable arrayInstance still has a value — the address of where the **NSMutableArray** instance used to exist. If you send a message to arrayInstance, it will cause a problem because that object no longer exists. However, if arrayInstance is set to nil, the problem goes away. (nil is the zero pointer. C programmers know it as NULL. Java programmers know it as null.)

```
arrayInstance = nil;
```

Now there is no danger of sending a message to the outdated memory address. Sending a message to nil is okay in Objective-C; nothing will happen. In a language like Java, sending messages to nil is illegal, so you see this sort of thing a lot:

```
if (rover != nil) {
    [rover doSomething];
}
```

In Objective-C, this check is unnecessary because a message sent to nil is just ignored. (A corollary: if your program doesn't do anything when you think it should be doing something, an unexpectedly nil pointer is often the culprit.)

Writing the RandomPossessions Tool

Before you dive into the UIKit (the set of libraries you use to create iPhone applications), you're going to write a command-line tool that will let you focus on the Objective-C language. Open Xcode and select New Project... from the File menu. On the lefthand table, select Application from underneath the Mac OS X section. Select Command Line Tool from the upper right panel. A list of options will appear in the pop-up menu of the bottom right panel. Choose Foundation from this pop-up menu as shown in Figure 2.3. Click the Choose... button.

Figure 2.3   Creating a command line utility

Name this project RandomPossessions. A project window will appear.

One source file (RandomPossessions.m) has been created for you in the Source group on the lefthand side of the project window (Figure 2.4).

Figure 2.4   Project window

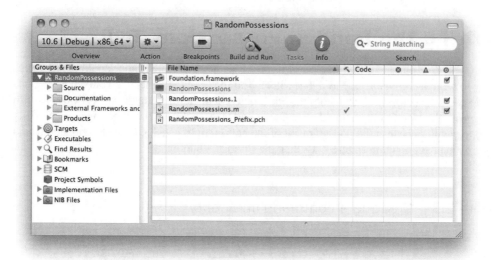

Double-click on this file to open it, and you'll see some code has already been written for you — most notably, a **main** function that is the entry point of any C (or Objective-C) application.

Time to put your knowledge of Objective-C basics to the test. Delete the line of code that **NSLog**s "Hello, World!" and replace it with a line that creates an instance of an **NSMutableArray**.

```
#import <Foundation/Foundation.h>
int main (int argc, const char * argv[])
{
    NSAutoreleasePool *pool = [[NSAutoreleasePool alloc] init];

    NSMutableArray *items = [[NSMutableArray alloc] init];

    [pool drain];
    return 0;
}
```

Once you have an instance of **NSMutableArray**, you can send it some messages. In this code, the receiver is the object pointed to by items. Add a few strings to this array instance.

```
    NSMutableArray *items = [[NSMutableArray alloc] init];
    [items addObject:@"One"];
    [items addObject:@"Two"];
    [items addObject:@"Three"];
    [items insertObject:@"Zero" atIndex:0];

    [pool drain];
```

When you want a string object in Objective-C, you prefix a literal C string with an @ symbol. This tells the compiler that you want to use an instance of **NSString** (another Objective-C class) to contain this string.

When this application executes, it creates an **NSMutableArray** and fills it with four **NSString** instances. However, you need to confirm your success. After adding the final object to the array, loop through every item in the array and print them to the console. (You can find out how many items are in an **NSMutableArray** by sending it the message **count**.)

```
[items insertObject:@"Zero" atIndex:0];
for(int i = 0; i < [items count]; i++) {
    NSLog(@"%@", [items objectAtIndex:i]);
}
[pool drain];
```

Select Build and Run from the Build menu. It may seem like nothing has happened since the program exits fairly quickly, but the console tells another story. From the Run menu, select Console. Ah, there we go — your hard work has paid off, and you now have output from your application (Figure 2.5).

Figure 2.5   Console output

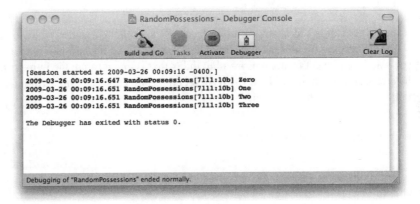

NSArray and NSMutableArray

What exactly is this **NSMutableArray**? An array is a collection object (also called a container). In the Cocoa Touch frameworks, there are a few collection objects, such as **NSDictionary** and **NSSet**, and each has a slightly different use. An array is an ordered list of objects that are accessed by an index. Other languages might call it a *list* or a *vector*. An **NSArray** is *immutable*, which means you cannot add or remove objects after the array is instantiated. You can, however, access objects within the array. **NSArray**'s mutable subclass, **NSMutableArray**, lets you add and remove objects dynamically.

In Objective-C, an array does not actually contain the objects that belong to it; instead it holds a pointer (a reference) to each object. When an object is added to an array,

```
[array addObject:object];
```

the address of that object in memory is stored inside the array.

Arrays can hold any type of Objective-C object. This means primitives and C structures cannot be added to an array. For example, you cannot have an array of ints. Also, because arrays only hold a pointer to an object, *you can have objects of different types in a single array.* This is different from many other compiled languages where an array can only hold objects of its declared type.

Note that you cannot add nil to an array. If you need to add holes to an array, you must use the **NSNull** object. **NSNull** is an object that represents nil and is used specifically for this task.

```
[array addObject:[NSNull null]];
```

To retrieve the pointer to an object later, you send the message **objectAtIndex:** to the array

```
NSString *object = [array objectAtIndex:0];
```

How do you know the order of the objects in an array? When an object is added to an array with the message **addObject:**, it is added at the end of the array. You can ask an array how many objects it is currently storing by sending it the message **count**. This information is important because if you ask for an object from an array at an index that is greater than the number of objects in the array, an exception will be thrown. (Exceptions are very bad; they will most likely ruin your application and cause it to crash.)

```
int numberOfObjects = [array count];
```

You can also insert objects at a specific index — as long as that index is less than or equal to the current number of objects in the array.

```
int numberOfObjects = [array count];
[array insertObject:object
            atIndex:numberOfObjects];
```

Objects added to an array are sent the message **retain**. When an object is removed from an array, it is sent the message **release**. When an array is deallocated, all of its objects are sent the message **release**. If you don't know what retain, release, and deallocate mean, that's okay; you'll learn about them in the next chapter.

So, to recap, you created an instance of **NSMutableArray** to which you added four instances of **NSString** as shown in Figure 2.6.

Figure 2.6   NSMutableArray instance

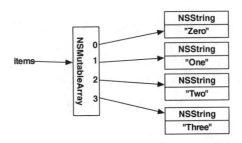

Then, you looped through every instance in that array. Each time you iterated through this loop, you called the C function **NSLog** with a single parameter. That single parameter was the description of the object at the *i*th index of the array.

The **NSLog** function is to Objective-C as the **printf** function is to C. The **NSLog** function uses the same format list with one addition: you can print Objective-C objects. To print an Objective-C object, the format is **"%@"**. When the format string is parsed, the **NSLog** function finds the matching argument in the argument list and sends it the message **description**. (Every object has a **description** method.) The string returned from that method then replaces the format string. And remember, the **NSLog** function expects an **NSString** for the format list, so you have to prefix an @ character before the string literal.

Subclassing an Objective-C Class

Where does the **description** method come from? Every class has exactly one superclass — except for the root class of the entire hierarchy: **NSObject**. That means, at minimum, every class inherits from **NSObject**. **NSObject** implements a method named **description**.

Sending the **description** message to an **NSObject** returns an **NSString** containing information about that instance. By default, that string is the object's class and its address in memory. A subclass of **NSObject**, like **NSString**, will override this method to return something that does a better job describing an instance of that subclass. For **NSString**, **description** just returns the string itself since that is the best way to describe an **NSString** instance.

So how do these subclasses get created? Glad you asked because now you are going to create one of your own. From the File menu, select New File.... Select Cocoa Class from the Mac OS X section in the lefthand table. Then select Objective-C class from the upper right panel. Choose NSObject from the pop-up menu, as shown in Figure 2.7.

Figure 2.7   Creating a class

Hit the Next button, and you will be given a chance to configure this new Objective-C class. Change the filename to Possession.m. The files for this class will be created and added to your project when you click Finish (Figure 2.8).

Figure 2.8   Configuring a new class

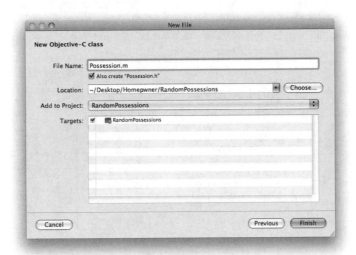

For every Objective-C class, there are two files: a header file and an implementation file. The *header file* (also called an interface file) declares the name of the new class, its superclass, the instance variables that each instance of this class has, and any methods this class implements. This file is suffixed with .h. Open Possession.h by double-clicking it in the Groups & Files table in the project window.

The goal of the header file is to declare an Objective-C class.

```
@interface Possession : NSObject {

}
@end
```

Let's break down this interface declaration to figure out what it all means. First, note that the C language retains all of its keywords, and any additional keywords from Objective-C are distinguishable by the @ prefix. To declare a class in Objective-C, you use the keyword @interface followed by the name of this new class. After a colon comes the name of the superclass. **Possession**'s superclass is **NSObject**. Objective-C only allows single inheritance, so you will only ever see the following pattern:

```
@interface ClassName : SuperclassName
```

Next comes the space for declaring instance variables. Instance variables must be declared *inside* the curly brace block immediately following the class and superclass declaration. After the closing curly brace, you declare any methods that this class implements. Once you declare methods here, you must implement them in the implementation file or the compiler will give you a warning. Finally, the @end keyword finishes off the declaration for your new class.

Instance variables

So far, the **Possession** class doesn't add a whole lot of interesting information to its superclass **NSObject**, so let's give it some possession-like instance variables. A possession, in our world, is going to have a name, serial number, value, and date of creation. You are going to declare an instance variable for each of these attributes (Figure 2.9).

Figure 2.9   A Possession instance

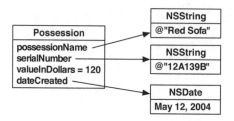

Type this new code into Possession.h. Also, make sure to change the imported header from Cocoa to Foundation. We are going to reuse this class later for an iPhone application, and the Cocoa framework doesn't exist on the iPhone.

```
// Don't forget to change this line from Cocoa/Cocoa.h!
#import <Foundation/Foundation.h>
@interface Possession : NSObject
{
    NSString *possessionName;
    NSString *serialNumber;
    int valueInDollars;
    NSDate *dateCreated;
}
@end
```

Accessors and properties

Now that you have instance variables, you need a way to get and set them. In object-oriented languages, we call methods that get and set instance variables *accessors*. Individually, we call them getters and setters. Without these methods, one object cannot access the instance variables of another object.

Prior to Objective-C version 2.0, we had to explicitly declare and define every accessor method. That was a lot of typing. Fortunately, Objective-C 2.0 introduces a shortcut called *properties*. By creating a property, you are declaring two accessor methods. Before properties were introduced, you would have declared those two accessor methods as follows:

```
// Getter
- (int)fido;

// Setter
- (void)setFido:(int)v;
```

You might wonder why the name of the getter is simply **fido** instead of **getFido**. This is another Objective-C style convention. The name of the instance variable you are accessing is the name of the getter method for it. While there is no compiler warning or error if you use **get**, stylish iPhone programmers stick to the convention.

With properties, you can declare the same two accessors in one line of code:

```
@property int fido;
```

When you create a property, the accessors are declared according to the naming convention above. Properties also declare how the accessors are implemented by setting property attributes. One attribute addresses how the setter method will set the variable. The default is simple assignment. You can change this to copy or retain. (The reasons why you might do this will make more sense after we talk about memory management in the next chapter.) Another attribute deals with whether the variable can be changed. The default is readwrite, but it can be set to readonly. In that case, only the getter method is declared. A third attribute tells us if the variable requires a lock. This attribute defaults to atomic, which means a lock must be acquired to get or set the variable. Specifying a property as nonatomic means no lock is required. In this book, you'll stick to nonatomic because it's a touch faster.

Property declarations are made in the same place as method declarations — after the closing curly brace. Add the following property declarations to Possession.h.

```
#import <Foundation/Foundation.h>
@interface Possession : NSObject
{
    NSString *possessionName;
    NSString *serialNumber;
    int valueInDollars;
    NSDate *dateCreated;
}
@property (nonatomic, copy) NSString *possessionName;
@property (nonatomic, copy) NSString *serialNumber;
@property (nonatomic) int valueInDollars;
@property (nonatomic, readonly) NSDate *dateCreated;
@end
```

Just declaring these properties doesn't implement the accessor methods; you have to *synthesize* them. To do this, you turn to the second file associated with an Objective-C class — the *implementation file* with the .m extension. This file is where you implement all of your methods and synthesize any properties. Synthesizing properties defines their accessor methods.

At the top of an implementation file, you always import the header (.h) file of that class. The implementation of a class needs to know how it has been declared. All of the method definitions in the implementation file will be inside an implementation block. An implementation block begins with the @implementation keyword followed by the name of the class that is being implemented. Methods are defined until you close out the block with the @end keyword.

Open Possession.m. Use the @synthesize keyword followed by a comma-delimited list of all properties you are synthesizing. Remember that this must occur inside the implementation block.

```
#import "Possession.h"

@implementation Possession
@synthesize possessionName, serialNumber, valueInDollars, dateCreated;
@end
```

If you chose to write your own accessors for valueInDollars, instead of using @synthesize, they would look like this:

```
// Getter
- (int)valueInDollars
{
    return valueInDollars;
}

// Setter
- (void)setValueInDollars:(int)x
{
    valueInDollars = x;
}
```

Build your application to ensure that there are no compiler errors or warnings. Now that your properties have been synthesized, you can send messages to **Possession** instances to get and set instance variables. For example, synthesizing valueInDollars allows you to send the messages **valueInDollars** and **setValueInDollars:** to instances of **Possession**.

Instance methods

Not all instance methods are accessors. You will regularly find yourself wanting to send messages to instances that perform other code, like **description**. Because **Possession** is a subclass of **NSObject** (the class that originally declares the **description** method), when you re-implement this method in the **Possession** class, you are said to be *overriding* the method.

When overriding a method, all you need to do is define it in the implementation file; you do not need to declare it in the header file because it has already been declared by the superclass. Override the **description** method in Possession.m. (Be sure to include the - in the first line of code. It denotes that **description** is an instance method, not a class method.)

```
- (NSString *)description
{
    NSString *descriptionString =
        [[NSString alloc] initWithFormat:@"%@ (%@): Worth $%d, Recorded on %@",
                            possessionName,
                            serialNumber,
```

```
        valueInDollars,
        dateCreated];

    return descriptionString;
}
```

Now whenever you send the message **description** to an instance of **Possession**, it returns an **NSString** that describes that instance. (To those of you familiar with Objective-C and managing memory, don't panic — you will fix the obvious problem with this code soon.)

What if you want to create an entirely new instance method, one that you are not overriding from its superclass? You typically declare a method in the header file and define it in the implementation file. A good method to begin with is an object's initializer.

Initializers

At the beginning of this chapter, we talked about how an instance is created: its class is sent the message **alloc**, which creates an instance of that class and returns a pointer to it, and that instance is sent the message **init**. The **init** message isn't a special type of instance method, though; it is simply a naming convention. Your initialization method *could* have a totally different name, like **finishMakingInstance**. However, by convention, all initialization methods begin with the word **init**. Objective-C is all about naming conventions, which you should strictly adhere to. (Seriously. Disregarding naming conventions in Objective-C results in problems that are worse than most beginners would imagine.)

The class **NSObject** implements a method named **init**. This is the initializer message you need to send to an instance of **NSObject** to initialize it. Because **init** is the main (or, in this case, only) initialization method for **NSObject**, we call it the *designated initializer*. Classes can have multiple initializers, but for every class, there is one designated initializer. The designated initializer must make sure that each of the instance variables has a valid value. Only then will the newly created instance be valid. ("Valid" has different meanings, but the meaning in this context is "when you send messages to this object after initializing it, you can predict the outcome and nothing bad will happen.") Typically, the designated initializer is the initializer with the most arguments.

Your **Possession** class has four instance variables, but only three are writeable. (The **NSDate** object used to set the read-only variable dateCreated is created inside the body of the method instead of being passed in.) **Possession**'s designated initializer needs to accept three arguments: one for each of the writable instance variables. In Possession.h, declare the designated initializer:

```
@property (nonatomic, readonly) NSDate *dateCreated;

- (id)initWithPossessionName:(NSString *)name
            valueInDollars:(int)value
             serialNumber:(NSString *)sNumber;
@end
```

Take another look at this method declaration. Its return type is id. The id type definition is "a pointer to any object." (This is a lot like void * in C.) **init** methods are always declared to return id. (Why? If **Possession** gets subclassed, its initializer will need to return the subclass's type. When you override a method, you cannot change its return type in the subclass. Therefore, initialization methods should always return id. Objects know which class created them anyway; the type they are declared is more or less a hint for the compiler.)

This method's name, or selector, is **initWithPossessionName:valueInDollars:serialNumber:**. This selector has three labels (**initWithPossessionName:**, **valueInDollars:**, and **serialNumber:**), and the method accepts three arguments.

These arguments each have a type and a parameter name. The type follows the label in parentheses. The parameter name then follows the type. So the label **initWithPossessionName:** is expecting an instance of type **NSString**. Within the body of that method, you can use name to reference the object that was passed in.

Now that you have declared the designated initializer, you need to implement it. Open Possession.m. Recall that the definitions for methods go within the implementation block in the implementation file. Add the designated initializer inside the implementation block.

```
@implementation Possession
@synthesize possessionName, serialNumber, valueInDollars, dateCreated;

- (id)initWithPossessionName:(NSString *)name
             valueInDollars:(int)value
             serialNumber:(NSString *)sNumber
{
    // Call the superclass's designated initializer
    [super init];

    // Give the instance variables initial values
    [self setPossessionName:name];
    [self setSerialNumber:sNumber];
    [self setValueInDollars:value];
    dateCreated = [[NSDate alloc] init];

    // Return the address of the newly initialized object
    return self;
}
```

In the designated initializer, you always call the superclass's designated initializer using super. The last thing you do is return a pointer to the successfully initialized object using self. So to understand what's going on in an initializer, you will need to know about self and super.

self

Inside a method, self is an implicit local variable. There is no need to declare it, and it is automatically initialized to the address of the object running the method. Typically, self is used so that an object can send a message to itself:

```
- (void)chickenDance
{
    [self pretendHandsAreBeaks];
    [self flapWings];
    [self shakeTailFeathers];
}
```

Most object-oriented languages have this concept, but some call it this instead of self.

In the last line of an **init** method, you always return the newly initialized object:

```
return self;
```

If things go badly and the **init** method fails, you will return nil instead of the new object.

super

Often when you are overriding a method in a subclass, you want to do some special subclass stuff and then invoke the implementation of the method as it was defined in the superclass. To make this possible, there is a compiler directive in Objective-C called super:

```
- (void)someMethod
{
    [self doSomeSpecialStuff];
    [super someMethod];
}
```

How does super work? Usually when you send a message to an object, the search for a method of that name starts in the object's class. If there is no such method, the search continues in the superclass of the object. The search will continue up the inheritance hierarchy until a suitable method is found. (If it gets to the top of the hierarchy and no method is found, an exception is thrown.) When you send a message to super, you are sending a message to self but demanding that the search for the method begin at the superclass.

In a designated initializer, the first thing you do is call the superclass's designated initializer using super. What if the superclass's initializer fails and returns nil? It is probably a good idea to save the return value of the superclass's initializer into the self variable and confirm that it is not nil before doing any further initialization. In Possession.m, edit your designated initializer to confirm the initialization of the superclass.

```
- (id)initWithPossessionName:(NSString *)name
              valueInDollars:(int)value
                serialNumber:(NSString *)sNumber
{
    // Call the superclass's designated initializer
        self = [super init];

    // Did the superclass's designated initializer fail?
    if (!self)
        return nil;

    // Give the instance variables initial values
    [self setPossessionName:name];
    [self setSerialNumber:sNumber];
    [self setValueInDollars:value];
    dateCreated = [[NSDate alloc] init];
```

```
    // Return the address of the newly initialized object
    return self;
}
```

Initializer chain

Let's say you are creating an instance of **Possession**, but you only know its name — not its value or serial number. You can create another initializer that accepts just one **NSString** meant for the possessionName instance variable. Declare another initializer for when you only know the name of the possession in Possession.h.

```
@property (nonatomic, readonly) NSDate *dateCreated;

- (id)initWithPossessionName:(NSString *)name
            valueInDollars:(int)value
             serialNumber:(NSString *)sNumber;

- (id)initWithPossessionName:(NSString *)name;
@end
```

An initializer that is not the designated initializer must always call its own class's designated initializer message with default values for the parameters that are not specified. To implement your new initializer in Possession.m, simply call the designated initializer using the passed-in parameter and default values for the other arguments. (Make sure this code is in between the @implementation and @end directives and not inside the curly brackets of another method!)

```
- (id)initWithPossessionName:(NSString *)name
{
    return [self initWithPossessionName:name
                        valueInDollars:0
                         serialNumber:@""];
}
```

When an instance of **Possession** is created with this initializer, it uses the name of the possession passed to it. The valueInDollars instance variable defaults to 0, and the serialNumber defaults to the empty string. Using initializers as a chain like this reduces the chance for error and makes maintaining code easier. You only write the core of the initializer once in the designated initializer; other initialization methods simply call that core with default values.

Furthermore, a subclass needs to override its superclass's designated initializer to invoke its own designated initializer. Right now, an instance of **Possession** could be sent the message **init**. To the programmer and compiler, the object would appear valid. However, only the superclass's (**NSObject**) instance variables would have been initialized — all of the stuff added by the **Possession** class would not be. To make sure this doesn't happen, override **init** to invoke **Possession**'s designated initializer with default values in Possession.m.

```
- (id)init
{
    return [self initWithPossessionName:@"Possession"
                         valueInDollars:0
                           serialNumber:@""];
}
```

(Remember, because you're overriding this method, you don't have to declare it in `Possession.h`.)

Class methods

So far, you have been creating instance methods. These are messages you can send to any instance of **Possession**. However, in Objective-C, classes can also receive messages. We call these class methods. (**alloc** is an example of a class method.) Class methods do not operate on an instance or have any access to instance variables.

Syntactically, class methods differ from instance methods by the first character in their declaration. An instance method uses the - character right before the return type, and a class method uses the + character. Also, class methods can only be sent to the class itself, never to an instance of that class.

One common use for class methods is to provide convenient ways to create instances of that class. For the **Possession** class, it would be nice if you could create a random possession. That way, you could test your possession class without having to think up a bunch of clever names. Declare a class method in `Possession.h` that will create a random possession.

```
@interface Possession : NSObject
{
    NSString *possessionName;
    NSString *serialNumber;
    int valueInDollars;
    NSDate *dateCreated;
}
@property (nonatomic, copy) NSString *possessionName;
@property (nonatomic, copy) NSString *serialNumber;
@property (nonatomic) int valueInDollars;
@property (nonatomic, readonly) NSDate *dateCreated;

+ (id)randomPossession;

- (id)initWithPossessionName:(NSString *)name
              valueInDollars:(int)value
                serialNumber:(NSString *)sNumber;

- (id)initWithPossessionName:(NSString *)name;
@end
```

Notice the order of the declarations for properties and methods. Properties come first, followed by class methods, followed by initialization methods. Further instance methods will follow after these. This is a convention that makes your header files easier to read.

Class methods that return an instance of their type are simply creating an instance as you normally would (with **alloc** and **init**), configuring it, and then returning it. In Possession.m, implement **randomPossession** to create, configure, and return a **Possession** instance:

```
+ (id)randomPossession
{
    // Create two arrays with a list of possible adjectives and nouns
    // Note: When using NSArray's arrayWithObjects:, you can pass as many
    // objects as you like. At the end of that list, you put nil to
    // signify that there are no more objects - otherwise you will crash.
    // The nil value is not added to the array, but is used by the method
    // to determine the end of the list.
    NSArray *randomAdjectiveList = [NSArray arrayWithObjects:@"Fluffy",
                                                    @"Rusty",
                                                    @"Shiny", nil];
    NSArray *randomNounList = [NSArray arrayWithObjects:@"Bear",
                                                @"Spork",
                                                @"Mac", nil];

    // Get the index of a random adjective/noun from the lists
    // Note: The % operator, called the modulo operator, gives
    // you the remainder. So adjectiveIndex is a random number
    // from 0 to 2 inclusive, in this case.
    int adjectiveIndex = random() % [randomAdjectiveList count];
    int nounIndex = random() % [randomNounList count];

    NSString *randomName = [NSString stringWithFormat:@"%@ %@",
                [randomAdjectiveList objectAtIndex:adjectiveIndex],
                [randomNounList objectAtIndex:nounIndex]];

    int randomValue = random() % 100;

    NSString *randomSerialNumber = [NSString stringWithFormat:@"%c%c%c%c%c",
                                        '0' + random() % 10,
                                        'A' + random() % 26,
                                        '0' + random() % 10,
                                        'A' + random() % 26,
                                        '0' + random() % 10];

    // Once again, ignore the memory problems with this method
    // We use "self" instead of the name of the class in class methods...
    // Keep reading to find out why
    Possession *newPossession =
        [[self alloc] initWithPossessionName:randomName
                            valueInDollars:randomValue
                                serialNumber:randomSerialNumber];
    return newPossession;
}
```

This method creates a string from a random adjective and noun, another string from some random numbers and letters, and a random integer value. It then creates an instance of **Possession** and sends it the designated initializer with these random objects as parameters.

You might notice that you actually used a class method of **NSString** in the implementation of this method. The message **stringWithFormat:** is sent directly to **NSString**; it is a class method that returns an **NSString** instance with the parameters that are sent to it. In Objective-C, class methods that return an object of their type (like **stringWithFormat:** and **randomPossession**) are called *convenience methods*.

Notice the use of self in **randomPossession**. This method is a class method, so self refers to the **Possession** class itself. Class methods should use self in convenience methods instead of their class name so that if you create a subclass of **Possession**, you can send that subclass the message **randomPossession**. Using self (instead of **Possession**) guarantees that the object returned by this method is the same type as the class being sent the message.

Now you get to use the neat little class you've created. Open RandomPossessions.m. In the **main** function, you were adding **NSString** instances to the **NSMutableArray** instance you created and then printing them to the console. Now you can add **Possession** instances to the array instead. Don't forget to import the header file Possession.h.

```
#import <Foundation/Foundation.h>

#import "Possession.h"

int main (int argc, const char * argv[])
{
    NSAutoreleasePool * pool = [[NSAutoreleasePool alloc] init];

    NSMutableArray *items = [[NSMutableArray alloc] init];

    for (int i = 0; i < 10; i++) {
        [items addObject:[Possession randomPossession]];
    }

    for (int i = 0; i < [items count]; i++) {
        NSLog(@"%@", [items objectAtIndex:i]);
    }
    [pool drain];
    return 0;
}
```

Build and run your application, making sure to show the console again. All you did was replace what objects you added to the array, and the code runs perfectly fine with a wildly different output (Figure 2.10). Creating this subclass was a success.

Figure 2.10   Application result

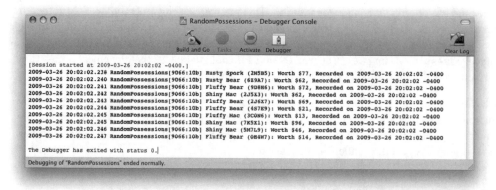

Check out the new #import statement at the top of RandomPossessions.m. Why did you have to import Possession.h when you didn't you have to import, say, NSMutableArray.h? Well, **NSMutableArray** comes from the Foundation framework, so it is included when you import Foundation/Foundation.h. On the other hand, your subclass exists in its own file, so you have to explicitly import it into RandomPossession.m. Otherwise, the compiler won't know it exists and will complain loudly.

Importing a file is the same as including a file in the C language except you are ensured that the file will only be included once.

If you don't want to import the header file for a class, but you want the compiler to know that the class exists, you can use a forward declaration like this:

```
@class Possession;
```

In a large project, judicious use of @class can speed up compiles considerably.

Exceptions and the Console Window

In a language like C, we have functions. When we call a function, code is executed. If we try and call a function that doesn't exist, the compiler says, "Hey, that's not right!" and the code will fail to compile. This is known as a compile-time error.

Objective-C, being a dynamically typed language, isn't able to figure out at compile time whether an object can *respond* to a message. An object can only respond to a message if its class implements the associated method. The compiler will warn you if it thinks you are sending a message to an object that won't respond, but the code will still compile. If, for some reason (and there are many), you end up sending a message to an object who doesn't respond, your application will throw an exception.

In RandomPossessions.m, add the following line of code after you create your array:

```
NSMutableArray *items = [[NSMutableArray alloc] init];
[items doSomethingWeird];
```

The class **NSMutableArray** does not implement a method called **doSomethingWeird**. Sending this message to an instance of **NSMutableArray** is going to throw an exception. Build and run your application.

Open the console window. When you ran this application before, the console contained the contents of the array. Now it is saying this:

```
2009-07-19 01:34:53.602 RandomPossessions[25326:10b]
*** -[NSCFArray doSomethingWeird]: unrecognized selector sent to instance 0x104b40
```

This is what an exception looks like. What exactly is this output saying? In every output statement to the console, the date, time, and name of the application are printed out. You can ignore that information. You are concerned with the information after the "***." That line tells us that an *unrecognized selector* was sent to an instance. You know that selector means message. You sent a message to an object, and that object does not implement that method.

The type of the receiver and the name of the message sent are also in this output. This makes it easier for you to debug. An instance of **NSCFArray** was sent the message **doSomethingWeird**. (The - at the beginning tells you the receiver was an instance of **NSCFArray**. A + would mean the class was the receiver.) Remove the line of code you added and take away this very important lesson: always keep the console window open. Run-time errors are just as important as compile-time errors.

(What does **NSCFArray** mean? The CF stands for Core Foundation. We'll get into that later in the book. For now, you can just drop the CF out of the name. An **NSArray**, the superclass of **NSMutableArray** is the type of the object that was sent this bad message.)

Some languages use try and catch blocks to handle exceptions. While Objective-C has this ability, we don't use it very often. Typically, an exception is a programmer error and should be fixed in the code instead of handled at runtime.

Objective-C 2.0 Additions

The newest version of Objective-C added a few syntax-level changes to the language specification. The most useful one is *fast enumeration*. Before Objective-C 2.0, iterating through an **NSArray** looked like this:

```
for (int i = 0; i < [items count]; i++) {
    Possession *item = [items objectAtIndex:i];
    NSLog(@"%@", item);
}
```

Now you can write that code segment much more succinctly with fast enumeration.

```
for (Possession *item in items)
    NSLog(@"%@", item);
```

Try changing the for loop in your **main** function to use fast enumeration.

Another addition to Objective-C 2.0 is dot-notation for property accessors. Instead of using brackets to invoke an accessor method, you can use a . operator instead and get the same results.

```
int v = [object foo];
[object setFoo:v];
```

...is identical to...

```
int v = object.foo;
object.foo = v;
```

According to the compiler, these two snippets are the same. There is no difference in speed — they are seriously identical.

Because these lines are identical, I think dot-notation is goofy. However, others do not. Whether to use dot-notation has become something of a religious war in the Objective-C community. (And no one is ever right in those wars.)

The argument for using dot-notation is that the dot signifies that the code is accessing the state of an object whereas using the brackets signifies that it is asking the object to perform some behavior. This supposedly gives the code clarity. The arguments against dot-notation are that it creates ambiguity with the C structure access operator and it confuses beginning programmers, especially when it comes to memory management.

This book will not use dot-notation because it is confusing to beginning programmers. If you choose to use dot-notation after you've mastered the concepts behind Objective-C, more power to you. For now, you will be better served by sticking with the brackets.

3

Memory Management

Understanding memory management in the Cocoa Touch framework is one of the first major roadblocks for newcomers. Unlike Objective-C on the Mac, Objective-C on the iPhone has no garbage collector. Thus, it is your responsibility to clean up after yourself.

Memory Management Concepts

This book assumes you are coming from a C background, so the words "pointer," "allocate," and "deallocate" shouldn't scare you. If your memory is a little fuzzy, here's a review. The iPhone has a limited amount of random access memory. Random access memory (RAM) is much faster to write to and read from than a hard drive, so when an application is executing, all of the memory it consumes is taken from RAM. When an operating system like iPhone OS launches your application, it reserves a heaping pile of the system's unused RAM for your application. Not-so-coincidentally, the memory your application has to work with is called the *heap*. The heap is your application's playground; it can do whatever it wants to it, and it won't affect the rest of the OS or any other applications.

When your application creates an instance of a class, it goes to the giant heap of memory it was given and takes a little scoop. Since you typically create objects during the course of your application's execution, you start using more and more of the heap. Most objects are not permanent, and when an object is no longer needed, the memory it was consuming should be returned to the heap. This way, it can be reused for another object created later.

There are two major problems in managing memory:

premature deallocation   You must never return memory to the heap until you are sure that no part of the program is still using it.

memory leaks   When a chunk of memory is no longer needed by any part of a program, it must be freed so that the memory can be used again.

Managing memory in C

In the C programming language, you have to explicitly ask the heap for a certain number of bytes. This is called *allocation*. It is the first stage of the heap life cycle shown in Figure 3.1. To do this, you use a function like `malloc`. If you want 100 bytes from that heap, you do something like this:

```
void function(void)
{
    char *buffer = malloc(100);
}
```

You then have 100 bytes with which you can perform some task like writing a string to it and then printing that string (which would require reading from those bytes). The location of the first of those 100 bytes is stored in the pointer buffer. You access the 100 bytes by using this pointer.

Figure 3.1   Heap allocation life cycle

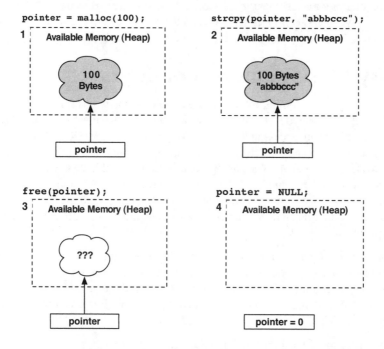

When you don't want to use those bytes anymore, you have to give them back to the heap by using the **free** function. This is called *deallocation*.

```
void function(void)
{
    char *buffer = malloc(100);
    ... Fill the buffer with text ...
    ... Print to the console ...
    free(buffer);
}
```

By calling **free**, those 100 bytes (starting at the address stored in buffer) are returned to the heap. If another **malloc** function is executed, any of these 100 bytes are fair game to be returned. Those bytes could be divvied up into smaller sections, or they could become part of a larger allocation.

Because you don't know what will happen with those bytes when they are returned to the heap, it isn't safe to access them through the `buffer` pointer anymore.

Managing memory with objects

Even though at the base level an object is bytes allocated from the heap, you never explicitly call `malloc` or `free` with objects.

Every class knows how many bytes of memory it needs to allocate for an instance. When you create an instance of a class by sending it the `alloc` message, the correct number of bytes is allocated from the heap. Like with `malloc`, you are returned a pointer to this memory (Figure 3.2). However, when using Objective-C, we think in terms of objects rather than raw memory. While our pointers are still pointing to a spot in memory, we don't need to know the details of that memory; we just know we have an object.

Figure 3.2   Allocating an object

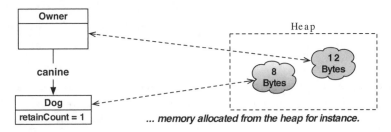

Of course, once you allocate memory from the heap, you need a way to return that memory back to the heap. Every object implements the method `dealloc`. When an object receives this message, it returns its memory back to the heap.

So, `malloc` is replaced with the class method `alloc`, and the function `free` is replaced with the instance method `dealloc`. However, you never explicitly send a `dealloc` message to an object; an object is responsible for sending `dealloc` to itself. That begs the question: if an object is in charge of destroying itself, how can it know if other objects are relying on its existence? This is where reference counting comes into play.

Reference Counting

In the Cocoa Touch framework, Apple has adopted *manual reference counting* to manage memory and avoid premature deallocation and memory leaks.

To understand reference counting, imagine a puppy. When the puppy is born, it has an owner. That owner later gets married, and the new spouse also becomes an owner of that dog. The dog is alive because they feed it. Later on, the couple gives the dog away. The new owner of the dog decides he doesn't like the dog and lets it know by kicking it out of the house. Having no owner, the dog runs away and, after a series of unfortunate events, ends up in doggy heaven.

What is the moral of this story? As long as the dog had an owner to care for it, it was fine. When it no longer had an owner, it ran away and ceased to exist. This is how reference counting works. When an object is created, it has an owner. Throughout its existence, it can have different owners, and it can have more than one owner at a time. When it has zero owners, it deallocates itself and goes to instance heaven.

Using retain counts

An object never knows *who* its owners are. It only knows its *retain count* (Figure 3.3).

Figure 3.3   Retain count for a dog

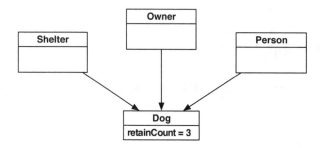

When an object is created — and therefore has one owner — its retain count is set to 1. When an object gains an owner, its retain count is incremented. When an object loses an owner, its retain count is decremented. When that retain count reaches 0, the object sends itself the message **dealloc**, which returns all of the memory it occupied to the heap.

Imagine how you would write the code to implement this scheme yourself:

```
- (id)retain
{
    retainCount++;
    return self;
}
- (void)release
{
    retainCount--;
    if (retainCount == 0)
        [self dealloc];
}
```

Simple, right? Now let's consider how retain counts work between objects. If object *A* creates object *B* (through **alloc** and **init**), *A* must send *B* the message **release** at some point in the future. Releasing *B* doesn't necessarily deallocate it; it is left to *B* to decide if it should be deallocated. (If *B* has another owner, it won't destroy itself.)

If some other object *C* wants to keep *B* around, *C* becomes an owner of *B* by sending it the message **retain**. What reason does *C* have to keep *B* around? *C* wants to send *B* messages.

Let's imagine you have a grocery list. You created it, so you own it. Later, you give that grocery list to your friend to do the shopping. You don't need to keep the grocery list anymore, so you release it. Your friend is smart, so he retained the list as soon as he was given it. Therefore, the grocery list will still exist whenever he needs it, and your friend is now the sole owner of the list.

Here is your code:

```
- (void)createAndGiveAwayTheGroceryList
{
   // Create a list
   GroceryList *g = [[GroceryList alloc] init];

   // (The retain count of g is 1)

   // Share it with your friend who retains it
   [smartFriend takeGroceryList:g];

   // (The retain count of g is 2)

   // Give up ownership
   [g release];

   // (The retain count of g is 1)
   // But we don't really care here, as this method's
   // responsibility is finished.
}
```

Here is your friend's code:

```
- (void)takeGroceryList:(GroceryList *)x
{
    // Take ownership
    [x retain];

    // Hold onto a pointer to the object
    myList = x
}
```

Retain counts can still go wrong in the two classic ways: leaks and premature deallocation. First, you could give the grocery list to your friend who retains it, but you don't release it. Your friend finishes the shopping and releases the list. You have forgotten where it is, but because you never released it, it still exists. Nobody has this grocery list anymore, but it still exists because its retain count is greater than 0. This is a leak.

Think of the grocery list as an **NSString**. You have a pointer to this **NSString** in the method where you created it. If you leave the scope of the method without releasing the **NSString**, you'll lose the pointer along with the ability to release the **NSString** later. Even if every other object releases the **NSString**, it will never be deallocated.

Consider the other way this process can go wrong — premature deallocation. You create a grocery list and give it to a friend, who doesn't retain it. When you release it (thinking it was safe with your friend), it is deallocated because you were its only owner. When your friend attempts to use the list, he can't find it because it doesn't exist anymore.

When an object attempts to access another object that no longer exists, your application accesses bad memory, starts to fail, and eventually (although sooner is better than later for debugging) crashes.

If an object retains another object, that other object is guaranteed to exist. So correct use of retain counts avoids premature deallocation. Now let's look more closely at memory leaks.

Avoiding memory leaks with autorelease

You already know that an object is responsible for returning its own bytes to the heap and that an object will do that when it has no owners. What happens when you want to create an object to give away, not to own? You own it by virtue of creating it, but you don't have any use for it.

Let's make this idea more concrete with an example from the RandomPossessions tool you wrote last chapter. In the **Possession** class, you implemented a convenience method called **randomPossession** that returns an instance of **Possession** with random parameters. The owner of this instance is the class **Possession** (because the object was created inside of a **Possession** class method), but **Possession** is only creating it because another object wants it. The pointer to the **Possession** instance is lost when the scope of **randomPossession** runs out, but the object still has a retain count of 1.

Now, in your **main** function, you could release the instance returned to you by this method. But, you didn't allocate the random possession in the **main** function. Therefore, releasing the memory isn't **main**'s responsibility. Since the **alloc** message was sent to the **Possession** class inside **randomPossession**'s implementation, it is **randomPossession**'s responsibility to release the memory. But looking at the following block of code, where could you safely release it?

```
+ (id)randomPossession
{
    ... Create random variables ...
    Possession *newPossession = [[self alloc]
                        initWithPossessionName:randomName
                             valueInDollars:randomValue
                               serialNumber:randomSerialNumber];
    // If we release newPossession here,
    // the object is deallocated before it is returned.
    return newPossession;
    // If we release newPossession here, this code is never executed.
}
```

How can you avoid this memory leak? You need some way of saying "Don't release this object yet, but I don't want to be an owner of it anymore." Fortunately, you can mark an object for future release by sending it the message **autorelease**. When an object is sent **autorelease**, it is not immediately released; instead, it is added to an instance of the **NSAutoreleasePool**. This **NSAutoreleasePool** keeps track of all the objects that have been autoreleased. Periodically, the autorelease pool is drained; it sends the message **release** to the objects in the pool and then removes them.

An object marked for autorelease after its creation has two possible destinies: it can either continue its death march to deallocation or another object can retain it. If another object retains it, its retain count is now 2. (It is owned by the retaining object, and it has not yet been sent **release** by the autorelease pool.) Sometime in the future, that autorelease pool will release it, which will set its retain count back to 1. The return value for **autorelease** is the instance that is sent the message, so you can method chain **autorelease**.

```
// Because autorelease returns the object being autoreleased, we can do this:
NSObject *x = [[[NSObject alloc] init] autorelease];
```

Sometimes the idea of "the object will be released some time in the future" confuses developers. When an iPhone application is running, there is a run loop that is continually cycling. This run loop checks for events (like a touch or a timer firing) and then processes that event by calling the methods you have written in your classes. Whenever an event occurs, it breaks from that loop and starts executing your code. When your code is finished executing, the application returns to the loop. At the end of the loop, all autoreleased objects are sent the message **release**, as shown in Figure 3.4. So, while you are executing a method, which may call other methods, you can safely assume that an autoreleased object will not be released.

Figure 3.4   Autorelease pool draining

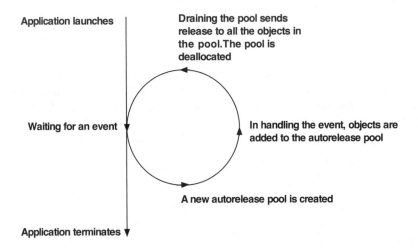

Managing memory in accessors and properties

Accessors are methods that get and set instance variables. Getter methods don't require any additional memory management:

```
- (Dog *)pet
{
    return pet;
}
```

Setters, however, need to take care to properly retain new values and release old ones.

```
- (void)setPet:(Dog *)d
{
    [d retain];         // Retain the new value
    [pet release];      // Release the old value
    pet = d;            // Make the pointer point at the new value
}
```

Notice that if pet hasn't been set, it is nil, and [pet release] would have no effect.

It is important to retain the new value before releasing the old one. Why? What if pet and d are pointers to the same object? What if that object has a retain count of 1? If you release it before you retain it, the retain count goes to 0, and the object is deallocated.

Here is the same thing in another style:

```
- (void)setPet:(Dog *)d
{
    if (pet != d) {
        [d retain];
        [pet release];
        pet = d;
    }
}
```

Once again, properties come to the rescue. If you use properties, all of the memory management code for your accessors is written for you when you synthesize the property. To have the compiler generate an accessor that properly releases and retains for you, you can use the retain attribute when declaring your properties in a header file:

```
@property (nonatomic, retain) Dog *pet;
```

Then, in the implementation file, synthesize the method:

```
@synthesize pet;
```

Retain count rules

Let's make a few rules from these ideas:

- If you send the message **alloc** to a class, the instance returned has a retain count of 1, and you are responsible for releasing it.

- If you send the message **copy** (or **mutableCopy**) to an instance, the instance returned has a retain count of 1, and you are responsible for releasing it (just as if you had allocated it).

- Assume that an object created through any other means (like a convenience method) has a retain count of 1 and is marked for autorelease.

- If an object wants to keep another object around (and the keeper didn't allocate it), it must send the wanted object the message **retain**.

- If an object no longer wants to keep another object around, it sends that object the message **release**.

There is one exception to the rules: in any method that starts with **new**, the object returned should be assumed to *not* be autoreleased.

Managing Memory in RandomPossessions

Now that you have the theory and some rules, you can implement better memory management in RandomPossessions. Open the RandomPossessions.xcodeproj file that you created in the last chapter. There are four memory management problems to fix in this project.

The first is found in the **main** function of RandomPossessions.m where you created an instance of **NSMutableArray** named items. You know two things about this instance: its owner is the **main** function and it has a retain count of one. It is then **main**'s responsibility to send this instance the message **release** when it no longer needs it. The last time you reference items in this function is when you print out all of its entries, so you can release it after that:

```
for(int i = 0; i < [items count]; i++) {
    NSLog(@"%@", [items objectAtIndex:i]);
}

[items release];
```

The object pointed to by items decrements its retain count when this line of code is executed. In this case, that object is deallocated because **main** was the only owner. If another object had retained items, it wouldn't have been deallocated.

There is one more detail to take care of. The instance of **NSMutableArray** that items pointed to is now gone. However, items is still storing the address that was the instance's location in memory. It is much safer to set the value of items to nil. Then any messages mistakenly sent to items will have no effect.

```
[items release];
items = nil;
```

The ordering of those two statements is important. Ordering them this way says, "Send the object release, and then clear my pointer to it." What would happen if you swapped the order of these statements? It would be the same thing as saying, "Set my pointer to this object to nil and then send the message **release** to.... Oh, no! I don't know where that object went!" You would leak the object: it wasn't released before you erased your pointer to it.

The second memory problem occurs when you create an instance of **NSMutableArray** and fill it with instances of **Possession** returned from the **randomPossession** convenience method:

```
NSMutableArray *items = [[NSMutableArray alloc] init];
for (int i = 0; i < 10; i++) {
    [items addObject:[Possession randomPossession]];
}
```

The implementation for **randomPossession** returns an instance of type **Possession** that it created by sending the message **alloc**. This object is owned by this class method and therefore has a retain count of 1.

When you add a **Possession** instance to an **NSMutableArray**, the array becomes an owner of that object, so its retain count is increased to 2. After **randomPossession** finishes executing, however, it loses its pointer to the **Possession** it created. The **Possession** instance still has two owners, but only one still has a pointer to it (items). Memory leak!

This is a perfect opportunity to use **autorelease**. The method **randomPossession** should send **autorelease** to an instance it creates and relinquish its ownership of that instance. The object will still exist temporarily and be retained when it is added to the **NSMutableArray**. The instance of **NSMutableArray** will then be the sole owner of this new **Possession**. In effect, you have transferred ownership of the instance from **randomPossession** to items. When the array deallocates itself and releases the objects it contains, each object will have a retain count of 0 and will deallocate itself. Memory leak solved.

Now fix the leak in the **randomPossession** method in Possession.m.

```
+ (id)randomPossession
{
    ... Create random variables ...
    Possession *newPossession = [[self alloc]
                            initWithPossessionName:randomName
                                    valueInDollars:randomValue
                                      serialNumber:randomSerialNumber];

    return [newPossession autorelease];
}
```

When working with an instance of **NSMutableArray**, three rules apply to object ownership:

• When an object is added to an **NSMutableArray**, that object gets sent the message **retain**; the array becomes an owner of that object and has a pointer to it.

• When an object is removed from an **NSMutableArray**, that object gets sent the message **release**; the array relinquishes ownership of that object and no longer has a pointer to it.

• When an **NSMutableArray** is deallocated, it sends the message **release** to all of its entries as shown in Figure 3.5.

Figure 3.5 Deallocating an NSMutableArray

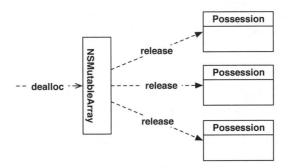

The third memory problem in RandomPossessions is in the **description** method that **Possession** implements. This method creates and returns an instance of **NSString** that needs to be autoreleased.

```
- (NSString *)description
{
    NSString *descriptionString =
        [[NSString alloc] initWithFormat:@"%@ (%@): Worth $%d, Recorded on %@",
                          possessionName,
                          serialNumber,
                          valueInDollars,
                          dateCreated];
    return [descriptionString autorelease];
}
```

You can make this even simpler by using a convenience method. **NSString** (as well as many other classes in the iPhone SDK) includes convenience methods that return autoreleased objects. Update **description** to use the convenience method **stringWithFormat:** to ensure that the **NSString** instance that **description** creates will be autoreleased.

```
- (NSString *)description
{
    return [NSString stringWithFormat:@"%@ (%@): Worth $%d, Recorded on %@",
                     possessionName,
                     serialNumber,
                     valueInDollars,
                     dateCreated];
}
```

The final memory problem has to do with the instance variables within **Possession** objects.

When the retain count of a **Possession** instance hits zero, it will send itself the message **dealloc**. The **dealloc** method of **Possession** has been implemented by its superclass, **NSObject**, but **NSObject** knows nothing about the instance variables added to **Possession**. So you must override **dealloc** in Possession.m to release any instance variables that have been retained.

```
- (void)dealloc
{
    [possessionName release];
    [serialNumber release];
    [dateCreated release];
    [super dealloc];
}
```

Always call the superclass implementation of **dealloc** at the end of the method. When an object is deallocated, it should release all of its own instance variables first. Then, it should go up its class hierarchy and release any instance variables of its superclass. In the end, the implementation of **dealloc** in **NSObject** will return the object's memory to the heap.

Now let's check your understanding of memory management concepts by looking more closely at instance variables and memory management.

Why send **release** to instance variables and not **dealloc**?

One object should never send **dealloc** to another. Always use **release** and let the object check its own retain count and decide whether to send itself **dealloc**.

Why do you need to release these instance variables in the first place? Where are the calls to **alloc**, **retain**, or **copy** that make an instance of **Possession** an owner of these objects?

Let's start with the instance variable dateCreated. Because it is allocated in the designated initializer for **Possession**, that instance of **Possession** becomes an owner and needs to release the object pointed to by dateCreated according to the first of the retain count rules described on page 52.

To figure out the other two instance variables, possessionName and serialNumber, you have to go back to their property declarations in Possession.h.

```
@property (nonatomic, copy) NSString *possessionName;
@property (nonatomic, copy) NSString *serialNumber;
```

Both of the properties associated with these instance variables have the copy attribute. When the message **setPossessionName:** is sent to an instance of **Possession**, the incoming parameter is sent the message **copy**. The instance variable possessionName is then set to point at that copied instance. If you wrote the code for **setSerialNumber:** instead of using @synthesize, it would look something like this:

```
- (void)setSerialNumber:(NSString *)newSerialNumber
{
    newSerialNumber = [newSerialNumber copy];
    [serialNumber release];
    serialNumber = newSerialNumber;
}
```

The second retain count rule states that, if an object copies something, the object becomes an owner of that thing. Therefore, the owning object needs to release the copied object in its **dealloc** method. The same would hold true of these instance variables if their property attribute was retain (but not if the attribute were assign, which is a simple pointer assignment).

Strings come in two flavors: **NSString** and **NSMutableString**. Because an **NSString** can never be changed, there is seldom a need to copy it. Thus, in the case of **NSString** (and most other immutable objects), the copy method looks like this:

```
- (id)copyWithZone:(NSZone *)z
{
    [self retain];
    return self;
}
```

This approach prevents unnecessary copying. For example, the code above is basically equivalent to this:

```
- (void)setSerialNumber:(NSString *)newSerialNumber
{
    NSString *newValue;

    // Is it a mutable string?
    if ([newSerialNumber isKindOfClass:[NSMutableString class]])
        // I need to copy it
        newValue = [newSerialNumber copy];
    else
        // It is sufficient to retain it
        newValue = [newSerialNumber retain];

    [serialNumber release];
    serialNumber = newValue;
}
```

Note, however, that this code is not exactly equivalent. Because of some underlying implementation details, both **NSString** and **NSMutableString** might return YES if asked whether they are of type **NSMutableString**.

Sometimes in this book, we will show you example code that does not exactly match the implementation in the SDK. We do this to give you a better understanding of the concepts being discussed. We're not lying to you; we're just sparing you some of the details until you're more comfortable with the concepts. Once you're there, you can divine all the details from the documentation. (In fact, we already did this when we gave an example of implementing **retain** and **release** earlier in this chapter. The implementations of these methods are actually much dirtier.)

Congratulations! You've implemented retain counts and fixed four memory leaks. Your RandomPossessions application now manages its memory like a champ!

Keep this code around because you are going to use it in later chapters.

4

Delegation and Core Location

In this chapter, we introduce delegation, a recurring design pattern of Cocoa Touch development, and demonstrate its use with the Core Location service, which provides the location-finding features of the iPhone.

Delegation

We spend a lot of time sending messages to objects. Sometimes, however, we want objects to send messages to us — a callback. A *callback* is a function that is triggered when an event occurs. Usually, this is an event that happens in response to user input. We don't exactly know when this event might occur, but we set up a callback so that when it does occur, our code will be called. In some systems, callbacks are sent to objects that are known as *listeners*.

In Cocoa Touch, callbacks are implemented using a technique known as *delegation*. Let's start with an example. Every instance of **UITextView** has a `delegate` property, which is a pointer to an object. That object is "the delegate" of the text view. You can set that pointer to refer to any object, as long as that object conforms to the protocol of the class for which it is a delegate. For instance, when you create a class that will be a **UITextView** delegate, you need to declare it to conform to the UITextViewDelegate protocol. You declare which protocols a class conforms to by listing the names of the protocols in a comma-delimited list in angled brackets after the name of the superclass:

```
// SuperGoodController conforms to the UITextViewDelegate
// and SomeOtherDelegate protocol.
@interface SuperGoodController : NSObject
    <UITextViewDelegate, SomeOtherDelegate>
```

A *protocol* is simply a list of method declarations. (Other languages, like Java, sometimes call them interfaces.) When a class conforms to a protocol, it is promising to implement all required methods from that protocol and is reserving the option to implement any optional methods. For example, here is the protocol that declares all the delegate methods for **UITextView**:

```
@protocol UITextViewDelegate

@optional
- (BOOL)textViewShouldBeginEditing:(UITextView *)textView;
- (BOOL)textViewShouldEndEditing:(UITextView *)textView;

- (void)textViewDidBeginEditing:(UITextView *)textView;
- (void)textViewDidEndEditing:(UITextView *)textView;

- (BOOL)textView:(UITextView *)textView
    shouldChangeTextInRange:(NSRange)range
            replacementText:(NSString *)text;

- (void)textViewDidChange:(UITextView *)textView;

- (void)textViewDidChangeSelection:(UITextView *)textView;
@end
```

Notice that this particular protocol doesn't have any required methods (which is not unusual). Also notice that the first argument to all of the delegate methods is a pointer to the object that is sending the callback. This lets the delegate know exactly which object is sending it a delegate message and is always the case with delegate methods.

In Apple's developer documentation, every protocol has its own page that lists and describes its methods. To get to the documentation, go to the Help menu and click Developer Documentation. There you can search for the protocol. By convention, the name of a delegate protocol is the name of the class doing the delegation suffixed with `Delegate`. For example, to find all of the delegate methods for a **UITextView**, search for **UITextViewDelegate**. The "UITextViewDelegate Protocol Reference" is shown in Figure 4.1.

Figure 4.1   UITextViewDelegate Documentation

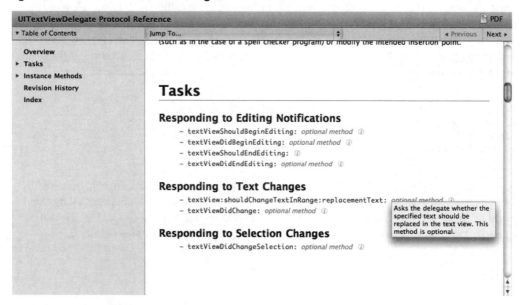

Once you have declared a class as conforming to a protocol, you find the methods you need in the documentation, implement them for that class, and you're good to go. For example, if the delegate of a **UITextView** has implemented the method **textViewDidChange:**, then that method will be called every time the user changes the text of that text view, as shown in Figure 4.2.

Figure 4.2   A UITextView delegate

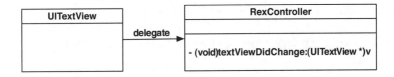

When implementing a delegate method, it is important to make sure you match the name and the types of arguments exactly as they are declared in the protocol. If you change the name in any way (capitalization or spelling errors are the most common "changes"), the method will not get called. If you change the types of the arguments, your application may not work as you intend it to.

There are two basic categories of delegate methods. Some are "for-your-information" methods. These methods are sent to a delegate to inform it that something has happened. For example, you would implement **textViewDidChange:** to be informed when the text in a **UITextView** changes.

Other delegate methods are "what-should-I-do?" methods. These methods expect a response back from the delegate that will dictate the behavior of the delegating object. For example, if a delegate implements **textView:shouldChangeTextInRange:replacementText:**, it can prevent an inappropriate edit by returning NO.

Sometimes protocols have required methods. A class that conforms to a protocol that has required methods must implement those methods or else the compiler will warn you and your application will probably crash. How can you tell if a method is required? In the protocol reference, the absence of the text optional method next to the method name indicates that it is a required method. (Some versions of the documentation label the required methods instead of optional methods.)

You can also determine which methods are required by looking at the header file in which the protocol is declared. Any required methods appear above the @optional directive in the protocol body. Methods that appear below the @optional directive are optional and do not have to be implemented by a class that conforms to that protocol. (If there is no @optional tag, then all methods in that protocol are required.)

```
// SuperCoolProtocol is a protocol that also
// includes methods from the NSObject protocol
@protocol SuperCoolProtocol <NSObject>
- (void)requiredMethod;
@optional
- (void)optionalMethod1;
- (void)optionalMethod2;
@end
```

Many classes use delegates: **AVAudioPlayer**, **CLLocationManager**, **NSNetServices**, **NSStream**, **NSURLConnection**, **NSXMLParser**, **CALayer**, **UIAccelerometer**, **UIApplication**, **UIPickerView**, **UIImagePickerController**, **UIScrollView**, **UITableView**, **UITextField**, **UIWebView**, and **UIWindow**. Take a moment to browse through some of these protocol references. (Here's a shortcut: in Xcode, hold down the Option and Command keys and double-click the name of the protocol. The documentation browser will appear displaying a list of every method for that protocol.)

To review, in order implement delegate methods for an object, you must

1. declare a class to conform to the object's delegate protocol

2. implement the necessary delegate methods (required ones and optional ones you want to use) in the class

3. set the delegate pointer of the object to point to an instance of your class

Beginning the Whereami Application

To help you understand delegation, you're going to write an application called Whereami that uses delegation over and over again. This application will display a map and allow the user to scroll, zoom, and tag the device's current location with a pin and a title. This exercise spans two chapters. At the end of this chapter, the application won't look like much, but the final product — and the clearer understanding of delegation — will be worth it. Create a Window-Based Application and name it Whereami.

Using frameworks

Open WhereamiAppDelegate.h and find the following line of code at the top. (You may have noticed it at the top of your other application delegate files, too.)

```
#import <UIKit/UIKit.h>
```

This translates to "From the UIKit framework, import the UIKit.h header." A *framework* is a collection of related classes, and Cocoa Touch is a set of frameworks. One of the benefits of Cocoa Touch being organized into frameworks is that you only need to import what your application needs. The UIKit framework is in every iPhone application because it contains all of the user interface classes like **UIButton** and **UILabel**. Whereami will also need the Core Location framework. It won't need, for example, the MediaPlayer framework.

The UIKit framework is added automatically by Xcode, but to use the code in the Core Location framework, you need to add it to your project. Select Edit Active Target from the Project menu. In the Target Info window that appears, select the General tab. At the bottom of the window is a list of Linked Libraries. Click the + button on the bottom-left corner of the window. A sheet will drop down from this window listing all of the available frameworks for iPhone OS. Choose CoreLocation.framework from that list and click the Add button as shown in Figure 4.3. This application can now use the classes and functions available in the Core Location framework.

Figure 4.3   Adding the Core Location framework

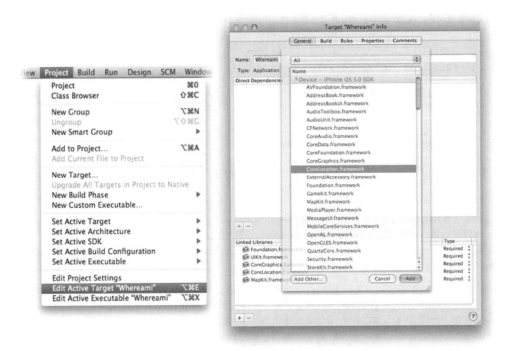

While there are other ways to add frameworks to your project, this is the recommended way because it allows you to switch freely between target SDKs. For example, you could recompile your application for a different version of the iPhone OS without making any other changes to your project in Xcode.

Make sure you remember how to add a framework to a project — you will have to do it fairly frequently!

Core Location

Location Services enables applications to determine the device's geographical location. Core Location is the framework that you use to talk to Location Services. No matter what type of device is being used, the Core Location code you write does not change.

The class that interfaces with the hardware is called **CLLocationManager**. Instances of this class are given a pointer to a delegate and then told to find the device's location in the world. At this point, the **CLLocationManager** starts doing its own thing while the rest of the application continues with other tasks — like accepting user input or updating the interface. This is possible because the location manager operates on another thread.

When a **CLLocationManager** instance succeeds or fails in determining the location of the device, it informs its delegate by sending it one of the messages in the CLLocationManagerDelegate protocol.

For the Whereami application, you need to create an instance of **CLLocationManager** and give it a delegate. **WhereamiAppDelegate** is the controller object for this exercise; it will contain a **CLLocationManager** and also be its delegate. Therefore, **WhereamiAppDelegate** must conform to the CLLocationManagerDelegate protocol. Add the following code to WhereamiAppDelegate.h

```
#import <UIKit/UIKit.h>
#import <CoreLocation/CoreLocation.h>

@interface WhereamiAppDelegate : NSObject
    <UIApplicationDelegate, CLLocationManagerDelegate>
{
    UIWindow *window;
    CLLocationManager *locationManager;
}
@property (nonatomic, retain) IBOutlet UIWindow *window;
@end
```

A **CLLocationManager** instance has properties you can set to specify how often it should update and how accurate it should be. The property distanceFilter determines how far the device must move in meters before **CLLocationManager** informs its delegate of a new location. Its setter method is **setDistanceFilter:**.

The second property, desiredAccuracy, can be set with the method **setDesiredAccuracy:**. The desired accuracy is important because it has consequences for battery power and CPU time. There is a tradeoff between the accuracy and the amount of battery life and CPU time required to determine a location. Moreover, the accuracy is ultimately dependent on the type of device the user has, the availability of cellular towers and satellites, and the availability of known wireless access points.

In the method **application:didFinishLaunchingWithOptions:**, you will instantiate a **CLLocationManager** to track a device's location. For this application, you will set its properties to request the most accurate location data available from the **CLLocationManager** as often as possible. (This will use the most amount of battery and take the longest amount of time.)

Add the following to WhereamiAppDelegate.m.

```
- (BOOL)application:(UIApplication *)application
    didFinishLaunchingWithOptions:(NSDictionary *)launchOptions
{
    // Create location manager object -
    locationManager = [[CLLocationManager alloc] init];

    // Make this instance of WhereamiAppDelegate the delegate
    // it will send its messages to our WhereamiAppDelegate
    [locationManager setDelegate:self];

    // We want all results from the location manager
    [locationManager setDistanceFilter:kCLDistanceFilterNone];

    // And we want it to be as accurate as possible
    // regardless of how much time/power it takes
    [locationManager setDesiredAccuracy:kCLLocationAccuracyBest];

    // Tell our manager to start looking for its location immediately
    [locationManager startUpdatingLocation];
```

```
    [window makeKeyAndVisible];
    return YES;
}
```

Notice that you have set the locationManager's delegate to self. Because we are within the implementation block for **WhereamiAppDelegate**, self refers to this instance of **WhereamiAppDelegate**. Therefore, all of the delegate methods for this instance of **CLLocationManager** will be implemented in WhereamiAppDelegate.m.

Also, the locationManager does *not* retain its delegate. In fact, delegates are never retained by the object doing the delegating. Why? Because a controller object usually owns the object for which it is a delegate. If an object then retains its delegate, it would create a problem called a *retain cycle*. Right now, you have other things to concentrate on, so we will leave the discussion of retain cycles for a future chapter; just remember that setting a delegate is always an assignment and that delegates are never retained or copied.

Because the delegate is not retained, it is important that the delegate pointer is never "dangling." For example, if the instance of **WhereamiAppDelegate** could get deallocated, we would be sure to set the delegate pointer to nil:

```
- (void)dealloc
{
    [locationManager setDelegate:nil];
    [super dealloc];
}
```

Receiving updates from CLLocationManager

When a **CLLocationManager** has enough data to produce a new location, it creates an instance of **CLLocation**. That **CLLocation** object is sent to the **CLLocationManager**'s delegate via the **locationManager:didUpdateToLocation:fromLocation:** delegate method as shown in Figure 4.4. (This method is from the CLLocationManagerDelegate protocol.)

Figure 4.4   A CLLocation object

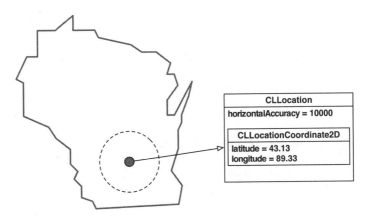

CLLocation objects contain the latitude and longitude of the user's device. Each location object will also contain the accuracy of its reading in the horizontalAccuracy property. Depending on the device, information like the elevation above sea level and the current heading of the device may also be recorded.

In order to start receiving **CLLocation** instances from the **CLLocationManager**, you must implement the delegate method **locationManager:didUpdateToLocation:fromLocation:** from the CLLocationManagerDelegate protocol. For now, implement this method in WhereamiAppDelegate.m so that it prints out the **CLLocation**'s **description** to the console. (Be careful that there are no typos in the method signature; remember, the name of the method must exactly match the declaration in the protocol. The compiler won't tell you if you made a mistake. It will just think you are defining a brand new method. Most developers copy and paste methods from the documentation.)

```
- (void)locationManager:(CLLocationManager *)manager
   didUpdateToLocation:(CLLocation *)newLocation
          fromLocation:(CLLocation *)oldLocation
{
    NSLog(@"%@", newLocation);
}
```

You also need to know if the **CLLocationManager** fails to find its location and why. When it fails, it sends a different message to its delegate # **locationManager:didFailWithError:**. Implement that method in WhereamiAppDelegate.m.

```
- (void)locationManager:(CLLocationManager *)manager
       didFailWithError:(NSError *)error
{
    NSLog(@"Could not find location: %@", error);
}
```

Build and run the application. After giving permission for the application to use location services and waiting for a few seconds while the location is determined, your console should read something like this:

```
<+37.33168900, -122.03073100> +/- 100.00m (speed -1.00 mps / course -1.00)
```

So that's how delegation works with a real example. If it feels odd or doesn't quite make sense, don't worry. It can be hard to understand at first, but you'll get it in time. In the next chapter, you are going to finish off the Whereami application. And yeah, you guessed it, you will be using more delegation in that chapter, too.

Releasing Controller Instance Variables

Deallocating objects while an application is running is important because it frees up memory for future objects. When an application terminates, the memory it was consuming is returned to the operating system. In most applications, however, controller objects exist the entire time an application is running. They never get released and therefore never get deallocated.

This holds true for Whereami: the instance of **WhereamiAppDelegate** will never get released because it needs to exist the entire time the application is running. Therefore, you do not need to implement the **dealloc** method for this class. Most of the applications in this book have controller objects that exist the entire time an application is running. This is the behavior for many controller objects in real applications for two reasons:

- Controller objects are the brains of an application. They take on a lot of roles and typically are needed throughout the execution of an application.

- Controller objects do not consume a lot of memory themselves. They only hold pointers to view and model objects, which are the two types of classes that consume the majority of memory. If memory is running low, the controller can get rid of the big objects it has pointers to (and, ideally, be able to reload those objects when needed).

Now, this isn't to say that *all* controller objects exist throughout an application's lifetime. Some controller objects can exist temporarily for a specific task. In these circumstances, you will need to release the appropriate instance variables in the controller's **dealloc** method.

We won't waste your time showing you the implementation of **dealloc** methods that will never get called, but you can't go wrong by getting in the habit of always writing correct **dealloc** methods. (An unused method never hurts you.)

In Snow Leopard, a static analyzer was added to Xcode. The static analyzer evaluates your code and looks for potential problems like memory leaks or uninitialized variables. (You can run the static analyzer on your code by selecting Build and Analyze from the Build menu.) It's not without flaws, though. If you have a controller object that you never intend to release, the static analyzer may warn you that you are leaking that object. You can ignore those warnings.

Challenge: Heading

Using delegation, retrieve the heading information from the **CLLocationManager** and print it to the console. (Hint: You need to implement at least one more delegate method and send another message to the location manager.)

For the More Curious: Compiler and Linker Errors

Building an application in Xcode is a multi-step process. Two of these steps are compiling and linking, and each comes with its own type of error.

Compiling, one of the first building steps, takes your Objective-C code and turns it into the binary code a computer understands. Each implementation file (suffixed with .m) is turned into an object file that contains that binary code.

If an error is found in your code during this phase, the compile fails. (And if an implementation file fails to compile, the corresponding object file is not created.) An error during this phase is called a *compile-time error* or *syntax error*. These errors mean that the compiler cannot understand your source code — usually because of little things like misplaced semicolons, unbalanced brackets ([]) or braces ({}), spelling or capitalization errors.

A syntax error is also generated if you declare a variable of a type that the compiler doesn't recognize. For each Objective-C class, there is a header file that declares it, and importing the header file tells the compiler about that class. To see an example of a syntax error, comment out the following line in WhereamiAppDelegate.h:

```
//#import <CoreLocation/CoreLocation.h>
```

Build your application again. It will fail, and the Build Results window will show you several errors (Figure 4.5).

Figure 4.5   Build results with compile-time error

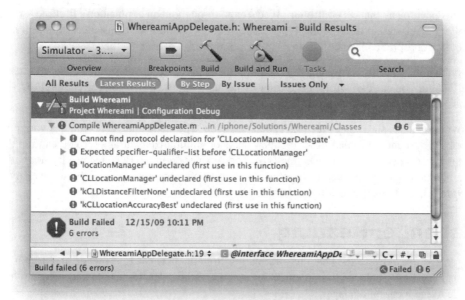

These errors tell you that the compiler doesn't know about **CLLocationManager** or its delegate protocol. That's because the declarations for these things are in CoreLocation/CoreLocation.h. Now that you've seen this error, you know how to fix it. Uncomment the #import directive, build again, and the errors will disappear. (So, what does importing a file really do? When an implementation file is compiled, each import directive is replaced with the text of the imported file. The text is effectively copied and pasted at the spot of the import directive.)

The next step in the building process is *linking*. The linker reads all of the object files, determines what functions and classes are being used, and then links them to the object file that contains the definition for those functions and classes. If the linker cannot find a definition, it generates a *linker error*. Typically, you get this error when you forget to add a framework to a project.

Linker errors are more difficult for new developers to understand because they use unfamiliar terms (like "symbol" and "literal-pointer"). So let's go ahead and cause a linker error just for practice. Select the CoreLocation.framework icon from the project window and press the delete key to remove it from your project. Build your application again, and the Build Results window will tell you of your folly (Figure 4.6).

Figure 4.6   Build results with linker error

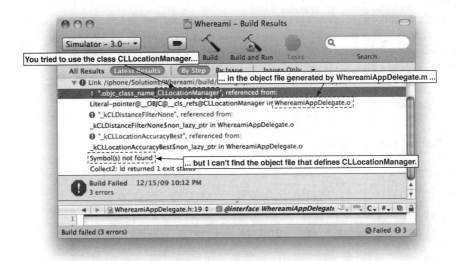

This error tells you that the compiler knew about **CLLocationManager** (because you imported the header file), but the linker can't find the object file that defines it. Add the Core Location framework back to your project to eliminate this error.

For the More Curious: Protocols

A protocol is a list of methods. Here's an example:

```
@protocol CLLocationManagerDelegate<NSObject>

@optional
- (void)locationManager:(CLLocationManager *)manager
     didUpdateToLocation:(CLLocation *)newLocation
            fromLocation:(CLLocation *)oldLocation;

- (void)locationManager:(CLLocationManager *)manager
        didUpdateHeading:(CLHeading *)newHeading;

- (BOOL)locationManagerShouldDisplayHeadingCalibration:
                                    (CLLocationManager *)manager;

- (void)locationManager:(CLLocationManager *)manager
        didFailWithError:(NSError *)error;

@end
```

In the iPhone SDK, most classes that have a delegate property define a protocol that declares the methods that can be sent to their delegate. Typically, a delegate protocol only has optional methods. (Not all protocols are delegate protocols; you'll work with other protocols later in this book. In fact, while "delegate protocol" is a handy term for a protocol that declares delegate methods, there is no such thing as a delegate protocol according to the compiler; a protocol is just a protocol.)

When an object wants to send an optional delegate message to its delegate, it first sends the message **respondsToSelector:** to see if the delegate implements the optional method. For example, when text is added to an instance of **UITextView**, it informs its delegate through an optional delegate method. If you were writing the **UITextView** class, the implementation of **UITextView** would look something like this:

```
@implementation UITextView
- (void)setText:(NSString *)t
{
    NSString *tCopy = [t copy];
    [text release];
    text = tCopy;

    // Find out if the delegate responds to textViewDidChange:
    if ([[self delegate] respondsToSelector:@selector(textViewDidChange:)]) {
        // Send the delegate a message saying the text did change!
        [[self delegate] textViewDidChange:self];
    }
}
```

However, with a required method, an object does not check before sending the message; it assumes that this method is implemented. If you don't implement a required delegate method for an object, your application will throw an unrecognized selector exception when the object sends the required message to its delegate.

Some classes in the iPhone SDK are borrowed from Mac OS X and do *not* declare a delegate protocol even if they have a delegate property. Usually these classes are prefixed with **NS** and are part of the Foundation framework. These classes were written before Objective-C 2.0 when there was no @optional directive. Back then, *every* method in a given protocol had to be implemented by a class that conformed to that protocol.

In order to have optional delegate methods, these classes declared their protocols in informal protocols. Informal protocols are a bit of a legacy and beyond the scope of this book. However, it's good to know about them for the purpose of reading the documentation. If you're looking for delegate methods for one of these classes, you'll find them in the same documentation page as the class that uses them instead of in a separate protocol reference.

5

MapKit and Text Input

In this chapter, you will finish the Whereami application using delegation with the MapKit framework and **UITextField**, a text input control from the UIKit framework (Figure 5.1). MapKit is the framework that allows you to display maps and the geographical data associated with them.

Figure 5.1   Finished Whereami

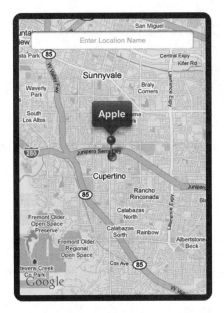

Object Diagrams

iPhone applications can get very large and use many classes and methods. One way to keep your head wrapped around a large and complex project is to draw an *object diagram*. Object diagrams show the major objects in an application and any objects they have as instance variables. (At Big Nerd Ranch, we use a program called OmniGraffle to draw our object diagrams.) Most exercises in this book will show you an object diagram to give you the "big picture" of the application you are developing. Figure 5.2 shows the object diagram for the complete Whereami application.

Figure 5.2   Whereami object diagram

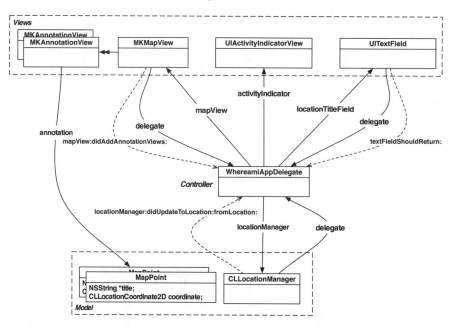

Let's look more closely at this diagram. At the top, there are three view objects:

- An **MKMapView** displays the map and the labels for the recorded locations.

- A **UIActivityIndicatorView** indicates that the device is working and not stalled.

- A **UITextField** allows the user to input text to label the current location on the map.

On the bottom are the model objects. One is an instance of **CLLocationManager**. A **CLLocationManager** interacts with the device's hardware to determine the user's location.

Finally, in the middle of everything is the controller object, **WhereamiAppDelegate**. **WhereamiAppDelegate** is responsible for processing updates and requests from objects and for updating the user interface. It is the delegate for **MKMapView**, **UITextField**, and **CLLocationManager**.

Now take a look at the messages sent to **WhereamiAppDelegate** by these objects. **MKMapView** sends **mapView:didAddAnnotationViews:** when a view (or views) is added. **UITextField** sends **textFieldShouldReturn:** when the user has finished entering text. **CLLocationManager** sends **locationManager:didUpdateToLocation:fromLocation:** to inform **WhereamiAppDelegate** of a location update.

MapKit Framework

The Core Location framework tells us where we are in the world; the MapKit framework shows us that world. At the end of this chapter, the user will be able place a *MapKit annotation* at the current location and name it. The default MapKit annotation appears as a red pin on the map.

Add the MapKit framework to your project. (If you've forgotten how, flip back to page 62 and refresh your memory.) Once you have added the MapKit framework, you must import the header file in any file that will use classes from that framework. At the top of WhereamiAppDelegate.h, import the MapKit header.

```
#import <CoreLocation/CoreLocation.h>
#import <MapKit/MapKit.h>
```

Most of MapKit's work is done by the class **MKMapView**. Instances of this type display a map, track touches, and display annotations. (They also do quite a bit more, but that's all you'll need for this application.) To determine the necessary instance variables for the Whereami project, review the object diagram in Figure 5.2. You'll need an instance of **MKMapView**, an instance of **UITextField**, and an instance of **UIActivityIndicatorView**. Declare these instance variables in WhereamiAppDelegate.h.

```
@interface WhereamiAppDelegate : NSObject
    <UIApplicationDelegate, CLLocationManagerDelegate>
{
    UIWindow *window;

    CLLocationManager *locationManager;

    IBOutlet MKMapView *mapView;
    IBOutlet UIActivityIndicatorView *activityIndicator;
    IBOutlet UITextField *locationTitleField;
}
@property (nonatomic, retain) IBOutlet UIWindow *window;

@end
```

In Interface Builder, open the file MainWindow.xib in the Resources group of the Whereami project. Then open the **UIWindow** instance in this XIB file by double-clicking on the Window object in the doc window.

Interface Properties

Drag an **MKMapView** onto the window. Then drop a **UITextField** and a **UIActivityIndicatorView** on the **MKMapView**. (If you are having trouble finding these objects, use the search box at the bottom of the Library window.) Reposition them and make the outlet connections as shown in Figure 5.3. When connecting the delegate for an object, remember to drag from the object that is delegating to the object that will be the delegate. For example, to set the **MKMapView**'s delegate, Control-click the **MKMapView** to bring up the connection panel and drag to the **WhereamiAppDelegate** instance.

Figure 5.3   Whereami XIB layout

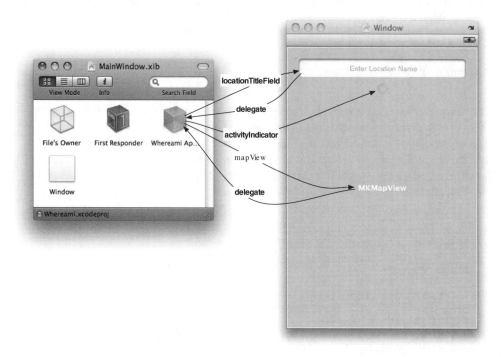

Now you're going to change some of the properties of your **UITextField** and
UIActivityIndicatorView to improve the user interface. When a **UITextField** is activated, a
keyboard appears on the screen. (We'll see why this happens later.) The keyboard's appearance is
determined by a set of the **UITextField**'s properties called **UITextInputTraits**. For Whereami,
the keyboard should display the placeholder text "Enter Location Name" and a blue-tinted Search
key. To make these changes, select the **UITextField** to get to its attributes in the Inspector
window. Change the values for Placeholder and Return Key to match what is shown in Figure 5.4.

Figure 5.4   UITextField attributes

Wouldn't it be nice if the **UIActivityIndicatorView** hid itself when it's not animating? Select **UIActivityIndicatorView** and check the box labeled Hide When Stopped in the Attributes panel as shown in Figure 5.5 to make this happen.

Figure 5.5   UIActivityIndicator attributes

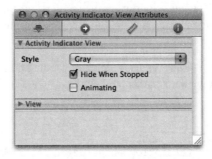

Save MainWindow.xib and quit Interface Builder.

Being a MapView Delegate

When Whereami launches, the user will be shown a map around the current location and be able to tag the location by entering a name in the **UITextField**. Core Location will get the latitude and longitude of the current location and create an object to represent it. **WhereamiAppDelegate** will then annotate the **MKMapView** at that location. In effect, the user will label locations that have been visited for future reference.

An **MKMapView** knows how to use Core Location to place the user's location on itself; you do not have to use Core Location directly when dealing with this type of object. If you set the showsUserLocation property of an **MKMapView** to YES, it will show the location of the user on the map. At the end of **application:didFinishLaunchingWithOptions:**, replace the message that tells the locationManager to update its location with one that tells the **MKMapView** to show the current location.

```
- (BOOL)application:(UIApplication *)application
    didFinishLaunchingWithOptions:(NSDictionary *)launchOptions
{
    locationManager = [[CLLocationManager alloc] init];
    [locationManager setDelegate:self];

    [locationManager setDistanceFilter:kCLDistanceFilterNone];
    [locationManager setDesiredAccuracy:kCLLocationAccuracyBest];

    // [locationManager startUpdatingLocation];
    [mapView setShowsUserLocation:YES];
    [window makeKeyAndVisible];

    return YES;
}
```

Build and run the application. A few moments after the application launches, the map will display a blue annotation dot on your current location. (If you are using the simulator, the current location is always Apple's Headquarters.) However, because you are still looking at the entire world, that blue dot is the size of Brazil and not exactly useful for figuring out where you are! Clearly, the application needs to zoom in closer to the current location.

To fix this problem, you *could* send some message to mapView telling it to zoom in on a region, but when would you do that? You can't do it when the application starts because mapView needs a moment to figure out where the user is. Nor do you want to continually tell the **MKMapView** to update its viewing region; that would be a waste of time.

Instead, how about delegation? **MKMapView** has a delegate — the **WhereamiAppDelegate** instance. So, first, declare that the **WhereamiAppDelegate** instance conforms to that protocol in WhereamiAppDelegate.h:

```
@interface WhereamiAppDelegate : NSObject
    <UIApplicationDelegate, CLLocationManagerDelegate, MKMapViewDelegate>
{
```

When an annotation is added to the map (like the blue dot that represents the user's current location), the map view should zoom in on a small area around the annotation. In the protocol documentation for MKMapViewDelegate, find a delegate method that will do that (Figure 5.6).

Figure 5.6 MKMapViewDelegate Protocol Reference

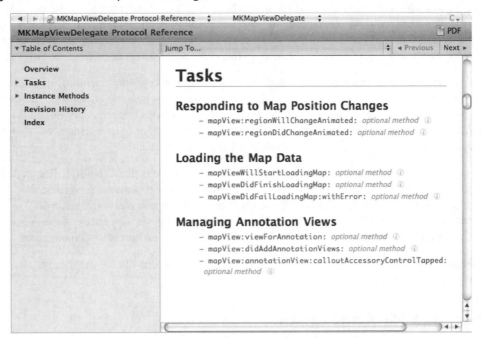

One method sticks out here: **mapView:didAddAnnotationViews:**. The documentation explains what the message name already makes rather clear — **mapView:didAddAnnotationViews:** will be called whenever an annotation is added to the map. This method can initiate the zoom any time an annotation is added. In WhereamiAppDelegate.m, implement **mapView:didAddAnnotationViews:**

```
- (void)mapView:(MKMapView *)mv didAddAnnotationViews:(NSArray *)views
{
    MKAnnotationView *annotationView = [views objectAtIndex:0];
    id <MKAnnotation> mp = [annotationView annotation];
    MKCoordinateRegion region =
        MKCoordinateRegionMakeWithDistance([mp coordinate], 250, 250);
    [mv setRegion:region animated:YES];
}
```

Take a closer look at this method body. You will need an **MKCoordinateRegion** to send to the **MKMapView**'s method **setRegion:animated:**. The **MKCoordinateRegion** is a structure (not an Objective-C object), so you can't send it messages. To create a region, you call the function **MKCoordinateRegionMakeWithDistance** with the center and two distances: meters east-west and meters north-south. The coordinate of the annotation is passed along with the number of meters that the region spans.

Skip the type declaration of the variable mp for a moment and focus on the array access. When the message **mapView:didAddAnnotationViews:** is sent to the delegate, an **NSArray** of **MKAnnotationView**s is passed as an argument. This array contains all of the views that were just added to the map. An **MKAnnotationView** is a view that is displayed on the **MKMapView**. It has a pointer to an object that contains the name, coordinate, and other annotation data. Here's where things get fun: the object that **MKAnnotationView** points to can be any object that conforms to the MKAnnotation protocol. You don't have to worry about what kind of object the annotation is; you know that you can send it the messages in the MKAnnotation protocol, and, therefore, its data can be used by an **MKAnnotationView**. (There may be more objects in the views array, depending on how many annotations were added to the map. In this exercise, you only care about the first one.)

Why is MKAnnotation a protocol and not a class? Any object can conform to a protocol, and that lets your application display different types of objects on one map. Imagine an application that maps everything in a neighborhood including restaurants and movie theaters. A restaurant has a menu, and a theater has a list of showtimes; they are different types of objects. However, both can be displayed on the map if they conform to MKAnnotation. It's brilliant!

Now consider the variable mp. Its type is id, which means "any Objective-C object." The angled brackets further specify "as long it conforms to this protocol." The MKAnnotation protocol says you can send the message **coordinate** to any conforming object, and it will return a **CLLocationCoordinate2D** structure. Here you use that structure to set the center of the region. Then, you hand the region off to the **MKMapView** with **setRegion:animated:** to do the zoom.

Build and run the application again. When the map figures out where you are in the world, it zooms in on that location.

Your own MKAnnotation

Now, you will write a class **MapPoint** that conforms to the MKAnnotation protocol and use instances of it for tagging locations in Whereami. From the File menu in Xcode, select New File.... A window will appear, and on the lefthand side of the window, select Cocoa Touch Class from the iPhone OS section. On the upper-right side, choose Objective-C class. Select NSObject from the pop-up menu and hit the Next button (Figure 5.7).

Figure 5.7 Creating an NSObject subclass

When prompted, name this class MapPoint.m and check the box labeled Also create "MapPoint.h". Click Finish, and the class files for this object will be added to your project (Figure 5.8).

Figure 5.8   Naming the subclass

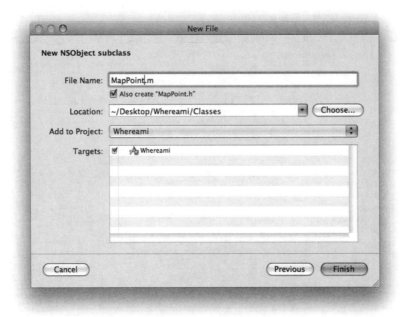

While most methods declared in the MKAnnotation protocol are optional, the **coordinate** method is required. If **MapPoint** is to conform to the MKAnnotation protocol, it must implement that method. (The protocol defines **coordinate** as a property, so you will as well. Recall from our discussion of accessors that a property is essentially a collection of method declarations.)

MKAnnotationView will interact with its annotation object through the methods declared in the MKAnnotation protocol. However, because a protocol can't declare instance variables, it is up to **MapPoint** to store the data that will be returned from the methods declared in the MKAnnotation protocol. Change MapPoint.h to read as follows:

```
#import <Foundation/Foundation.h>
#import <CoreLocation/CoreLocation.h>
#import <MapKit/MapKit.h>

@interface MapPoint : NSObject <MKAnnotation>
{
    NSString *title;
    CLLocationCoordinate2D coordinate;
}
@property (nonatomic, readonly) CLLocationCoordinate2D coordinate;
@property (nonatomic, copy) NSString *title;

- (id)initWithCoordinate:(CLLocationCoordinate2D)c title:(NSString *)t;

@end
```

Switch to MapPoint.m to enter the implementation. (The keyboard shortcut for switching between the header file and the implementation file is Command-Option-Up Arrow.)

```
#import "MapPoint.h"

@implementation MapPoint
@synthesize coordinate, title;

- (id)initWithCoordinate:(CLLocationCoordinate2D)c title:(NSString *)t
{
    [super init];
    coordinate = c;
    [self setTitle:t];
    return self;
}

- (void)dealloc
{
    [title release];
    [super dealloc];
}
@end
```

Note that you don't release coordinate in the **dealloc** method because it is not an Objective-C object and can't receive messages. The CLLocationCoordinate2D structure's memory will live inside each instance of **MapPoint**, and it will be created and destroyed automatically along with the object.

Tagging locations

Now that you have your own class that conforms to MKAnnotation, you can start tagging locations on the **MKMapView**. As we decided earlier, the user can enter text into the **UITextField** and tap the Search button on the keyboard to tag a location. But you don't have an IBAction hooked up to that button, so how will you know when the Search button was tapped?

Delegation, once again, comes to the rescue. Whenever a keyboard is dismissed from the screen by its return key, the **UITextField** that displayed the keyboard is told to return. When that happens, the **UITextField** sends its delegate the message **textFieldShouldReturn:** to see if it really should return. Because you set up locationTitleField's delegate to be **WhereamiAppDelegate**, you can implement this delegate method in WhereamiAppDelegate.m.

```
- (BOOL)textFieldShouldReturn:(UITextField *)tf
{
    [self findLocation];
    [tf resignFirstResponder];
    return YES;
}
```

Text input and the first responder

For now, ignore **findLocation**. You will write the implementation for that in a moment. Let's talk about text editing and the *first responder*.

There is a class in the UIKit framework named **UIResponder**. A responder is responsible for receiving events and processing them. A **UITextField** is a direct subclass of **UIControl**, which is a subclass of **UIView**, which is a subclass of **UIResponder** (Figure 5.9). Thus, **UITextField** can receive events, like a touch.

Figure 5.9   Class hierarchy of a UIControl object

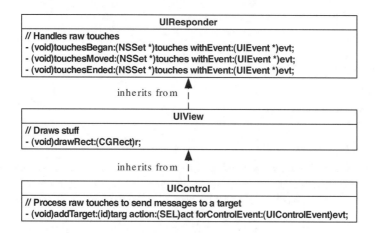

When a **UITextField** receives a touch, it becomes a special type of responder: the *first responder*. On the iPhone, the first responder only has a few uses. (On the Desktop, it has significantly more.) There can only be one first responder for a window at a time, and, since there is only one window in an application, there can only be one first responder for an application.

Every **UIResponder** has a pointer called nextResponder. A view's nextResponder is typically its superview. Thus, you can think of the responder chain as a linked list of objects — each responder has a pointer to the next responder in the chain.

When an object is the first responder, it gets a chance to handle keyboard and motion events (like shakes) first. (Touch events go to whatever view was touched first, regardless of what object is the first responder.) If the first responder doesn't handle the event, the event is passed to its nextResponder. If the nextResponder doesn't handle that event, it goes to *its* nextResponder, and so on.

When a **UITextField** becomes the first responder, it slides a keyboard onto the screen. This keyboard will remain on the screen as long as the **UITextField** remains the first responder. When you want to dismiss the keyboard, you send the message **resignFirstResponder** to the text field that put it there.

(Everything about **UITextField** holds true for instances of **UITextView**, too. The difference between **UITextView** and **UITextField** is that a **UITextView** allows for multi-line editing. As a result, a text view's Return key enters the newline character whereas a text field's Return key dispatches the delegate method **textFieldShouldReturn:**.)

Putting the pieces together

Now you need to implement the method **findLocation**. This method tells the locationManager to start looking for the current location. It also updates the user interface so that the user can't re-enter text into the text field and starts the activity indicator spinning. Declare **findLocation** in WhereamiAppDelegate.h along with its counterpart, **foundLocation**.

```
@interface WhereamiAppDelegate : NSObject
    <UIApplicationDelegate, CLLocationManagerDelegate, MKMapViewDelegate>
{
    UIWindow *window;

    CLLocationManager *locationManager;

    IBOutlet MKMapView *mapView;
    IBOutlet UIActivityIndicatorView *activityIndicator;
    IBOutlet UITextField *locationTitleField;
}

@property (nonatomic, retain) IBOutlet UIWindow *window;

- (void)findLocation;
- (void)foundLocation;

@end
```

In WhereamiAppDelegate.m, implement these two methods. They set the state of your UI elements and the locationManager.

```
- (void)findLocation
{
    [locationManager startUpdatingLocation];
    [activityIndicator startAnimating];
    [locationTitleField setHidden:YES];
}

- (void)foundLocation
{
    [locationTitleField setText:@""];
    [activityIndicator stopAnimating];
    [locationTitleField setHidden:NO];
    [locationManager stopUpdatingLocation];
}
```

One last bit: when the locationManager finds the current location, it should create a new **MapPoint** and add it to the **MKMapView** instead of printing the description on the console. Add the following code to **locationManager:didUpdateToLocation:fromLocation:** in WhereamiAppDelegate.m.

```
- (void)locationManager:(CLLocationManager *)manager
    didUpdateToLocation:(CLLocation *)newLocation
          fromLocation:(CLLocation *)oldLocation
{
    NSLog(@"%@", newLocation);
    // How many seconds ago was this new location created?
    NSTimeInterval t = [[newLocation timestamp] timeIntervalSinceNow];
    // CLLocationManagers will return the last found location of the
    // device first, you don't want that data in this case.
    // If this location was made more than 3 minutes ago, ignore it.
    if (t < -180) {
        // This is cached data, you don't want it, keep looking
        return;
    }
    MapPoint *mp = [[MapPoint alloc]
                        initWithCoordinate:[newLocation coordinate]
                                     title:[locationTitleField text]];
    [mapView addAnnotation:mp];
    [mp release];

    [self foundLocation];
}
```

Of course, WhereamiAppDelegate.m needs to know about the **MapPoint** class in order to use it. So, at the top of this file, import the **MapPoint** header.

```
#import "WhereamiAppDelegate.h"
#import "MapPoint.h"

@implementation WhereamiAppDelegate
```

Note that you use quotation marks for this import and angled brackets for frameworks. Angled brackets tell the compiler, "Only look in your system libraries for this file." Quotation marks say, "Look in all the directories for this project first, and if you don't find something, then look in the system libraries."

Build and run the application. Enter a title into the text field and watch as an annotation with that title is displayed on the map at your current location!

Challenge: Annotation Extras

Using the **NSDate** and **NSDateFormatter** classes, have your tagged annotations show the dates they were tagged.

Challenge: Reverse Geocoding

Use delegation and the class **MKReverseGeocoder** to display the city and state of a **MapPoint** on the map.

Challenge: Changing the Map Type

Add a `UISegmentedControl` to the interface. Have this segmented control switch the `MKMapView` between the standard, satellite, and hybrid maps.

For the More Curious: Renaming an Application

When you create an application, you give it a name. But you aren't stuck with that name for life, and there are at least a couple of reasons you might want to change it.

You can change your mind. Usually when I'm working on a new application, I come up with a totally cool name. I show all of my friends every time I see them and talk non-stop about how "SupercoolApp" is going to be so great. When I finish the application, however, I look at the name and think, "That's a really stupid name."

Or you can be too late. Once in a blue moon, I write an application and still love the name when I'm finished. (Baaahlast, for example, still makes me laugh when I see it.) Then reality hits, and I find out someone else has already used the name! Whereami is one of those applications. Another iPhone book has a Whereami application example, so our (way cooler) application needs a name change. How does Wherewasi sound?

To change the name of an application, choose Edit Active Target from the Project menu. You've been here before, but this time select the Build tab at the top of the window. Select All Configurations from the Configuration: pop-up button. While there are many groups in the table (and each contains plenty of settings for the target), you are looking for the Packaging group. Find the Product Name setting within that group and double-click on that row (Figure 5.10).

Figure 5.10   Renaming an application

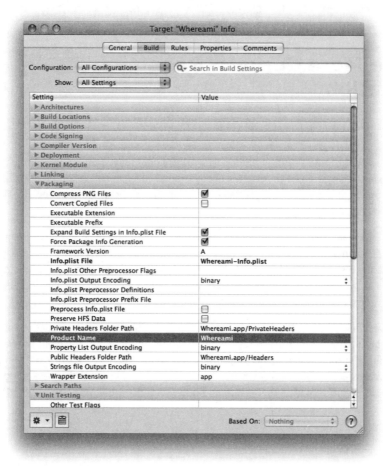

A sheet will drop down. Enter Wherewasi into this box and hit OK. Build and run your application again. Check out the name of the application on the home screen now.

6

Subclassing UIView

In previous chapters, you've created several views: a **UIButton**, a **UILabel**, etc. But what exactly is a view?

- A view is an instance of a subclass of **UIView**.

- A view knows how to draw itself on the application's window.

- A view is arranged within a hierarchy: the window (an instance of **UIWindow**) is itself a view and the root of the hierarchy. It has subviews (that appear on the window). Those views can also have subviews.

- A view handles touch events.

In this chapter, you are going to create your own **UIView** subclass that fills the screen with concentric circles as shown in Figure 6.1. You will also learn how to add text and enable scrolling and zooming.

Figure 6.1   View that draws concentric circles

Creating a Custom View

In Xcode, create a new Window-based Application. Name it Hypnosister.

To create a new **UIView** subclass, select New File... from the File menu. On the lefthand side of the next window, select Cocoa Touch Class within the iPhone OS group. Choose the Objective-C class option for the template. In the pop-up menu labeled Subclass of, select UIView. (Figure 6.2)

Figure 6.2   Creating a UIView subclass

Apple frequently (and pointlessly) changes this interface, so your window may look different. If it does, make sure you are finding a template that is a subclass of **UIView** (not **UIViewController**). Click the Next button.

Name this file HypnosisView.m and make sure that Also create "HypnosisView.h" is toggled on, as shown in Figure 6.3. Click the Finish button.

Figure 6.3   Creating a HypnosisView

The HypnosisView.h file will open automatically. Open its counterpart, HypnosisView.m. Locate the **drawRect:** method in this file.

The drawRect: method

Every **UIView** subclass implements the method **drawRect:**. The **drawRect:** method is where the drawing code for the view goes. For example, a **UIButton**'s **drawRect:** method draws a rounded rectangle with a title string in the center.

Each time an instance of **UIView** is drawn, the system prepares a graphics context specifically for that view. The context is then activated, and the message **drawRect:** is sent to the instance of **UIView** that is being drawn. The graphics context's type is **CGContextRef** (*Core Graphics Context Reference*), and it is responsible for aggregating drawing commands and producing an image as a result. This image is the appearance of the view instance. A graphics context also stores its drawing state, which includes things like the current drawing color, coordinate system, and the width of lines.

When drawing a view, you will sometimes use Objective-C to make calls defined in UIKit that implicitly use the active graphics context. Other times, you will get hold of the graphics context explicitly and draw using the C functions of the Core Graphics framework. In this chapter, you will do both.

In HypnosisView.m, change the **drawRect:** method:

```objc
- (void)drawRect:(CGRect)rect
{
    // What rectangle am I filling?
    CGRect bounds = [self bounds];

    // Where is its center?
    CGPoint center;
    center.x = bounds.origin.x + bounds.size.width / 2.0;
    center.y = bounds.origin.y + bounds.size.height / 2.0;

    // From the center how far out to a corner?
    float maxRadius = hypot(bounds.size.width, bounds.size.height) / 2.0;

    // Get the context being draw upon
    CGContextRef context = UIGraphicsGetCurrentContext();

    // All lines will be drawn 10 points wide
    CGContextSetLineWidth(context, 10);

    // Set the stroke color to light gray
    [[UIColor lightGrayColor] setStroke];

    // Draw concentric circles from the outside in
    for (float currentRadius = maxRadius; currentRadius > 0; currentRadius -= 20)
    {
        CGContextAddArc(context, center.x, center.y,
                        currentRadius, 0.0, M_PI * 2.0, YES);
        CGContextStrokePath(context);
    }
}
```

Notice that you are passed a CGRect structure. This is the rectangle that needs to be redrawn, sometimes called a *dirty rectangle*. Typically, you ignore the dirty rectangle and issue the drawing instructions as though the entire view needed to be redrawn. If, however, your drawing code is particularly intricate, you might be more careful and only redraw the parts in the dirty rectangle to speed up drawing.

A CGRect structure (Figure 6.4) contains the members origin and size. These two members are also structures. The origin is of type CGPoint and contains two more float members: x and y. The size is of type CGSize and also has two float members: width and height. These three structures are the basic building blocks of Core Graphics routines.

Figure 6.4   CGRect

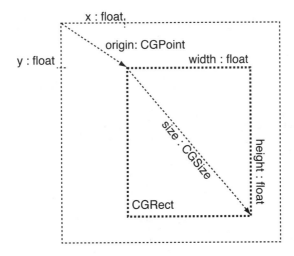

Instantiating a UIView

Recall that there are two ways to create an instance of your view:

- create it in Interface Builder

- create it programmatically with **alloc** and **initWithFrame:** and make the new view a subview of the window

In this chapter, you are going to create the view programmatically.

Open HypnosisterAppDelegate.h and add an instance variable for the new view:

```
#import <UIKit/UIKit.h>
@class HypnosisView;

@interface HypnosisterAppDelegate : NSObject <UIApplicationDelegate>
{
    UIWindow *window;
    HypnosisView *view;
}
@property (nonatomic, retain) IBOutlet UIWindow *window;

@end
```

In HypnosisterAppDelegate.m, create the new instance and place it on the window:

```
#import "HypnosisterAppDelegate.h"
#import "HypnosisView.h"

@implementation HypnosisterAppDelegate

@synthesize window;

- (BOOL)application:(UIApplication *)application
    didFinishLaunchingWithOptions:(NSDictionary *)launchOptions
{
    CGRect wholeWindow = [window bounds];
    view = [[HypnosisView alloc] initWithFrame:wholeWindow];
    [view setBackgroundColor:[UIColor clearColor]];
    [window addSubview:view];

    [window makeKeyAndVisible];
    return YES;
}
// A dealloc method that will never get called because
// HypnosisterAppDelegate will exist for the life of the application
- (void)dealloc
{
    [view release];
    [window release];
    [super dealloc];
}

@end
```

Notice that you are calling **initWithFrame:**, the designated initializer for **UIView**. The view then has a size and position. When it is added to a view hierarchy (**addSubview:**), its position will be in the coordinate system of its superview (window).

(Retain count trivia: Because you created the view with **alloc** and added it to the window, the view is being retained by **HypnosisterAppDelegate** and the window and therefore has a retain count of two. But note that neither **HypnosisterAppDelegate** nor the window will ever get released or deallocated because they exist the entire time the application is running.)

Build and run your application.

Drawing Text and Shadows

While we are talking about drawing, let's add some text with a shadow to the view, as shown in Figure 6.5.

Figure 6.5 View that draws text

Open `HypnosisView.m` and add the following code to the end of your **drawRect:** method:

```
for (float currentRadius = maxRadius; currentRadius > 0; currentRadius -= 20)
{
    CGContextAddArc(context, center.x, center.y,
                    currentRadius, 0, M_PI * 2.0, YES);
    CGContextStrokePath(context);
}

// Create a string
NSString *text = @"You are getting sleepy.";

// Get a font to draw it in
UIFont *font = [UIFont boldSystemFontOfSize:28];

// Where am I going to draw it?
CGRect textRect;
textRect.size = [text sizeWithFont:font];
textRect.origin.x = center.x - textRect.size.width / 2.0;
textRect.origin.y = center.y - textRect.size.height / 2.0;

// Set the fill color
[[UIColor blackColor] setFill];

// Set the shadow
CGSize offset = CGSizeMake(4, 3);
CGColorRef color = [[UIColor darkGrayColor] CGColor];
CGContextSetShadowWithColor(context, offset, 2.0, color);
```

```
    // Draw the string
    [text drawInRect:textRect
            withFont:font];
}
```

Build and run the application. You will see the text with a shadow appear on the view.

Notice that you only call drawing routines inside **drawRect:**. Outside of a **drawRect:** method, there is no active **CGContextRef**, and drawing routines will fail. (In a later chapter, you will manage your own **CGContextRef** for offscreen drawing. Only then can you draw outside of **drawRect:**.)

Using UIScrollView

When you want to let the user scroll around your view, you typically make your view the subview of a **UIScrollView**, as shown in Figure 6.6.

Figure 6.6   Object diagram

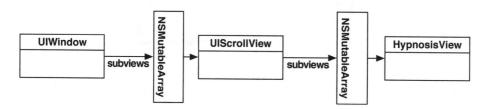

In HypnosisterAppDelegate.m, put your view inside a scroll view and add that scroll view to the window:

```
- (BOOL)application:(UIApplication *)application
    didFinishLaunchingWithOptions:(NSDictionary *)launchOptions
{
    CGRect wholeWindow = [window bounds];

    UIScrollView *scrollView = [[UIScrollView alloc] initWithFrame:wholeWindow];
    [window addSubview:scrollView];
    [scrollView release];

    // Make your view twice as large as the window
    CGRect reallyBigRect;
    reallyBigRect.origin = CGPointZero;
    reallyBigRect.size.width = wholeWindow.size.width * 2.0;
    reallyBigRect.size.height = wholeWindow.size.height * 2.0;
    [scrollView setContentSize:reallyBigRect.size];

    // Center it in the scroll view
    CGPoint offset;
    offset.x = wholeWindow.size.width * 0.5;
    offset.y = wholeWindow.size.height * 0.5;
```

```
    [scrollView setContentOffset:offset];

    // Create the view
    view = [[HypnosisView alloc] initWithFrame:reallyBigRect];
    [view setBackgroundColor:[UIColor clearColor]];
    [scrollView addSubview:view];

    [window makeKeyAndVisible];
    return YES;
}
```

Build and run your application. You will be able to push your view up and down, left and right, as shown in Figure 6.7.

Figure 6.7 HypnosisView in UIScrollView

However, zooming doesn't work. Yet.

Zooming

To add zooming, you need to give the scroll view a delegate. The delegate will tell the scroll view which view needs to be transformed. In HypnosisterAppDelegate.h, declare that **HypnosisterAppDelegate** conforms to the UIScrollViewDelegate protocol:

```
@interface HypnosisterAppDelegate : NSObject
    <UIApplicationDelegate, UIScrollViewDelegate>
```

Open HypnosisterAppDelegate.m. In **application:didFinishLaunchingWithOptions:**, set the delegate and the limits of the zoom:

```
- (BOOL)application:(UIApplication *)application
    didFinishLaunchingWithOptions:(NSDictionary *)launchOptions
{
    CGRect wholeWindow = [window bounds];

    UIScrollView *scrollView = [[UIScrollView alloc] initWithFrame:wholeWindow];
    [window addSubview:scrollView];
    [scrollView release];

    // Make your view twice as large as the window
    CGRect reallyBigRect;
    reallyBigRect.origin = CGPointZero;
    reallyBigRect.size.width = wholeWindow.size.width * 2.0;
    reallyBigRect.size.height = wholeWindow.size.height * 2.0;
    [scrollView setContentSize:reallyBigRect.size];

    // Center it in the scroll view
    CGPoint offset;
    offset.x = wholeWindow.size.width * 0.5;
    offset.y = wholeWindow.size.height * 0.5;
    [scrollView setContentOffset:offset];

    // Enable zooming
    [scrollView setMinimumZoomScale:0.5];
    [scrollView setMaximumZoomScale:5];
    [scrollView setDelegate:self];

    // Create the view
    view = [[HypnosisView alloc] initWithFrame:reallyBigRect];
    [view setBackgroundColor:[UIColor clearColor]];
    [scrollView addSubview:view];

    [window makeKeyAndVisible];
    return YES;
}
```

In that same file, implement the necessary delegate method:

```
- (UIView *)viewForZoomingInScrollView:(UIScrollView *)scrollView
{
    return view;
}
```

Build and run the application and zoom away!

Hiding the Status Bar

When you're being hypnotized, you probably don't want to see the time or your remaining battery charge; these things cause anxiety. So, hide the status bar before you make the window visible. Add a line near the end of **application:didFinishLaunchingWithOptions:** in HypnosisterAppDelegate.m:

```
[scrollView addSubview:view];

[[UIApplication sharedApplication] setStatusBarHidden:YES
                           withAnimation:UIStatusBarAnimationFade];


[window makeKeyAndVisible];
return YES;
}
```

Build and run the application again. The status bar will fade out after the application launches. However, sometimes you may want the status bar to be hidden before your application appears on the screen. To do this, you must add a new key-value pair to the application's info property list. Open Hypnosister-Info.plist.

Figure 6.8   Info property list with hidden status bar

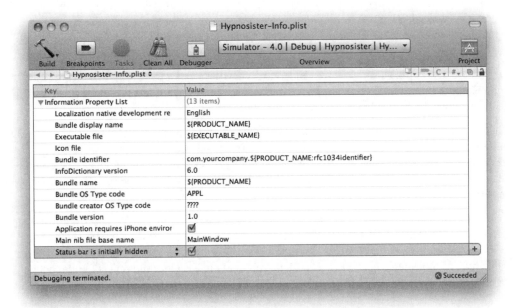

Select the last row in Hypnosister-Info.plist and click the + icon on the righthand side of the window. A new row will appear, and a pop-up menu will open in the Key column. Choose Status bar is initially hidden from this list and hit return. A checkbox will appear in the Value column. Check this box, and then build and run the application again. The status bar will be hidden as soon as you launch the application.

Challenge: Colors

Make the circles appear in assorted colors.

For the More Curious: Retain Cycles

A view hierarchy is made up of many parent-child relationships. When we talk about view hierarchies, we call parents *superviews* and their children *subviews*. When a view is added to a view hierarchy, it is retained by its superview, as shown in Figure 6.9.

Figure 6.9   View hierarchy ownership

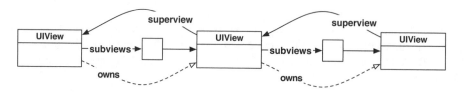

It is sometimes necessary for a subview to send a message to its superview. Every subview, then, has a pointer back to its superview. The superview property of a **UIView** is set to its superview when the view is added to a view hierarchy. (When a view is not part of a view hierarchy, superview is nil.)

Superviews are *not* retained by their subviews. Why not? Well, imagine what would happen if they were. Every time a subview was added to a view (let's call it **BigView**), **BigView** would increment its retain count. For example, if **BigView** had six subviews, it would have a retain count of seven — one for each subview and one for its superview.

What would happen if **BigView**'s superview wanted to get rid of **BigView**? The superview would send **BigView** the message **release**. However, **BigView** would still be retained by each of its subviews and would not be deallocated. As a result, **BigView**'s subviews would never be sent the message **release**. **BigView** and all of its subviews would be cut off from the rest of the application and exist in their own little cycle of independent objects where no other object could reach them.

We call this problem a *retain cycle*, and it can arise in any parent-child relationship, not just with view objects. The solution is simple: *children should never retain their parents*. In fact, a child should never retain its parent's parent, or its parent's parent's parent, and so on. When you adhere to this rule, deallocating a parent object will appropriately release its child objects. If the parent is the only owner of its children, these child objects will be deallocated.

For the More Curious: Redrawing Views

When a **UIView** instance is sent the message **setNeedsDisplay**, that view is marked for re-display. View subclasses send themselves the message **setNeedsDisplay** when their drawable content changes. For example, **UITextField** will be marked for re-display if it is sent the message **setText:**. (It has to redraw if the text it displays changes, right?)

When a view is marked for re-display, it is not immediately redrawn; it is simply added to a list of views that need to be updated. Why? Because your application is actually one giant infinite loop called the *run loop*. The run loop's job is to check for input (a touch, Core Location updates, data coming in through a network interface, etc.) and then find the appropriate handlers for that event (like an action or delegate method for an object). Those handler methods call other methods, those other methods call more methods, and so on. Views are not redrawn until *after* your methods have completed and control returns to the run loop, as shown in Figure 6.10.

Figure 6.10 Redrawing views with the run loop

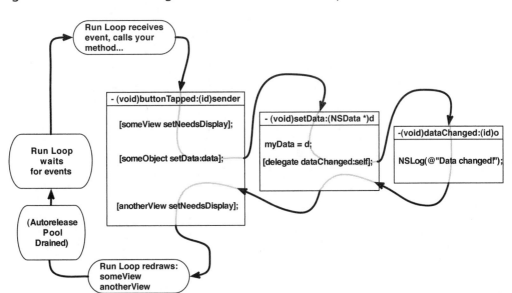

When control returns to the run loop, it says, "Well, a bunch of code was just executed. I'm going to check if any views need to be redrawn." The run loop prepares the necessary drawing contexts and sends the message **drawRect:** to all of the views that have been sent **setNeedsDisplay** in this iteration of the loop. Any subviews of a redrawn view are also redrawn.

7

View Controllers

View Controllers and XIB Files

In the Quiz application, you had one "screen," one controller, and one XIB file:

Figure 7.1   Quiz, a single screen application

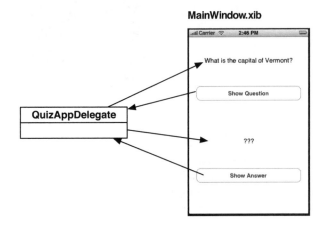

But what about applications with multiple "screens"? Typically, each screen gets its own controller and XIB file. Figure 7.2 shows an example application with two screens and the resulting controllers and XIB files.

Figure 7.2   Example of an application with two screens

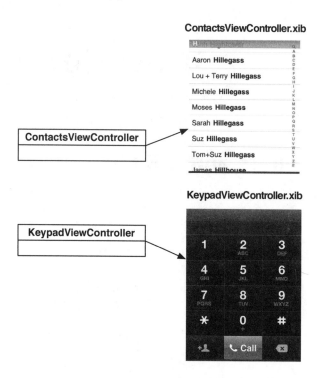

Each controller has a view that gets placed on the window. (The view often has subviews like buttons and labels.) Thus, we call these controllers *view controllers*. A view controller is a subclass of **UIViewController** that acts as the controller for its view. And, we typically need an object to take care of the view swapping for us. In the example application below, the swapping is done by a **UITabBarController**. The object diagram for this application is shown in Figure 7.3.

Figure 7.3   Object diagram for tab bar application

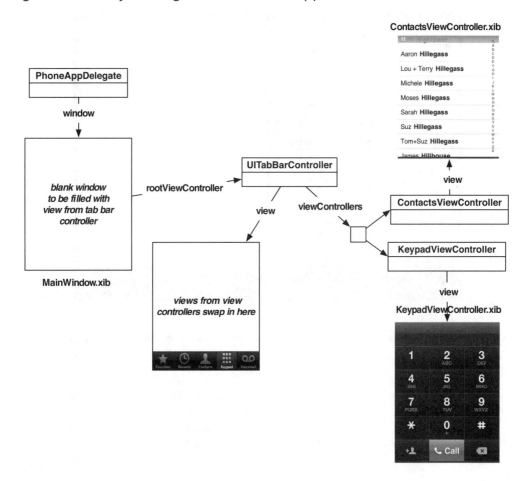

Note that this approach means that when you write an application with seven screens, you will typically write seven subclasses of **UIViewController**. Therefore, you may have up to eight XIB files (one for the window and one for each view controller).

However, sometimes there are fewer XIB files. When a view controller has just one view, it is usually easier to create a single view programmatically as you did in the last chapter.

Ready to have your mind blown a little? **UITabBarController** is also a subclass of **UIViewController**. It is a view controller that swaps in and out other view controllers.

Using View Controllers

In this chapter, you are going to write an application with two screens. One will display the **HypnosisView** you created in the last chapter, and the other will let the user get the current time by tapping a button (Figure 7.4). We will swap in the views using a **UITabBarController**.

Figure 7.4   HypnoTime screens

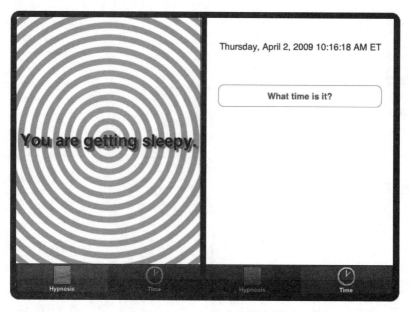

In Xcode, create a new Window-based Application project named HypnoTime. (Yes, there is a Tab Bar Application project template, but using that template makes things seem more complicated and magical than they are. Do not use it for this application.)

You will re-use **HypnosisView** in this application. Use Finder to locate HypnosisView.h and HypnosisView.m and drag them into the Classes group in Xcode (*not* the Classes directory in the filesystem). When the next sheet appears, check the box labeled Copy items into destination group's folder and click Add. Also, add the icons Hypno.png and Time.png (available at http://www.bignerdranch.com/solutions/iPhoneProgramming.zip) to the Resources group.

Creating the UITabBarController

In HypnoTimeAppDelegate.m, create the tab bar controller and set it as the rootViewController of the window:

```
- (BOOL)application:(UIApplication *)application
    didFinishLaunchingWithOptions:(NSDictionary *)launchOptions
{
    // Create the tabBarController
    UITabBarController *tabBarController = [[UITabBarController alloc] init];

    // Set tabBarController as rootViewController of window
    [window setRootViewController:tabBarController];

    // The window retains tabBarController, we can release our reference
    [tabBarController release];
```

```
    // Show the window
    [window makeKeyAndVisible];

    return YES;
}
```

Build and run the application. Notice that the black tab bar appears at the bottom of the window, but there are no tab bar items. This is the **UITabBar**, a subview of the **UITabBarController**'s view. Notice, also, the big white space where your views will get swapped in.

In previous applications, you manipulated the view hierarchy directly. For example, in Chapter 5, you added subviews to the window using Interface Builder. In Chapter 6, you added subviews to the window using the method **addSubview:**.

When using view controllers, you don't have to manipulate the view hierarchy directly. As of iOS 4.0, **UIWindow** implements a method named **setRootViewController:**. Passing an instance of **UIViewController** as the argument to this method automatically installs the view of that view controller into the view hierarchy and resizes the view to fit the window. The window also retains its root view controller.

Figure 7.5   View hierarchy with UITabBarController

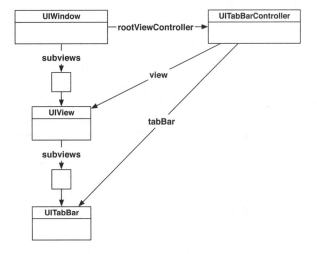

Before iOS 4.0, you had to grab a pointer to a view controller's view and add it as a subview of the window. That looked like this:

```
    tabBarController = [[UITabBarController alloc] init];
    [window addSubview:[tabBarController view]];
    // Note that tabBarController is NOT released, because
    // it is not retained by the window here.
```

Setting the rootViewController of the window still adds the view controller's view to the window. It will also clear out any other subviews of the window, thus making the rootViewController's view the sole subview of the window. (At the time of this writing, the iPad does not support 4.0. Therefore, you must use the pre-4.0 version of adding a view controller's view to the window hierarchy.)

Creating view controllers and tab bar items

To create the first view controller for HypnoTime, select the New File... menu item and then UIViewController subclass. For this view controller, toggle on the checkbox titled With XIB for user interface (Figure 7.6). Name the file CurrentTimeViewController.m.

Figure 7.6   Creating CurrentTimeViewController

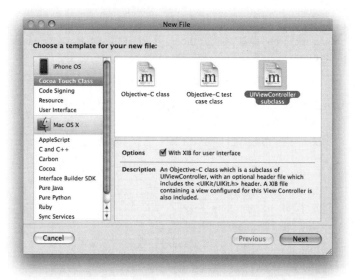

Now create another **UIViewController** subclass. This time, toggle off the XIB checkbox. Name this file HypnosisViewController.m.

Every view controller has a tab bar item that controls the text or icon that appears in the tab bar as shown in Figure 7.7.

Figure 7.7   UITabBarItem example

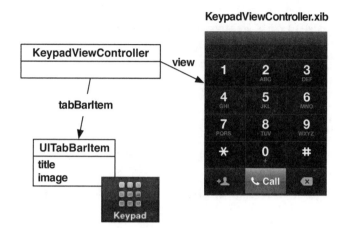

Let's start by putting a title on the tab bar items.

Open HypnosisViewController.m. Create a new **init** method, override the designated initializer for the superclass (**UIViewController**), and edit the **viewDidLoad** method to match the code below:

```
- (id)init
{
    // Call the superclass's designated initializer
    [super initWithNibName:nil
                    bundle:nil];

    // Get the tab bar item
    UITabBarItem *tbi = [self tabBarItem];

    // Give it a label
    [tbi setTitle:@"Hypnosis"];

    return self;
}

- (id)initWithNibName:(NSString *)nibName bundle:(NSBundle *)bundle
{
    // Disregard parameters - nib name is an implementation detail
    return [self init];
}

// This method gets called automatically when the view is created
- (void)viewDidLoad
{
    [super viewDidLoad];

    // Set the background color of the view so we can see it
    [[self view] setBackgroundColor:[UIColor orangeColor]];
}
```

Open `CurrentTimeViewController.m` and do the same thing:

```
- (id)init
{
    // Call the superclass's designated initializer
    [super initWithNibName:nil
                    bundle:nil];

    // Get the tab bar item
    UITabBarItem *tbi = [self tabBarItem];

    // Give it a label
    [tbi setTitle:@"Time"];

    return self;
}

- (id)initWithNibName:(NSString *)nibName bundle:(NSBundle *)bundle
{
    // Disregard parameters - implementation detail
    return [self init];
}

- (void)viewDidLoad
{
    [super viewDidLoad];

    // Set the background color of the view so we can see it
    [[self view] setBackgroundColor:[UIColor greenColor]];
}
```

Now you need to create instances of the view controllers and add them to the tab bar controller. Open `HypnoTimeAppDelegate.m` and make the following changes:

```
#import "HypnoTimeAppDelegate.h"
#import "HypnosisViewController.h"
#import "CurrentTimeViewController.h"

@implementation HypnoTimeAppDelegate

@synthesize window;


- (BOOL)application:(UIApplication *)application
    didFinishLaunchingWithOptions:(NSDictionary *)launchOptions
{
    // Create the tabBarController
    UITabBarController *tabBarController = [[UITabBarController alloc] init];

    // Create two view controllers
    UIViewController *vc1 = [[HypnosisViewController alloc] init];
    UIViewController *vc2 = [[CurrentTimeViewController alloc] init];

    // Make an array containing the two view controllers
    NSArray *viewControllers = [NSArray arrayWithObjects:vc1, vc2, nil];

    // The viewControllers array retains vc1 and vc2, we can release
```

```
    // our ownership of them in this method
    [vc1 release];
    [vc2 release];

    // Attach them to the tab bar controller
    [tabBarController setViewControllers:viewControllers];

    // Put the tabBarController's view on the window
    [window setRootViewController:tabBarController];
    [tabBarController release];

    // Show the window
    [window makeKeyAndVisible];

    return YES;
}

// A dealloc method that will never get called
- (void)dealloc
{
    [window release];
    [super dealloc];
}

@end
```

Build and run the application. Two labeled tab bar items will appear on the tab bar (Figure 7.8).
Tap one and then the other, and you will see that the views for the view controllers are getting
swapped in.

Figure 7.8   Tab bar items with labels

Now let's add icons. Open HypnosisViewController.m and edit the **init** method:

```
- (id)init
{
    [super initWithNibName:nil
                    bundle:nil];

    UITabBarItem *tbi = [self tabBarItem];
    [tbi setTitle:@"Hypnosis"];

    // Create a UIImage from a file
    UIImage *i = [UIImage imageNamed:@"Hypno.png"];

    // Put that image on the tab bar item
    [tbi setImage:i];

    return self;
}
```

Next, open `CurrentTimeViewController.m` and edit its **init** method:

```
- (id)init
{
    [super initWithNibName:nil
                    bundle:nil];

    UITabBarItem *tbi = [self tabBarItem];
    [tbi setTitle:@"Time"];
    UIImage *i = [UIImage imageNamed:@"Time.png"];
    [tbi setImage:i];

    return self;
}
```

Now when you build and run the application, you will also see icons in the tab bar (Figure 7.9).

Figure 7.9   Tab bar items with labels and icons

Creating views for the view controllers

Now that you have a perfectly nice tab bar with two view controllers (and the two corresponding tab bar items), it's time to give your view controllers views. There are two ways to do this:

- create the view programmatically

- create a XIB file

How do you know when to do one versus the other? Here's a good rule-of-thumb: if the view has no subviews, create it programmatically; if it has subviews, create a XIB file.

When the view needs to be created, the view controller is sent the message **loadView**. In **HypnosisViewController**, you are going to override this method so that it creates an instance of **HypnosisView** programmatically. When an instance of a **UIViewController** is instantiated, its view is not created right away. A **UIViewController**'s view is created when it is placed in a view hierarchy (also known as "the first time it appears on screen"). Add the following method to `HypnosisViewController.m`:

```
- (void)loadView
{
    HypnosisView *hv = [[HypnosisView alloc] initWithFrame:CGRectZero];
    [hv setBackgroundColor:[UIColor whiteColor]];
    [self setView:hv];
    [hv release];
}
```

HypnosisViewController.m needs to know about the class **HypnosisView**. At this top of this file, import **HypnosisView**'s header file.

```
#import "HypnosisViewController.h"
#import "HypnosisView.h"

@implementation HypnosisViewController
```

We no longer want the background of the view to be orange, so delete the following line from the **viewDidLoad** method in HypnosisViewController.m:

```
[[self view] setBackgroundColor:[UIColor orangeColor]];
```

Also, delete the corresponding line of code from the **viewDidLoad** method in CurrentTimeViewController.m.

```
[[self view] setBackgroundColor:[UIColor greenColor]];
```

Build and run the application. You should see a **HypnosisView** like the one in Figure 7.10.

Figure 7.10   HypnosisViewController

Double-click on `CurrentTimeViewController.xib` to open it in Interface Builder. Double-click on the View object in the doc window to open it. From the Library, drop a button and a label on the View's window. Make them both nearly as wide as the window. Change the title on the button to What time is it?. Change the label to ??? and set the alignment to centered (Figure 7.11).

Figure 7.11 Button and Label

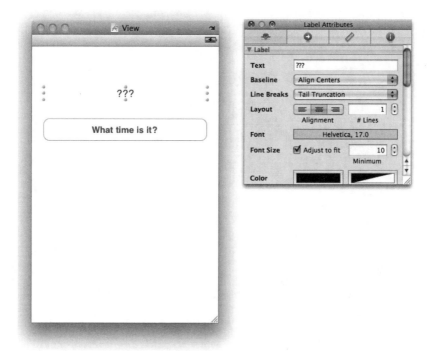

See that icon labeled File's Owner? It is a placeholder for an object to be supplied when the XIB file is read in. When the view controller loads the XIB file, it says "Load the XIB named CurrentTimeViewController.xib, and I will act as File's Owner." Thus, you can know that the file's owner is the view controller for this XIB. You know it is going to be an instance of **CurrentTimeViewController**, but Interface Builder does not.

In Xcode, add the necessary outlet and action to CurrentTimeViewController.h:

```
#import <UIKit/UIKit.h>

@interface CurrentTimeViewController : UIViewController
{
    IBOutlet UILabel *timeLabel;
}
- (IBAction)showCurrentTime:(id)sender;

@end
```

Save that file and return to Interface Builder.

Control-click on File's Owner to see its connection panel (Figure 7.12). Drag from timeLabel to the **UILabel**.

Figure 7.12   Connecting timeLabel and UILabel

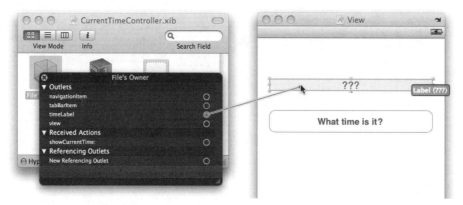

The view controller has a pointer called view that needs to point to the entire view that is to be displayed. Notice that the view outlet is already connected to the instance of **UIView** in the doc window. (The template did this for you.)

Control-drag from the button to the File's Owner (Figure 7.13). Choose the action showCurrentTime:.

Figure 7.13   Setting the showCurrentTime: action

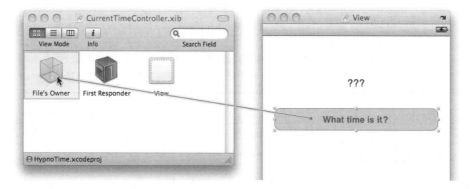

Return to Xcode and open CurrentTimeViewController.m. In **init**, tell it the name of the XIB file it is to load. Also delete the line that sets the background color to green:

```
- (id)init
{
    [super initWithNibName:@"CurrentTimeViewController"
                    bundle:nil];

    UITabBarItem *tbi = [self tabBarItem];
    [tbi setTitle:@"Time"];
```

```
    UIImage *i = [UIImage imageNamed:@"Time.png"];
    [tbi setImage:i];

    return self;
}
```

Finally, implement the action method:

```
- (IBAction)showCurrentTime:(id)sender
{
    NSDate *now = [NSDate date];

    // Static here means "only once." The variable formatter
    // is created when the program is first loaded into memory.
    // The first time this method is invoked, formatter will
    // be nil and the if-block will execute, creating
    // an NSDateFormatter object that formatter will point to.
    // Subsequent entry into this method will reuse the same
    // NSDateFormatter object.
    static NSDateFormatter *formatter = nil;
    if (!formatter) {
        formatter = [[NSDateFormatter alloc] init];
        [formatter setTimeStyle:NSDateFormatterShortStyle];
    }
    [timeLabel setText:[formatter stringFromDate:now]];
}
```

Build and run the application. You will be able to switch back and forth between the two views. Clicking the button on the time view will display the current time.

viewWillAppear:

UIViewController has several methods that get called at certain times:

viewWillAppear:	when its view is about to be added to the window
viewDidAppear:	when its view has been added to the window
viewWillDisappear:	when its view is about to be dismissed, covered, or otherwise hidden from view
viewDidDisappear:	when its view has been dismissed, covered, or otherwise hidden from view

These methods are useful because a view controller is only created once but usually gets displayed (and dismissed or hidden) several times. You often need a way to override the default behavior at these times in the life of view controller. For example, you may want to do some sort of initialization each time the view controller is moved on screen. Here you would use **viewWillAppear:** or **viewDidAppear:**. Similarly, if you had a large data structure that you only need while the view controller is being displayed, you might want to do some clean-up each time the view controller is moved off screen. Then you would use **viewWillDisappear:** or **viewDidDisappear:**.

Note that these methods, as defined in **UIViewController**, do nothing. They are there so that your subclasses can override them.

```
- (void)viewWillAppear:(BOOL)animated;
- (void)viewDidAppear:(BOOL)animated;
- (void)viewWillDisappear:(BOOL)animated;
- (void)viewDidDisappear:(BOOL)animated;
```

Now let's override **viewWillAppear:** to initialize the time label of the **CurrentTimeViewController** to the current time each time it is displayed. In CurrentTimeViewController.m, make the following changes:

```
- (void)viewWillAppear:(BOOL)animated
{
    [super viewWillAppear:animated];
    [self showCurrentTime:nil];
}
```

Build and run the application. Note that each time you return to the Time page, the time label is updated.

The Lifecycle of a View Controller

A view controller is created through **alloc** and **init**. It does not, however, create its view at that time. Instead, it waits until the view is really needed before it executes **loadView**. (Remember that the default implementation of **loadView** reads in a NIB file, but you can override it to create the view programmatically.) This lazy creation of the view is good. For example, if you have a tab view with a dozen view controllers, the view for any particular view controller will only be created if that particular tab is selected.

First rule: *Never* manipulate your view in **init**. Wait until **loadView** or **viewDidLoad** before sending messages to the view. Trying to interact with the view in **init** will cause it to be created, which will destroy the lazy nature of your view controller.

Furthermore, a view controller's view may get created and destroyed several times. Let's say that you have several view controllers in memory (but only one on screen) and that all their views have been created. This could take up a lot of memory and trigger a low memory warning. At that point, **didReceiveMemoryWarning** is sent to all the view controllers. The default implementation of **didReceiveMemoryWarning** releases the view if it has no superview. (No superview indicates it is not on screen and no other view cares about it.) After the view is released, the view controller is sent **viewDidUnload**.

If the view is needed again, the view controller is sent **loadView** again. Thus, **loadView** may be called many times on a single view controller. However, **init** is only sent to a view controller once. If you were to send messages to a view controller's view in **init**, they would not be sent to a reloaded view.

(When the view controller is deallocated, it releases its view, but **viewDidUnload** is not called.)

Second rule: For a view controller, any outlets that you set in Interface Builder must be released and set to nil in **viewDidUnload**. They must also be released in **dealloc**.

By default, any outlet from your view controller to a subview is retained by that view controller. For example, **CurrentTimeViewController** retains a **UILabel** because it has the outlet timeLabel. Thus, the timeLabel has a retain count of two: it is being retained by its superview *and* by **CurrentTimeViewController** directly. Thus, if the view is unloaded because of a low memory warning, it will not be correctly deallocated. Add a **viewDidUnload** method to CurrentTimeViewController.m to release timeLabel: and fix this problem:

```
- (void)viewDidUnload
{
    NSLog(@"Must have received a low memory warning. Releasing timeLabel");
    [super viewDidUnload];
    [timeLabel release];
    timeLabel = nil;
}
```

(Low memory warnings are discussed in more depth in Chapter 15.)

Also, you need to release timeLabel in **dealloc**. While **CurrentTimeViewController** will never be deallocated in HypnoTime, other view controllers in other applications may. Accordingly, subviews of a view controller's view that are also retained by the view controller must be released in **dealloc**:

```
- (void)dealloc
{
    [timeLabel release];
    [super dealloc];
}
```

Build and run the application in the simulator. While the **CurrentTimeViewController** is off-screen, simulate a low memory warning by selecting Simulate Low Memory Warning from the Hardware menu. You should see the log statement from **viewDidUnload** on the console.

Challenge: Map Tab

Add another view controller to the tab bar controller that displays an **MKMapView**. When the map view appears on the screen, have it show the user's location.

For the More Curious: Paging

Some applications, like Weather, allow you to "page" through views by swiping your finger from left to right. People occasionally mistake this behavior for something that **UITabBarController** can do. It is actually the work of another class you have already used, **UIScrollView**.

Each page is a **UIView** subclass. All of the pages are typically controlled by a single **UIViewController**, and the **UIScrollView** is responsible for managing which view is currently on screen. There actually is not a whole lot to it once you have used a **UIScrollView**.

Let's say you wanted two views to be pages within a **UIScrollView** that is controlled by a **UIViewController**. The view controller's view would be an instance of **UIScrollView**, and the scroll view's subviews would be the two pages.

```
- (void)loadView
{
    CGRect frame = [[UIScreen mainScreen] applicationFrame];
    UIScrollView *sv = [[[UIScrollView alloc]
                initWithFrame:frame] autorelease];

    frame.origin.y = 0;
    UIView *aView = [[[UIView alloc]
                initWithFrame:frame] autorelease];

    frame.origin.x += frame.size.width;
    UIView *bView = [[[UIView alloc]
                initWithFrame:frame] autorelease];

    [aView setBackgroundColor:[UIColor redColor]];
    [bView setBackgroundColor:[UIColor greenColor]];

    [sv addSubview:aView];
    [sv addSubview:bView];

    // ContentSize should be wide enough for 2 pages
    [sv setContentSize:CGSizeMake(2 * frame.size.width, frame.size.height)];
    [self setView:sv];
}
```

Notice how the second page view is offset from the first page view by the width of the screen. This puts the two views side-by-side, but the second one is off to the righthand side of the screen. The contentSize of the scroll view accommodates this by having a width that is twice the size of the screen (and a height that is the same as the screen).

If you stopped here, the scroll view will work normally: the user can move around the double screen-sized area and see the content of the two pages. However, a scroll view can also automatically stop at each page. To enforce the display of only one page at a time, the scroll view needs to enable paging:

```
[sv setPagingEnabled:YES];
```

Now when the user swipes to the left or right, one of the pages will lock itself onto the screen. The scroll view will automatically stop and recenter its content based on the bounds of the scroll view. Just make sure the **UIScrollView**'s size matches the size of each page and that the contentSize has enough room for all of the pages.

8

The Accelerometer

One of the flashiest features of the iPhone is the *accelerometer*. The accelerometer detects the device's real-world orientation by tracking the force of the earth's gravity on its X, Y, and Z axes. You can also use the accelerometer data to detect changes in the device's velocity.

In this chapter, you are going to use the accelerometer to skew the center of the **HypnosisView** according to orientation: when the user tilts the phone, the center will slide in the direction of the tilt, as shown in Figure 8.1.

Figure 8.1   HypnosisView

Setting Up the Accelerometer

To receive accelerometer data, your application needs to give the single instance of **UIAccelerometer** an updateInterval and a delegate. The delegate needs to implement the method **accelerometer:didAccelerate:**. This method reports changes in the accelerometer data every updateInterval seconds in the form of a **UIAcceleration** object.

Open your HypnoTime project. Before you add any code, you need to decide which object will be the **UIAccelerometer** delegate. There are two options:

- Make the **HypnosisView** the delegate. It will handle changing the center of drawing internally.

- Make the **HypnosisViewController** the delegate. In this case, you will also need to set a "center" property for view when the orientation of the device changes.

If the **HypnosisView** is the accelerometer delegate, it becomes a self-contained object, which makes reusing it simpler. However, there can only be one accelerometer delegate. If other objects need input from the accelerometer, **HypnosisView**, a view object, can't forward that information on to those objects — it's not a controller. Therefore, the more stylish option is to let the controller object, **HypnosisViewController**, be the delegate and receive the accelerometer updates as shown in Figure 8.2. **HypnosisViewController** can easily inform the **HypnosisView** of a change in orientation, and it can inform other objects if necessary.

Figure 8.2   Object diagram for HypnoTime

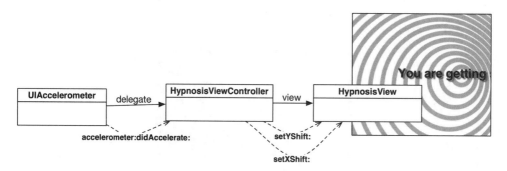

In HypnosisViewController.m, instantiate the accelerometer and set its update interval and delegate in **viewWillAppear:**.

```
- (void)viewWillAppear:(BOOL)animated
{
    [super viewWillAppear:animated];

    NSLog(@"Monitoring accelerometer");
    UIAccelerometer *a = [UIAccelerometer sharedAccelerometer];
    // Receive updates every 1/10th of a second.
    [a setUpdateInterval:0.1];
    [a setDelegate:self];
}
```

When the **HypnosisViewController**'s view is moved off of the screen, the controller should stop receiving accelerometer updates. Also, when the singleton instance of **UIAccelerometer** does not have a delegate object, the accelerometer hardware is powered down to conserve battery life. In general, you should set the accelerometer's delegate to `nil` when it is not in use. Make this change in `HypnosisViewController.m`:

```
- (void)viewWillDisappear:(BOOL)animated
{
    [super viewWillDisappear:animated];
    [[UIAccelerometer sharedAccelerometer] setDelegate:nil];
}
```

Getting Accelerometer Data

Write a stub implementation of the **UIAccelerometer** delegate method in `HypnosisViewController.m`. Notice that the parameters for this method are two different types even though they look similar:

```
- (void)accelerometer:(UIAccelerometer *)meter
        didAccelerate:(UIAcceleration *)accel
{
    NSLog(@"%f, %f, %f", [accel x], [accel y], [accel z]);
}
```

In `HypnosisViewController.h`, declare that the class conforms to the `UIAccelerometerDelegate` protocol:

```
#import <UIKit/UIKit.h>

@interface HypnosisViewController : UIViewController <UIAccelerometerDelegate>
{
}

@end
```

Build and run the application on your device. Watch the console as you rotate and shake the phone to get a feel for the data that the accelerometer will produce.

Orientation and Scale of Acceleration

The device's acceleration is measured in Gs. 1G is the force due to the earth's gravity. (When the device is still, the accelerometer doesn't know if it is moving at a constant velocity in the earth's gravity well or if it is far out in space and accelerating upwards at 9.8 meters per second every second.)

While the application is running, hold the device vertically in front of your face as if you were using it. The y-component of the acceleration is about -1, and the x- and z-components are approximately 0. If you lay the device on its back, the z-component of the acceleration is about -1, and the others are approximately 0. If you balance the device on the edge with the volume switch down, the x-component of the acceleration is about -1, and the others are approximately 0. If you drop your device, it will feel weightless as it falls: all three components will be 0. Well, until it hits the floor.

Using Accelerometer Data

This application will use the accelerometer data to offset the center of drawing in the **HypnosisView**. **HypnosisViewController** receives the accelerometer data and must send it to the view. Therefore, **HypnosisView** needs two properties to define the offset. Add them in HypnosisView.h.

```
@interface HypnosisView : UIView
{
    float xShift, yShift;
}
@property (nonatomic, assign) float xShift;
@property (nonatomic, assign) float yShift;
@end
```

Now synthesize these properties in HypnosisView.m:

```
@implementation HypnosisView
@synthesize xShift, yShift;
```

HypnosisView needs to know how to use these properties when it draws. In HypnosisView.m, add code to **drawRect:** that uses the xShift and yShift instance variables:

```
    // Draw concentric circles
    for (float currentRadius = maxRadius; currentRadius > 0; currentRadius -= 20)
    {
        center.x += xShift;
        center.y += yShift;
        CGContextAddArc(context, center.x, center.y,
                        currentRadius, 0, M_PI * 2.0, YES);
        CGContextStrokePath(context);
    }
```

Using the **UIAcceleration** object the accelerometer gives you, set xShift and yShift and redraw the view. In HypnosisViewController.m, replace the following method:

```
- (void)accelerometer:(UIAccelerometer *)meter
        didAccelerate:(UIAcceleration *)accel
{
    HypnosisView *hv = (HypnosisView *)[self view];
    [hv setXShift:10.0 * [accel x]];
    [hv setYShift:-10.0 * [accel y]];

    // Redraw the view
    [hv setNeedsDisplay];
}
```

Build and run your application. The center of the view will move as the phone is rotated and shaken.

Smoothing Accelerometer Data

The movement of the **HypnosisView** has a jerky feel that is not conducive to hypnosis. Each time the accelerometer updates, the center of the view changes to represent the orientation of the device. Because the updateInterval is constant and the device's movement is not, the center appears to jump around. It would be more appropriate to "smooth" the data from the accelerometer, thus smoothing the movement of the center of the view. To smooth the accelerometer data, you need to apply a low-pass filter.

In HypnosisViewController.m, apply a low-pass filter to the accelerometer data:

```
- (void)accelerometer:(UIAccelerometer *)meter
        didAccelerate:(UIAcceleration *)accel
{
    HypnosisView *hv = (HypnosisView *)[self view];
    float xShift = [hv xShift] * 0.8 + [accel x] * 2.0;
    float yShift = [hv yShift] * 0.8 - [accel y] * 2.0;
    [hv setXShift:xShift];
    [hv setYShift:yShift];

    // Redraw the view
    [hv setNeedsDisplay];
}
```

Build and run your application. The application will have a smoother response and a nicer feel.

Detecting Shakes

In the original iPhone SDK, developers had to implement their own shake-detection algorithms in the accelerometer delegates. However, the 3.0 SDK contains three new methods for **UIResponder** (the superclass of **UIView**) that make detecting shakes easier.

```
// Triggered when a shake is detected
- (void)motionBegan:(UIEventSubtype)motion
        withEvent:(UIEvent *)event;

// Triggered when the shake is complete
- (void)motionEnded:(UIEventSubtype)motion
        withEvent:(UIEvent *)event;

// Triggered when a shake is interrupted (by a call for example)
// Or if a shake lasts for more than a second
- (void)motionCancelled:(UIEventSubtype)motion
            withEvent:(UIEvent *)event;
```

In this chapter, you are going to override **motionBegan:withEvent:** to change the stripe color when the phone is shaken. First, add an instance variable to HypnosisView.h to hold on to the new color:

```
#import <UIKit/UIKit.h>

@interface HypnosisView : UIView {
    UIColor *stripeColor;
    float xShift, yShift;
}
@property (nonatomic, assign) float xShift;
@property (nonatomic, assign) float yShift;
@end
```

Now initialize stripeColor in the **initWithFrame:** method of HypnosisView.m:

```
- (id)initWithFrame:(CGRect)r
{
    [super initWithFrame:r];
    // Notice we explicitly retain the UIColor instance
    // returned by the convenience method lightGrayColor,
    // because it is autoreleased and we need to keep it around
    // so we can use it in drawRect:.
    stripeColor = [[UIColor lightGrayColor] retain];
    return self;
}
```

Finally, use the stripeColor in your **drawRect:** method of HypnosisView.m.

```
    CGContextSetLineWidth(context, 10);

    // Set the stroke color to light gray
    [stripeColor setStroke];

    // Draw concentric circles
    for (float currentRadius = maxRadius; currentRadius > 0; currentRadius -= 20)
    {
```

Build and run the application just to make sure you haven't broken anything. It should work exactly as before.

Because stripeColor is owned by **HypnosisView**, it must be released in the view's **dealloc** method.

```
- (void)dealloc
{
    [stripeColor release];
    [super dealloc];
}
```

Now override **motionBegan:withEvent:** to change the color and redraw the view in HypnosisView.m.

```
- (void)motionBegan:(UIEventSubtype)motion withEvent:(UIEvent *)event
{
    // Shake is the only kind of motion for now,
    // but we should (for future compatibility)
    // check the motion type.
    if (motion == UIEventSubtypeMotionShake) {
        NSLog(@"shake started");
        float r, g, b;
        r = random() % 256 / 256.0;
        g = random() % 256 / 256.0;
        b = random() % 256 / 256.0;
        [stripeColor release];
        stripeColor = [UIColor colorWithRed:r
                                      green:g
                                       blue:b
                                      alpha:1];
        [stripeColor retain];
        [self setNeedsDisplay];
    }
}
```

There's one more important detail: the window's firstResponder is the only object that gets sent motion events. Right now, **HypnosisView** is not the first responder, but you can make it so in two steps. First, you need to override **canBecomeFirstResponder** so that your view can become a first responder. Add this method to HypnosisView.m:

```
- (BOOL)canBecomeFirstResponder
{
    return YES;
}
```

(You may remember that instances of **UITextField** become the first responder of the window when tapped, and then the keyboard slides onto the screen. **UITextField** implements this same method to return YES.)

Then, when your view appears on the screen, you need to make it the first responder. In HypnosisViewController.m, add the following line of code:

```
- (void)viewWillAppear:(BOOL)animated
{
    [super viewWillAppear:animated];
    NSLog(@"Monitoring accelerometer");
    UIAccelerometer *a = [UIAccelerometer sharedAccelerometer];
    [a setUpdateInterval:0.1];
    [a setDelegate:self];

    [[self view] becomeFirstResponder];
}
```

Build and run the application. Shake the device and watch the color of the stripes change. Notice that the color does not continue to change if you continue shaking it. This is because motion events happen when a motion begins and when a motion ends, but not in the middle. There is no "while motion continues" method. To change the color, you have to shake the device, stop shaking it, and then shake it again. (The fix for this would be to use an **NSTimer** to send periodic "change the color now" messages. Create the timer in **motionBegan:withEvent:**, and destroy it in **motionEnded:withEvent:** and **motionCancelled:withEvent:**.)

Also note that motion events have nothing to do with the **UIAccelerometer** delegate. The system determines there is a shake by querying the accelerometer hardware and then sending the appropriate messages to the firstResponder of the application. The accelerometer data is delivered to the **UIAccelerometer** delegate separately.

Challenge: Changing Colors

Change the colors of the stripes based on the orientation of the device. There are three color channels (Red, Green, Blue) and three axes of movement (X, Y, Z). Assign a color to each axis. When the G force on an axis is closer to -1, set its color channel to 0 and when it is closer to 1 set its color channel to 1. Use the documentation!

For the More Curious: Filtering and Frequency

In general, there are two ways of altering the accelerometer data in order to suit your needs: you can change the frequency of accelerometer data updates and you can apply a filter to the data. An application that relies on accelerometer data needs to be carefully tuned to find an update interval and filtering algorithm that gives the user the best experience.

Here are some examples of types of applications and their recommended update frequencies to give you a starting point:

Orientation Applications	If your application relies on the current orientation of the device, for example, to rotate an arrow to point in a certain direction, the accelerometer can update infrequently. A value of 1/20 to 1/10 seconds for the updateInterval is sufficient.
Game Applications	An application that uses accelerometer data as input for controlling a visual object in real-time needs a slightly faster update interval. For applications like this, the updateInterval should be between 1/30 to 1/60 seconds.
High-Frequency Applications	Applications that need to squeeze every little update out of the accelerometer should set the updateInterval between 1/70 and 1/100 seconds (the smallest possible interval). An application that detects shakes is updating at a high frequency.

Once you have chosen the right update interval, you need to choose what type of filter is best for your application. Typically, you'll choose either a low-pass filter or a high-pass filter.

Using a *low-pass filter*, as you did in the exercise, isolates the gravity component of the acceleration data and reduces the effect of sudden changes in the device's orientation. In most situations, it gives you just the orientation of the device. A basic low-pass filter equation looks like this:

```
float filteringFactor = 0.1;
lowPassed = newValue * filteringFactor + lowPassed * (1.0 - filteringFactor);
```

where `lowPassed` is the output. Notice that the previous output is used the next time the equation is solved and that the new value produced by the accelerometer is blended with all of the previous values. The output of a low-pass filter is essentially a weighted average of previous inputs. Therefore, sudden movements will not affect the output as much as they would with unfiltered data.

On the other hand, sometimes you want to ignore the orientation (which is usually constant) and focus on sudden changes such as a shake. For this, you would use a *high-pass filter*. Now that you have mastered the low-pass filter, the high-pass signal is what's left if you subtract out the low-pass signal:

```
float filteringFactor = 0.1;
lowPassed = newValue * filteringFactor + lowPassed * (1.0 - filteringFactor);
highPassed = newValue - lowPassed;
```

There are other algorithms for high-pass filtering, but this one is especially easy to understand.

Figure 8.3 is a graph over time of low-pass and high-pass filtering on a shaking phone.

Figure 8.3   Low- and high-pass filter graphs

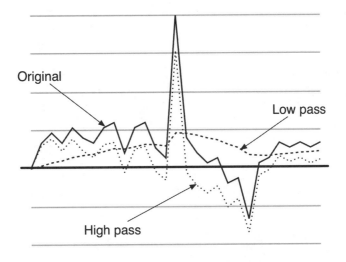

Notification and Rotation

9

Objective-C code is all about objects sending messages to other objects. This communication usually occurs between two objects — the sender and receiver. However, sometimes a bunch of objects are concerned with one object. They all want to know when this object does something interesting. But it's just not feasible for that object to keep track of every interested object and send every one a message.

Instead, an object can post notifications about what it is doing to a centralized notification center. Interested objects can register to receive a message when a particular notification is posted or when a particular object posts. In this chapter, you will learn how to use a notification center to handle these notifications. You will also learn about the autorotation behavior of **UIViewController**.

Notification Center

In every application, there is an instance of **NSNotificationCenter**, which works like a smart bulletin board. An object can register as an observer ("Send any 'lost dog' notifications to me."). When another object posts a notification ("I lost my dog."), the notification center forwards that notification to the appropriate registered observers.

These notifications are instances of **NSNotification**. Every **NSNotification** object has a name and a pointer back to the object that posted it. When you register as an observer, you can specify a notification name and a posting object that you care about.

Here's is a snippet of code that shows how you would register for notifications named LostDog posted by any object:

```
NSNotificationCenter *nc = [NSNotificationCenter defaultCenter];
[nc addObserver:self
       selector:@selector(thatMethodThatShouldBeTriggered:)
           name:@"LostDog"
         object:nil];
```

Note that nil works as a wildcard; in this case, the code requests that this method be triggered regardless of who posts the notification.

The method that is triggered when the notification arrives takes an **NSNotification** object as the argument:

```
- (void)thatMethodThatShouldBeTriggered:(NSNotification *)note
{
    id poster = [note object];
    NSString *name = [note name];
    NSDictionary *extraInformation = [note userInfo];
    ....
}
```

Notice that the notification object may also have a `userInfo` dictionary attached to it. This dictionary is used to pass added information. For example, when a keyboard is coming onto the screen, it posts a `UIKeyboardDidShowNotification` that has a `userInfo` dictionary. This dictionary contains the on-screen region that the newly visible keyboard occupies.

Here's an example of an object posting a notification:

```
NSDictionary *extraInfo = ...;
NSNotification *note = [NSNotification notificationWithName:@"LostDog"
                                                    object:self
                                                  userInfo:extraInfo];
[[NSNotificationCenter defaultCenter] postNotification:note];
```

This is important: the notification center does not retain the observers. If you have an object that registered itself with the notification center, that object should unregister itself before it is deallocated. If an object does not unregister itself from the notification center, the next time any notification it was registered for is posted, the center will try and send the object a message. But that object will have been deallocated, and your application will crash.

```
- (void)dealloc
{
    [[NSNotificationCenter defaultCenter] removeObserver:self];
    [super dealloc];
}
```

UIDevice Notifications

One object that regularly posts notifications is **UIDevice**. Here are the constants for the notifications that a **UIDevice** posts:

```
UIDeviceOrientationDidChangeNotification
UIDeviceBatteryStateDidChangeNotification
UIDeviceBatteryLevelDidChangeNotification
UIDeviceProximityStateDidChangeNotification
```

Wouldn't it be cool to get a message when the phone rotates? Or when the phone is placed next to the user's face? These notifications do just that.

Create a new Window-based Application project and name it HeavyRotation. In HeavyRotationAppDelegate.m, register to receive notifications when the orientation of the device changes:

```
- (BOOL)application:(UIApplication *)application
    didFinishLaunchingWithOptions:(NSDictionary *)launchOptions
{
    // Get the device object
    UIDevice *device = [UIDevice currentDevice];

    // Tell it to start monitoring the accelerometer for orientation
    [device beginGeneratingDeviceOrientationNotifications];

    // Get the notification center for the app
    NSNotificationCenter *nc = [NSNotificationCenter defaultCenter];

    // Add yourself as an observer
    [nc addObserver:self
          selector:@selector(orientationChanged:)
              name:UIDeviceOrientationDidChangeNotification
            object:device];

    [window makeKeyAndVisible];

    return YES;
}
```

Now, whenever the device's orientation changes, the message **orientationChanged:** will be sent to the instance of **HeavyAppDelegate**. In the same file, add an **orientationChanged:** method:

```
- (void)orientationChanged:(NSNotification *)note
{
    // Log the constant that represents the current orientation
    NSLog(@"orientationChanged: %d", [[note object] orientation]);
}
```

Build and run the application. (This is best run on the device because the simulator won't let you achieve some orientations.)

Many classes post notifications including **UIApplication**, **NSManagedObjectContext**, **MPMoviePlayerController**, **NSFileHandle**, **UIWindow**, **UITextField**, and **UITextView**. See the reference pages for these classes in the docs for details.

Autorotation

Many applications rotate and resize all of their views when the user rotates the phone. You could implement this using notifications, but it would be a lot of work. Thankfully, Apple created *autorotation* to simplify the process.

When the device is rotated and if the view on screen is controlled by a view controller, the view controller is asked if it is okay to rotate the view. If the view controller agrees, the view is resized and rotated. The subviews are also resized and rotated.

To implement autorotation in HeavyRotation, you must

- override **shouldAutorotateToInterfaceOrientation:** in **HeavyViewController** to allow autorotation

- carefully set the autoresize mask on each subview so that it acts reasonably when the superview is resized to fill the rotated window.

In Xcode, create a UIViewController subclass with a XIB file and name it HeavyViewController.m.

In HeavyViewController.m, you could create an **init** method that specifies the NIB to load and override the designated initializer of the superclass to call that **init** method:

```
- (id)init
{
    [super initWithNibName:@"HeavyViewController"
                    bundle:nil];
    return self;
}

- (id)initWithNibName:(NSString *)nibName bundle:(NSBundle *)bundle
{
    return [self init];
}
```

However, it really isn't necessary. The **init** method of **UIViewController** calls [self initWithNibName:nil bundle:nil]. And if the nibName is nil, the view controller assumes that the name of the NIB file is the same as the name of the view controller. Because you don't need to initialize any instance variables, this class doesn't need an initializer at all; the default behavior is perfect.

Have your view controller allow autorotation for any orientation except upside-down:

```
- (BOOL)shouldAutorotateToInterfaceOrientation:(UIInterfaceOrientation)x
{
    // Return YES if incoming orientation is Portrait
    // or either of the Landscapes, otherwise, return NO
    return (x == UIInterfaceOrientationPortrait)
        || UIInterfaceOrientationIsLandscape(x);
}
```

(Other **UIDevice** orientation constants can be found in the documentation page for **UIDevice**.)

Drag any image from Finder into your project under the Resources group. (Or you can use the file joeeye.jpg in the downloadable solutions at http://www.bignerdranch.com/solutions/ iPhoneProgramming.zip.)

Double-click HeavyViewController.xib to open it in Interface Builder. Drop a slider, an image view, and two buttons onto the window. In the Attributes panel of the Inspector for the image view, set Image to your image file. Choose Aspect Fit mode to fit the image to the view without changing its aspect ratio and set the background color to gray as shown in Figure 9.1.

Figure 9.1   UIImageView

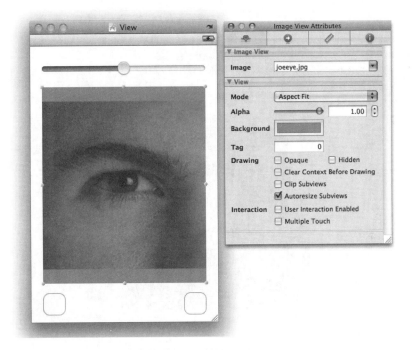

Now you need to set the autoresize mask for each view. The autoresize mask controls what happens to the view when its superview resizes. In the Size inspector, a view is a rectangle within a rectangle. The inner rectangle represents the selected view, and the outer rectangle represents its superview (Figure 9.2).

Figure 9.2   Autosizing in Size inspector

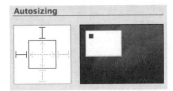

Clicking to turn on a red arrow inside the inner box means "It's okay if this view resizes in this dimension." Turning on a red strut between the inner and outer box means "The distance between this edge of the view and the corresponding edge of the superview is never allowed to change." Still confused? Check out the little movie inside the inspector that demonstrates these choices.

Select each view and set the autoresize mask appropriately. The image view should resize with the window. The slider should get wider but not taller. The buttons should stay with their respective corners but not resize (Figure 9.3).

Figure 9.3 Autoresizing mask for views

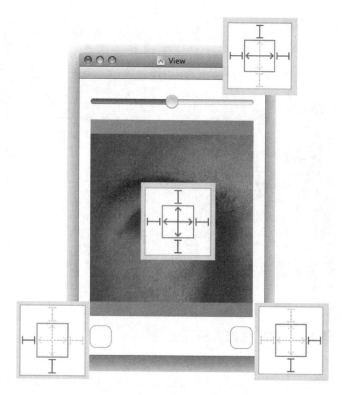

Finally, you need to create an instance of **HeavyViewController** and set it as the rootViewController of the window. Add the following lines of code to **application:didFinishLaunchingWithOptions:** in HeavyRotationAppDelegate.m. Make sure to include the import statement at the top of the file.

```
#import "HeavyViewController.h"

@implementation HeavyRotationAppDelegate
- (BOOL)application:(UIApplication *)application
    didFinishLaunchingWithOptions:(NSDictionary *)launchOptions
{
    ...
    HeavyViewController *hvc = [[[HeavyViewController alloc] init] autorelease];
    [window setRootViewController:hvc];

    [window makeKeyAndVisible];

    return YES;
}
```

Build and run the application. It should autorotate when you rotate the device as shown in Figure 9.4.

Figure 9.4   Running rotated

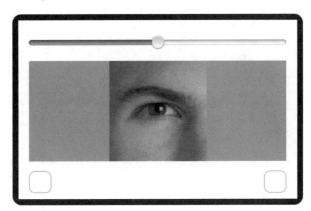

For the More Curious: Forcing Landscape Mode

If your application only makes sense in landscape mode, you can force it to run that way. First, make your view controller only allow autorotation to landscape orientations:

```
- (BOOL)shouldAutorotateToInterfaceOrientation:(UIInterfaceOrientation)x
{
    return UIInterfaceOrientationIsLandscape(x);
}
```

In an application's Info.plist, you can specify that the device be launched in a particular orientation. Double-click on the application's Info.plist to open it. Add a key-value pair by selecting a row and clicking the + button next to it (Figure 9.5). From the Key column's pop-up menu, choose Initial interface orientation (or type in UIInterfaceOrientation) and select the desired orientation from the pop-up list in the Value column.

Figure 9.5   Choosing the initial orientation

Build and run your application. Regardless of how you rotate the device, it will only appear in landscape mode.

Challenge: Proximity Notifications

Register for proximity notifications too. You will need to turn on proximity monitoring:

```
[device setProximityMonitoringEnabled:YES];
```

For the More Curious: Overriding Autorotation

In most cases, autorotation does the right thing as long as the autoresizing masks are properly set. However, you might want to take additional action on an autorotation or override the autorotation process altogether to change the way the view looks when it rotates. You can do this by overriding **willAnimateRotationToInterfaceOrientation:duration:** in a view controller subclass.

When a view controller is about to autorotate its view, it checks to see if you have implemented this method. If you have, it invokes this method during the animation block of the rotation code. Therefore, all changes to subviews in this method will be animated as well. You can also perform some custom code within this method. Here is an example that will reposition a button and change the background color on autorotation:

```
- (void)willAnimateRotationToInterfaceOrientation:(UIInterfaceOrientation)x
                                duration:(NSTimeInterval)duration
{
    // Assume "button" is a subview of this view controller's view

    UIColor *color = nil;
    CGRect bounds = [[self view] bounds];
    // If the orientation is rotating to Portrait mode...
    if (UIInterfaceOrientationIsPortrait(x)) {

        // Put the button in the top right corner
        [button setCenter:CGPointMake(bounds.size.width - 30,
                                20)];

        // the background color of the view will be red
        color = [UIColor redColor];
    } else {  // If the orientation is rotating to Landscape mode

        // Put the button in the bottom right corner
        [button setCenter:CGPointMake(bounds.size.width - 30,
                                bounds.size.height - 20)];

        // the background color of the view will be blue
        color = [UIColor blueColor];
    }
    [[self view] setBackgroundColor:color];
}
```

Overriding this method is useful when you want to update your user interface for a different orientation. For example, you could change the zoom or position of a scroll view or a table view (which you will learn about shortly) or even swap in an entirely different view. Make sure, however, that you do not replace the view of the view controller in this method. If you wish to swap in another view, you must swap a subview of the view controller's view.

This method is only available in iPhone OS 3.0 or later. In earlier versions of the OS, autorotation was performed in two steps. To implement additional actions for applications that support earlier versions of the OS, you can override two methods, **willAnimateFirstHalfOfRotationToInterfaceOrientation:duration:** and **willAnimateSecondHalfOfRotationFromInterfaceOrientation:duration:**. One caveat: if you implement either of these two methods, the one-step method, **willAnimateRotationToInterfaceOrientation:duration:**, will not be invoked.

10

UITableView and UITableViewController

iPhone applications frequently show an interactive list of items that allows a user to select, delete, or reorder items on the list. Whether it's a list of people in the user's address book or a list of items on the App Store, a **UITableView** is doing the work. A **UITableView** displays a single column of data with a variable number of rows. Figure 10.1 shows some examples of **UITableView**.

Figure 10.1   Examples of UITableView

Beginning the Homepwner Application

Over the next six chapters, you're going to develop an application called Homepwner that keeps an inventory of all your possessions. In the case of a fire or other catastrophe, you'll have a record for your insurance company. So far, all of your iPhone projects have been small, but Homepwner will grow into a realistically complex application. This will give you a feeling for what it is like to work on a large iPhone application. (By the way, "Homepwner" is not a typo. If you need a definition for the word "pwn," please visit http://www.urbandictionary.com.)

Select New Project from the File menu. In the New Project window, select Window-Based Application template (without Core Data). Click the Choose... button and name this project Homepwner. At that point, you will be taken to the familiar project window.

By the end of this chapter, Homepwner will present a list of **Possession** objects in a **UITableView**, as shown in Figure 10.2.

Figure 10.2   Homepwner: phase 1

UITableViewController

UITableView is a view object, so, according to Model-View-Controller, it knows how to draw itself, but it doesn't handle application logic or data. Thus, when using a **UITableView**, you must consider what helper objects are necessary. A **UITableView** usually occupies the entire screen, so it needs a **UIViewController** to handle placing it on the screen. A **UITableView** also typically needs a delegate so that other objects can be informed of events involving the **UITableView**. The delegate can be any object that (you guessed it!) conforms to the UITableViewDelegate protocol.

Additionally, a **UITableView** *always* needs a data source. A **UITableView** will ask its data source for the number of rows, the data to be shown in those rows, and many other tidbits that make a **UITableView** useful. Without a data source, a table view would be just an empty container. The dataSource for a **UITableView** can be any type of Objective-C object as long as it conforms to the UITableViewDataSource protocol.

Meet **UITableViewController**, a class that can fill all three roles: view controller, delegate, and data source. A **UITableViewController** is a subclass of **UIViewController**, and it handles most of the preparation and presentation of a **UITableView**. A **UITableViewController**'s view is always an instance of **UITableView**. The delegate and dataSource instance variables of the **UITableView** are automatically set to point at its **UITableViewController** (Figure 10.3).

Figure 10.3   UITableViewController-UITableView relationship

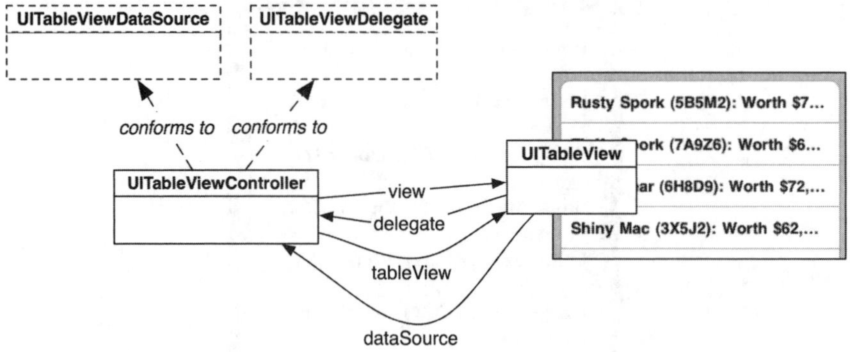

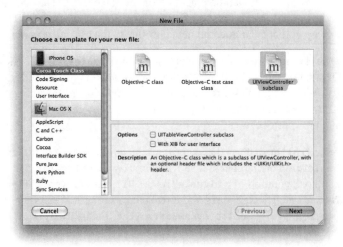

Subclassing UITableViewController

Now you're going to write a subclass of **UITableViewController** for Homepwner. To create a **UITableViewController** subclass, select New File... from the File menu and select UIViewController subclass from iPhone OS's Cocoa Touch Classes group. While there is a checkbox for a UITableViewController, *do not* check this. (The Xcode template for a **UITableViewController** subclass fills in too much code.) Also, uncheck the box for With XIB for user interface (Figure 10.4). Click the Next button, and you will be prompted for the name of this subclass. Call it ItemsViewController.m and click the Finish button.

Figure 10.4   Creating a UITableViewController subclass

Open ItemsViewController.h. Change the superclass of **ItemsViewController** from **UIViewController** to **UITableViewController**.

```
#import <UIKit/UIKit.h>
@interface ItemsViewController : UITableViewController
{

}

@end
```

Once you have a **UITableViewController** subclass, you need to add its **UITableView** to the window's view hierarchy in order for the **UITableView** to appear on the screen.

Every **UIViewController** has a property named view. A **UITableViewController**'s view is always its **UITableView**. Every **UITableViewController** also has a property named tableView. This property will return the same object as view, but the compiler will see the object's type as **UITableView** instead of the generic **UIView**. This is useful for sending messages to a **UITableViewController**'s table view that are specific to table views.

Once you have a **UITableViewController** instantiated and thus have a pointer to its **UITableView**, you can add the table view to the window. You have access to your application's **UIWindow** in **HomepwnerAppDelegate** where the template connected it in Interface Builder. But first, **HomepwnerAppDelegate** needs to know about **ItemsViewController**. Open the file HomepwnerAppDelegate.m and import the header for **ItemsViewController**.

```
#import "HomepwnerAppDelegate.h"
#import "ItemsViewController.h"
```

When your application launches, you will create an instance of **ItemsViewController** and add its view to the window. Once this happens, user events will go to the **UITableView** and get handled by its controller, **ItemsViewController**. Add an instance variable to HomepwnerAppDelegate.h to hold on to the the instance of **ItemsViewController**.

```
#import <UIKit/UIKit.h>

@class ItemsViewController;

@interface HomepwnerAppDelegate : NSObject <UIApplicationDelegate>
{
    UIWindow *window;
    ItemsViewController *itemsViewController;
}

@property (nonatomic, retain) IBOutlet UIWindow *window;

@end
```

In **application:didFinishLaunchingWithOptions:** in HomepwnerAppDelegate.m, create an instance of **ItemsViewController** and set it as the rootViewController of the window.

```
- (BOOL)application:(UIApplication *)application
   didFinishLaunchingWithOptions:(NSDictionary *)launchOptions
{
    // Create a ItemsViewController
    itemsViewController = [[ItemsViewController alloc] init];

    // Place ItemsViewController's table view in the window hierarchy
    [window setRootViewController:itemsViewController];

    // We won't release itemsViewController here, as we have an
    // instance variable that points to it as well, and therefore,
    // truly has two owners.

    [window makeKeyAndVisible];
    return YES;
}
```

(Note that the itemsViewController doesn't leak or need to be released because it will be alive the entire time the application is running. If you did release it here, you would also release the data source and delegate for its **UITableView**. That would be bad.)

Build and run your application. You will see the default appearance of a plain **UITableView** with no content, as shown in Figure 10.5.

Figure 10.5   Empty UITableView

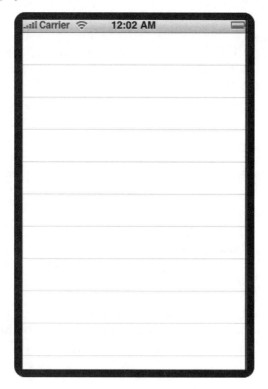

Poor empty table view! You should give it some rows to display. In Chapter 2, you wrote a class that can describe a possession. Now you're going to use that class again to have each row of your table view display an instance of **Possession**. Locate the interface and implementation files for **Possession** (Possession.h and Possession.m) and drag them onto Homepwner's project window and into the Classes group on the Groups & Files table.

When dragging these files into your project window, make sure to select the checkbox labeled Copy items into destination group's folder, as shown in Figure 10.6.

Figure 10.6   Adding files to a project

This will copy the files from their current directory to your project's directory on the filesystem and add them to your project. The project window will now appear as shown in Figure 10.7.

Figure 10.7   Project window with possession files added

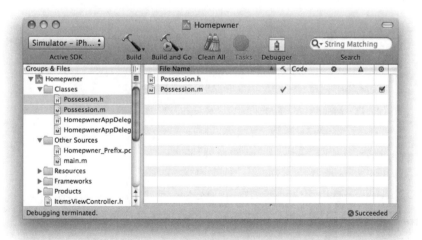

UITableView's Data Source

The process of providing a **UITableView** with rows in Cocoa Touch is different from a procedural programming task. In a procedural design, you tell the table view what it should display. In Cocoa Touch, the table view asks another object — its datasource — what it should display. Its data source is prepared to answer that question; it just needs to know for which row it should provide the content.

As a view object, a **UITableView** displays rows but doesn't store the data used to populate those rows. That's the job of the data source; therefore, **ItemsViewController** needs a way to store possession data. In Chapter 2, you used an **NSMutableArray** to store **Possession** instances and then print them out. You'll do the same thing in this exercise, but instead of printing to the console, you'll "print" to a **UITableView** (Figure 10.8).

Figure 10.8   Homepwner object diagram

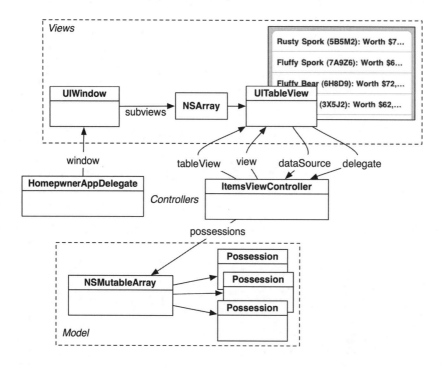

First, add an instance variable to ItemsViewController.h.

```
@interface ItemsViewController : UITableViewController
{
    NSMutableArray *possessions;
}
@end
```

The possessions array will be a list of **Possession** instances, and the **UITableView** will display these objects in its rows. Fortunately, you've already written a convenience method to create random **Possession** objects, and you already know how to populate an **NSMutableArray**. Implement the initialization methods in ItemsViewController.m.

```
#import "ItemsViewController.h"
#import "Possession.h"

@implementation ItemsViewController

- (id)init
{
    // Call the superclass's designated initializer
    [super initWithStyle:UITableViewStyleGrouped];

    // Create an array of 10 random possession objects
    possessions = [[NSMutableArray alloc] init];
    for(int i = 0; i < 10; i++) {
        [possessions addObject:[Possession randomPossession]];
    }
    return self;
}

- (id)initWithStyle:(UITableViewStyle)style
{
    return [self init];
}
```

In the code above, **initWithStyle:** (the designated initializer of the superclass) is overridden to call the new designated initializer, **init**. One reason for this change is users of this class now only have to send it the message **init**; they don't have to worry about passing it any arguments. It also forces **ItemsViewController** to appear in grouped table view style. (It looks prettier this way.)

UITableViewDataSource protocol

Now that **ItemsViewController** has some possessions, you need to teach it how to turn those possessions into rows that its **UITableView** can display. When a **UITableView** needs to know what to display, it has a set of messages it sends to its dataSource. These methods are declared in the UITableViewDataSource protocol.

Once again, you will peer into the iPhone SDK documentation to find these methods. In ItemsViewController.h, Command-Option-double click on the string **UITableViewController** to pull up the Developer Documentation window and the class reference for **UITableViewController** (Figure 10.9).

Figure 10.9   Documentation window

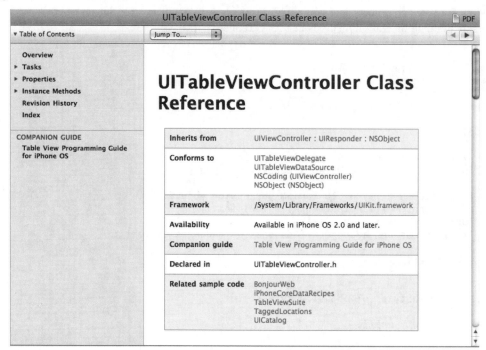

This reference will tell you everything you would ever want to know about
UITableViewController. The basic information about the class is in a table at the top of the page.
For instance, the Inherits from section tells you the class hierarchy of **UITableViewController**;
ItemsViewController will also respond to any methods these classes implement. You can click
on any of the items in this table to get to the reference for them.

Experienced iPhone developers spend a lot of time in the documentation. Many developers new to
the Apple way of doing things don't understand the importance of the documentation. Regardless
of the amount of experience you have with the iPhone SDK, you will still spend a lot of time
checking the documentation for the method or class you need. (The documentation browser is
always open on any Big Nerd Ranch employee's computer.) When starting or struggling with an
implementation, browse the documentation to find the appropriate classes and methods to work
with. Remember, if a common task is difficult in Cocoa Touch, you are probably doing it wrong.
The documentation will usually show you the easy way.

Right now, you are looking for the methods from the UITableViewDataSource protocol that
ItemsViewController could implement to turn **Possession** instances into rows for the table
view. Click on UITableViewDataSource in the Conforms to section to get to the protocol
reference. There you can scroll down and see all the messages that a **UITableView** can send to its
dataSource.

There are many methods here, but the two that are marked required method *must* be implemented.
For **UITableViewController** to properly conform to UITableViewDataSource, it must implement
tableView:numberOfRowsInSection: and **tableView:cellForRowAtIndexPath:**. These methods
tell the table view how many rows it should display and what content to display in each row.

Whenever a **UITableView** needs to display itself, it sends a series of messages (the required methods plus any optional ones that have been implemented) to its dataSource. The required method **tableView:numberOfRowsInSection:** returns an integer value for the number of rows that the **UITableView** should display. Because there needs to be a row for each entry in the possessions array, the implementation of this method should return the number of entries in the array as shown in Figure 10.10.

Figure 10.10   Obtaining the number of rows

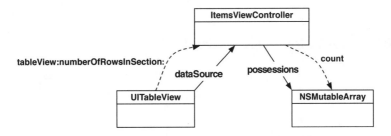

Now implement **tableView:numberOfRowsInSection:** in ItemsViewController.m.

```
- (NSInteger)tableView:(UITableView *)tableView
  numberOfRowsInSection:(NSInteger)section
{
    return [possessions count];
}
```

(You might be wondering what a "section" means in this method name. Table views can be broken up into sections, and each section can have its own set of rows. For example, in the address book, all the names beginning with "D" are grouped together in a section. By default, a table view has one section, and for this exercise, we will work with only one section. Once you understand how a table view works, it's not hard to use multiple sections. In fact, using multiple sections is one of the challenges at the end of this chapter.)

UITableViewCells

A **UITableViewCell** is a subclass of **UIView**, and each row in a **UITableView** is represented by a **UITableViewCell**. (Recall that a table on the iPhone can only have one column, so a row will only have one cell.) **UITableView** is a container for **UITableViewCells**. A cell consists of a content view where the cell displays data and an accessory view (Figure 10.11). In the accessory view, the cell can display an action-oriented icon — like a checkbox, a disclosure button, or a fancy blue dot with a chevron inside. These icons are accessed through pre-defined constants for the appearance of the accessory view. (See the docs for **UITableViewCell** for details.)

Figure 10.11   UITableViewCell layout

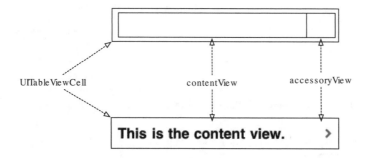

However, the real meat of a **UITableViewCell** is the content view. Each cell's contentView has three subviews. Two of those subviews are **UILabel** instances, textLabel and detailTextLabel. The third is a **UIImageView** called imageView (Figure 10.12).

Figure 10.12   UITableViewCell hierarchy

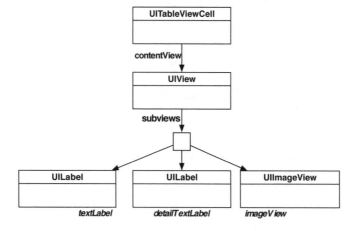

Each cell also has a UITableViewCellStyle that determines which of these subviews are used and their position within the contentView. These styles are shown in Figure 10.13.

Figure 10.13   UITableViewCellStyles

In this chapter, each cell will display the **description** of a **Possession**. To make this happen, you will implement the **tableView:cellForRowAtIndexPath:** in the data source (**ItemsViewController**). This method will create a cell, set its textLabel to the **description** of the corresponding **Possession**, and return it to the **UITableView** that requested it (Figure 10.14).

Figure 10.14   UITableViewCell retrieval

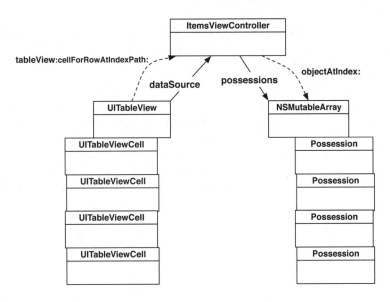

How do you decide which cell a **Possession** corresponds to? One of the parameters sent to **tableView:cellForRowAtIndexPath:** is an **NSIndexPath**, which has two properties, section and row. When this message is sent to a data source, the table view is asking, "Can I have a cell to display in section X at row Y?" Because there is only one section in this exercise, the row is the only value of consequence. Therefore, implement this method in `ItemsViewController.m` so that the *n*th row displays the *n*th entry in the `possessions` array.

```
- (UITableViewCell *)tableView:(UITableView *)tableView
        cellForRowAtIndexPath:(NSIndexPath *)indexPath
{
    // Create an instance of UITableViewCell, with default appearance
    UITableViewCell *cell =
        [[[UITableViewCell alloc] initWithStyle:UITableViewCellStyleDefault
                            reuseIdentifier:@"UITableViewCell"] autorelease];

    // Set the text on the cell with the description of the possession
    // that is at the nth index of possessions, where n = row this cell
    // will appear in on the tableview
    Possession *p = [possessions objectAtIndex:[indexPath row]];
    [[cell textLabel] setText:[p description]];
    return cell;
}
```

You can build and run the application now, and you'll see a **UITableView** populated with a list of random **Possession**s. Yep, it was that easy! Thanks, Cocoa Touch! Also note that you didn't have to change anything about **Possession** — you simply changed the controller object to interface with a different view. This is why Model-View-Controller is such a powerful concept. With a minimal amount of code, you were able to show the same data in an entirely different way.

Reusing UITableViewCells

The iPhone has a limited amount of memory. If we were displaying a list with thousands of entries in a **UITableView**, we would have thousands of instances of **UITableViewCell**. And the iPhone would sputter and die. In its dying breath, it would say "You only needed enough cells to fill the screen... arrrghhh!" It would be right.

Reusing **UITableViewCell**s prevents senseless iPhone death. A **UITableView** retains any **UITableViewCell** returned to it by the method **tableView:cellForRowAtIndexPath:** (which is why you can autorelease it in **tableView:cellForRowAtIndexPath:**). When the user scrolls the table, some cells are moved offscreen and put into a pool of cells available for reuse. Then, instead of creating a brand new cell for every request, the data source can check the pool. If there is an unused cell, the data source configures it with new data and returns it to the table view.

Figure 10.15 Reusable UITableViewCells

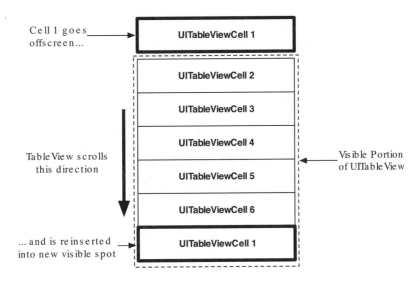

There is one problem: sometimes a **UITableView** has different types of cells. Occasionally, you have to subclass **UITableViewCell** to create a special look or behavior. However, subclasses floating around the pool of reusable cells create the possibility of getting back a cell of the wrong type. You must be sure of the type of the cell returned to you so that you can be sure of what properties and methods it has.

Note that you don't care about getting any *specific cell* out of the pool because you're going to change the cell data anyway. What you want is a cell of a *specific type*. The good news is every cell has a reuseIdentifier (an **NSString**) that the table view uses to distinguish it from other cells. If the reuse identifier is the name of the cell class, then it becomes easy to ask for a specific type of a cell. Update **tableView:cellForRowAtIndexPath:** to implement reusable cells:

```
- (UITableViewCell *)tableView:(UITableView *)tableView
        cellForRowAtIndexPath:(NSIndexPath *)indexPath
{
    // Check for a reusable cell first, use that if it exists
    UITableViewCell *cell =
        [tableView dequeueReusableCellWithIdentifier:@"UITableViewCell"];

    // If there is no reusable cell of this type, create a new one
    if (!cell) {
        cell = [[[UITableViewCell alloc]
                initWithStyle:UITableViewCellStyleDefault
                reuseIdentifier:@"UITableViewCell"] autorelease];
    }


    Possession *p = [possessions objectAtIndex:[indexPath row]];
    [[cell textLabel] setText:[p description]];
    return cell;
}
```

Reusing cells means that you only have to create a handful of cells. When one needs to be reinserted in the table, you simply update its contents with new information. Your iPhone (and your application's users) will thank you for it. Build and run the application. The behavior of the application should remain the same.

In the next chapter, you're going to expand Homepwner and allow the user to reorder, delete, and insert new rows.

Challenge: Sections

Have the **UITableView** display two sections — one for possessions worth more than $50 and one for the rest. To make this process easier, use two separate possessions arrays. Before you start this challenge, copy the folder containing the project and all of its source files in Finder. Then tackle the challenge in the copied project; you'll need the original to build on in the coming chapters.

11

Editing UITableView

In the last chapter, you began an application that displayed a list of **Possession** instances in a **UITableView**. The next step in this application is allowing the user to interact with that table by moving, deleting, and inserting rows. Figure 11.1 shows what your Homepwner application will look like by the end of this chapter.

Figure 11.1 Homepwner in editing mode

Editing Mode

Every **UITableView** has an editing variable. When this boolean variable is set to YES, the **UITableView** enters editing mode, and the rows of the table can be manipulated by the user. The user can change the order of the rows, add rows, or remove rows. Editing mode, however, does not allow the user to edit the *content* of a row.

But before any of this can happen, the user needs a way to put the **UITableView** in editing mode. For now, you're going to display a button that toggles editing mode in the *header view* of the table. A header view appears at the top of a section of a table and is useful for adding section-wide or table-wide titles or controls. It can be any **UIView** subclass. There's also a footer view for the bottom of a section that works the same way. Figure 11.2 shows a table with two sections. Each section has a **UISlider** for a header view and a **UILabel** for a footer view.

Figure 11.2   UITableView header and footer views

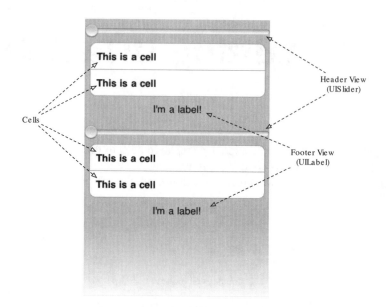

Open Homepwner.xcodeproj again. In ItemsViewController.h, declare an instance variable of type **UIView** for your header view. Also, declare a new method that will create this header view.

```
@interface ItemsViewController : UITableViewController
{
    UIView *headerView;
    NSMutableArray *possessions;
}
- (UIView *)headerView;
@end
```

The standard **UIView** you've declared will be a container for a **UIButton** that toggles editing mode on and off. Now implement **headerView** in ItemsViewController.m.

```
- (UIView *)headerView
{
    if (headerView)
        return headerView;

    // Create a UIButton object, simple rounded rect style
    UIButton *editButton = [UIButton buttonWithType:UIButtonTypeRoundedRect];

    // Set the title of this button to "Edit"
    [editButton setTitle:@"Edit" forState:UIControlStateNormal];

    // How wide is the screen?
    float w = [[UIScreen mainScreen] bounds].size.width;
```

```
    // Create a rectangle for the button
    CGRect editButtonFrame = CGRectMake(8.0, 8.0, w - 16.0, 30.0);
    [editButton setFrame:editButtonFrame];

    // When this button is tapped, send the message
    // editingButtonPressed: to this instance of ItemsViewController
    [editButton addTarget:self
                   action:@selector(editingButtonPressed:)
         forControlEvents:UIControlEventTouchUpInside];

    // Create a rectangle for the headerView that will contain the button
    CGRect headerViewFrame = CGRectMake(0, 0, w, 48);
    headerView = [[UIView alloc] initWithFrame:headerViewFrame];

    // Add button to the headerView's view hierarchy
    [headerView addSubview:editButton];

    return headerView;
}
```

In the method above, you added the target-action pair for the button in the code as opposed to previous chapters where you used Interface Builder. Remember when you Control-clicked a button and dragged back to the application delegate or view controller in the doc window? You were adding a target-action pair to that button so that whenever it received an event, it would send the action message to the target object. When you added this bit of code to **headerView**

```
    [editButton addTarget:self
                   action:@selector(editingButtonPressed:)
         forControlEvents:UIControlEventTouchUpInside];
```

you were doing the same thing as making the connection in Interface Builder. Now, whenever the editButton is tapped (UIControlEventTouchUpInside), it will send the message **editingButtonPressed:** to the instance of **ItemsViewController** as shown in Figure 11.3.

Figure 11.3   Target-Action pair

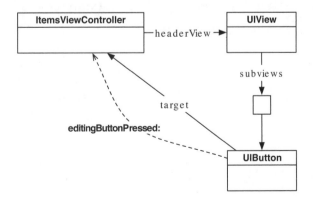

To get your header view to appear in a **UITableView**, you need to implement two UITableViewDelegate methods to check for a header view and obtain the view and its height. Implement these two methods in ItemsViewController.m.

```
- (UIView *)tableView:(UITableView *)tv viewForHeaderInSection:(NSInteger)sec
{
    return [self headerView];
}

- (CGFloat)tableView:(UITableView *)tv heightForHeaderInSection:(NSInteger)sec
{
    return [[self headerView] frame].size.height;
}
```

Build and run the application. An Edit button will appear at the top of the table, but pressing it will generate an exception, of course, because you haven't yet implemented its action — **editingButtonPressed:**.

The implementation of **editingButtonPressed:** needs to toggle the editing mode of the table view. In this method, you could set the editing property of **UITableView** directly. However, a **UITableViewController**, like every **UIViewController**, also has an editing property. A **UITableViewController** instance automatically sets the editing property of its table view to the same value as its own editing property. To set the editing property for a view controller and toggle editing mode, you send it the message **setEditing:animated:**. Therefore, both the view controller and the table view will know whether editing is occurring, which will be important for implementing controller logic. Implement **editingButtonPressed:** in ItemsViewController.m.

```
- (void)editingButtonPressed:(id)sender
{
    // If we are currently in editing mode...
    if ([self isEditing]) {
        // Change text of button to inform user of state
        [sender setTitle:@"Edit" forState:UIControlStateNormal];
        // Turn off editing mode
        [self setEditing:NO animated:YES];
    } else {
        // Change text of button to inform user of state
        [sender setTitle:@"Done" forState:UIControlStateNormal];
        // Enter editing mode
        [self setEditing:YES animated:YES];
    }
}
```

Build and run your application and touch the Edit button. The **UITableView** will enter editing mode (Figure 11.4).

Figure 11.4   UITableView in editing mode

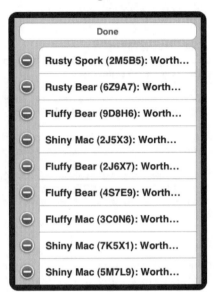

Deleting Rows

The red circles with the dash (shown in Figure 11.4) are deletion controls, and touching one will delete that row. However, at this point, touching a deletion control deletes nothing. (Test it for yourself.) Before a row can be deleted, the table view needs to ask the data source *how* to delete that row. This includes choosing what type of animation to display and how the data being displayed is affected by the deletion of that row.

A **UITableView** asks its data source for the cells it should display when it is first added to the screen and at least three other times:

- when the user scrolls the table view

- when the table view is removed from the view hierarchy and then added back to the view hierarchy

- when your code sends the message **reloadData** to the **UITableView**

Now consider what would happen if deleting a row only removed the row from the table view and not the data source. The possessions array would still have the **Possession** instance displayed by that row, and the next time the **UITableView** reloaded its rows, the data source would create a cell for the supposedly deleted **Possession**. The unwanted row would rise from the dead and return to the table.

Therefore, when a row is deleted, you must remove the object that the row displayed from the data source. The method to implement is **tableView:commitEditingStyle:forRowAtIndexPath:**. When that message is sent to your data source, two extra arguments are passed along

with it. The first is the **UITableViewCellEditingStyle**, which, in this case, will be
UITableViewCellEditingStyleDelete. The other argument is the **NSIndexPath** of the row within
the table. Implement this method in ItemsViewController.m.

```
- (void)tableView:(UITableView *)tableView
    commitEditingStyle:(UITableViewCellEditingStyle)editingStyle
    forRowAtIndexPath:(NSIndexPath *)indexPath
{
    // If the table view is asking to commit a delete command...
    if (editingStyle == UITableViewCellEditingStyleDelete) {

        // We remove the row being deleted from the possessions array
        [possessions removeObjectAtIndex:[indexPath row]];

        // We also remove that row from the table view with an animation
        [tableView deleteRowsAtIndexPaths:[NSArray arrayWithObject:indexPath]
                    withRowAnimation:UITableViewRowAnimationFade];
    }
}
```

Build and run your application and then delete a row. It will disappear. Now scroll the list, return
to where the deleted row was, and check to see if your data source was updated. No zombie cell —
hooray!

Moving Rows

To change the order of rows in a **UITableView**, you will use another data source method —
tableView:moveRowAtIndexPath:toIndexPath:. The implementation of this method needs to
remove the object at fromIndexPath from the possessions array and re-insert it at toIndexPath.
Implement this method in ItemsViewController.m.

```
- (void)tableView:(UITableView *)tableView
    moveRowAtIndexPath:(NSIndexPath *)fromIndexPath
        toIndexPath:(NSIndexPath *)toIndexPath
{
    // Get pointer to object being moved
    Possession *p = [possessions objectAtIndex:[fromIndexPath row]];

    // Retain p so that it is not deallocated when it is removed from the array
    [p retain];
        // Retain count of p is now 2

    // Remove p from our array, it is automatically sent release
    [possessions removeObjectAtIndex:[fromIndexPath row]];
        // Retain count of p is now 1

    // Re-insert p into array at new location, it is automatically retained
    [possessions insertObject:p atIndex:[toIndexPath row]];
        // Retain count of p is now 2

    // Release p
    [p release];
        // Retain count of p is now 1
}
```

When you were deleting a row, you had to explicitly send the message **deleteRowsAtIndexPaths:withRowAnimation:** to the **UITableView**. When moving rows, however, you don't have to send a message to the table view that it's okay to move a row; the table view will move it without further instruction. You just have to catch the message to update your data source. Build and run your application. Then touch and hold the reordering control (the three horizontal lines) on the side of a row and move it to a new position (Figure 11.5).

Figure 11.5   Moving a row

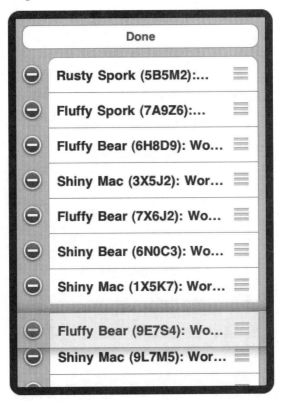

Note that before you implemented this method, the reordering controls did not appear on the table view. Simply implementing this method made them appear. This is because Objective-C is a very smart language. The **UITableView** can ask its data source whether it implements **tableView:moveRowAtIndexPath:toIndexPath:** at runtime. If it does, the table view says, "Good, you can handle moving rows. I'll add the re-ordering controls." If not, it says, "You bum. If you are too lazy to implement that method, I'm not putting the controls there."

Inserting Rows

Deleting and moving rows is easy; inserting them is trickier. First, let's discuss the one way of inserting a row that isn't tricky at all: sending the message **reloadData**. You know that a **UITableView** displays rows based on what its dataSource tells it to display. If you wanted to add a row, you could simply insert an entry into possessions and send the message **reloadData** to the **UITableView**. The method **reloadData** restarts the process of asking the data source for the number of rows and getting the cells, and the new row would be added as part of that process. (You could do the same thing for deleting and moving rows, too, but the implementation would be more difficult — how would the user select which row to delete or move?)

The approach you're going to implement is more difficult but totally worth it in terms of user experience. What you want is a row at the bottom of the table that has an insertion control (a green icon with a plus symbol) next to it (Figure 11.6). This row will only be visible during editing mode, and touching it will place a new random **Possession** at the bottom of the list along with an animation.

Figure 11.6   Adding a row

To begin, the table view needs to display an additional row when it is in editing mode. Override **setEditing:animated:** for **ItemsViewController** so that it either adds or removes a row at the bottom of the table depending on whether you are entering or leaving editing mode. (Recall that this is the method that is invoked when the editing button is tapped.)

```
- (void)setEditing:(BOOL)flag animated:(BOOL)animated
{
    // Always call super implementation of this method, it needs to do work
    [super setEditing:flag animated:animated];

    // You need to insert/remove a new row in to table view
    if (flag) {
        // If entering edit mode, we add another row to our table view
        NSIndexPath *indexPath =
            [NSIndexPath indexPathForRow:[possessions count] inSection:0];
```

```
        NSArray *paths = [NSArray arrayWithObject:indexPath];

        [[self tableView] insertRowsAtIndexPaths:paths
                            withRowAnimation:UITableViewRowAnimationLeft];
    } else {
        // If leaving edit mode, we remove last row from table view
        NSIndexPath *indexPath =
            [NSIndexPath indexPathForRow:[possessions count] inSection:0];
        NSArray *paths = [NSArray arrayWithObject:indexPath];

        [[self tableView] deleteRowsAtIndexPaths:paths
                            withRowAnimation:UITableViewRowAnimationFade];
    }
}
```

Notice that you send the same message to the superclass. This is to take advantage of **UITableViewController**'s special property that matches the **UITableView**'s editing property with its own.

When the user enters editing mode, another row is added to the bottom. However, now the view is out of sync with the data source: there are eleven rows visible, but the data source only has ten entries in possessions. Change the following method in ItemsViewController.m to resolve this conflict:

```
- (NSInteger)tableView:(UITableView *)tableView
 numberOfRowsInSection:(NSInteger)section
{
    int numberOfRows = [possessions count];
    // If we are editing, we will have one more row than we have possessions
    if ([self isEditing])
        numberOfRows++;

    return numberOfRows;
}
```

The **UITableView** will now have the correct number of rows while it is being edited. Now update **tableView:cellForRowAtIndexPath:** in ItemsViewController.m so that the last row in editing mode displays something useful like "Add New Item...":

```
- (UITableViewCell *)tableView:(UITableView *)tableView
        cellForRowAtIndexPath:(NSIndexPath *)indexPath
{
    UITableViewCell *cell =
            [tableView dequeueReusableCellWithIdentifier:@"UITableViewCell"];

    if (!cell) {
        cell = [[[UITableViewCell alloc]
                    initWithStyle:UITableViewCellStyleDefault
                 reuseIdentifier:@"UITableViewCell"] autorelease];
    }

    // If the table view is filling a row with a possession in it, do as normal
    if ([indexPath row] < [possessions count]) {
        Possession *p = [possessions objectAtIndex:[indexPath row]];
        [[cell textLabel] setText:[p description]];
```

```
    } else { // Otherwise, if we are editing we have one extra row...
        [[cell textLabel] setText:@"Add New Item..."];
    }

    return cell;
}
```

Build and run your application. Touch the Edit button and scroll down to the bottom of the table. There's your new row... but it still has a deletion control next to it. To give this row an insertion control instead, you'll need to change the row's editing style. When a **UITableView** begins editing, it asks its delegate for the editing style at each row. Implement the following method in ItemsViewController.m so that the last row has a UITableViewCellEditingStyleInsert style.

```
- (UITableViewCellEditingStyle)tableView:(UITableView *)tableView
          editingStyleForRowAtIndexPath:(NSIndexPath *)indexPath
{
    if ([self isEditing] && [indexPath row] == [possessions count]) {

        // The last row during editing will show an insert style button
        return UITableViewCellEditingStyleInsert;
    }
    // All other rows remain deleteable
    return UITableViewCellEditingStyleDelete;
}
```

Building and running now shows an insertion control next to the last row.

Now you have to implement code to handle what happens when this control is touched. You have already written the data source method for this; you just need to write some additional code to handle inserts. Add the following code to **tableView:commitEditingStyle:forRowAtIndexPath:** in ItemsViewController.m.

```
- (void)tableView:(UITableView *)tableView
    commitEditingStyle:(UITableViewCellEditingStyle)editingStyle
     forRowAtIndexPath:(NSIndexPath *)indexPath
{
    if (editingStyle == UITableViewCellEditingStyleDelete) {
        [possessions removeObjectAtIndex:[indexPath row]];
        [tableView deleteRowsAtIndexPaths:[NSArray arrayWithObject:indexPath]
                withRowAnimation:UITableViewRowAnimationFade];
    } else if (editingStyle == UITableViewCellEditingStyleInsert) {

        // If the editing style of the row was insertion,
        // we add a new possession object and new row to the table view
        [possessions addObject:[Possession randomPossession]];
        [tableView insertRowsAtIndexPaths:[NSArray arrayWithObject:indexPath]
                withRowAnimation:UITableViewRowAnimationLeft];
    }
}
```

Adding the Add New Item... row introduces two potential bugs in Homepwner. First, the user could use the reordering control to move the Add New Item... row. This would blow up the entire application. (Try it — it's fun!) The table view assumes that all rows can move in editing mode because its data source implemented the method to move rows. However, you can trim the set of moveable rows by implementing another data source method, `tableView:canMoveRowAtIndexPath:`, in ItemsViewController.m. This method will return NO for the last row, and that row will not show a reordering control.

```
- (BOOL)tableView:(UITableView *)tableView
    canMoveRowAtIndexPath:(NSIndexPath *)indexPath
{
    // Only allow rows showing possessions to move
    if ([indexPath row] < [possessions count])
        return YES;
    return NO;
}
```

The second problem will occur if the user moves another row beneath the Add New Item... row. This will cause all sorts of havoc in the data source methods. Fixing this problem requires another delegate method, and yes, you may scream "I knew it!" This method gives you the **NSIndexPath** of the row that wants to move as well as the row it wants to occupy. If you don't want to allow the proposed move to take place, you return the **NSIndexPath** of the row that it should move to instead. Add the following implementation to ItemsViewController.m.

```
- (NSIndexPath *)tableView:(UITableView *)tableView
    targetIndexPathForMoveFromRowAtIndexPath:(NSIndexPath *)sourceIndexPath
    toProposedIndexPath:(NSIndexPath *)proposedDestinationIndexPath

{
    if ([proposedDestinationIndexPath row] < [possessions count]) {
        // If we are moving to a row that currently is showing a possession,
        // then we return the row the user wanted to move to
        return proposedDestinationIndexPath;
    }
    // We get here if we are trying to move a row to under the "Add New Item..."
    // row, have the moving row go one row above it instead.
    NSIndexPath *betterIndexPath =
        [NSIndexPath indexPathForRow:[possessions count] - 1 inSection:0];

    return betterIndexPath;
}
```

Build and run the application. Try moving the last row. Now try moving another row beneath it. Ha! You can't! Homepwner is so safe that even a child could use it. Now if we could just add real possessions instead of generating random ones....

UINavigationController

Earlier in this book, you learned about **UITabBarController** and how it allows a user to access different screens. A tab bar controller is great when you have screens that don't rely on each other, but what if you want to move between related screens?

For example, the iPhone Settings application has multiple related screens of information: a list of settings (like Sounds), a detailed page for each setting, and a selection page for each detail. This type of interface is called a *drill-down interface*. In this chapter, you will use a **UINavigationController** to add a drill-down interface to Homepwner (Figure 12.1).

Figure 12.1   Homepwner with UINavigationController

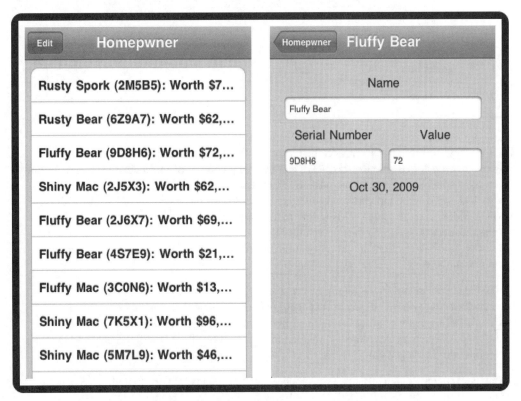

UINavigationController

When you have an application that presents multiple screens of information, **UINavigationController** maintains a stack of those screens. The stack is an **NSArray** of view controllers, and each screen is the view instance controlled by a **UIViewController**. When a **UIViewController** is on top of the stack, its view is visible.

When you initialize an instance of **UINavigationController**, you give it one **UIViewController**. This **UIViewController** is called the *root view controller*, and its position in the stack is shown in Figure 12.2. In the Homepwner application, the root view controller will be **ItemsViewController**. It is the first screen the user sees and can navigate from.

Figure 12.2   UINavigationController's stack

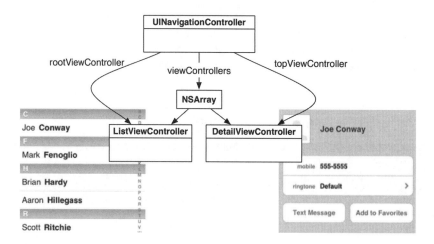

The root view controller is always on the bottom of the stack (which is also the top if there is only one item). More **UIViewController**s can be pushed on top of this stack during execution. When this happens, the view of the pushed **UIViewController** slides onto the screen. When the stack is popped, the top view controller is removed from the stack, and the view of the one below it slides onto the screen. This ability to add to the stack during execution is missing in **UITabBarController**, which must have all of the view controllers it maintains at initialization time. Navigation controllers are more dynamic, and only the root view controller is guaranteed to always be in the stack.

The **UIViewController** that is on top of the stack can be accessed by sending the message **topViewController** to the **UINavigationController** instance. You can also get the entire stack as an **NSArray** by sending the navigation controller the message **viewControllers**. The viewControllers array is ordered so that the root view controller is the first entry and the top view controller is the last entry.

UINavigationController is actually a subclass of **UIViewController**, so it also has a view instance. Its view always has at least two subviews: a **UINavigationBar** and the view of the

UIViewController that is on top of the stack (Figure 12.3). The only requirements for using a **UINavigationController** are that you add its view to the visible view hierarchy and give it a root view controller.

Figure 12.3 A UINavigationController's view

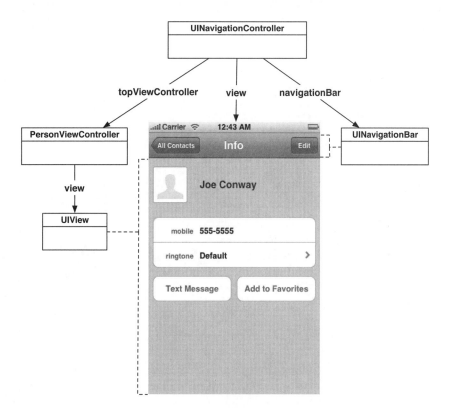

In this chapter, you will be adding a **UINavigationController** to the Homepwner application. When a user selects one of the possession rows, a new **UIViewController**'s view will slide onto the screen. That view controller will allow the user to view and edit the properties of the **Possession**. The object diagram for the updated Homepwner application is shown in Figure 12.4.

Figure 12.4   Homepwner object diagram

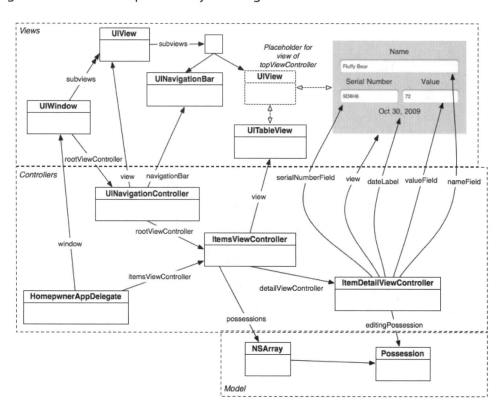

This application is starting to get fairly large, as demonstrated by the massive object diagram. Fortunately, view controllers and **UINavigationController** know how to deal with this type of complicated object diagram. When writing iPhone applications, it is important to treat each **UIViewController** as its own little world. The stuff that has already been implemented in Cocoa Touch will do the heavy lifting.

In Homepwner.xcodeproj that you created earlier, open the file HomepwnerAppDelegate.m. The **UINavigationController** instance will now be the window's rootViewController (whereas, previously, the root view controller of the window was **ItemsViewController**). This **UINavigationController** will be initialized with **ItemsViewController** as its root view controller. Make these changes in **application:didFinishLaunchingWithOptions:**.

```
- (BOOL)application:(UIApplication *)application
    didFinishLaunchingWithOptions:(NSDictionary *)launchOptions
{
    itemsViewController = [[ItemsViewController alloc] init];

    // Create an instance of a UINavigationController
    // its stack contains only itemsViewController
```

```
UINavigationController *navController = [[UINavigationController alloc]
        initWithRootViewController:itemsViewController];

// Place navigation controller's view in the window hierarchy
[window setRootViewController:navController];
[navController release];


[window makeKeyAndVisible];
return YES;
}
```

Build and run the application. Homepwner will look the same as it did before — except now it has a **UINavigationBar** at the top of the screen (Figure 12.5). Notice how **ItemsViewController**'s view was resized to fit the screen with a navigation bar. **UINavigationController** did this for you.

Figure 12.5   Homepwner with an empty navigation bar

UINavigationBar

The **UINavigationBar** isn't very interesting right now. At a minimum, a **UINavigationBar** should display a descriptive title for the **UIViewController** that is currently on top of the **UINavigationController**'s stack.

Every **UIViewController** has a property navigationItem of type **UINavigationItem**. While **UINavigationBar** is a subclass of **UIView** (which means it can be appear on screen), **UINavigationItem** is not. However, it supplies the navigation bar with the content it needs to draw. When a **UIViewController** comes to the top of a **UINavigationController**'s stack, the navigation controller's **UINavigationBar** uses the **UIViewController**'s navigationItem to configure itself, as shown in Figure 12.6.

Figure 12.6   UINavigationItem

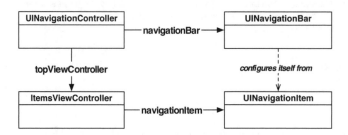

That's not the easiest thing to understand at first glance. So, consider the following analogy. Think of **UIViewController** as an NFL football team, and moving to the top of the stack as going to the Super Bowl. The **UINavigationItem** is the team logo design, and, no matter what, its team logo remains unchanged; it's an internal design. The **UINavigationController** is the stadium, and the **UINavigationBar** is an end zone. When a team makes it to the Super Bowl, its team logo is painted on one end zone of the stadium. And when a **UIViewController** is moved to the top of the stack, its **UINavigationItem** is painted on the **UINavigationBar** within the **UINavigationController**.

By default, a **UINavigationItem** is empty. At the most basic level, a **UINavigationItem** has a simple title string. When a **UIViewController** is moved to the top of the navigation stack and its navigationItem has a valid string for its title property, the navigation bar will display that string (Figure 12.7).

Figure 12.7   UINavigationItem with title

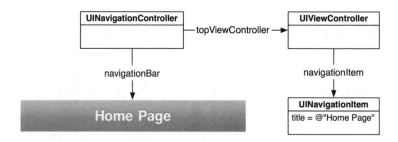

A navigation item can hold more than just a title string, as shown in Figure 12.8. There are three customizable areas for each **UINavigationItem**: a titleView, a leftBarButtonItem, and a rightBarButtonItem. The left and right bar button items are pointers to instances of **UIBarButtonItem**, a type of button that can only be displayed on a **UINavigationBar** or a **UIToolbar**.

Figure 12.8   UINavigationItem with everything

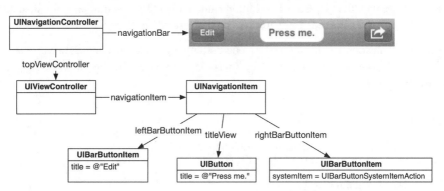

Like **UINavigationItem**, **UIBarButtonItem** is not a subclass of **UIView** but supplies the content that a **UINavigationBar** needs to draw. Consider the **UINavigationItem** and its **UIBarButtonItem**s to be containers for strings, images, and other content. A **UINavigationBar** knows how to look in those containers and draw the content that's there.

The third customizable area of a **UINavigationItem** is its titleView. You have a choice with each navigation item: use a basic string as the title (as you'll do in this chapter) or have any subclass of **UIView** sit in the center of the navigation item. You cannot have both. If it suits the context of a specific view controller to have a custom view (such as a button, a slider, an image view, or even a map) instead of a title, you would set the titleView of the navigation item to that custom view. Typically, however, a title string is sufficient.

Set up **ItemsViewController** to have a proper navigationItem. Update the **init** method by adding the following lines of code to ItemsViewController.m.

```objc
- (id)init
{
    [super initWithStyle:UITableViewStyleGrouped];

    possessions = [[NSMutableArray alloc] init];
    for (int i = 0; i < 10; i++) {
        [possessions addObject:[Possession randomPossession]];
    }

    // Set the nav bar to have the pre-fab'ed Edit button when
    // ItemsViewController is on top of the stack
    [[self navigationItem] setLeftBarButtonItem:[self editButtonItem]];

    // Set the title of the nav bar to Homepwner when ItemsViewController
    // is on top of the stack
    [[self navigationItem] setTitle:@"Homepwner"];

    return self;
}
```

Building and running the application now will show a lovely **UINavigationBar** with a title and — surprise! — an Edit button. Go ahead and tap that Edit button and watch the **UITableView** enter editing mode! Where did **editButtonItem** come from? Every **UIViewController** has a editButtonItem property. When sent **editButtonItem**, the view controller creates a **UIBarButtonItem** with the title Edit. This button came with a target-action pair: it will send the message **setEditing:animated:** to its **UIViewController** when tapped.

This means you can simplify the code a bit. You no longer need the header view with the button labeled Edit. To get rid of the header view, delete the following two methods from ItemsViewController.m.

```
// Delete these!

- (UIView *)tableView:(UITableView *)aTableView
    viewForHeaderInSection:(NSInteger)section
{
    return [self headerView];
}

- (CGFloat)tableView:(UITableView *)tableView
    heightForHeaderInSection:(NSInteger)section
{
    return [[self headerView] frame].size.height;
}
```

The headerView will no longer be used, and your code will still build the correct application. Also, you will want to remove the instance variable headerView along with the implementation of the methods **headerView** and **editingButtonPressed:**.

Now you can build and run again. The old Edit button is gone, and you have a much more efficient editButtonItem in the **UINavigationBar** that does the same thing (Figure 12.9).

Figure 12.9   Homepwner with navigation bar

An Additional UIViewController

To see the real power of **UINavigationController**, you need another **UIViewController** to put on its stack. Create a new **UIViewController** subclass by selecting New File... from the File menu. Choose UIViewController subclass and select With XIB for user interface only. Name this class ItemDetailViewController and add it to the Homepwner project (Figure 12.10).

Figure 12.10   Creating ItemDetailViewController

In Homepwner, the user will be able to tap one of the rows and have another view slide onto the screen with editable text fields for each property of that **Possession**. This view will be controlled by an instance of **ItemDetailViewController**.

You need four subviews — one for each instance variable of a **Possession** instance. **ItemDetailViewController**'s view will display these and allow the user to edit them. And because you need to be able to access these subviews during runtime, **ItemDetailViewController** needs outlets for these subviews. Add the following instance variables to ItemDetailViewController.h.

```
@interface ItemDetailViewController : UIViewController
{
    IBOutlet UITextField *nameField;
    IBOutlet UITextField *serialNumberField;
    IBOutlet UITextField *valueField;
    IBOutlet UILabel *dateLabel;
}
@end
```

Save this file. The IBOutlet in front of each of these instance variables should clue you into the fact you are going to use Interface Builder to lay out the interface for **ItemDetailViewController**'s view. When you created **ItemDetailViewController**, a XIB file of the same name was created and added to the project. Open ItemDetailViewController.xib now.

The XIB file and File's Owner

You have seen XIB files in previous exercises. You've also added subviews to the window, made outlet connections, and connected action messages. In those XIB files, there was a File's Owner object in the doc window that you used without really understanding. Now it is time to learn what the File's Owner really is.

File's Owner is a placeholder for an object that is supplied when the NIB file is read in. That is, File's Owner is a hole, and whatever causes the NIB file to be unarchived, supplies something to go into that hole.

This is a little abstract because you have never explicitly unarchived a NIB file. Instead, the **UIApplication** object implicitly unarchived the MainWindow.nib file, and your view controllers have implicitly unarchived their NIB files. How does this work? When a view controller loads its NIB file, it will supply itself to fill the role of File's Owner. The implementation of **loadView** in **UIViewController** looks something like this:

```
- (void)loadView
{
    NSBundle *bundle = [self nibBundle];
    NSString *nibName = [self nibName];
    if (bundle == nil)
        bundle = [NSBundle mainBundle];
    if (nibName == nil)
        nibName = NSStringFromClass([self class]);

    [bundle loadNibNamed:nibName owner:self options:nil];
}
```

So, this object (which exists before the NIB file is read in) gets wired to the newly created objects.

Setting up ItemDetailViewController

Back in ItemDetailViewController.xib, double-click the View object in the doc window. This view will be the view of **ItemDetailViewController** when it is loaded from this XIB file. (Don't believe me? Check the connections for the File's Owner.) Drag four **UILabel**s and three **UITextField**s from the Library window onto the view so that it matches Figure 12.11.

Figure 12.11   ItemDetailViewController's configured view

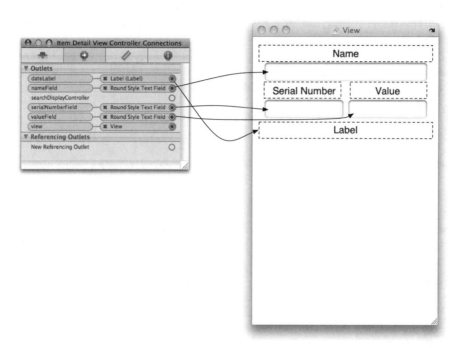

Make connections from the File's Owner to each of these objects, as shown in Figure 12.11.

For each **UITextField** instance, uncheck the Clear When Editing Begins checkbox on the Inspector window (Figure 12.12). Save this XIB file and quit Interface Builder.

Figure 12.12   UITextField attributes

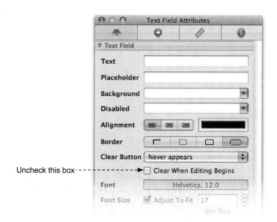

While you are here, fancy the application up a bit. Right now, the view for
ItemDetailViewController has a plain white background. Let's give it the same background
as the **UITableView**. When should you do this? After a **UIViewController** loads its view, it is
immediately sent the message **viewDidLoad**. Whether that view is loaded from a XIB file or using
the method **loadView**, this message gets sent to the view controller. If you need to do any extra
initialization to a **UIViewController** that requires its view to already exist, you must override
viewDidLoad. (Remember, instantiating a view controller doesn't create the view. The view is
created only when it is needed.) Override **viewDidLoad** in ItemDetailViewController.m.

```
- (void)viewDidLoad
{
    [super viewDidLoad];
    [[self view] setBackgroundColor:[UIColor groupTableViewBackgroundColor]];
}
```

When **ItemDetailViewController**'s view gets unloaded, its subviews will still be retained by
ItemDetailViewController. They need to be released and set to nil in **viewDidUnload**. Override
this method in ItemDetailViewController.m.

```
- (void)viewDidUnload
{
    [super viewDidUnload];

    [nameField release];
    nameField = nil;

    [serialNumberField release];
    serialNumberField = nil;

    [valueField release];
    valueField = nil;

    [dateLabel release];
    dateLabel = nil;
}
```

And, finally, you need a **dealloc** method:

```
- (void)dealloc
{
    [nameField release];
    [serialNumberField release];
    [valueField release];
    [dateLabel release];
    [super dealloc];
}
```

Navigating with UINavigationController

Now you have a navigation controller, a navigation bar, and two view controllers. Time to put
all the pieces together. The user should be able to tap one of the rows in **ItemsViewController**'s

table view and have the **ItemDetailViewController**'s view slide onto the screen and display the properties of the selected **Possession** instance.

Of course, you then need to create an instance of **ItemDetailViewController**. Where should this object be created and what object should hold the pointer to it? Think back to previous exercises where you instantiated all of your controllers in the method **application:didFinishLaunchingWithOptions:**. For example, in the tab bar controller chapter, you created both view controllers and immediately added them to tab bar controller's viewControllers array.

However, when using a **UINavigationController**, you cannot simply store all of the possible view controllers in its stack. The viewControllers array of a navigation controller is dynamic — you start with a root view controller, and additional view controllers are added depending on user input. Therefore, some object other than the navigation controller needs to own the instance of **ItemDetailViewController** and be responsible for adding it to the stack. This owner needs two things: it needs to know when to push **ItemDetailViewController** onto the stack, and it needs a pointer to the navigation controller. Why must this object have a pointer to the navigation controller? If it is to dynamically add view controllers to the navigation controller's stack, it must be able to send the navigation controller messages, namely, **pushViewController:animated:**.

ItemsViewController meets both of these needs. Whenever a row is tapped in a table view, the table view's delegate receives the message **tableView:didSelectRowAtIndexPath:**. Therefore, **ItemsViewController** knows when to push the other view controller on the stack. Furthermore, when a view controller belongs to a navigation controller's stack, it can be sent the message **navigationController** to get a pointer to the navigation controller it belongs to. As the root view controller, **ItemsViewController** always belongs to the navigation controller and thus can always access it.

In any application that uses a **UINavigationController**, there is one root view controller. It often owns the next view controller, and the next view controller owns the one after that and so on. Some applications, like the Photos application, may have more than one combination of view controllers that can be on the stack at a given time. In Photos, there are four view controllers:

AlbumListViewController	This view controller displays a list of all of the albums in the user's media library. It is the root view controller.
AlbumViewController	This view controller displays thumbnails for all of the videos and images.
ImageViewController	When an image is selected in the **AlbumViewController**, this view controller is pushed onto the stack, and it will display that image.
VideoViewController	If the user chooses to view a video, this view controller is pushed on the stack to play the movie.

Therefore, **AlbumListViewController** owns **AlbumViewController**. **AlbumViewController** owns both **ImageViewController** and **VideoViewController** (Figure 12.13).

Figure 12.13   Controller hierarchy in Photos

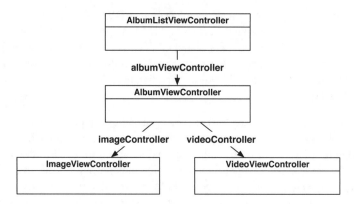

Back in ItemsViewController.h, add an instance variable for an **ItemDetailViewController**.

```
@class ItemDetailViewController;

@interface ItemsViewController : UITableViewController
{
    ItemDetailViewController *detailViewController;
```

Recall that when a row is tapped, its delegate is sent a message containing the index path of the selected row. In ItemsViewController.m, implement this method to lazily allocate the **ItemDetailViewController** and then push it on top of the navigation controller's stack.

```
- (void)tableView:(UITableView *)aTableView
    didSelectRowAtIndexPath:(NSIndexPath *)indexPath
{
    // Do I need to create the instance of ItemDetailViewController?
    if (!detailViewController) {
        detailViewController = [[ItemDetailViewController alloc] init];
    }

    // Push it onto the top of the navigation controller's stack
    [[self navigationController] pushViewController:detailViewController
                                          animated:YES];
}
```

Finally, at the top of ItemsViewController.m, import the header file for **ItemDetailViewController**.

```
#import "ItemsViewController.h"
#import "ItemDetailViewController.h"

@implementation ItemsViewController
```

Build and run the application. Select one of the rows from the **UITableView**. Not only will you be taken to **ItemDetailViewController**'s view, but you will get a free animation *and* a button in the **UINavigationBar** titled Homepwner. Tapping this button will take you back to **ItemsViewController**. All of that comes for free. Thanks, **UINavigationController**!

Of course, the **UITextField**s on the screen are currently empty. How do you pass data between these two **UIViewController**s? You have all of the **Possession**s in **ItemsViewController**, and you want to display a single **Possession** in **ItemDetailViewController**. You need to implement a method in **ItemDetailViewController** that will take a **Possession** instance and fill the contents of its **UITextField**s with it. **ItemsViewController** will select the appropriate possession from its array and pass it through that method to the **ItemDetailViewController**.

In ItemDetailViewController.h, add an instance variable to hold the **Possession** that is being edited and declare a method to set that instance variable. The class declaration should now look like this:

```
#import <UIKit/UIKit.h>

@class Possession;
@interface ItemDetailViewController : UIViewController
{
    IBOutlet UITextField *nameField;
    IBOutlet UITextField *serialNumberField;
    IBOutlet UITextField *valueField;
    IBOutlet UILabel *dateLabel;

    Possession *editingPossession;
}
@property (nonatomic, assign) Possession *editingPossession;
@end
```

Use @synthesize to create accessors for editingPossession in ItemDetailViewController.m.

```
@implementation ItemDetailViewController

@synthesize editingPossession;
```

At the top of ItemDetailViewController.m, make sure to import the header file for the **Possession** class.

```
#import "ItemDetailViewController.h"
#import "Possession.h"

@implementation ItemDetailViewController
```

When the **ItemDetailViewController**'s view appears on the screen, it needs to set the values of its subviews to match the properties of the editingPossession. Override **viewWillAppear:** in ItemDetailViewController.m to transfer the editingPossession's properties to the various **UITextField**s.

```
- (void)viewWillAppear:(BOOL)animated
{
    [super viewWillAppear:animated];

    [nameField setText:[editingPossession possessionName]];
    [serialNumberField setText:[editingPossession serialNumber]];
    [valueField setText:[NSString stringWithFormat:@"%d",
                           [editingPossession valueInDollars]]];

    // Create a NSDateFormatter that will turn a date into a simple date string
    NSDateFormatter *dateFormatter = [[[NSDateFormatter alloc] init]
                                       autorelease];
    [dateFormatter setDateStyle:NSDateFormatterMediumStyle];
    [dateFormatter setTimeStyle:NSDateFormatterNoStyle];

    // Use filtered NSDate object to set dateLabel contents
    [dateLabel setText:
        [dateFormatter stringFromDate:[editingPossession dateCreated]]];

    // Change the navigation item to display name of possession
    [[self navigationItem] setTitle:[editingPossession possessionName]];
}
```

Now you must invoke this method when the **ItemDetailViewController** is being pushed onto the navigation stack. Add the following line of code to this method in ItemsViewController.m.

```
- (void)tableView:(UITableView *)aTableView
    didSelectRowAtIndexPath:(NSIndexPath *)indexPath
{
    // Do I need to create the instance of ItemDetailViewController?
    if (!detailViewController) {
        detailViewController = [[ItemDetailViewController alloc] init];
    }

    // Give detail view controller a pointer to the possession object in row
    [detailViewController setEditingPossession:
                [possessions objectAtIndex:[indexPath row]]];

    [[self navigationController] pushViewController:detailViewController
                                          animated:YES];}
```

Many programmers new to the iPhone SDK struggle with how data is passed between **UIViewController**s. The technique you just implemented, having all of the data in the root view controller and passing subsets of that data to the next **UIViewController**, is a very clean and efficient way of performing this task.

Build and run your application. Select one of the rows of the **UITableView**, and the view that appears on your screen will contain all of the information for the **Possession** that was in that row. While you can edit this data, the **UITableView** won't have changed when you return to it. To fix this problem, you need to implement code to update the properties of the **Possession** being edited.

Appearing and disappearing views

Whenever a **UINavigationController** is about to swap views, it sends out two messages:
viewWillDisappear: and **viewWillAppear:**. The **UIViewController** that is about to be popped
off the stack is sent the message **viewWillDisappear:**. The **UIViewController** that will then be
on top of the stack is sent **viewWillAppear:**.

When **ItemDetailViewController** is popped off the stack, you will set the properties of the
editingPossession to the values in the **UITextField**s. When implementing these methods for
views appearing and disappearing, it is important to call the superclass's implementation — it has
some work to do as well. Implement **viewWillDisappear:** in ItemDetailViewController.m.

```
- (void)viewWillDisappear:(BOOL)animated
{
    [super viewWillDisappear:animated];

    // Clear first responder
    [nameField resignFirstResponder];
    [serialNumberField resignFirstResponder];
    [valueField resignFirstResponder];


    // "Save" changes to editingPossession
    [editingPossession setPossessionName:[nameField text]];
    [editingPossession setSerialNumber:[serialNumberField text]];
    [editingPossession setValueInDollars:[[valueField text] intValue]];
}
```

Now the values of the **Possession** will be updated when the user taps the Homepwner back button
on the **UINavigationBar**. When **ItemsViewController** appears back on the screen, it is sent
the message **viewWillAppear:**. Take this opportunity to reload its **UITableView** so the user can
immediately see the changes. Implement that **viewWillAppear:** in ItemsViewController.m.

```
- (void)viewWillAppear:(BOOL)animated
{
    [super viewWillAppear:animated];
    [[self tableView] reloadData];
}
```

Build and run your application now. You will be able to move back and forth between each of the
UIViewControllers you created and change the data with ease.

Challenge: Number Pad

The keyboard for the **UITextField** that displays a **Possession**'s valueInDollars is a QWERTY
keyboard. It would be better if it was a number pad. Change the Keyboard Type of that
UITextField to the Number Pad. (Hint: You can do this in Interface Builder in the Attributes tab of
the Inspector.)

Camera and UIPopoverController

In this chapter, you're going to use **UIImagePickerController**, a subclass of **UIViewController**, to add photos to the Homepwner application. You will present a **UIImagePickerController** so that the user can take and save a picture of each possession. The image will then be associated with a **Possession** instance, stored in an image cache, and viewable in the possession's detail view. Then, when the insurance company demands proof, the user has a visual record of owning that 70" HDTV.

Figure 13.1 Homepwner with camera addition

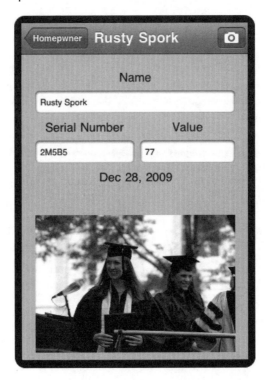

ImageCache: a Singleton

First, you are going to create an image cache to hold all the pictures the user will take. In Chapter 14, you will have the **Possession** objects write out their instance variables to a file, which will then be read in when the application starts. However, images tend to be very large, so you're going to keep them in the image cache and separate from the other possession data. The image cache will fetch the images as they are needed and flush the cache when the device runs low on free memory.

All of that nifty saving/fetching/loading stuff comes later; in this chapter, the image cache is little more than a dictionary of key-value pairs in which the keys are unique strings and the values are images. Open Homepwner.xcodeproj and, in Xcode, create a new subclass of **NSObject** (from the Cocoa Touch Class section) called **ImageCache**. Open ImageCache.h and create its interface:

```
#import <UIKit/UIKit.h>

@interface ImageCache : NSObject
{
    NSMutableDictionary *dictionary;
}
+ (ImageCache *)sharedImageCache;
- (void)setImage:(UIImage *)i forKey:(NSString *)s;
- (UIImage *)imageForKey:(NSString *)s;
- (void)deleteImageForKey:(NSString *)s;

@end
```

NSDictionary

The dictionary is an instance of **NSMutableDictionary**, the mutable subclass of **NSDictionary**. An **NSDictionary** is a collection object similar to an **NSArray**. However, an **NSArray** is an ordered list of pointers to objects that can be accessed by an index. When you have an array, you can ask it for the object at the *n*th index:

```
// Put some object at the end of an array
[someArray addObject:someObject];
// Get that same object out
someObject = [someArray objectAtIndex:[someArray count] - 1];
```

On the other hand, dictionary objects are not ordered within the collection. So instead of accessing entries with an index, you use a *key*. The key is usually an instance of **NSString**.

```
// Add some object to a dictionary for the key, "MyKey"
[someDictionary setObject:someObject forKey:@"MyKey"];
// Get that same object out
someObject = [someDictionary objectForKey:@"MyKey"];
```

Here are some more important facts about **NSDictionary**:

- Whenever you add an object to a dictionary, the dictionary retains it. Whenever you remove an object from a dictionary, the dictionary releases it.

- There can only be one object for each key. Therefore, if you add an object to a dictionary and an object is already stored with that key, the new object is added to the dictionary and the previous one is removed.

- To associate multiple objects with one key, add them to the dictionary as an array.

- An **NSDictionary** is useful when you want to name the entries within a collection. In other development environments, this is called a *hash map* or *hash table* (Figure 13.2).

Figure 13.2   NSDictionary diagram

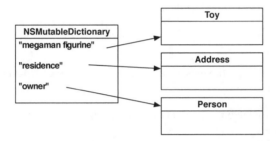

Open `ImageCache.m` and add the following methods to save and retrieve images from a dictionary:

```objc
- (id)init
{
    [super init];
    dictionary = [[NSMutableDictionary alloc] init];
    return self;
}

#pragma mark Accessing the cache

- (void)setImage:(UIImage *)i forKey:(NSString *)s
{
    [dictionary setObject:i forKey:s];
}

- (UIImage *)imageForKey:(NSString *)s
{
    return [dictionary objectForKey:s];
}

- (void)deleteImageForKey:(NSString *)s
{
    [dictionary removeObjectForKey:s];
}
```

Note that there is no **dealloc** method because the cache itself will live for the entire life of the application.

Singletons

Note that there will be exactly one instance of **ImageCache** that will hold all the images and be accessible to all the controllers in the application. We call this a *singleton*. A singleton is a class that can only be instantiated once. (You've already used a singleton: **UIAccelerometer**.) The instance of a singleton class often represents a single resource that must be shared by many objects. Singletons also might contain instance variables that act as global variables without the possibility of a namespace collision.

Add a static variable in ImageCache.m that will hold on to the single instance:

```
#import "ImageCache.h"

static ImageCache *sharedImageCache;

@implementation ImageCache
```

(Some object-oriented languages have *class variables*. Static variables declared in the .m file serve the same purpose for Objective-C programmers.)

Now make it impossible to decrement the retain count of that instance or create another instance. Add the following methods to ImageCache.m:

```
#pragma mark Singleton stuff

+ (ImageCache *)sharedImageCache
{
    if (!sharedImageCache) {
        sharedImageCache = [[ImageCache alloc] init];
    }
    return sharedImageCache;
}

+ (id)allocWithZone:(NSZone *)zone
{
    if (!sharedImageCache) {
        sharedImageCache = [super allocWithZone:zone];
        return sharedImageCache;
    } else {
        return nil;
    }
}
```

```
- (id)copyWithZone:(NSZone *)zone
{
    return self;
}

- (void)release
{
    // No op
}
```

@end

Displaying Images and UIImageView

Once you have an image cache, you'll want to get and display images from it using the **ItemDetailViewController**. An easy way to display an image is to put an instance of **UIImageView** on the window. Open ItemDetailViewController.h and add an outlet for an image view:

```
@interface ItemDetailViewController : UIViewController
{
    IBOutlet UIImageView *imageView;
```

Save ItemDetailViewController.h, or Interface Builder won't recognize the changes.

As a new subview of **ItemDetailViewController**'s view that is instantiated by loading a XIB file, imageView needs to be released and its pointer cleared in **viewDidUnload**. Make the following changes to ItemDetailViewController.m.

```
- (void)viewDidUnload
{
    [super viewDidUnload];

    [nameField release];
    nameField = nil;

    [serialNumberField release];
    serialNumberField = nil;

    [valueField release];
    valueField = nil;

    [dateLabel release];
    dateLabel = nil;

    [imageView release];
    imageView = nil;
}
```

Also release the image view in **dealloc**:

```
- (void)dealloc
{
    [nameField release];
    [serialNumberField release];
    [valueField release];
    [dateLabel release];
    [imageView release];
    [super dealloc];
}
```

Open ItemDetailViewController.xib. Double-click on the View instance in the doc window and drag a **UIImageView** onto it. The interface of **ItemDetailViewController** should look like Figure 13.3.

Figure 13.3   ItemDetailViewController's interface with a UIImageView

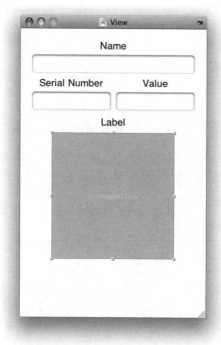

The **UIImageView** will display an image according to its contentMode property. This property determines where to position and how to resize the content of a view within its frame. The default value for contentMode is UIViewContentModeCenter, which centers but does not appropriately resize the content to fit within the bounds of the view. If you keep the default, the large image produced by the camera takes up most of the screen.

To change the contentMode of the image view so that it resizes the image, select the **UIImageView** and open the Inspector window to the first tab, Attributes. Change the pop-up button titled Mode

to Aspect Fit, as shown in Figure 13.4. This will resize the image to fit within the bounds of the
UIImageView.

Finally, make the connection from File's Owner to the **UIImageView**, selecting imageView
as the outlet. (Remember, anything you can do in Interface Builder can be done in code; to
change the contentMode a **UIImageView** programmatically, you would send it the message
setContentMode:.)

Figure 13.4   Image view attributes

Before exiting Interface Builder, find the **UITextField**s that display **Possession** instance
variables and hook up their delegate outlets to the File's Owner object. This is necessary
because you're going to implement a method from the UITextFieldDelegate protocol in
ItemDetailViewController.m later in this chapter. Save the XIB file and quit Interface Builder.

Taking pictures and UIImagePickerController

Now you need a button to initiate the photo-taking process. There is plenty of room on the
UINavigationBar to add a **UIBarButtonItem**. **UIBarButtonItem**s have a few stock icons they
can display including a camera icon. Create a bar button item with a camera icon and add it to
right slot of the **ItemDetailViewController**'s navigationItem. You also need to instantiate the
imageCache instance variable. In ItemDetailViewController.m, override the method **init**:

```
- (id)init
{
    [super initWithNibName:@"ItemDetailViewController" bundle:nil];

    // Create a UIBarButtonItem with a camera icon, will send
    // takePicture: to our ItemDetailViewController when tapped
    UIBarButtonItem *cameraBarButtonItem =
        [[UIBarButtonItem alloc]
```

```
                   initWithBarButtonSystemItem:UIBarButtonSystemItemCamera
                                     target:self
                                     action:@selector(takePicture:)];

    // Place this image on our navigation bar when this viewcontroller
    // is on top of the navigation stack
    [[self navigationItem] setRightBarButtonItem:cameraBarButtonItem];

    // cameraBarButton is retained by the navigation item
    [cameraBarButtonItem release];
    return self;
}
- (id)initWithNibName:(NSString *)nibName bundle:(NSBundle *)bundle
{
    return [self init];
}
```

When this button is tapped, it sends the message **takePicture:** to the instance of
ItemDetailViewController. This method will create an instance of **UIImagePickerController**,
if one has not yet been created, and then present it on the screen.

Figure 13.5 Interface with camera button

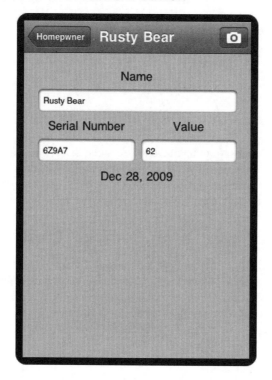

When creating an instance of **UIImagePickerController**, you must set its sourceType property. The sourceType is a constant that tells the image picker where to get the images. There are three possible values:

- UIImagePickerControllerSourceTypeCamera — The image picker will allow the user to take a new picture.

- UIImagePickerControllerSourceTypePhotoLibrary — The user will be prompted to select an album and then a photo from that album.

- UIImagePickerControllerSourceTypeSavedPhotosAlbum — The user picks from the most recently taken photos.

Figure 13.6 shows the results of using each constant.

Figure 13.6   UIImagePickerControllerTypes

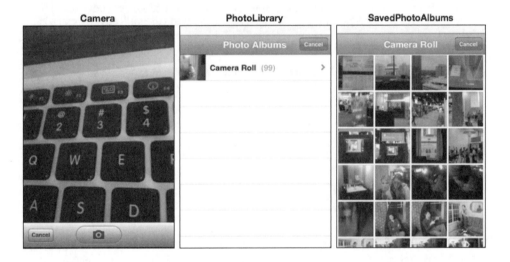

The first source type, UIImagePickerControllerSourceTypeCamera, won't work on a device that doesn't have a camera. So you have to check for device support before using this type by sending the **UIImagePickerController** class method **isSourceTypeAvailable:**. When you send this message to the **UIImagePickerController** class with one of the image picking constants, you are returned a boolean value for whether the device supports that source type.

In addition to a source type, the **UIImagePickerController** also needs a delegate to handle requests from its view. When the user taps the Use button on the **UIImagePickerController**'s interface, the delegate is sent the message **imagePickerController:didFinishPickingMediaWithInfo:**. (The delegate receives another message — **imagePickerControllerDidCancel:** — if the process was cancelled.)

Once the **UIImagePickerController** has a source type and a delegate, it's time to put its view on the screen. Unlike other **UIViewController** subclasses you've used before, **UIImagePickerController**s are presented *modally*. When a view controller is *modal*, it takes over the entire screen until it has finished its work. (On the desktop, modal windows are windows that cannot be dismissed until a specific task is completed.) To present a view modally, **presentModalViewController:animated:** is sent to the **UIViewController** whose view is on the screen. The view controller to be presented is passed to it, and its view slides up from the bottom of the screen.

Implement the method **takePicture:** in ItemDetailViewController.m to create, configure, and present the **UIImagePickerController**.

```
- (void)takePicture:(id)sender
{
    UIImagePickerController *imagePicker =
            [[UIImagePickerController alloc] init];

    // If our device has a camera, we want to take a picture, otherwise, we
    // just pick from photo library
    if ([UIImagePickerController
            isSourceTypeAvailable:UIImagePickerControllerSourceTypeCamera]) {
        [imagePicker setSourceType:UIImagePickerControllerSourceTypeCamera];
    } else {
        [imagePicker setSourceType:UIImagePickerControllerSourceTypePhotoLibrary];
    }
    // image picker needs a delegate so we can respond to its messages
    [imagePicker setDelegate:self];

    // Place image picker on the screen
    [self presentModalViewController:imagePicker animated:YES];

    // The image picker will be retained by ItemDetailViewController
    // until it has been dismissed
    [imagePicker release];
}
```

On the iPhone or iPod Touch, you can build and run the application on your device. (Hang on till the next section if you are interested in displaying the image picker on the iPad). Navigate to the **ItemDetailViewController** and tap the camera button on the **UINavigationBar**. **UIImagePickerController**'s interface will appear on the screen, and you can take a picture (or choose an existing image if you're developing on a device that doesn't have a camera). Tapping the Use Photo button will dismiss the **UIImagePickerController**. But, wait — you don't yet have a reference to the image anywhere in the code! You need to implement the delegate method **imagePickerController:didFinishPickingMediaWithInfo:** in **ItemDetailViewController** to hold on to the selected image.

Figure 13.7   UIImagePickerController preview interface

Before you implement this method, you have to address the two warnings that appeared when you last built the application: "**ItemDetailViewController** does not conform to the UIImagePickerControllerDelegate or UINavigationControllerDelegate protocol." In ItemDetailViewController.h, add the protocols to the class declaration. (Why UINavigationControllerDelegate? **UIImagePickerController** is a subclass of **UINavigationController**.)

```
@interface ItemDetailViewController : UIViewController
    <UINavigationControllerDelegate, UIImagePickerControllerDelegate>
{
```

When the Use Photo button is tapped, the message **imagePickerController:didFinishPickingMediaWithInfo:** will be sent to its delegate. In this method, put the image into the **UIImageView** you created earlier. Implement this method in ItemDetailViewController.m.

```
- (void)imagePickerController:(UIImagePickerController *)picker
didFinishPickingMediaWithInfo:(NSDictionary *)info
{
    // Get picked image from info dictionary
    UIImage *image = [info objectForKey:UIImagePickerControllerOriginalImage];
```

```
// Put that image onto the screen in our image view
[imageView setImage:image];

// Take image picker off the screen -
// you must call this dismiss method
[self dismissModalViewControllerAnimated:YES];
}
```

Build and run the application again. Take a photo and tap the Use Photo button. After the image picker slides off the screen, you will see a scaled version of the image in the **UIImageView**. Note that if you choose another item from the table view, the same image will appear in the detail view controller until you take a new image. You will fix this shortly.

UIPopoverController

On the iPad, you cannot present a **UIImagePickerController** modally. Instead, an image picker must be presented by a **UIPopoverController**. A popover controller shows a view controller's view in an overlay on top of an existing interface. A popover controller is useful for giving the user a directed choice: select something from this popover controller or tap anywhere else to cancel. To use a **UIPopoverController**, you create an instance of it and give it a contentViewController. Then, you present the popover controller on the screen.

When the user taps the camera bar button item, you will present a popover controller that displays the image picker. In ItemDetailViewController.h, add an instance variable for the popover controller and declare that **ItemDetailViewController** conforms to the UIPopoverControllerDelegate protocol.

```
@interface ItemDetailViewController : UIViewController
    <UINavigationControllerDelegate, UIImagePickerControllerDelegate,
    UIPopoverControllerDelegate>
{
    IBOutlet UITextField *nameField;
    IBOutlet UITextField *serialNumberField;
    IBOutlet UITextField *valueField;
    IBOutlet UILabel *dateLabel;
    Possession *editingPossession;
    IBOutlet UIImageView *imageView;

    UIPopoverController *imagePickerPopover;
}
```

In ItemDetailViewController.m, add the following code to **takePicture:**.

```
[imagePicker setDelegate:self];

// Place image picker on the screen
// -- If the application is being run on an iPad as opposed to a iPhone/iPod...
if([[UIDevice currentDevice] userInterfaceIdiom] == UIUserInterfaceIdiomPad) {
    // Get rid of the previous popover controller that we may have been using
    [imagePickerPopover release];
```

```
    // Create a new popover controller that will display the imagePicker
    imagePickerPopover = [[UIPopoverController alloc]
                            initWithContentViewController:imagePicker];

    // Display the popover controller - sender here
    // is the camera bar button item
    [imagePickerPopover presentPopoverFromBarButtonItem:sender
                        permittedArrowDirections:UIPopoverArrowDirectionAny
                        animated:YES];
} else {
    // If on the iPhone/iPod, then present imagePicker modally as before
    [self presentModalViewController:imagePicker animated:YES];
}
// The image picker will be retained until it has been dismissed
[imagePicker release];
```

In order to run this code on an iPad, you will have to set up your project to run natively on the iPad. Select the Homepwner target from underneath the Targets group in the project window (Figure 13.8). Right-click and choose Upgrade Current Target for iPad.... Choose One Universal application from the sheet that appears and hit OK.

Figure 13.8   Universalizing Homepwner

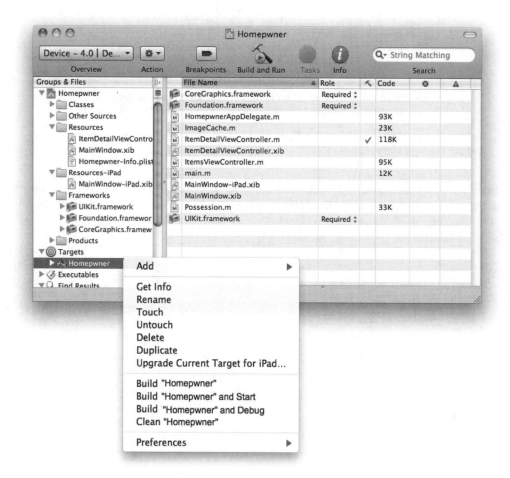

At the time of this writing, there is a little bug with the universalization process. Open `MainWindow-iPad.xib`. (It was created and added to your project in the previous step.) Select the Window object and open the Inspector window to the first tab. Check the box titled Full Screen at Launch and save the file. Build and run the application on an iPad and tap the camera button.

Right now, when you select an image from the popover controller, the popover remains on the screen. At the end of **imagePickerController:didFinishPickingMediaWithInfo:**, dismiss the popover when an image is selected.

```
// Take image picker off the screen - this line does nothing on the iPad
[self dismissModalViewControllerAnimated:YES];

// This line does nothing on the iPhone
[imagePickerPopover dismissPopoverAnimated:YES];
```

Creating and using keys

How can a **Possession** know which photo in the cache is its very own? Because you're using a dictionary as the image cache, a **Possession** only needs to know the key for its image to find the right one in the cache. Add an instance variable to Possession.h to store the key.

```
    NSDate *dateCreated;
    NSString *imageKey;
}
@property (nonatomic, copy) NSString *imageKey;
```

Synthesize this new property in the implementation file.

```
@implementation Possession
@synthesize imageKey;
```

You also need to release this object when a **Possession** is deallocated. Add this code to Possession.m.

```
- (void)dealloc
{
    [imageKey release];
```

The image keys need to be unique in order for your dictionary to work. While there are many ways to hack together a unique string, Cocoa Touch has a mechanism for creating universally unique identifiers (UUIDs), also known as globally unique identifiers (GUIDs). Objects of type **CFUUIDRef** can represent a UUID and are generated using the time, a counter, and a hardware identifier, usually the MAC address of the ethernet card.

However, **CFUUIDRef** is not an Objective-C object; it is a C structure and part of the Core Foundation API. Core Foundation is a C API that is already included in the template projects and contains the building blocks for applications including strings, arrays, and dictionaries. Core Foundation "classes" are prefixed with CF and suffixed with Ref. Other examples include **CFArrayRef** and **CFStringRef**. Many objects in Core Foundation have an Objective-C counterpart, and **NSString** is the Objective-C counterpart of **CFStringRef**. However, **CFUUIDRef** does not have an Objective-C counterpart and knows nothing at all about Objective-C. Thus, when it produces a UUID as a string, that string cannot be an **NSString** — it must be a **CFStringRef**.

Recall that your instance variable for the image key is of type **NSString**. Do you have to change it to **CFStringRef**? Nope. Many Core Foundation objects can simply be *typecast* as their Objective-C counterparts. Here's an example:

```
// Create an instance of a CFStringRef
CFStringRef someString = CFSTR("String");
// Turn it in to an NSString
NSString *coolerString = (NSString *)someString;
```

We call this *toll-free bridging*. (And it works because the structures in memory are equivalent. How smart is that?)

Now, in ItemDetailViewController.m, make changes to
imagePickerController:didFinishPickingMediaWithInfo: to create and use a key for a possession image.

```
- (void)imagePickerController:(UIImagePickerController *)picker
        didFinishPickingMediaWithInfo:(NSDictionary *)info
{
    NSString *oldKey = [editingPossession imageKey];

    // Did the possession already have an image?
    if (oldKey) {

        // Delete the old image
        [[ImageCache sharedImageCache] deleteImageForKey:oldKey];
    }

    UIImage *image = [info objectForKey:UIImagePickerControllerOriginalImage];

    // Create a CFUUID object - it knows how to create unique identifiers
    CFUUIDRef newUniqueID = CFUUIDCreate (kCFAllocatorDefault);

    // Create a string from unique identifier
    CFStringRef newUniqueIDString =
            CFUUIDCreateString (kCFAllocatorDefault, newUniqueID);

    // Use that unique ID to set our possessions imageKey
    [editingPossession setImageKey:(NSString *)newUniqueIDString];

    // We used "Create" in the functions to make objects, we need to release them
    CFRelease(newUniqueIDString);
    CFRelease(newUniqueID);

    // Store image in the ImageCache with this key
    [[ImageCache sharedImageCache] setImage:image
                                    forKey:[editingPossession imageKey]];

    // Put that image on to the screen in our image view
    [imageView setImage:image];
```

```
    // Take image picker off the screen
    [self dismissModalViewControllerAnimated:YES];
}
```

In this method, we call the C functions **CFUUIDCreate** and **CFUUIDCreateString**. When a C
function name contains the word Create, you are responsible for releasing its memory just as
if you had sent the message **alloc** to a class. To release a Core Foundation object, you call the
function **CFRelease** with the object as a parameter.

Figure 13.9   Cache

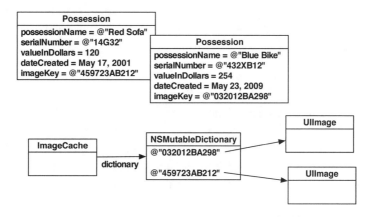

Now, when **ItemDetailViewController**'s view appears on the screen, it should grab an
image from the imageCache using the imageKey of the **Possession** to be displayed. Then, it
should place the image in the **UIImageView**. Add the following code to **viewWillAppear:** in
ItemDetailViewController.m.

```
- (void)viewWillAppear:(BOOL)animated
{
    [super viewWillAppear:animated];

    [nameField setText:[editingPossession possessionName]];
    [serialNumberField setText:[editingPossession serialNumber]];
    [valueField setText:[NSString stringWithFormat:@"%d",
                                   [editingPossession valueInDollars]]];

    NSDateFormatter *dateFormatter = [[NSDateFormatter alloc] init];
    [dateFormatter setDateStyle:NSDateFormatterMediumStyle];
    [dateFormatter setTimeStyle:NSDateFormatterNoStyle];

    [dateLabel setText:
            [dateFormatter stringFromDate:[editingPossession dateCreated]]];
    [dateFormatter release];

    [[self navigationItem] setTitle:[editingPossession possessionName]];
```

```
    NSString *imageKey = [editingPossession imageKey];

    if (imageKey) {
        // Get image for image key from image cache
        UIImage *imageToDisplay =
                [[ImageCache sharedImageCache] imageForKey:imageKey];

        // Use that image to put on the screen in imageView
        [imageView setImage:imageToDisplay];
    } else {
        // Clear the imageView
        [imageView setImage:nil];
    }
}
```

Notice that if no image exists in the cache for that key (or there is no key for that possession), the pointer to the image will be nil and that **UIImageView** just won't display an image.

Make sure to import the header file that contains the **ImageCache** class declaration at the top of ItemDetailViewController.m.

```
#import "ImageCache.h"
@implementation ItemDetailViewController
```

Build and run the application. Select the first row of the **UITableView** and tap the camera button. After taking a picture, return to the list of possessions, tap a different row, and take another picture. Now verify that the appropriate image is displayed for each possession.

Dismissing the keyboard

When the keyboard appears on the screen in the possession detail view, it obscures **ItemDetailViewController**'s imageView. Because this is annoying when you're trying to see an image, the user may want to get rid of the keyboard. You're going to allow the user to dismiss the keyboard by implementing the delegate method **textFieldShouldReturn:** in ItemDetailViewController.m. (This is why you hooked up the delegate outlets earlier in the chapter.)

```
- (BOOL)textFieldShouldReturn:(UITextField *)textField
{
    [textField resignFirstResponder];
    return YES;
}
```

However, it would also be stylish to dismiss the keyboard automatically when the user taps the camera button. In order to dismiss the keyboard, you must send the message **resignFirstResponder** to the first responder. Unfortunately, when the camera button is tapped, you don't know which **UITextField** in the detail view is currently the first responder. While you could send **resignFirstResponder** to every **UITextField**, it's easier to let **UIView** do it. **UIView** implements an **endEditing:** method that will send **resignFirstResponder** to all of its subviews. In ItemDetailViewController.m, send this message to **ItemDetailViewController**'s view when the camera button is tapped.

```
- (void)takePicture:(id)sender
{
    [[self view] endEditing:YES];

    UIImagePickerController *imagePicker = [[UIImagePickerController alloc] init];

    if ([UIImagePickerController
            isSourceTypeAvailable:UIImagePickerControllerSourceTypeCamera]) {
        [imagePicker setSourceType:UIImagePickerControllerSourceTypeCamera];
    } else {
        [imagePicker
                setSourceType:UIImagePickerControllerSourceTypePhotoLibrary];
    }
    [imagePicker setDelegate:self];

    [self presentModalViewController:imagePicker animated:YES];

    [imagePicker release];
}
```

You've done a lot in this chapter with Homepwner: accessed the camera, created an image cache, stored images in the cache, and tied them to possessions with unique identifiers. In the next chapter, you'll learn more about the nuts and bolts of saving and loading data in an iPhone application and add that ability to Homepwner.

Challenge: Removing an Image

Add a button that clears the image for a possession.

For the More Curious: Recording Video

Once you understand how to use **UIImagePickerController** to take pictures, making the transition to recording video is trivial. Recall that an image picker controller has a sourceType property that determines whether an image comes from the camera, photo library, or saved photos album. Image picker controllers also have a mediaTypes property, an array of strings that contains identifiers for what types of media can be selected from the three source types.

There are two types of media a **UIImagePickerController** can select: still images and video. By default, the mediaTypes array only contains the constant string kUTTypeImage. Thus, if you do not change the mediaTypes property of an image picker controller, the camera will only allow the user to take still photos, and the photo library and saved photos album will only display images.

Adding the ability to record video or choose a video from the disk is as simple as adding the constant string kUTTypeMovie to the mediaTypes array. However, not all devices support video through the **UIImagePickerController**. Just like the class method **isSourceTypeAvailable:** allows you to determine if the device has a camera, the **availableMediaTypesForSourceType:** method is for checking if that camera can capture video. To set up an image picker controller that can record video or take still images, you would write the following code:

```
UIImagePickerController *ipc = [[UIImagePickerController alloc] init];
NSArray *availableTypes = [UIImagePickerController
    availableMediaTypesForSourceType:UIImagePickerControllerSourceTypeCamera];
[ipc setMediaTypes:availableTypes];
[ipc setSourceType:UIImagePickerControllerSourceTypeCamera];
[ipc setDelegate:self];
```

Now when this image picker controller interface is presented to the user, there will be a switch that allows them to choose between the still image camera or the video recorder. If the user chooses to record a video, you need to handle that in the **UIImagePickerController** delegate method **imagePickerController:didFinishPickingMediaWithInfo:**. When dealing with images, the info dictionary that is passed as an argument to this method contains the full image as a **UIImage** object.

However, there is no "UIVideo" class (loading an entire video into memory at once would be tough to do with the iPhone's memory constraints). Therefore, recorded video is written to disk in a temporary directory. When the user finalizes the video recording, **imagePickerController:didFinishPickingMediaWithInfo:** is sent to the image picker controller's delegate, and the path of the video on the disk will be in the info dictionary. You can get the path in the delegate method like so:

```
- (void)imagePickerController:(UIImagePickerController *)picker
didFinishPickingMediaWithInfo:(NSDictionary *)info
{
    NSURL *mediaURL = [info objectForKey:UIImagePickerControllerMediaURL];
}
```

While we will talk about the filesystem in the next chapter in depth, what you should know now is that the temporary directory is not a safe place to store the video. It needs to be moved to another location.

```
- (void)imagePickerController:(UIImagePickerController *)picker
didFinishPickingMediaWithInfo:(NSDictionary *)info
{
    NSURL *mediaURL = [info objectForKey:UIImagePickerControllerMediaURL];
    if (mediaURL) {

        // Make sure this device supports videos in its photo album
        if (UIVideoAtPathIsCompatibleWithSavedPhotosAlbum([mediaURL path])) {

            // Save the video to the photos album
            UISaveVideoAtPathToSavedPhotosAlbum([mediaURL path], nil, nil, nil);

            // Remove the video from the temporary directory it was saved at
            [[NSFileManager defaultManager] removeItemAtPath:[mediaURL path]
                                                       error:nil];
        }
    }
}
```

That is really all there is to it. There is just one situation that requires some additional information: suppose you want to restrict the user to choosing *only videos*. Restricting the user to images only is simple (leave mediaTypes as the default). Allowing the user to choose between images and videos is just as simple (pass the return value from **availableMediaTypesForSourceType:**). However, to allow video only, you have to jump through a few hoops. First, you must make sure the device supports video and then set the mediaTypes property to an array containing the identifier for video only.

```
NSArray *availableTypes = [UIImagePickerController
    availableMediaTypesForSourceType:UIImagePickerControllerSourceTypeCamera];

if([availableTypes containsObject:(NSString *)kUTTypeMovie])
    [ipc setMediaTypes:[NSArray arrayWithObject:(NSString *)kUTTypeMovie]];
```

If you build this code it will fail, and Xcode will complain about not knowing what kUTTypeMovie is. Oddly enough, both kUTTypeMovie and kUTTypeImage are declared and defined in another framework — MobileCoreServices. You will have to explicitly add this framework and import its header file into your project to use these two constants.

You might also wonder why kUTTypeMovie is cast to an **NSString**. This constant is declared as:

```
const CFStringRef kUTTypeVideo;
```

A **CFStringRef** is the standard string type in Core Foundation. Core Foundation is another API that is a bit lower-level than Cocoa Touch. Core Foundation technically doesn't know anything about Objective-C — it is a C API. Some bits of the iPhone SDK, like this constant, use Core Foundation and C instead of Cocoa Touch and Objective-C.

The string pointed to by kUTTypeMovie is of type **CFStringRef**. Two methods in this code snippet (**containsObject:** and **arrayWithObject:**) want Objective-C objects as arguments — not a Core Foundation C object. To fix this problem, some Core Foundation objects are *toll-free bridged* with Cocoa Touch objects. A toll-free bridged object can be cast back and forth between its Core Foundation and Cocoa Touch counterpart. Underneath the hood, the objects are essentially the same and by casting them, the compiler won't complain that an object is the wrong type. **CFStringRef** and **NSString** are toll-free bridged. Note that casting an object changes nothing about it — only the compiler cares about this detail.

Saving, Loading and Multitasking

On iPhone OS, every application has its own *application sandbox*. An application sandbox is a directory on the filesystem that is barricaded from the rest of the filesystem. Your application must stay in its sandbox, and no other application can access its sandbox.

Application Sandbox

Figure 14.1   Application sandbox

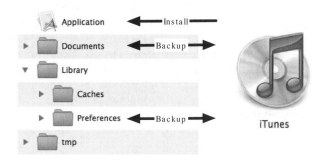

The application sandbox has a number of directories, and each of them has a different use.

Application bundle	This directory contains all the resources and the executable. It is read-only.
Library/Preferences/	This directory is where any preferences are stored and where the Settings application will look for application preferences. Library/Preferences is handled automatically by the class **NSUserDefaults** (which you will learn about in Chapter 25) and is backed up when the device is synchronized with iTunes.
tmp/	This directory is where you write data that you will use temporarily during an application's runtime. You should

remove files from this directory when done with them, but the operating system may purge them while your application is not running. It does not get backed up when the device is synchronized with iTunes. The convenience function for getting the path to the tmp directory in the application sandbox is:

```
NSString *tmpDirectory = NSTemporaryDirectory();
```

Documents/

This directory is where you write data that the application generates during runtime that you want to persist between runs of the application. It is backed up when the device is synchronized with iTunes. If something goes wrong with the device, files in this directory can be restored from iTunes. For example, if you were writing a game, the saved game files would be stored here.

Library/Caches/

This directory is where you write data that the application generates during runtime that you want to persist between runs of the application. However, unlike the Documents directory, it does not get backed up when the device is synchronized with iTunes. A major reason for not backing up cached data is that the data can be very large and extend the time it takes to synchronize your device. Data stored somewhere else — like a web server — can be placed in this directory. If the user ever needs to restore the device, this data can be downloaded from the web server again.

To get the full path for one of these directories in the sandbox, you use the C function **NSSearchPathForDirectoriesInDomains**. This function takes three parameters: the type of directory, the domain mask, and a boolean value that decides if it should expand a tilde (~) if one exists in the path. The last two parameters are always the same on the iPhone: NSUserDomainMask and YES. The first parameter is an **NSSearchPathDirectory** constant. For example, if you wanted to get the Documents directory for an application, you would call the function as follows:

```
NSArray *documentPaths =
    NSSearchPathForDirectoriesInDomains(NSDocumentDirectory,
                                        NSUserDomainMask, YES);
NSString *ourDocumentPath = [documentPaths objectAtIndex:0];
```

The function returns an **NSArray** because this function comes from Mac OS X where there could be multiple directories for the parameters. On the iPhone, however, there is only one directory for the possible constants, and it is safe to grab the first **NSString** from the array.

You can also get the path for the sandbox itself and navigate within it using the function **NSHomeDirectory**.

```
NSString *sandboxPath = NSHomeDirectory();
// Once you have the full sandbox path, you can create a path from it
NSString *documentPath = [sandboxPath
        stringByAppendingPathComponent:@"Documents"];
```

However, you cannot write files or create directories at the root-level of the sandbox (the path returned by the **NSHomeDirectory** function). Any new directories or files must be created within one of the writable directories in the sandbox: Documents, Library, or tmp.

Armed with these functions, you can read and write to the appropriate directories within the application sandbox.

Archiving

There are many ways to write data to the disk on the iPhone, and one of the most important is called *archiving*. Archiving is handled by concrete subclasses of **NSCoder** and the NSCoding protocol and its two required methods: **encodeWithCoder:** and **initWithCoder:**. You can implement these two methods in any class, and instances of that class will know how to save and load themselves from disk. Therefore, when a class conforms to the NSCoding protocol, it can be archived and later reloaded into an application. (In fact, this is exactly what a XIB file is — a bunch of archived objects.)

In this chapter, you will make **Possession** instances in Homepwner conform to the NSCoding protocol. These possessions will then persist between runs of the application. Open Homepwner.xcodeproj.

Implementing the two NSCoding methods is easy. First, declare that **Possession** conforms to NSCoding. In Possession.h, declare the protocol in the interface declaration.

```
@interface Possession : NSObject <NSCoding>
```

When an object needs to be archived, it is sent the message **encodeWithCoder:**. An **NSCoder** instance is passed to the object, and all of the instance variables are encoded into it. If any of those instance variables are objects, those objects are then told to **encodeWithCoder:** (Figure 14.2). So archiving is a recursive process that starts at one object that encodes his friends, and they encode their friends, and so on. Thus, you can only encode objects and supported primitives like int that conform to the NSCoding protocol.

Figure 14.2   Encoding an object

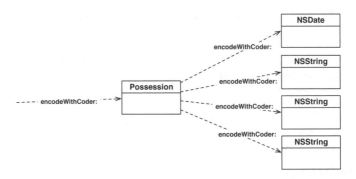

Implement **encodeWithCoder:** in Possession.m.

```
- (void)encodeWithCoder:(NSCoder *)encoder
{
    // For each instance variable, archive it under its variable name
    [encoder encodeObject:possessionName forKey:@"possessionName"];
    [encoder encodeObject:serialNumber forKey:@"serialNumber"];
    [encoder encodeInt:valueInDollars forKey:@"valueInDollars"];
    [encoder encodeObject:dateCreated forKey:@"dateCreated"];
    [encoder encodeObject:imageKey forKey:@"imageKey"];
}
```

So what exactly is this **NSCoder** instance? It is an abstract superclass for different types of data transfers. On the iPhone, **NSCoder** has only one available mode of data transfer: keyed archiving. (Desktop Cocoa has two more options.) There are two concrete subclasses of **NSCoder** for keyed archiving: an **NSKeyedArchiver** knows how transfer data to disk from RAM and an **NSKeyedUnarchiver** can read that data back into RAM from the disk. Keyed archives work a lot like an **NSMutableDictionary**; you add an object to it with a key. When you want that object back, you use the key to retrieve it. Typically, you use the name of the instance variable you are encoding as the key.

To unarchive an instance of **Possession**, you allocate a **Possession** instance and send it the message **initWithCoder:**. This method will use the keys to decode the same objects you encoded with **encodeWithCoder:**. Implement **initWithCoder:** in Possession.m.

```
- (id)initWithCoder:(NSCoder *)decoder
{
    [super init];

    // For each instance variable that is archived, we decode it,
    // and pass it to our setters. (Where it is retained)
    [self setPossessionName:[decoder decodeObjectForKey:@"possessionName"]];
    [self setSerialNumber:[decoder decodeObjectForKey:@"serialNumber"]];
    [self setValueInDollars:[decoder decodeIntForKey:@"valueInDollars"]];
    [self setImageKey:[decoder decodeObjectForKey:@"imageKey"]];
```

```
        // dateCreated is read only, we have no setter. We explicitly
        // retain it and set our instance variable pointer to it
        dateCreated = [[decoder decodeObjectForKey:@"dateCreated"] retain];

        return self;
}
```

Build your application to check for any syntax errors. Your application should run the same as before.

Note that **initWithCoder:** does not replace the other initialization methods. If you wish to create a **Possession** in code, you use the other initialization methods. If you want to create an instance from an archive, you use **initWithCoder:**.

Now, you actually don't create an **NSCoder** instance explicitly; instead one of the **NSCoder** subclasses creates it for you and sends the appropriate messages to your **Possession** instances. In fact, you never invoke **initWithCoder:** or **encodeWithCoder:** on your own; **NSKeyedUnarchiver** and **NSKeyedArchiver** handle these processes.

You've implemented these two methods, and now the **Possession** class conforms to the NSCoding protocol. Not only can **Possession** instances be written to a file by themselves, but other NSCoding-compliant objects that contain **Possession** instances can also be written to a file.

What object in your code contains **Possession** instances? The possessions array in **ItemsViewController**. Its type, **NSMutableArray**, also conforms to NSCoding. Because the array and its contents conform to NSCoding, you can simply archive the entire array and unarchive it the next time the application launches. Brilliant!

To archive this array, you need to have a path on the filesystem to write to. You will create a function that will return the full path of a file in the Documents directory. This function will not be part of an Objective-C class but a stand-alone C function. You are going to want to use this function many different places, so create a separate file for it. From the New File... window, select C and C++ from underneath the Mac OS X group. Choose C File from the template list as shown in Figure 14.3. Name this file FileHelpers.m. (Make sure to change the file suffix to .m!)

Figure 14.3   Creating a C file

Open `FileHelpers.h`, import the header file from UIKit, and declare this new function.

```
#import <UIKit/UIKit.h>

NSString *pathInDocumentDirectory(NSString *fileName);
```

In `FileHelpers.m`, define the following function. To use this function, you pass it a file name, and it will construct the full path for that file in the `Documents` directory.

```
NSString *pathInDocumentDirectory(NSString *fileName)
{
    // Get list of document directories in sandbox
    NSArray *documentDirectories =
            NSSearchPathForDirectoriesInDomains(NSDocumentDirectory,
                                                NSUserDomainMask, YES);

    // Get one and only document directory from that list
    NSString *documentDirectory = [documentDirectories objectAtIndex:0];

    // Append passed in file name to that directory, return it
    return [documentDirectory stringByAppendingPathComponent:fileName];
}
```

When the application launches, you are going to unarchive an array of **Possession** instances from the disk and pass it to **ItemsViewController**. When the user quits using the application, you will archive that array to the disk. The object that receives messages for these two events (launching and quitting) is **HomepwnerAppDelegate**. Change the interface of **HomepwnerAppDelegate** to the following:

```
@interface HomepwnerAppDelegate : NSObject <UIApplicationDelegate>
{
    UIWindow *window;
    ItemsViewController *itemsViewController;
}
- (NSString *)possessionArrayPath;
@property (nonatomic, retain) IBOutlet UIWindow *window;
@end
```

The method **possessionArrayPath** will return the full path to where you will save the possessions array. Implement that method in HomepwnerAppDelegate.m.

```
- (NSString *)possessionArrayPath
{
    return pathInDocumentDirectory(@"Possessions.data");
}
```

Because HomepwnerAppDelegate.m uses **pathInDocumentDirectory**, it must import the header file that this function was declared in. You could import FileHelpers.h at the top of HomepwnerAppDelegate.m, but you are going to use this function in other files, too. You would then have to import this file in every file that used **pathInDocumentDirectory**. Wouldn't it be great if you could tell the compiler, "Import FileHelpers.h into ALL of my files."? Well, you can.

Every project has a *prefix file*, and any declarations or compiler directives in this file are prefixed to all of your source code. Open the prefix file for this project, Homepwner_Prefix.pch (pch stands for *precompiled header*). In this file, import FileHelpers.h.

```
#ifdef __OBJC__
    #import <Foundation/Foundation.h>
    #import <UIKit/UIKit.h>
    #import "FileHelpers.h"
#endif
```

Now that you can construct the appropriate path on the file system and your **Possession** instances can be archived, you need to write code to kick off the processes of saving and loading. Because **HomepwnerAppDelegate** will be receiving messages when the application launches or terminates, it will be responsible for starting these processes. Currently, the array of **Possession** instances is pointed to by an instance variable in **ItemsViewController**. **HomepwnerAppDelegate** needs a way to get a reference to this array. Therefore, you will expose **ItemsViewController**'s possessions array as a property. Declare this property in ItemsViewController.h.

```
}
@property (nonatomic, retain) NSMutableArray *possessions;
@end
```

Synthesize it in `ItemsViewController.m`.

```
@implementation ItemsViewController
@synthesize possessions;
```

Archiving Objects

To write objects that conform to `NSCoding` to disk, you use the class method
archiveRootObject:toFile: of **NSKeyedArchiver**. The *root object*, the first argument to
this method, can be any object that conforms to `NSCoding`. This method creates an instance of
NSKeyedArchiver and then encodes the root object into it.

When an object is encoded into an **NSKeyedArchiver**, it is sent the message **encodeWithCoder:**,
just like the one you implemented for **Possession**. The argument passed to **encodeWithCoder:**
is the instance of **NSKeyedArchiver** that will be responsible for writing all of the archived objects
it contains to disk. When an array is encoded, all of the objects it contains are encoded with it
(Figure 14.4).

Figure 14.4   Archiving an array

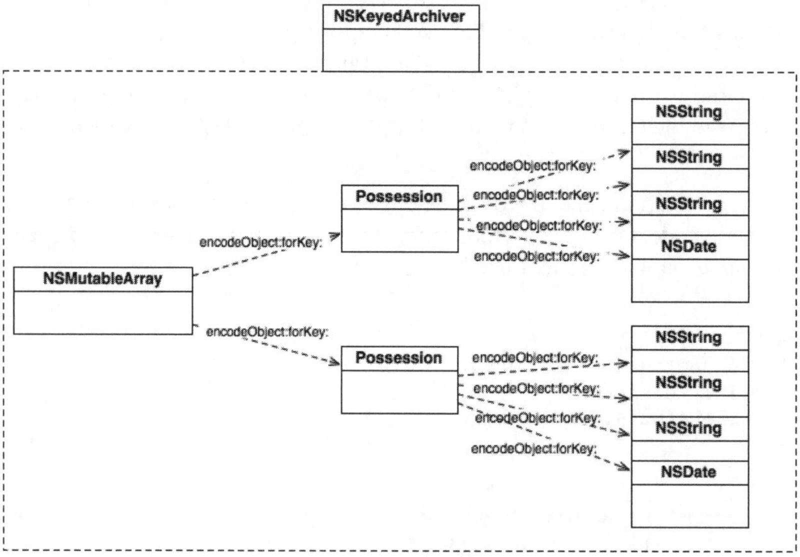

Therefore, passing an array full of **Possession** instances to the method
archiveRootObject:toFile: kicks off a chain reaction of encoding. The root object is
encoded, and thus sent **encodeWithCoder:**. Each object in the array is encoded and also sent
encodeWithCoder:. Each of those objects then encodes their instance variables, triggering the
encodeWithCoder: for each of those objects. This process continues until the entire subgraph

of objects starting at the root object has been encoded. The data contained in the archive is then written to the disk at the path specified by the second argument of `archiveRootObject:toFile:`.

Figure 14.5   Archived object

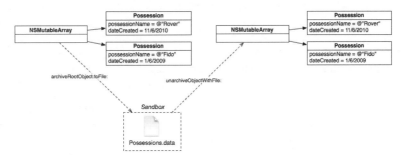

To kick off this chain reaction, you will write a new method named **archivePossessions** in HomepwnerAppDelegate.m. In this method, you will get a pointer to the possessions array from the **ItemsViewController** instance and archive it to **possessionArrayPath** (Figure 14.5).

Declare this method in HomepwnerAppDelegate.h.

```
- (NSString *)possessionArrayPath;
- (void)archivePossessions;
@end
```

Implement this method in HomepwnerAppDelegate.m.

```
- (void)archivePossessions
{
    // Get full path of possession archive
    NSString *possessionPath = [self possessionArrayPath];

    // Get the possession list
    NSMutableArray *possessionArray = [itemsViewController possessions];

    // Archive possession list to file
    [NSKeyedArchiver archiveRootObject:possessionArray
                                toFile:possessionPath];
}
```

Supporting Multitasking

When the user quits the application, you will archive all of the **Possession** instances to disk by invoking the method **archivePossessions**. In previous versions of iOS, when the user pressed the device's Home button, the active application would be terminated. The application delegate would get sent the message **applicationWillTerminate:**, and you would have invoked **archivePossessions** in its implementation. However, in iOS 4.0 and later, applications do not get terminated when the user presses the home button. Therefore, you must save data to the disk at another time.

To know when to save an application's data, you must understand the various states an application will transition to during its lifetime (Figure 14.6). When an application is not running, it is said to be in the *not running state*. In this state, the application does not execute any code nor does it have any memory reserved in RAM.

When the user launches an application, it enters the *active state*. When in the active state, the application is truly running; its interface is on the screen, it is accepting events and your code is handling those events. There is also a *inactive state* and it is similar to the active state, except that the application is not currently receiving events. An application is in the inactive state when it is first being launched (and the run loop hasn't been created yet) or when a phone call or other system-event (like a SMS message) occurs. (An application typically spends very little time in the inactive state.)

Figure 14.6   States of typical application

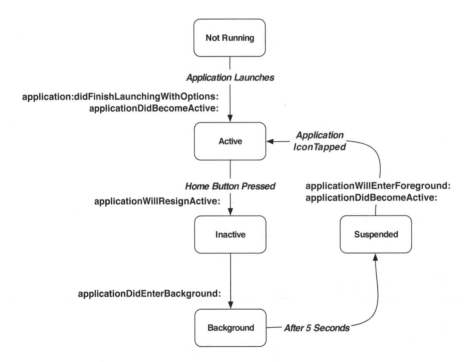

An application also briefly enters the inactive state before it enters the *background state*. When the user presses the Home button while an application is running, it goes from active, to inactive, to the background. While an application is in the background state, it can still execute code, but it is no longer visible. Its icon appears in the dock (accessible by double-clicking the Home button). By default, an application that enters the background state has five seconds before it enters the *suspended state*. (An application can stay in the background state for longer if requested. This will be covered later in the book.)

A suspended application cannot execute code, and any resources it doesn't need while in the suspended state are released. An application in the suspended state is essentially freeze-dried so it can be quickly thawed when the user launches it later. The resources that are released can be reloaded, and they include unreferenced cached images, system-managed caches, and other graphics data. You don't have to worry about these resources; your application will handle the destruction and renewal of them automatically.

Figure 14.7 Background and suspended applications in the dock

An application in the suspended state also appears in the dock and will remain in the dock as long as there is adequate system memory. When the operating system believes memory is getting low, it will immediately terminate suspended applications as needed. A suspended application that gets terminated gets no notification that it is terminated; it is simply removed from memory and the dock. (Note that a multitasking application never sends the message `applicationWillTerminate:` to its delegate. There is one exception to this that will be discussed later in the book.)

With all of these states, when should you save your data? Clearly, the not running and suspended states are out of the question; no code can be executed in these states. You could periodically "autosave" your data while still in the active state, but that will slow down the user experience if you are writing a lot of data at once. (In that case, you will be better served using SQLite or Core Data to do partial writes, and these tools handle writing data to the disk for you.) That leaves two options:

- The inactive state is entered when a phone call or system-event occurs, or when it is on its way to the background state, but your application is still running in the foreground. Saving data when transitioning to this state is a waste of time because the application will either become active again shortly, or it will enter the background. Therefore, the inactive state is not a likely candidate for saving data.

- When transitioning to the background state, the application is being removed from the screen. It is likely that it is on its way to being suspended, at which point, it is subject to being terminated by the operating system. Therefore, transitioning to the background state is the best time to save any application data.

For the majority of application state transitions, the application delegate is sent the appropriate message. (An application is not sent a message when it enters the suspended state, but it is sent one for the rest of the states.) The message sent to the application delegate when the application enters the background state is **applicationDidEnterBackground:**.

Implement this method in HomepwnerAppDelegate.m so that it calls the **archivePossessions** method.

```
- (void)applicationDidEnterBackground:(UIApplication *)application
{
    [self archivePossessions];
}
```

This will properly archive all of the **Possession** instances to disk when the user presses the Home button. However, not all iOS devices support multitasking. For iOS devices that do not support multitasking, when you press the Home button, the active application will terminate and the application delegate is sent the message **applicationWillTerminate:**. Implement this method to perform the same task as its multitasking counterpart in HomepwnerAppDelegate.m.

```
- (void)applicationWillTerminate:(UIApplication *)application
{
    [self archivePossessions];
}
```

Unarchiving Objects

In **application:didFinishLaunchingWithOptions:**, you will unarchive all of the possession instances from disk. To do this, you will use the class method **unarchiveObjectWithFile:** of **NSKeyedUnarchiver**. By passing this method a path, the contents at that path are unarchived by reading the data and sending the message **initWithCoder:** to the root object. Replace the code for **application:didFinishLaunchingWithOptions:** in HomepwnerAppDelegate.m. (Because there are subtle changes to the previous lines of code in this method, replace the whole thing — don't try and edit it!)

```
- (BOOL)application:(UIApplication *)application
    didFinishLaunchingWithOptions:(NSDictionary *)launchOptions
{
    // Get the full path of our possession archive file
    NSString *possessionPath = [self possessionArrayPath];

    // Unarchive it into an array
    NSMutableArray *possessionArray =
            [NSKeyedUnarchiver unarchiveObjectWithFile:possessionPath];

    // If the file did not exist, our possession array will not either
```

```
    // Create one in its absence.
    if (!possessionArray)
        possessionArray = [NSMutableArray array];

    // Create an instance of ItemsViewController
    itemsViewController = [[ItemsViewController alloc] init];

    // Give it the possessionArray
    [itemsViewController setPossessions:possessionArray];

    // Push it onto the navController's stack
    UINavigationController *navController = [[UINavigationController alloc]
            initWithRootViewController:itemsViewController];

    // Place navigation controller's view into window hierarchy
    [window setRootViewController:navController];
    [navController release];

    [window makeKeyAndVisible];
    return YES;
}
```

Notice that the object returned from **unarchiveObjectWithFile:** is of type **NSMutableArray**. That's because the root object that was archived to this path was an **NSMutableArray**. However, an archive's root object does not have to be an array in all cases, it just so happens to be in our application. Remember that the root object can be any object that conforms to NSCoding. When you unarchive data, you should know the type of the root object that was archived to that file to make your code work properly.

Also, notice that you create an empty **NSMutableArray** if nothing was returned from unarchiving the data at possessionPath. This is important because the first time the application launches, there won't be any data at that path, and nil will be returned from **unarchiveObjectWithFile:**. You must create an empty array if this happens so that you can add **Possession**s to it during execution.

Let's review what you have done so far. When the application launches, it creates an **NSMutableArray** (either by unarchiving one from disk or by making a brand new one) and passes it to **ItemsViewController**. **ItemsViewController** uses the array as its possessions instance. When the application exits, you grab that array back from **ItemsViewController** and write it to disk. Simple enough, right?

Now that your data can persist between runs of the application, you will no longer fill the possessions array with random possessions. Remove the following code in the **init** method in ItemsViewController.m.

```
    // Delete this stuff!
    possessions = [[NSMutableArray alloc] init];
    for(int i = 0; i < 10; i++) {
        [possessions addObject:[Possession randomPossession]];
    }
```

Build and run the application. There will be an empty table on the screen. Add some possessions using the Edit button. Play with some of the values of the **Possession**s and exit the application.

(If you are using the simulator to run this application, you must click the Home button on the simulator window for the application to exit properly and archive the possessions. Quitting the simulator or stopping execution in Xcode will not properly exit the application.) Reopen the application, and your possessions will be there. So far, so good. However, because the image for each **Possession** is not archived, you still have to write out the images for the possessions to disk another way.

Application State Transitions

Before you move on to saving the image data, it might help to write some code to get a better understanding of application state transitions. As you know, there is an implicit variable named self that is available in every method body that points to the instance that is currently running that method. There is actually another implicit variable for every method. It is called _cmd and it is the selector for the method currently being run. You can get the **NSString** representation of a selector with the function **NSStringFromSelector**. In HomepwnerAppDelegate.m, implement all of the state transition delegate methods so that they print out the name of the method:

```
- (void)applicationWillResignActive:(UIApplication *)application
{
    NSLog(@"%@", NSStringFromSelector(_cmd));
}
- (void)applicationWillEnterForeground:(UIApplication *)application
{
    NSLog(@"%@", NSStringFromSelector(_cmd));
}
- (void)applicationDidBecomeActive:(UIApplication *)application
{
    NSLog(@"%@", NSStringFromSelector(_cmd));
}
```

Also, add the following **NSLog** statements to the top of
application:didFinishLaunchingWithOptions:, **applicationWillTerminate:** and
applicationDidEnterBackground:.

```
- (BOOL)application:(UIApplication *)application
   didFinishLaunchingWithOptions:(NSDictionary *)launchOptions
{
    NSLog(@"%@", NSStringFromSelector(_cmd));
    ...
}
- (void)applicationDidEnterBackground:(UIApplication *)application
{
    NSLog(@"%@", NSStringFromSelector(_cmd));
    [self archivePossessions];
}
- (void)applicationWillTerminate:(UIApplication *)application
{
    NSLog(@"%@", NSStringFromSelector(_cmd));
    [self archivePossessions];
}
```

Build and run the application. You will see that the application gets sent `application:didFinishLaunchingWithOptions:` and then `applicationDidBecomeActive:`. Click the home button, and the console will report that the application briefly inactivated and then went to the background state. Relaunch the application by tapping its icon on the Home screen or in the dock. The console will report that the application entered the foreground and then became active. Double-click the home button to launch the dock and then tap and hold the Homepwner icon until it begins to jiggle. Tap the red terminate button in the icon's upper left corner and note that no message is sent to your application delegate, it is simply terminated immediately.

Writing to Disk with NSData

The images for **Possession** instances are created by user interaction and are only stored within the application. Therefore, the `Documents` directory is the best choice to store them. Let's extend the image cache to save images as they are added and fetch them as they are needed. You can use the image key generated when the user takes a picture to name the image in the file system.

In this section, you are going to copy the JPEG representation of an image into a buffer in memory. Instead of just malloc'ing a buffer, Objective-C programmers have found it handy to have an object to create, maintain, and destroy these sorts of buffers. Thus, **NSData** instances hold some number of bytes of binary data, and you'll use **NSData** in this exercise.

Open `ImageCache.m` and extend the `setImage:forKey:` method to write a JPEG of the image to the `Documents` directory.

```
- (void)setImage:(UIImage *)i forKey:(NSString *)s
{
    // Put it in the dictionary
    [dictionary setObject:i forKey:s];

    // Create full path for image
    NSString *imagePath = pathInDocumentDirectory(s);

    // Turn image into JPEG data,
    NSData *d = UIImageJPEGRepresentation(i, 0.5);

    // Write it to full path
    [d writeToFile:imagePath atomically:YES];
}
```

When an image is deleted from the cache, make sure to delete it from the filesystem:

```
- (void)deleteImageForKey:(NSString *)s
{
    [dictionary removeObjectForKey:s];
    NSString *path = pathInDocumentDirectory(s);
    [[NSFileManager defaultManager] removeItemAtPath:path
                                               error:nil];
}
```

The function **UIImageJPEGRepresentation** takes two parameters: a **UIImage** and a compression quality. The compression quality is a `float` from 0 to 1, where 1 is the highest quality. The function returns an instance of **NSData**, a wrapper for a buffer of bytes. This **NSData** instance can be written to disk by sending it the message **writeToFile:atomically:**. The bytes held in this **NSData** instance are then written to the path of the first parameter. The second parameter, **atomically,** is a boolean value. If it is YES, the file is written to a temporary place on the disk, and, once the writing operation is complete, that file is renamed to the path of the first parameter, replacing any previously existing file. This prevents data corruption should your application crash during the write procedure.

It is worth noting that the way you are writing the image data to disk is *not* archiving. While **NSData** instances can be archived, using the method **writeToFile:atomically:** is a binary write to disk. Other classes, like **NSString**, have similar methods, and those are not archiving either. When an **NSString** is written to disk by sending it the message **writeToFile:atomically:encoding:error:**, the data written is a text file. These methods are useful when you are saving binary or text data to the disk.

Now when the user takes a picture, the image is stored to disk, and **ImageCache** will need to load that image when it is requested. The class method **imageWithContentsOfFile:** of **UIImage** will read in an image from a file, given a path. In ImageCache.m, replace the method **imageForKey:**.

```
- (UIImage *)imageForKey:(NSString *)s
{
    // If possible, get it from the dictionary
    UIImage *result = [dictionary objectForKey:s];

    if (!result) {
        // Create UIImage object from file
        result = [UIImage imageWithContentsOfFile:pathInDocumentDirectory(s)];

        // If we found an image on the file system, place it into the cache
        if (result)
            [dictionary setObject:result forKey:s];
        else
            NSLog(@"Error: unable to find %@", pathInDocumentDirectory(s));
    }
    return result;
}
```

Build and run the application again. Take a photo of one of the possessions and exit the application. Launch the application again. Selecting that same possession will reveal the photo you took.

Challenge: Archiving Wherewasi

Another application you wrote could benefit from archiving: Wherewasi. Go back to that application and archive the **MapPoint** objects so they can be reused.

For the More Curious: Reading and Writing to Disk

In addition to archiving and **NSData**'s binary read and write methods, there are a few more methods for transferring data to and from the disk. A few of them, like SQLite and Core Data, will be discussed in their own chapters later. The others are worth mentioning here.

You have access to the standard file I/O functions from the C library. These functions look like this:

```
FILE *inFile = fopen("textfile", "rt");
char* buffer = malloc(someSize);
fread(buffer, byteCount, 1, inFile);

FILE *outFile = fopen("binaryfile", "w");
fwrite(buffer, byteCount, 1, outFile);
```

You won't see these functions used much because there are more convenient ways of reading and writing binary and text data. You already implemented code in this chapter that reads and writes binary data when you save and load the images for a **Possession**. For text data, **NSString** has two instance methods **writeToFile:atomically:encoding:error:** and **initWithContentsOfFile:**. They are used as follows:

```
// A local variable to store an error object if one comes back
NSError *err;

NSString *someString = @"Text Data";
BOOL success = [someString writeToFile:@"/some/path/"
                            atomically:YES
                              encoding:NSUTF8StringEncoding
                                 error:&err];
if (!success) {
    NSLog(@"Error writing file: %@", [err localizedDescription]);
}

NSString *x = [[NSString alloc] initWithContentsOfFile:@"/some/path/"
                                              encoding:NSUTF8StringEncoding
                                                 error:&err];
if (!x) {
    NSLog(@"Error reading file: %@", [err localizedDescription]);
}
```

What's that **NSError** object? Some methods might fail for a variety of reasons — for example, writing to disk might fail because the path is invalid or the user doesn't have permission to write to the specified path. **NSError** objects contain the reasons for failure. You can send the message **localizedDescription** to an instance of **NSError** for a human-readable description of the error. This is something you can show to the user or print out to a debug console.

Error objects also have **code** and **domain** properties. The code is an integer representing the error. The domain represents the error domain. For example, not having permission to write to a directory results in error code 513 in error domain NSCocoaErrorDomain. Each domain has its own set of error codes, and those codes within different domains can have the same integer value; therefore, an error is uniquely specified by its code within an error domain. You can check out most of the error codes for the NSCocoaErrorDomain in the file Foundation/FoundationErrors.h.

The syntax for getting back an **NSError** instance is a little strange, though. An error object is only created if an error occurred; otherwise, there is no need for the object. When a method can return an error through one of its arguments, you create a local variable that is a pointer to an **NSError** object. Notice that you don't instantiate the error object — that is the job of the method you are calling. You pass the *address* of the pointer variable you have to the method that might generate an error. If an error occurs in the implementation of that method, an **NSError** instance is created, and your pointer is set to point at that new object. (The error object is autoreleased.) If you don't care about the error object, you can always pass `nil`.

In addition to **NSString**, two other objects have **writeToFile:** and **initWithContentsOfFile:** methods: **NSDictionary** and **NSArray**. In order to write objects of these types to disk in this fashion, they must contain only *property list serializable* objects. The only objects that are *property list serializable* are **NSString**, **NSNumber**, **NSDate**, **NSData**, **NSArray**, and **NSDictionary**. When an **NSArray** or **NSDictionary** is written to disk with these methods, an *XML property list* is created. (XML is a markup language, similar to HTML.) An XML property list is therefore a collection of values that are tagged.

```
<?xml version="1.0" encoding="UTF-8"?>
<!DOCTYPE plist PUBLIC "-//Apple//DTD PLIST 1.0//EN"
        "http://www.apple.com/DTDs/PropertyList-1.0.dtd">
<plist version="1.0">
<array>
    <dict>
        <key>firstName</key>
        <string>Joe</string>
        <key>lastName</key>
        <string>Conway</string>
    </dict>
    <dict>
        <key>firstName</key>
        <string>Aaron</string>
        <key>lastName</key>
        <string>Hillegass</string>
    </dict>
</array>
</plist>
```

XML property lists are a convenient way to store data because they can be read on nearly any system. Many web service applications use property lists as input and output. The code for writing and reading a property list looks like this:

```
NSMutableDictionary *d = [NSMutableDictionary dictionary];
[d setObject:@"A string" forKey:@"String"];
[d writeToFile:@"/some/path" atomically:YES];

NSMutableDictionary *anotherD = [[NSMutableDictionary alloc]
                        initWithContentsOfFile:@"/some/path"];
```

For the More Curious: The Application Bundle

When you build an iPhone application project in Xcode, you create an *application bundle*. The application bundle contains the application executable and any resources you have bundled with your application. Resources are things like NIB files, images, audio files — any files that will be used at runtime. When you add a resource file to a project, Xcode is smart enough to realize that it should be bundled with your application and categorizes it accordingly.

How can you tell which files are being bundled with your application? In the Homepwner project window, open the Targets group by clicking the disclosure button next to it. The Homepwner target will appear. Click the disclosure button next to it. Three gray boxes will appear underneath it, as shown in Figure 14.8.

Figure 14.8   Target Details

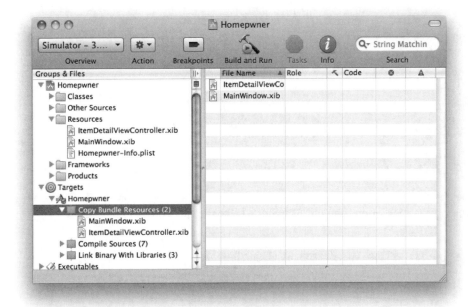

Each item in the Homepwner target group is one of the phases that occurs when you build a project. The Copy Bundle Resources phase is where all of the resources in your project get copied into the application bundle.

You can check out what an application bundle looks like on the filesystem after you install an application on the simulator. Navigate to ~/Library/Application Support/iPhone Simulator/ (version number)/Applications. The directories within this directory are the application sandboxes for applications installed on your computer's iPhone Simulator. Opening one of these directories will show you what you expect in an application sandbox: an application bundle and the Documents, tmp, and Library directories. Right or Command-click the application bundle and choose Show Package Contents from the contextual menu.

Figure 14.9   Viewing an Application Bundle

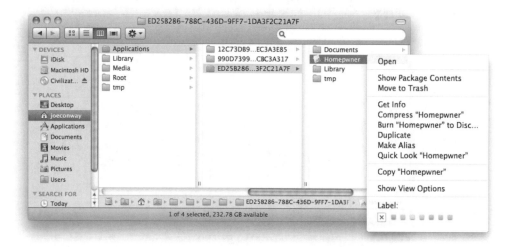

A Finder window will appear showing you the contents of the application bundle. When a user downloads your application from the App Store, these files are copied to their device.

Figure 14.10   The Application Bundle

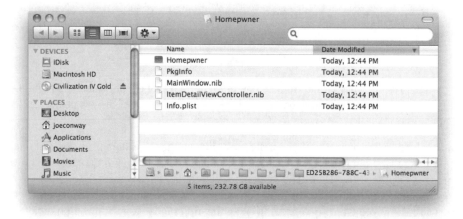

You can load files in the application's bundle at runtime. To get the full path for files in the application bundle, you need to get a pointer to the application bundle and then ask it for the path of a resource.

```
// Get a pointer to the application bundle
NSBundle *applicationBundle = [NSBundle mainBundle];

// Ask for the path to a resource named myImage.png in the bundle
NSString *path = [applicationBundle pathForResource:@"myImage"
                                             ofType:@"png"];
```

If you ask for the path to a file that is not in the application's bundle, this method will return nil. If the file does exist, then the full path is returned, and you can use this path to load the file with the appropriate class.

Also, files within the application bundle are read-only. You cannot modify them nor can you dynamically add files to the application bundle at runtime. Files in the application bundle are typically things like button images, interface sound effects, or the initial state of a database you ship with your application. You will use this method in later chapters to load these types of resources at runtime.

15

Low-Memory Warnings

The iPhone, while extremely powerful, still has its limitations. One of the most important and often overlooked limitations is the amount of memory an application can consume before the device simply gives up. iPhone OS constantly monitors an application's memory usage and alerts the application when it is in danger of running out of memory.

When the operating system detects that it is low on memory, it sends your application a low-memory warning. A low-memory warning will occur when the device is consuming a large percentage of the available RAM. Overuse of graphical memory is typically the reason why an application receives a low-memory warning. Apple suggests that you don't use more than 24 MB of graphics memory. For an image the size of the iPhone screen, the amount of memory used is over half a megabyte. Each **UIView**, image, Core Animation layer, and anything else that can be displayed on the screen consumes some of the allotted 24 MB. (Apple doesn't suggest any maximum for other types of data like **NSString**s.)

It is up to your application to release reloadable resources or unneeded memory back to the heap. If your application does not release enough memory for the operating system to continue running it, iPhone OS will terminate your application. Unfortunately, there is no indication of how much memory should be released or at what percentage of used memory a low-memory warning occurs. Therefore, handling a low-memory warning is not an exact science, and you should simply free up any memory that you can.

Handling Low-Memory Warnings

When an application receives a low-memory warning, it forwards that event to its delegate by sending the message **applicationDidReceiveMemoryWarning:**, as shown in Figure 15.1. You can also register any object for the low-memory warning notification, UIApplicationDidReceiveMemoryWarningNotification.

If Homepwner receives a low-memory warning, the culprit is likely the **ImageCache**. The **ImageCache** is maintaining a dictionary of images and could be huge. It'd be a good idea to have the cache register to receive memory warning notifications and to clear the cache when a notification arrives. In ImageCache.m, extend the **init** method:

```
- (id)init
{
    [super init];
    dictionary = [[NSMutableDictionary alloc] init];
    NSNotificationCenter *nc = [NSNotificationCenter defaultCenter];
    [nc addObserver:self
            selector:@selector(clearCache:)
                name:UIApplicationDidReceiveMemoryWarningNotification
              object:nil];

    return self;
}
```

Now implement **clearCache:** in ImageCache.m:

```
- (void)clearCache:(NSNotification *)note
{
    NSLog(@"flushing %d images out of the cache", [dictionary count]);
    [dictionary removeAllObjects];
}
```

Build and run your application on the device. Take a few pictures and watch the output from the **NSLog** statement in the console. The operating system will see these memory-hogging images being allocated and will issue a low-memory warning to your application. If your application doesn't shut down and the user is not at all interrupted after the memory warning is issued, your memory warning was handled successfully.

Figure 15.1   Low-memory warning handlers

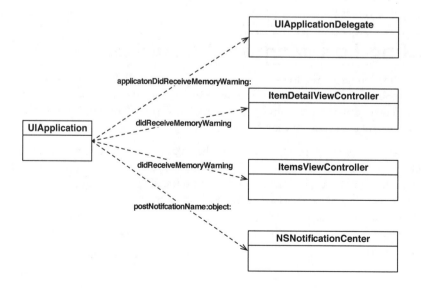

Remember that the notification center does not retain its observers. If the image cache were ever deallocated, it would also need to remove itself from the notification center. The dealloc method would look like this:

```
- (void)dealloc
{
    [dictionary release];
    [[NSNotificationCenter defaultCenter] removeObserver:self];
    [super dealloc];
}
```

View controller memory warnings

In addition to the application delegate and registered observers, every instantiated **UIViewController** is sent the message **didReceiveMemoryWarning** when a low-memory warning occurs. Thus, in Homepwner, the instances of **ItemsViewController** and **ItemDetailViewController** are both sent the message **didReceiveMemoryWarning** when the operating system decides too much memory is being used (Figure 15.1).

The default implementation of this method will release the view of the view controller if it has no superview. (A view controller typically only has a superview when it is on the screen.) The view of a **UIViewController** is a reloadable resource. View controllers know how to reload their views by reloading from the XIB file or invoking their **loadView** method. A view controller's view will be reloaded if it needs to go back on the screen; you don't have to handle this yourself.

Figure 15.2   View controller memory warning cycle

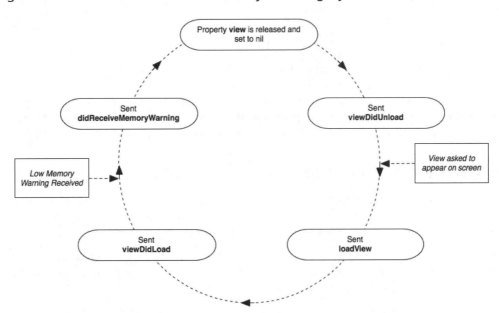

There are three steps to take when handling a low-memory warning for a view controller.

First, if a view controller needs to free up any memory for objects that are not views but can be reloaded later, you will override **didReceiveMemoryWarning**. It is important to always invoke the superclass's implementation of this method because it is responsible for destroying the view of the view controller.

```
// Example implementation:
- (void)didReceiveMemoryWarning
{
    [self cleanupCaches];
    [super didReceiveMemoryWarning];
}
```

Second, if a view controller is initialized with a XIB file and its view has subviews that are IBOutlets connected in that XIB file, the subviews are being retained twice: once by their superview and once by the controller with the outlets. You will need to override **viewDidUnload** to release them and set them to nil. Because the view controller still exists after a memory warning, it is possible that a message might be sent to one of its instance variables after that object was released. By releasing the object and setting the pointer to it to nil, you avoid sending a message to an object that doesn't exist anymore.

```
// Example implementation - myButton declared as: IBOutlet UIButton *myButton;
- (void)viewDidUnload
{
    // the view property has already been released and set to
    // nil by the time this method is invoked.
    [super viewDidUnload];

    [myButton release];
    myButton = nil;
}
```

Last, make sure that you can fully reconstruct a view controller's view hierarchy with the **loadView** and **viewDidLoad** methods. These two messages will be sent to a view controller when it needs to reload its view after a low-memory warning occurs. Some view controllers may dynamically change their interface during runtime. It is important that you keep track of those changes so that you can replicate them if a view controller receives a memory warning.

Simulating Low-Memory Warnings

Most applications will not consume the entirety of the iPhone's memory on their own; however, as a developer, you must always plan for the worst. The simulator allows you to simulate a low-memory warning by selecting Simulate Low-Memory Warning from the Hardware menu.

In general, you should simulate a low-memory warning for every **UIViewController** in an application. Navigate to each view controller in Homepwner, simulate a warning, and then make sure your application doesn't crash and can still run smoothly.

Finally, remember that just releasing some memory during a low-memory warning doesn't guarantee that your application will survive. If you are simply using too much memory, the OS will have no choice but to shut down your application.

Subclassing UITableViewCell

UITableViews display a list of **UITableViewCell**s. For many applications, the basic cell, with its textLabel, detailTextLabel, and imageView, is sufficient. However, when you need a cell with more detail or a different layout, you subclass **UITableViewCell**.

In this chapter, you are going to create a subclass of **UITableViewCell** to display **Possession** instances more eloquently. Each one of these cells will show a **Possession**'s name, its value in dollars, and a thumbnail of its image as shown in Figure 16.1.

Figure 16.1   Homepwner with subclassed UITableViewCells

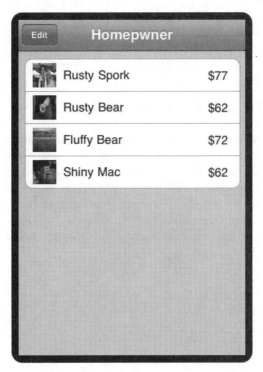

Open Homepwner.xcodeproj. Select the New File... menu item from the File menu and create a new subclass of **UITableViewCell** (Figure 16.2). Name this subclass HomepwnerItemCell.m.

Figure 16.2   Creating a UITableViewCell subclass

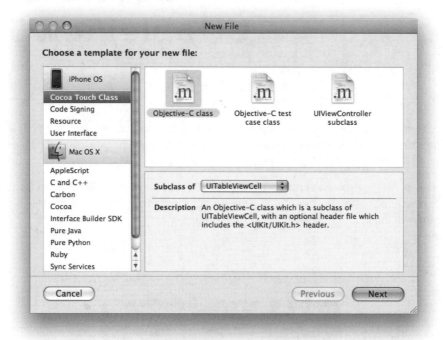

Creating HomepwnerItemCell

A **UITableViewCell** is a **UIView** subclass. When subclassing **UIView** (or any of its subclasses), you typically override its **drawRect:** method to customize the view's appearance. However, subclassing **UITableViewCell** requires a different approach. Each cell has a subview named contentView, which is a container for the various view objects that will make up the layout of a cell subclass (Figure 16.3). For instance, you could create instances of the classes **UITextField**, **UILabel**, and **UIButton** and add them to the contentView. (If you wanted something even more daring, you could create a **UIView** subclass, override its **drawRect:**, and add an instance of it to the contentView.)

Figure 16.3   HomepwnerItemCell hierarchy

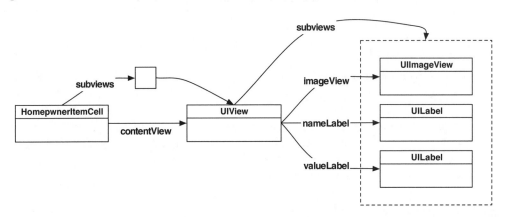

The contentView is important because it knows about the editing controls on either side of the row and automatically adjusts its subviews to allow for the presence of these controls when a cell enters editing mode (Figure 16.4). If you were to add subviews directly to the **UITableViewCell**, these editing controls would appear on top and obscure the cell's content.

Figure 16.4   Table view cell layout in standard and editing mode

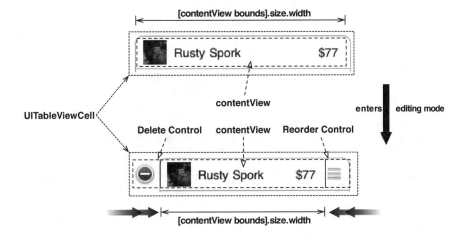

Create subviews

In your cell subclass, you need an instance variable for each subview so that you can set its content as it is displayed in a table view. In HomepwnerItemCell.h, create instance variables for the necessary subviews and declare a method to set their values with a **Possession** instance.

```
@class Possession;
@interface HomepwnerItemCell : UITableViewCell
{
    UILabel *valueLabel;
    UILabel *nameLabel;
    UIImageView *imageView;
}
- (void)setPossession:(Possession *)possession;
@end
```

When an instance of **HomepwnerItemCell** is created, its valueLabel, nameLabel, and
imageView are instantiated. Then, these subviews are added to the cell's contentView.
Override the designated initializer in HomepwnerItemCell.m to create each of the subviews.
HomepwnerItemCell.m should now look like this:

```
#import "HomepwnerItemCell.h"
#import "Possession.h"
@implementation HomepwnerItemCell
- (id)initWithStyle:(UITableViewCellStyle)style
    reuseIdentifier:(NSString *)reuseIdentifier
{
    if (self = [super initWithStyle:style reuseIdentifier:reuseIdentifier])
    {
        // Create a subview - don't need to specify its position/size
        valueLabel = [[UILabel alloc] initWithFrame:CGRectZero];

        // Put it on the content view of the cell
        [[self contentView] addSubview:valueLabel];

        // It is being retained by its superview
        [valueLabel release];

        // Same thing with the name
        nameLabel = [[UILabel alloc] initWithFrame:CGRectZero];
        [[self contentView] addSubview:nameLabel];
        [nameLabel release];

        // Same thing with the image view
        imageView = [[UIImageView alloc] initWithFrame:CGRectZero];
        [[self contentView] addSubview:imageView];

        // Tell the imageview to resize its image to fit inside its frame
        [imageView setContentMode:UIViewContentModeScaleAspectFit];
        [imageView release];
    }
    return self;
}
@end
```

Layout subviews

Note that you don't set the size or position of the cell's subviews here in the initialization method;
you need to know the dimensions of the cell itself before you can set the subviews. Instead,
the subviews should be sized and positioned in the method **layoutSubviews**. This message is

sent to the cell right before it is displayed and, thus, after its size has been determined. (In fact, **layoutSubviews** is an instance method of **UIView** and is sent to any instance of **UIView** that is about to be displayed.)

Implement **layoutSubviews** in HomepwnerItemCell.m. (If you have a hard time picturing the sizes of frame rectangles in your head, draw them out on a piece of paper first.)

```
- (void)layoutSubviews
{
    // We always call this, the table view cell needs to do its own work first
    [super layoutSubviews];

    float inset = 5.0;
    CGRect bounds = [[self contentView] bounds];
    float h = bounds.size.height;
    float w = bounds.size.width;
    float valueWidth = 40.0;

    // Make a rectangle that is inset and roughly square
    // (using the height of the contentView as the width
    //  and height of the image view)
    CGRect innerFrame = CGRectMake(inset, inset, h, h - inset * 2.0);
    [imageView setFrame:innerFrame];

    // Move that rectangle over and resize the width for the nameLabel
    innerFrame.origin.x += innerFrame.size.width + inset;
    innerFrame.size.width = w - (h + valueWidth + inset * 4);
    [nameLabel setFrame:innerFrame];

    // Move that rectangle over again and resize the width for valueLabel
    innerFrame.origin.x += innerFrame.size.width + inset;
    innerFrame.size.width = valueWidth;
    [valueLabel setFrame:innerFrame];
}
```

This method is fairly ugly, but let's look at it more closely. First, you always invoke the superclass's implementation of **layoutSubviews**. Invoking this method allows the **UITableViewCell** to layout its subview, its contentView. Then, you get the bounds of the contentView to find out how much area you have to work with when sizing and positioning all of the subviews. (If you don't invoke the superclass' implementation of **layoutSubviews**, the bounds of the contentView may not be correct.) Finally, you set the frame of each subview relative to the contentView's bounds. This process ensures that instances of **HomepwnerItemCell** will have an appropriate layout regardless of the size of the **UITableViewCell**.

Using the custom cell

Now let's look at the two options for setting the content of the subviews (imageView, nameLabel, and valueLabel). The first option is to create a property for each subview to use when you set the cell content in **tableView:cellForRowAtIndexPath:** (similar to the way you have been accessing the textLabel property of each cell). The second option is to pass the cell an instance of **Possession** and have it fill its own subviews. In this chapter, you will use the second option. Either way is perfectly reasonable; however, in the second option, the cell is made specifically to represent a **Possession** instance, so the code is written in a way that's easier to follow. (The drawback is that **HomepwnerItemCell** will only be able to represent **Possession** instances.) Implement the method **setPossession:** in HomepwnerItemCell.m to extract values from a **Possession** instance and display them in the cell.

```
- (void)setPossession:(Possession *)possession
{
    // Using a Possession instance, we can set the values of the subviews
    [valueLabel setText:
            [NSString stringWithFormat:@"$%d", [possession valueInDollars]]];
    [nameLabel setText:[possession possessionName]];
}
```

You can build the application to make sure there are no compile errors. Running it won't show anything new because you aren't yet returning **HomepwnerItemCell**s from the **UITableView** data source method implemented by **ItemsViewController**. In ItemsViewController.m, import the header file for **HomepwnerItemCell**.

```
#import "HomepwnerItemCell.h"

@implementation ItemsViewController
```

Replace the method **tableView:cellForRowAtIndexPath:** to return instances of your new cell subclass. However, for the Add New Item..., you still need to return a standard cell. Check the incoming **NSIndexPath** before you decide what type of cell to return.

```
- (UITableViewCell *)tableView:(UITableView *)tableView
        cellForRowAtIndexPath:(NSIndexPath *)indexPath
{
    // This will occur when editing, extra row that shows "Add New Item..."
    if ([indexPath row] >= [possessions count]) {

        // Create a basic cell
        UITableViewCell *basicCell = [tableView
                        dequeueReusableCellWithIdentifier:@"UITableViewCell"];
        if (!basicCell)
            basicCell = [[[UITableViewCell alloc]
                            initWithStyle:UITableViewCellStyleDefault
                            reuseIdentifier:@"UITableViewCell"] autorelease];

        // Set its label to say "Add New Item..."
        [[basicCell textLabel] setText:@"Add New Item..."];

        return basicCell;
    }

    // Get instance of a HomepwnerItemCell - either an unused one or a new one
    HomepwnerItemCell *cell = (HomepwnerItemCell *)[tableView
                    dequeueReusableCellWithIdentifier:@"HomepwnerItemCell"];
    if (!cell)
        cell = [[[HomepwnerItemCell alloc]
                        initWithStyle:UITableViewCellStyleDefault
                        reuseIdentifier:@"HomepwnerItemCell"] autorelease];
```

```
    // Instead of setting each label directly, we pass it a possession object
    // it knows how to configure its own subviews
    Possession *p = [possessions objectAtIndex:[indexPath row]];
    [cell setPossession:p];

    return cell;
}
```

When creating a cell for a row that is intended to display Add New Item..., this method creates and returns a standard **UITableViewCell**. When creating a cell to display a **Possession** instance, this method creates and returns your new **HomepwnerItemCell**. Notice that you use different reuse identifiers for each type of cell; if you didn't, you might get a **UITableViewCell** back for a cell intended to display a **Possession**. Then, the **UITableViewCell**'s lack of response to the message **setPossession:** would throw an exception and kill the application. (That's bad.)

Build and run the application. Your new cells will display the name and value of a **Possession**. However, remember that you also want to display an image of the **Possession** within the cell.

Image Manipulation

To display an image within a cell, you could just resize the 1024x1024 image of the possession already in the image cache. However, it would be better to create and use a thumbnail of the image instead. Using the larger image would incur a performance penalty because a larger number of bytes would need to be read, filtered, and resized to fit within the cell whereas a thumbnail requires far fewer bytes. To create a thumbnail of an image, you are going to draw a scaled-down version of the full image to an offscreen context and keep a pointer to that new image inside a **Possession** instance.

However, this application will only create a thumbnail when an image is taken, and, if the user exits the application, the thumbnails will be lost. Therefore, you need a place to store this thumbnail image so that it can be reloaded when the application launches again — like the archive along with the rest of the **Possession** instance variables. (It's okay to store thumbnails in the archive because they are so much smaller than the original images. Those images are still in the image cache where they can easily be flushed if there is a low memory warning.)

Big problem, though: **UIImage** doesn't conform to the NSCoding protocol, so it can't be encoded in an **NSCoder**. The thumbnail can, however, be encoded as *data* (JPEG format) and wrapped in an **NSData** object (which does conform to NSCoding). Open Possession.h. Declare two instance variables: a **UIImage** and an **NSData**. You will also want a method to turn a full-sized image into a thumbnail.

```
@interface Possession : NSObject <NSCoding> {
    NSString *possessionName;
    NSString *serialNumber;
    int valueInDollars;
    NSDate *dateCreated;
    NSString *imageKey;
    UIImage *thumbnail;
    NSData *thumbnailData;
}
@property (readonly) UIImage *thumbnail;
- (void)setThumbnailDataFromImage:(UIImage *)image;
```

In `Possession.m`, create a getter method for `thumbnail` that will create it from the data if necessary:

```
- (UIImage *)thumbnail
{
    // Am I imageless?
    if (!thumbnailData) {
        return nil;
    }

    // Is there no cached thumbnail image?
    if (!thumbnail) {

        // Create the image from the data
        thumbnail = [[UIImage imageWithData:thumbnailData] retain];
    }
    return thumbnail;
}
```

Both objects (the data and the image) will be retained. Therefore, you need to send a matching **release** message to them when a **Possession** instance is deallocated.

```
- (void)dealloc
{
    [thumbnail release];
    [thumbnailData release]
    [possessionName release];
    [serialNumber release];
    [dateCreated release];
    [imageKey release];
    [super dealloc];
}
```

The **setThumbnailDataFromImage:** method will take a full size image, create a smaller representation of it in an offscreen context object, and set the `thumbnail` pointer to the image produced by the offscreen context. The iPhone SDK provides a convenient function suite to create offscreen contexts and produce images from them. To create an offscreen image context, you use the function **UIGraphicsBeginImageContext**. This function accepts a `CGSize` structure that specifies the width and height of the image context.

When this function is called, a new **CGContextRef** is created and becomes the current context. To draw to a **CGContextRef**, you use Core Graphics, just as though you were implementing a **drawRect:** method for a **UIView** subclass. To get a **UIImage** from this context after it has been drawn, you call the function **UIGraphicsGetImageFromCurrentImageContext**. Finally, once you have produced an image from an image context, you must clean up that context with the function **UIGraphicsEndImageContext**.

Implement the following method in `Possession.m` to create a thumbnail using an offscreen context.

```
- (void)setThumbnailDataFromImage:(UIImage *)image
{
    // Release the old thumbnail data
    [thumbnailData release];

    // Release the old thumbnail
    [thumbnail release];

    // Create an empty image of size 70 x 70
    CGRect imageRect = CGRectMake(0, 0, 70, 70);
    UIGraphicsBeginImageContext(imageRect.size);

    // Render the big image onto the image context
    [image drawInRect:imageRect];


    // Make a new one from the image context
    thumbnail = UIGraphicsGetImageFromCurrentImageContext();

    // Retain the new one
    [thumbnail retain];

    // Clean up image context resources
    UIGraphicsEndImageContext();


    // Make a new data object from the image
    thumbnailData = UIImageJPEGRepresentation(thumbnail, 0.5);
    // You may get malloc warnings from the simulator on this line
    // That is a bug in the simulator.

    // Retain it
    [thumbnailData retain];
}
```

Because you create a thumbnail when the camera takes the original image, you need to add the following line of code to **imagePickerController:didFinishPickingMediaWithInfo:** in ItemDetailViewController.m.

```
- (void)imagePickerController:(UIImagePickerController *)picker
didFinishPickingMediaWithInfo:(NSDictionary *)info
{
    NSString *oldKey = [editingPossession imageKey];

    if (oldKey) {

        // Delete the old image
        [[ImageCache sharedImageCache] deleteImageForKey:oldKey];
    }
    UIImage *image = [info objectForKey:UIImagePickerControllerOriginalImage];

    CFUUIDRef newUniqueID = CFUUIDCreate (kCFAllocatorDefault);

    CFStringRef newUniqueIDString =
                CFUUIDCreateString (kCFAllocatorDefault, newUniqueID);

    [editingPossession setImageKey:(NSString *)newUniqueIDString];
```

```
    CFRelease(newUniqueIDString);
    CFRelease(newUniqueID);

    [[ImageCache sharedImageCache] setImage:image
                              forKey:[editingPossession imageKey]];

    [imageView setImage:image];

    [editingPossession setThumbnailDataFromImage:image];

    // Take image picker off the screen
    [self dismissModalViewControllerAnimated:YES];
}
```

Because you use this thumbnail to set the imageView of the cells when they are configured for the table view, add the following line of code to setPossession: in HomepwnerItemCell.m.

```
- (void)setPossession:(Possession *)possession
{
    [valueLabel setText:
            [NSString stringWithFormat:@"$%d", [possession valueInDollars]]];
    [nameLabel setText:[possession possessionName]];
    [imageView setImage:[possession thumbnail]];
}
```

Build and run the application now. Take a picture for a **Possession** instance. That row will display a thumbnail image along with the name and value of the **Possession**.

Don't forget to add the thumbnail data to your archive! Open Possession.m:

```
- (id)initWithCoder:(NSCoder *)decoder
{
    self = [super init];
    [self setPossessionName:[decoder decodeObjectForKey:@"possessionName"]];
    [self setSerialNumber:[decoder decodeObjectForKey:@"serialNumber"]];
    [self setValueInDollars:[decoder decodeIntForKey:@"valueInDollars"]];
    [self setImageKey:[decoder decodeObjectForKey:@"imageKey"]];
    dateCreated = [[decoder decodeObjectForKey:@"dateCreated"] retain];

    thumbnailData = [[decoder decodeObjectForKey:@"thumbnailData"] retain];

    return self;
}

- (void)encodeWithCoder:(NSCoder *)encoder
{
    // For each instance variable, archive it under its variable name
    [encoder encodeObject:possessionName forKey:@"possessionName"];
    [encoder encodeObject:serialNumber forKey:@"serialNumber"];
    [encoder encodeInt:valueInDollars forKey:@"valueInDollars"];
    [encoder encodeObject:dateCreated forKey:@"dateCreated"];
    [encoder encodeObject:imageKey forKey:@"imageKey"];

    [encoder encodeObject:thumbnailData forKey:@"thumbnailData"];
}
```

Build and run the application. Take some photos of possessions and then exit and relaunch the application. The thumbnails will now appear for saved possession objects.

Challenge: Accessory Views

`HomepwnerItemCell` only displays three properties of a `Possession` instance in the content. Allow `HomepwnerItemCell` to have an accessory view. When that accessory view is tapped, it will toggle between two different display modes: one that shows the serial number and date created of a `Possession` and another that shows the name and value in dollars.

Challenge: Make it Pretty

The thumbnail could be much prettier. Make it preserve the aspect ratio of the original image. Round the corners. You could even add a nice glossy gradient to make it look 3-dimensional.

17

Multi-Touch, UIResponder, and Using Instruments

In Chapter 6, you created a **UIScrollView** that dealt with multi-touch events to translate and scale your view. You have also used **UIControl** when you set a target/action pair to be triggered for certain types of events. What if you want to do something else, something special or unique, with touch events?

In this chapter, your are going to create a view that lets the user draw lines by dragging across the view (Figure 17.1). Using multi-touch, the user will be able to draw more than one line at a time. Double-tapping will clear the screen and allow the user to begin again.

Figure 17.1   A drawing program

Touch Events

A **UITouch** object represents one finger touching the screen. Because you can use multiple fingers simultaneously, touches are processed in sets. **NSSet** is a container class like **NSArray**, but it has no order and an object can only appear in a set once.

As a subclass of **UIResponder**, your view can override four methods to handle touch events:

- a finger or fingers touches the screen

  ```
  - (void)touchesBegan:(NSSet *)touches
            withEvent:(UIEvent *)event;
  ```

- a finger or fingers move across the screen (This message is sent repeatedly as a finger moves.)

  ```
  - (void)touchesMoved:(NSSet *)touches
            withEvent:(UIEvent *)event;
  ```

- a finger or fingers is removed from the screen

  ```
  - (void)touchesEnded:(NSSet *)touches
            withEvent:(UIEvent *)event;
  ```

- a system event, like an incoming phone call, interrupts a touch before it ends

  ```
  - (void)touchesCancelled:(NSSet *)touches
              withEvent:(UIEvent *)event;
  ```

When the user touches the screen, a **UITouch** instance is created. The same **UITouch** object is updated and reused for all touch events associated with an individual finger. It holds all of the information about that finger: where it is, its state, when its state last changed, the view it is on, the number of times it has tapped the screen, and where it has been most recently. When that finger is removed from the screen, the **UITouch** is discarded.

After the **UITouch** instance is created, it is sent to the **UIView** on which the touch occurred via the message **touchesBegan:withEvent:**. This method has two arguments: an **NSSet** and a **UIEvent**. The **NSSet** instance contains the touch object. Why send an **NSSet** and not a **UITouch**? An **NSSet** is necessary in case two (or more) fingers touch the screen at the exact same time. (In practice, this is very unlikely; we humans are not as precise as we think we are.) If simultaneous touches occur, multiple **UITouch** instances can be sent in the **NSSet**.

(Apple could have used **NSArray** instead of **NSSet**, but the implementation of **NSSet** makes it faster to use in this context. The good news is you can iterate over an **NSSet** in the same way you do an array using fast enumeration in Objective C 2.0.)

Creating the TouchTracker Application

Now let's get started with your application. In Xcode, create a new Window-based Application and name it TouchTracker. Create a new UIView subclass called **TouchDrawView**.

The **TouchDrawView** is going to need an object that can hold the two end points of a line. Create a new NSObject subclass named **Line**. In Line.h, declare two CGPoint instance variables and the accessors for setting and getting them:

```
#import <Foundation/Foundation.h>

@interface Line : NSObject {
    CGPoint begin;
    CGPoint end;
}
@property (nonatomic) CGPoint begin;
@property (nonatomic) CGPoint end;
@end
```

In Line.m, synthesize the accessors:

```
#import "Line.h"

@implementation Line

@synthesize begin, end;

@end
```

In TouchDrawView.h, declare two collections: an array to hold complete lines and a dictionary to hold lines that are still being drawn.

```
#import <UIKit/UIKit.h>

@interface TouchDrawView : UIView {
    NSMutableDictionary *linesInProcess;
    NSMutableArray *completeLines;
}

@end
```

You might be surprised to see that you are using a dictionary to hold the lines that are in the process of being drawn. What do lines have to do with key-value pairs? In this case, you're using a dictionary to keep track of which **UITouch** created which **Line**. So you'll want to use the **UITouch** as the key and the **Line** as the value. However, only objects that have a **copyWithZone:** method (from the NSCoding protocol) can be used as keys in a dictionary. **UITouch** does not implement this method, so you can't use **UITouch** instances themselves as keys. However, you can wrap a pointer to the **UITouch** in an **NSValue** instance and use the **NSValue** as the key.

Figure 17.2 shows the object diagram for TouchTracker. Take a moment to look it over before continuing on with the creation of your view.

Figure 17.2   Object diagram for TouchTracker

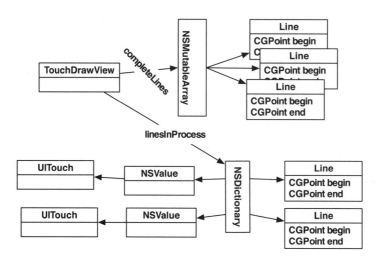

In Chapter 6, you instantiated your custom view programmatically. This time, you will instantiate a custom view in Interface Builder. Open up MainWindow.xib. From the Library, drag an instance of **UIView** onto the window. In the Identity panel of the Inspector, set its class to **TouchDrawView** as shown in Figure 17.3.

Figure 17.3 Identity Inspector

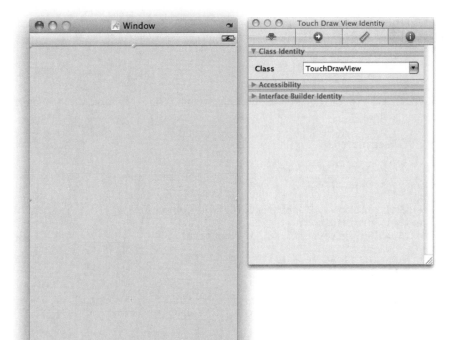

Views created programmatically have their **initWithFrame:** method called; views created in Interface Builder are unarchived using **initWithCoder:**. Thus, for **TouchDrawView**, you will override **initWithCoder:** instead of **initWithFrame:**.

Save MainWindow.xib and return to Xcode. In TouchDrawView.m, take care of the creation and destruction of the two collections:

```
#import "TouchDrawView.h"
#import "Line.h"

@implementation TouchDrawView

- (id)initWithCoder:(NSCoder *)c
{
    [super initWithCoder:c];
    linesInProcess = [[NSMutableDictionary alloc] init];
    // Don't let the autocomplete fool you on the next line,
    // make sure you are instantiating an NSMutableArray
    // and not an NSMutableDictionary!
    completeLines = [[NSMutableArray alloc] init];
    [self setMultipleTouchEnabled:YES];
    return self;
}
```

```
- (void)dealloc
{
    [linesInProcess release];
    [completeLines release];
    [super dealloc];
}
```

Notice that you had to explicitly enable multi-touch events. Without this, only one touch at a time can be active on a view.

Now edit the **drawRect:** method:

```
- (void)drawRect:(CGRect)rect
{
    CGContextRef context = UIGraphicsGetCurrentContext();
    CGContextSetLineWidth(context, 10.0);
    CGContextSetLineCap(context, kCGLineCapRound);

    // Draw complete lines in black
    [[UIColor blackColor] set];
    for (Line *line in completeLines) {
        CGContextMoveToPoint(context, [line begin].x, [line begin].y);
        CGContextAddLineToPoint(context, [line end].x, [line end].y);
        CGContextStrokePath(context);
    }

    // Draw lines in process in red
    [[UIColor redColor] set];
    for (NSValue *v in linesInProcess) {
        Line *line = [linesInProcess objectForKey:v];
        CGContextMoveToPoint(context, [line begin].x, [line begin].y);
        CGContextAddLineToPoint(context, [line end].x, [line end].y);
        CGContextStrokePath(context);
    }
}
```

Finally, create a method that clears the collections and redraws the view:

```
- (void)clearAll
{
    // Clear the containers
    [linesInProcess removeAllObjects];
    [completeLines removeAllObjects];

    // Redraw
    [self setNeedsDisplay];
}
```

Turning Touches Into Lines

When a touch begins, you will create a new **Line** instance and store it in an **NSMutableDictionary**. The key to retrieve the line is the address of the **UITouch** object stored in an **NSValue**.

Override **touchesBegan:withEvent:** in TouchDrawView.m.

```
- (void)touchesBegan:(NSSet *)touches
          withEvent:(UIEvent *)event
{
    for (UITouch *t in touches) {

        // Is this a double tap?
        if ([t tapCount] > 1) {
            [self clearAll];
            return;
        }

        // Use the touch object (packed in an NSValue) as the key
        NSValue *key = [NSValue valueWithPointer:t];

        // Create a line for the value
        CGPoint loc = [t locationInView:self];
        Line *newLine = [[Line alloc] init];
        [newLine setBegin:loc];
        [newLine setEnd:loc];

        // Put pair in dictionary
        [linesInProcess setObject:newLine forKey:key];

        // There is a memory leak in this method
        // You will find it using Instruments later in the chapter
    }
}
```

In **touchesMoved:withEvent:**, you will update the end point of the line associated with the moving touch. Override this method in TouchDrawView.m.

```
- (void)touchesMoved:(NSSet *)touches
          withEvent:(UIEvent *)event
{
    // Update linesInProcess with moved touches
    for (UITouch *t in touches) {
        NSValue *key = [NSValue valueWithPointer:t];

        // Find the line for this touch
        Line *line = [linesInProcess objectForKey:key];

        // Update the line
        CGPoint loc = [t locationInView:self];
        [line setEnd:loc];
    }
    // Redraw
    [self setNeedsDisplay];
}
```

When a touch ends, you need to finalize the line. However, a touch can end for two reasons: the user lifts the finger off the screen or the operating system interrupts your application. A phone call, for example, will interrupt your application. In many applications, you'll want to handle these two events differently. However, for TouchTracker, you're going to write one method to handle both cases. Implement these methods in TouchDrawView.m.

```
- (void)endTouches:(NSSet *)touches
{
    // Remove ending touches from dictionary
    for (UITouch *t in touches) {
        NSValue *key = [NSValue valueWithPointer:t];
        Line *line = [linesInProcess objectForKey:key];

        // If this is a double tap, 'line' will be nil
        if (line) {
            [completeLines addObject:line];
            [linesInProcess removeObjectForKey:key];
        }
    }
    // Redraw
    [self setNeedsDisplay];
}

- (void)touchesEnded:(NSSet *)touches
        withEvent:(UIEvent *)event
{
    [self endTouches:touches];
}

- (void)touchesCancelled:(NSSet *)touches
            withEvent:(UIEvent *)event
{
    [self endTouches:touches];
}
```

Build and run the application. Then draw lines with one or more fingers.

The Responder Chain

Every **UIResponder** can receive touch events. **UIView** is one example, but there are many other **UIResponder** subclasses including **UIViewController**, **UIApplication**, and **UIWindow**. You are probably thinking, "But you can't touch a **UIViewController**. It's not an on-screen object!" And you are right — you can't send a touch event *directly* to a **UIViewController**. (And you get two bonus points for keeping the view controller and its view separate in your brain.)

In Chapter 4, you learned a little about the *responder chain*. When a responder doesn't handle an event, it passes it to its nextResponder. How does a **UIResponder** *not* handle an event? For starters, the default implementation of methods like **touchesBegan:withEvent:** simply passes the message to the next responder. So if a method is not overridden, you ensure its next responder will attempt to handle the touch event.

You can explicitly send a message to a next responder, too. Let's say there is a view that wants to track touches, but if a double tap occurs, its next responder should handle it. The code would look like this:

```
- (void)touchesBegan:(NSSet *)touches withEvent:(UIEvent *)event
{
    UITouch *touch = [touches anyObject];
    if ([touch tapCount] == 2)
        [[self nextResponder] touchesBegan:touches withEvent:event];

    ... Go on to do code that isn't a double tap
}
```

Figure 17.4 shows the objects that make up the responder chain. An event starts at the view that was touched. The nextResponder of a view is its **UIViewController**. If that view has a view controller that owns it, then the controller is next in line. After that, the superview of the view is given a chance to handle the event. If the touch runs out of views and view controllers, it goes to the window. If the window doesn't handle it, the singleton instance of **UIApplication** does. (Note that the window and application objects won't do anything with an event unless you subclass them.) If the application doesn't handle the event, then it is discarded.

Figure 17.4 Responder chain

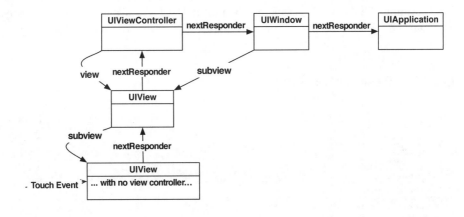

Instruments

After Xcode and Interface Builder, the most important tool that Apple gives developers is Instruments. When you run your applications in Instruments, it shows you the objects that are allocated, where the CPU is spending all its time, file I/O, network I/O, etc. Instruments has plug-ins that enable you to inspect these issues in more detail. Each plug-in is known as an Instrument. Together, they can help you track down inefficiencies in your application and optimize your code.

The ObjectAlloc Instrument

There is a memory leak in TouchTracker. When the user double-taps, the screen clears. At this point, all instances of **Line** should be deallocated, but they aren't. You're now going to use the ObjectAlloc instrument to confirm this.

While you can profile the application running on the simulator, you'll get more accurate data on the device. So, build the application for the device, and under the Run menu, choose Run with Performance Tool -> Object Allocations.

Instruments will launch, and, as you interact with your application, it will keep track of every object created and destroyed. Draw a while, double-tap a few times to clear the lines, switch back to Instruments, and click the Stop button to stop recording.

In the Instruments window, find the row for instances of **Line** by scrolling through the table or using the search bar underneath the table. Notice two counts for the instances, Overall and Living.

Overall is a count of all the instances of **Line** that have been created during this run of the application. It is the number of times **alloc** has been sent to the class **Line**. Living is a count of all the instances of **Line** that have been created minus those that have been deallocated (the number of **Line** objects that exist currently). Because the overall and living **Line** counts are the same in this sampling, you know that no instances of **Line** were deallocated when you double-tapped to clear lines from the screen. These **Line**s were leaked.

At the top of Instruments, there is a graph next to the ObjectAlloc instrument. Right now, it is graphing all memory allocations. You can modify that list by checking and unchecking the boxes in the Graph column of the table. Uncheck the box next to "* All Allocations *" and check Line as shown in Figure 17.5. (If you don't see "* All Allocations *", clear the search bar.)

Figure 17.5   Basic ObjectAlloc

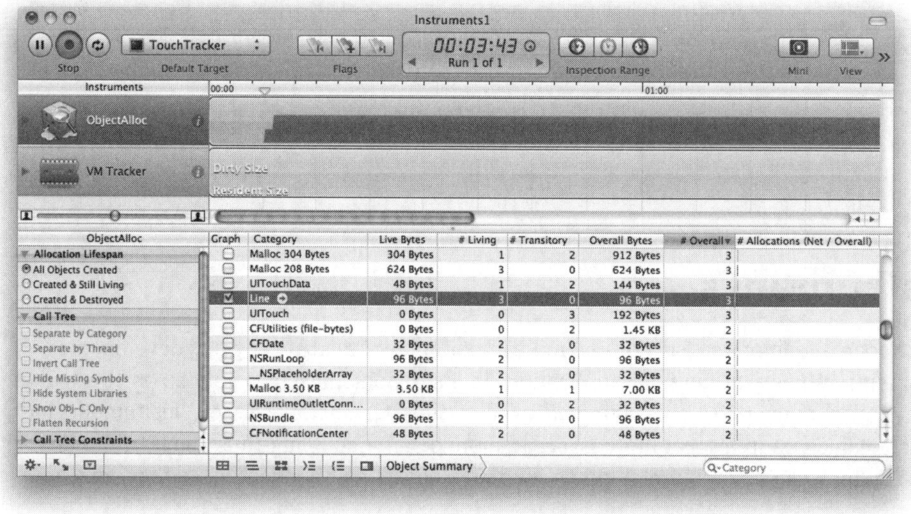

If your **Line** objects were being properly deallocated, the graph would drop to zero when you double-tapped to clear the drawing. Want to know more about those pesky **Line** instances that won't die? If you select the row for **Line**, a small arrow will appear in the Category column next to the word Line. Click that arrow to see the detailed view (Figure 17.6). Select a particular instance to see the call stack as it appeared when the instance was allocated. If you don't see the stack, choose View -> Extended Detail from the menu. Also, if the stack does not show the names of the methods being called, make sure your application is being built with the most recent version of the SDK. (In Xcode, choose the most recent version from the Project menu's Set Active SDK menu item and rebuild.)

Figure 17.6   Detail of one instance's allocation

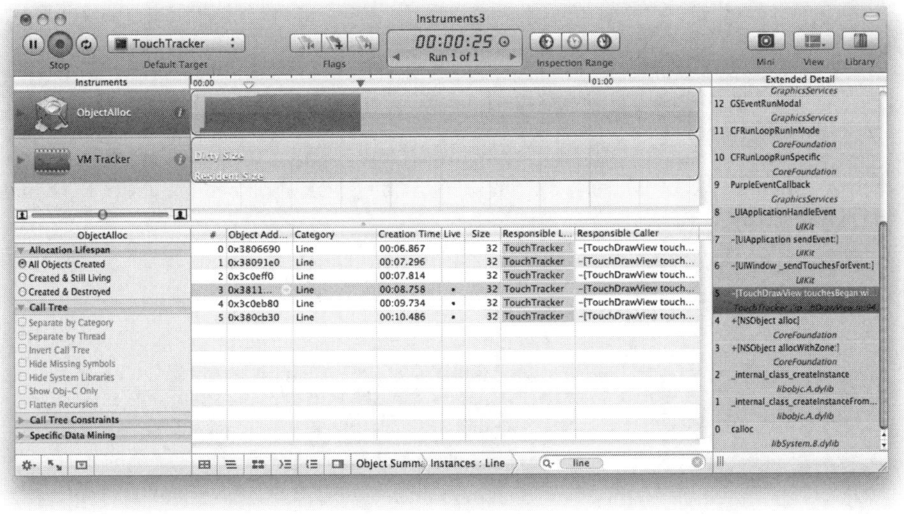

You can also set Instruments to show you every **retain** and **release**. While Instruments is not recording, open the Inspector for the ObjectAlloc instrument by clicking on the info button next to it. Check Record Reference Counts, as shown in Figure 17.7. Run the application again by clicking the Record button.

Figure 17.7   Record reference counts

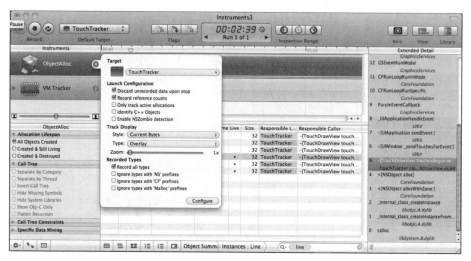

Now when you browse the instances, you can see how the stack appeared for every **retain** and **release** (Figure 17.8).

Figure 17.8   Inspecting a release

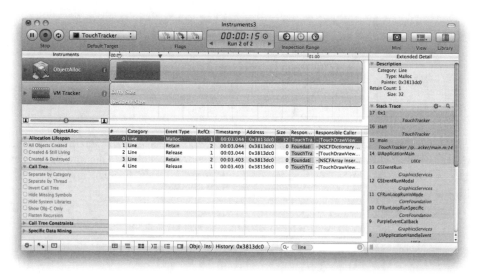

OK, time to fix the memory leak. In **touchesBegan:withEvent:**, release newLine after you add it to the dictionary:

```
- (void)touchesBegan:(NSSet *)touches
           withEvent:(UIEvent *)event
{
    for (UITouch *t in touches) {
        if ([t tapCount] > 1) {
            [self clearAll];
            return;
        }
        NSValue *key = [NSValue valueWithPointer:t];
        CGPoint loc = [t locationInView:self];
        Line *newLine = [[Line alloc] init];
        [newLine setBegin:loc];
        [newLine setEnd:loc];
        [linesInProcess setObject:newLine forKey:key];
        [newLine release];
    }

}
```

The Sampler Instrument

Now that you have hunted down wasted memory, let's look for wasted CPU cycles using the Sampler instrument. Add the following CPU wasting code to the end of your **drawRect:** method:

```
float f = 0.0;
for (int i = 0; i < 1000; i++) {
    f = f + sin(sin(time(NULL) + i));
}
NSLog(@"f = %f", f);
```

Build your application. (Make sure you do this; otherwise Instruments will use the previously built application.) Under the Run menu, select Run with Performance Tool->CPU Sampler to install the application on your device and launch Instruments with the Sampler and the CPU Monitor instruments. Run your application by clicking the Record button and then draw something pretty.

CPU Sampler is useful for finding bottlenecks in your code. The time that your application takes to call each function is compared to the total running time of your application and expressed as a percentage. In a responsive application, the majority of time will be spent in a function called **mach_msg_trap**. This is the function your application sits in when it is doing nothing. Therefore, you want most of your application's time to be spent in this function.

Many developers using Instruments for the first time will be concerned over this **mach_msg_trap** function. Don't worry about it — a responsive application may report near 100% for this function. However, just because your application does not spend near 100% of its time in **mach_msg_trap** does not mean it is performing poorly. An application might spend a lot of time performing a task that requires no user input — like processing an image after the user takes a picture. This application would report a lot of time spent in some image processing method. Therefore, there is no rule that says, "If X percentage is spent in this function, your application has a problem."

Without a handy rule, how do you determine if you have a problem, then? You need to use the results of Instruments in conjunction with the user experience of your application. If, for example, you draw a line in TouchTracker and the application feels unresponsive, you should be concerned with the amount of time being spent in methods while your finger is on the screen. When you want to look at a specific time interval (like when your finger is on the screen), you can drag the playhead on top of the graph and click on the Inspection Range buttons to set the start and stop time of the interval you are interested in.

Now, TouchTracker purposely wastes CPU time by calling the **sin** function over and over again every time the view is redrawn. Find the number of samples that your CPU spent running the **sin** function by locating **sin** symbol name in the table (Figure 17.9).

Figure 17.9   Sampler

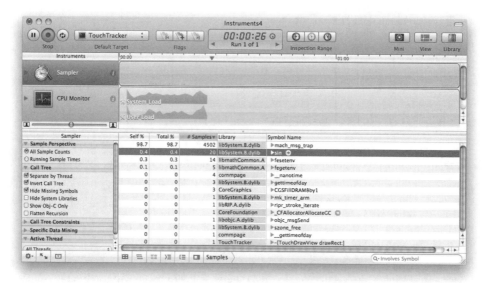

You will notice that a small percentage of time is spent in this function; however, relative to the rest of the function calls, the percentage is very high. You can select the row with **sin** in it and click the arrow next to it to see the call stack trace for when this function is called. This will show you where you can optimize your code. In this case, you aren't using **sin** for anything other than learning how to use Instruments, so the optimization is just to delete the CPU wasting code from **drawRect:**.

When you get more comfortable with Instruments, you will see some common function calls that always use a lot of CPU time. Most of the time, these are harmless and unavoidable. For example, the **objc_msgSend** function will occasionally creep up to the top of the list when you are sending lots of messages to objects. (It is the central dispatch function for any Objective-C message.) Usually, it's nothing to worry about. However, if you are spending more time dispatching messages than actually doing the work in the methods that are triggered and your application isn't performing well, there is a problem that needs solving.

As a real world example, some Objective-C developers might be tempted to create classes for things like vectors, points, and rectangles for drawing. These classes would likely have methods to add, subtract, or multiply instances in addition to accessor methods to get and set instance variables. When such classes are used, however, the drawing code has to send a lot of messages to do simple things, like creating two vectors and adding them together. These messages add excessive overhead to the simple operation that is being performed. Therefore, the better alternative is to create data types like these as structures and access their memory directly. (This is why CGRect and CGPoint are structures and not Objective-C classes.)

This should give you a good start with the Instruments application. The more you play with it, the more adept at using it you will become. However, there is one final word of warning before you invest a significant amount of your development time using Instruments: if there is no performance problem, don't fret over every little row in Instruments. It is a tool for finding problems, not for creating them. Write clean code that works first; then, if there is a problem, you can find and fix it with the help of Instruments.

Challenge: Saving and Loading

Save the lines when the application terminates. Reload them when the application resumes.

Challenge: Circles

Use two fingers to draw circles. Try having each finger represent one corner of the bounding box around the circle. (Hint: This is much easier if you track touches that are working on a circle in a separate dictionary.) You can simulate two fingers on the simulator by holding down the option button.

For the More Curious: UIControl

The class **UIControl** is the superclass for many objects in Cocoa Touch: **UIButton**, **UISlider**, **UITextField**, etc. These objects seem magical — when a touch event occurs in one of these views, an action message is dispatched to a target. But there is no magic to any of these; **UIControl** simply overrides **UIResponder** methods.

Consider a very common control event: UIControlEventTouchUpInside. You've used this control event for the target-action pairs of all of the buttons in this book. Now it's time to see how **UIControl** implements it:

```
// In UIControl.m - Not the exact code. There is a bit more going on!
- (void)touchesEnded:(NSSet *)touches withEvent:(UIEvent *)event
{
    // Reference to the touch that is ending
    UITouch *touch = [touches anyObject];

    // Location of that point in this control's coordinate system
    CGPoint touchLocation = [touch locationInView:self];

    // Is that point still in my viewing bounds?
    if (CGRectContainsPoint([self bounds], touchLocation))
    {
        // Send out action messages to all targets registered for this event!
        [self sendActionsForControlEvents:UIControlEventTouchUpInside];
    } else {
        [self sendActionsForControlEvents:UIControlEventTouchUpOutside];
    }
}
```

Pretty simple, right? Let's look at UIControlEventTouchDownRepeat:

```
// In UIControl.m - Not the exact code. There is a bit more going on!
- (void)touchesBegan:(NSSet *)touches withEvent:(UIEvent *)event
{
    if ([[touches anyObject] tapCount] > 1)
        [self sendActionForControlEvents:UIControlEventTouchDownRepeat];
}
```

Those are easy. What about a **UISlider**? When a touch is dragged across a slider, the control knob moves, and then all targets are sent their action message for UIControlEventValueChanged.

```
// In UISlider.m - Not the exact code. There is a bit more going on!
- (void)touchesMoved:(NSSet *)touches withEvent:(UIEvent *)event
{
    UITouch *touch = [touches anyObject];
    CGPoint touchLocation = [touch locationInView:self];
    CGRect bounds = [self bounds];
    float sliderWidth = bounds.size.width;

    // Make sure the knob stays within the bounds
    if (touchLocation.x < bounds.origin.x)
        touchLocation.x = bounds.origin.x;
    if (touchLocation.x > bounds.origin.x + sliderWidth)
        touchLocation.x = bounds.origin.x + sliderWidth;

    // Update interface
    [self moveSliderKnobTo:touchLocation];

    // Figure out the new value
    float normalizedPositionOfKnob
        = (touchLocation.x - bounds.origin.x)  / sliderWidth;
    float range = [self maximumValue] - [self minimumValue];
    float newValue = [self minimumValue]
                                + normalizedPositionOfKnob * range;
    [self setValue:newValue];

    [self sendActionsForControlEvents:UIControlEventValueChanged];
}
```

So how do these actions get sent to the right target? The method **sendActionsForControlEvents:** sends the message **sendAction:to:from:forEvent:** to the singleton **UIApplication** instance for each target-action pair registered for that event. **UIApplication** then delivers the message to the appropriate target.

The controls could send the action messages to the target on their own, but controls can also have nil-targeted actions. In fact, having nil-targeted actions can be very useful. If a **UIControl**'s target is nil, **UIApplication** finds the *first responder* of its **UIWindow** and sends the action message to it. This is exactly how keyboard input works — each of the buttons on the keyboard has nil-targeted actions, and **UIApplication** sends the action message to the first responder, which is the active **UITextField**. How cool is that?

18

Core Animation Layer

One of the things that makes iPhone interfaces so beautiful is the use of animation. When used properly, animation can increase the functionality of an application by giving the user visual cues about the application's workflow. On the iPhone, the Core Animation API contains the classes and functions needed to animate an application's interface.

There are two classes that make Core Animation work: **CALayer** and **CAAnimation**.

CALayer is, at its core, a buffer containing a bitmap. When you draw a layer (or, more importantly, a stack of layers), the rendering is hardware-accelerated. This makes drawing a layer to the screen incredibly fast. The idea of layers may be new, but you've been been using layers this entire time: every view has a layer, and when a view draws, it is drawing on its layer.

CAAnimation is an object that causes a change over time. Typically, it is changing one property (like opacity) of a layer while being driven by a timer object.

In this chapter, we are going to focus on **CALayer**, and in the next chapter, we'll focus on **CAAnimation**.

To use any part of Core Animation, you need to add the QuartzCore framework to your project. Open your HypnoTime project. Double-click on the Target called HypnoTime. In the General page of the info panel, add QuartzCore.framework to the linked libraries for the project, as shown in Figure 18.1.

Figure 18.1   QuartzCore.framework

Creating a CALayer

Like views, layers are arranged hierarchically: each layer can have sublayers. Your **HypnosisView**, like all views, already has one layer. In this section, you are going to explicitly add a sublayer to it.

Figure 18.2 Object diagram

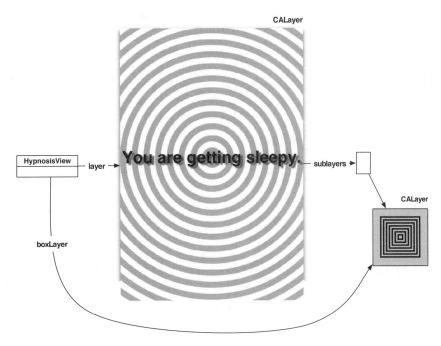

Add an instance variable to HypnosisView.h to hold on to the layer object you are about to create:

```
#import <UIKit/UIKit.h>
#import <QuartzCore/QuartzCore.h>
@interface HypnosisView : UIView {
    CALayer *boxLayer;
    UIColor *stripeColor;
    float xShift, yShift;
}

@end
```

The designated initializer for a **CALayer** is simply **init**. After you instantiate a layer, you set its size, position (relative to its superlayer), and contents. In HypnosisView.m, change the **initWithFrame:** method to create a new layer and add it as a sublayer to **HypnosisView**'s layer.

```
- (id)initWithFrame:(CGRect)r
{
    [super initWithFrame:r];

    stripeColor = [[UIColor lightGrayColor] retain];

    // Create the new layer object
    boxLayer = [[CALayer alloc] init];
```

```
    // Give it a size
    [boxLayer setBounds:CGRectMake(0.0, 0.0, 85.0, 85.0)];

    // Give it a location
    [boxLayer setPosition:CGPointMake(160.0, 100.0)];

    // Make half-transparent red the background color for the layer
    UIColor *reddish = [UIColor colorWithRed:1.0 green:0.0 blue:0.0 alpha:0.5];

    // Get a CGColor object with the same color values
    CGColorRef cgReddish = [reddish CGColor];
    [boxLayer setBackgroundColor:cgReddish];

    // Make it a sublayer of the view's layer
    [[self layer] addSublayer:boxLayer];

    // boxLayer is retained by its superlayer
    [boxLayer release];

    return self;
}
```

Build and run the application. You will see a semi-transparent, red block appear on the view as shown in Figure 18.3.

Figure 18.3   Red layer

Layer Content

Layers interpret their size and position a little differently than views do. With a **UIView**, we typically define the frame of the view to establish its size and position. The origin of the frame rectangle is the upper-left corner of the view, and the size stretches right and down from the origin.

For a **CALayer**, instead of defining a frame, you set the bounds and position properties of the layer. By default, the position is the *center* of the layer in its superlayer. (The anchorPoint property determines where the position lies within the layer's bounds: the default value is (0.5, 0.5), the center.) Therefore, you can change the size of the layer, but if the position remains constant, the layer will still be centered on the same point.

You can still set or get the frame of a layer by sending it the messages **setFrame:** and **frame**. However, it is considered better practice to use the position and bounds properties. Why? You cannot animate a layer's frame. In fact, layers do not have a frame property at all. When a layer is sent the message **frame**, it computes a rectangle from its position and bounds properties. Similarly, when sending a layer the message **setFrame:**, it does some math and then sets the bounds and position properties. The mental math you will need to do to animate a layer will be much simpler if you stick to setting the bounds and position properties separately.

A layer is simply a bitmap. We refer to a layer's appearance as its *contents*, which can be set from an image or programmatically. To draw to a layer programmatically, you either subclass **CALayer** or assign a delegate to an instance of **CALayer**. The delegate will then implement drawing routines. The drawing in these methods is done using Core Graphics. We will discuss these two approaches for drawing a layer at the end of this chapter. For now, however, you will use an image file to set the contents of the layer. Add the following code to the **initWithFrame:** method:

```
- (id)initWithFrame:(CGRect)r
{
    [super initWithFrame:r];

    stripeColor = [[UIColor lightGrayColor] retain];

    boxLayer = [[CALayer alloc] init];
    [boxLayer setBounds:CGRectMake(0.0, 0.0, 85.0, 85.0)];
    [boxLayer setPosition:CGPointMake(160.0, 100.0)];

    UIColor *reddish = [UIColor colorWithRed:1.0 green:0.0 blue:0.0 alpha:0.5];
    CGColorRef cgReddish = [reddish CGColor];
    [boxLayer setBackgroundColor:cgReddish];

    // Create a UIImage
    UIImage *layerImage = [UIImage imageNamed:@"Hypno.png"];

    // Get the underlying CGImage
    CGImageRef image = [layerImage CGImage];

    // Put the CGImage on the layer
    [boxLayer setContents:(id)image];

    // Inset the image a bit on each side
    [boxLayer setContentsRect:CGRectMake(-0.1, -0.1, 1.2, 1.2)];

    // Let the image resize (without changing the aspect ratio)
    // to fill the contentRect
    [boxLayer setContentsGravity:kCAGravityResizeAspect];
```

```
    [[self layer] addSublayer:boxLayer];
    [boxLayer release];
    return self;
}
```

Build and run the application. You will see an image on the layer as shown in Figure 18.4.

Figure 18.4   Layer with image

The contents and backgroundColor properties of the **CALayer** were set with objects of type **CGImageRef** and **CGColorRef**, respectively. You are used to working with **UIImage** and **UIColor**, so why doesn't Core Animation just use these types of objects?

UIKit (where we get **UIImage** and anything else prefixed with UI) only exists on the iPhone. Core Animation, however, exists on the iPhone and on the Mac. This means using the Core Graphics types makes your code portable between systems. Fortunately, UIKit objects have methods to easily switch between themselves and their Core Graphics counterparts (for example, **UIImage**'s **CGImage** and **initWithCGImage:** methods).

Just like with views, layers have a pointer to their parent layer. While views call this pointer superview, layers, as you may have guessed, call this pointer superlayer. When a layer is drawn, it copies its contents to the screen, and then each sublayer copies its contents to the screen. Therefore, a layer always draws on top of its superlayer.

Each layer has a property, zPosition, that determines how far away it is from the plane of the screen. If two layers are siblings (that is, they have the same superlayer) and they overlap, then the layer with the higher z-position is drawn last. (A sublayer *always* draws on top of its superlayer, regardless of zPosition.) A layer's zPosition defaults to 0 and can be set to a negative value.

```
[aLayer setZPosition:-5];
[bLayer setZPosition:5];
[parentLayer addSublayer:bLayer];
[parentLayer addSublayer:aLayer];

// bLayer draws on top of aLayer!
```

Figure 18.5   Perspective vs. Orthographic

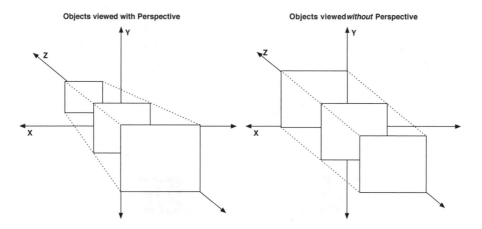

When the Z-axis is discussed, some developers think there is perspective applied, and they expect a layer to appear larger as its zPosition increases. However, Core Animation layers are presented orthographically, so they will not appear to be different sizes based on their zPositions. (You can of course fake perspective by changing the transform or bounds properties of a layer, but at that point, you might be better served using OpenGL ES directly.)

Implicitly Animatable Properties

Several of the properties of **CALayer** are *implicitly animatable*. Changes to these properties are animated just by invoking the setter method for them. The property position is an example of an implicitly animatable property. Therefore, sending the message **setPosition:** to a **CALayer** will trigger an animation that changes the position of that layer over a small amount of time.

In this section, you are going to add a response to user taps: the layer will move to wherever the user starts a touch by sending it the message **setPosition:**. The motion will be animated because position is an implicitly animatable property. Add the following to HypnosisView.m:

```
- (void)touchesBegan:(NSSet *)touches
         withEvent:(UIEvent *)event
{
    UITouch *t = [touches anyObject];
    CGPoint p = [t locationInView:self];
    [boxLayer setPosition:p];
}
```

Build and run the application. The layer will move smoothly to where you start a touch.

What if the user drags? The layer should follow the user's finger. Implement a similar method:

```
- (void)touchesMoved:(NSSet *)touches
           withEvent:(UIEvent *)event
{
    UITouch *t = [touches anyObject];
    CGPoint p = [t locationInView:self];
    [boxLayer setPosition:p];
}
```

Build and run the application. Notice how the animation makes the layer lag behind the drag. This makes the application seem sluggish.

Figure 18.6   Animation missing waypoints

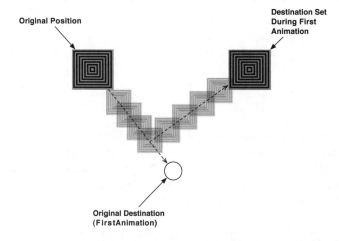

Implicit animation is convenient, but it causes problems in some cases. All implicitly animatable properties change to their destination value over a constant time interval. However, changes to the property of a layer while it is currently being animated restarts an implicit animation. Therefore, if a layer is in the middle of traveling from point A to point B, and you tell it to go to point C, it will never reach B; and that little instantaneous change of direction coupled with the timer restarting is what makes the animation look choppy. (Figure 18.6)

If you wish to disable an implicit animation, you can use an *animation transaction*. Animation transactions allow you to batch implicit animations and set the parameters of the animation, like the duration and animation curve. To begin a transaction, you send the message **begin** to the class **CATransaction**. To end a transaction, you send **commit** to **CATransaction**. Within the **begin** and **commit** block, you can set properties of a layer as normal and also set values for **CATransaction**. In **touchesMoved:withEvent:**, use **CATransaction** to disable the animation during a drag:

```
- (void)touchesMoved:(NSSet *)touches
            withEvent:(UIEvent *)event
{
    UITouch *t = [touches anyObject];
    CGPoint p = [t locationInView:self];
    [CATransaction begin];
    [CATransaction setValue:[NSNumber numberWithBool:YES]
                     forKey:kCATransactionDisableActions];
    [boxLayer setPosition:p];
    [CATransaction commit];
}
```

Build and run the application. Dragging should feel much more responsive.

For the More Curious: Programmatically Generating Content

In this chapter, you provided the content of a layer with the instance method **setContents:**. There are two other ways of drawing to a layer that use Core Graphics: subclassing and delegation. In practice, subclassing is the last thing you want to do. The only reason to subclass **CALayer** to provide custom content is if you need to draw differently depending on the state of the layer. If this is the approach you wish to take, you must override the method **drawInContext:**.

```
@implementation LayerSubclass

- (void)drawInContext:(CGContextRef)ctx
{
    UIImage *layerImage = nil;
    if (hypnotizing)
        layerImage = [UIImage imageNamed:@"Hypno.png"];
    else
        layerImage = [UIImage imageNamed:@"Plain.png"];

    CGRect boundingBox = CGContextGetClipBoundingBox(ctx);
    CGContextDrawImage(ctx, boundingBox, [layerImage CGImage]);
}
@end
```

Delegation is the more common way to programmatically draw to a layer. A layer sends the message **drawLayer:inContext:** to its delegate object when it is being displayed. The delegate can then perform Core Graphics calls on this context.

```
@implementation Controller

- (void)drawLayer:(CALayer *)layer inContext:(CGContextRef)ctx
{
    if (layer == hypnoLayer)
    {
        UIImage *layerImage = [UIImage imageNamed:@"Hypno.png"];
        CGRect boundingBox = CGContextGetClipBoundingBox(ctx);
        CGContextDrawImage(ctx, boundingBox, [layerImage CGImage]);
    }
}
@end
```

For both subclassing and delegation, you must send an explicit **setNeedsDisplay** to the layer in order for these methods to be invoked. Otherwise, the layer thinks it doesn't have any content and won't draw. Another fun tip: don't ever set the delegate of an explicit layer to a **UIView**. We'll discuss why in the next section.

For the More Curious: Layers and Views

In conversation, we talk about a view as though it is visible object that is drawn to the screen — and this works well for discussing views and understanding higher level concepts. However, this is technically inaccurate. A view doesn't know how to draw to the screen; it only knows how to draw to a layer. A layer is the *only* thing that draws to the screen in iPhone OS. (On the Desktop, Core Animation was introduced later in the game, so views and layers draw differently.)

Figure 18.7   View and corresponding layer hierarchy

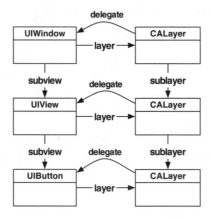

Okay, take a deep breath, slow down. It's crazy, but it's true. Every view has a layer, and there is a matching layer hierarchy that mimics the view hierarchy (Figure 18.7). We call layers created automatically by a view *implicit layers* (and we call layers created by sending **alloc** to the class **CALayer** *explicit layers*). You might hear implicit layers referred to as the layer in *layer-backed views*, but this only makes sense on the Desktop where views are the focus and layers are optional.

A layer is simply a bitmap — a chunk of memory that holds the red, green, blue, and alpha values of each pixel. When you send the message **setNeedsDisplay** to a **UIView** instance, that method is forwarded to the view's layer. After the run loop is done processing an event, every layer marked for re-display prepares a **CGContextRef**. Drawing routines called on this context generate pixels that end up in the layer's bitmap.

How do drawing routines get called on the layer's context? After an implicit layer prepares its context, it sends the message **drawLayer:inContext:** to its delegate. *The delegate of an implicit layer is its view*. In the implementation for **drawLayer:inContext:**, the view sends **drawRect:** to itself. Therefore, when you see this line at the top of your **drawRect:** implementations,

```
- (void)drawRect:(CGRect)r
{
    CGContextRef ctx = UIGraphicsGetCurrentContext();
}
```

you are getting a pointer to the layer's context. All of the drawing in **drawRect:** is filling the layer's bitmap, which is then copied to the screen. Need to see for yourself? Set an Xcode breakpoint in **HypnosisView**'s **drawRect:** and check out the stack trace, as shown in Figure 18.8.

Figure 18.8   Stack trace in drawRect:

A few paragraphs up, we mentioned that the pixels generated by drawing routines end up in the layer's bitmap. What exactly does that mean? When you want to create a bitmap context in Cocoa Touch (as you did when you created the thumbnails for the possessions), you typically do something like this:

```
// Create context
UIGraphicsBeginImageContext(size);
    ... Do drawing here ...

// Get image result
UIImage *result = UIGraphicsGetImageFromCurrentImageContext();

// Clean up image context
UIGraphicsEndImageContext();
```

A bitmap context is created and drawn to, and the resulting pixels are stored in a **UIImage** instance.

The UIGraphics suite of functions is a convenient way of creating a bitmap **CGContextRef** and writing that data to a **UIImage** object by calling the following code:

```
// Create a color space to use for the context
CGColorSpaceRef colorSpace = CGColorSpaceCreateDeviceRGB();

// Create a context of appropriate width and height
// with 4 bytes per pixel - RGBA
CGContextRef ctx =
    CGBitmapContextCreate(NULL, width, height, 8, width * 4,
                colorSpace, kCGImageAlphaPremultipliedLast);

// Make this context the current one
UIGraphicsPushContext(ctx);

... Do drawing here ...

// Get image result
CGImageRef image = CGBitmapContextCreateImage(ctx);
UIImage *result = [[[UIImage alloc] initWithCGImage:image] autorelease];

// Clean up image context - make previous context current if one exists
UIGraphicsPopContext();
CGImageRelease(image);
CGContextRelease(ctx);
CGColorSpaceRelease(colorSpace);
```

A layer creates the same kind of context when it needs to redraw its contents. However, it does it a little differently. See the NULL as the first parameter to **CGBitmapContextCreate**? That is where you pass a data buffer to hold the pixels generated by drawing routines in this context. By passing NULL, we say, "Core Graphics, figure out how much memory is needed for this buffer, create it, and then dispose of it when the context is destroyed." A **CALayer** already has a buffer (its contents), so it would call the function as follows:

```
CGContextRef ctx =
    CGBitmapContextCreate(myBitmapPixels, width, height, 8, width * 4,
                colorSpace, kCGImageAlphaPremultipliedLast);
```

Therefore, when this context is drawn to, all of the resulting pixels are immediately written to the bitmap that is the layer. Cool, huh?

So what is the point of having views when we have layers? **UIView** is a subclass of **UIResponder** and can handle touches. A view is really an abstraction of a visible object that can be interacted with on the screen, conveniently wrapped into a tidy class.

Challenge: Dynamic Layer Content

Give boxLayer a delegate to draw its content. When the layer is near the top of the screen, draw the Hypno image to the layer in the delegate method with full opacity. As the layer approaches the bottom of the screen, draw the image more transparently.

This is a very difficult challenge, so you can have three hints:

1. The delegate of boxLayer cannot be **HypnosisView**.

2. You must send **setNeedsDisplay** to the layer every time it changes position.

3. To set the opacity of drawing in a context, use the function **CGContextSetAlpha**.

Happy coding!

19

Controlling Animation with CAAnimation

An animation object drives change over time. While you have not yet used animation objects explicitly, all the animation in iPhone OS is driven by instances of the different animation classes. An animation object is an instruction set ("Move from point A to point B over 2 seconds") that can be added to a **CALayer** instance. Many properties of **CALayer** can be animated by animation objects: opacity, position, transform, bounds, and contents are just a few. When an animation object is added to a layer, that layer begins following the instructions of the animation.

Animation Objects

The abstract superclass for all animation objects is **CAAnimation**. **CAAnimation** is responsible for handling timing; it has a duration property that specifies the length of the animation. As an abstract superclass, you do not use **CAAnimation** objects directly. Instead, you will use one of its concrete subclasses shown in Figure 19.1.

Figure 19.1   Inheritance

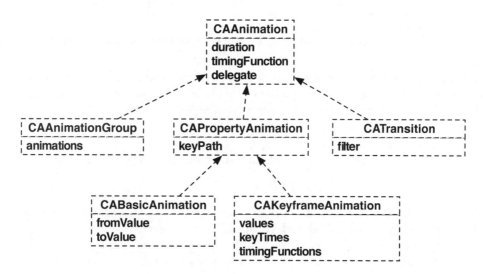

CAPropertyAnimation is a subclass of **CAAnimation** and extends on the ability of its superclass to keep track of time by adding functionality to change the properties of a layer. Each property animation has a *key path* of type **NSString**. This string is the name of an animatable property of a **CALayer**. Many of **CALayer**'s properties are animatable; the documentation has an Animatable Properties section for a list of the possibilities (Figure 19.2).

Figure 19.2   Animatable Properties in the documentation

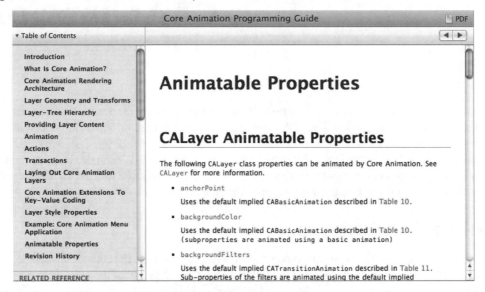

Typically, the key path matches the name of the property. For example, a property animation that will animate a layer's opacity property will have a key path of opacity.

```
// This property animation will be able to modify the opacity
// property of any layer it is added to
CAPropertyAnimation *propAnimation =
              [CAPropertyAnimation animationWithKeyPath:@"opacity"];
```

Sometimes properties whose type is a structure (like position, whose type is CGPoint) can have each of their members accessed by a key path. (The available options for this are in the documentation under Core Animation Extensions To Key-Value Coding.)

```
CAPropertyAnimation *propAnimation =
              [CAPropertyAnimation animationWithKeyPath:@"position.x"];
```

However, just like with **CAAnimation**, you do not create instances of type **CAPropertyAnimation**. To create animation objects that modify a property of a layer, you use one of the two concrete subclasses of **CAPropertyAnimation**: **CABasicAnimation** or **CAKeyframeAnimation**. Instances of these two classes allow you to specify the actual values that the key path property will change to over the duration of an animation. Most of the time you will spend with Core Animation will involve these two classes.

Figure 19.3 Interpolating a CABasicAnimation that animates the position of a layer

CABasicAnimation is the simpler version of the two. It has two properties: fromValue and toValue. When a basic animation is added to a layer, the property it is modifying is set to the value in fromValue. As the animation progresses, the value of the property is interpolated linearly from fromValue to toValue as shown in Figure 19.3.

```
// This animation object will act on a layer's opacity property
CABasicAnimation *fader = [CABasicAnimation animationWithKeyPath:@"opacity"];
// ... it will last for 1 second ...
[fader setDuration:1.0];
// ... the layer's opacity will start at 1.0 at t = 0 and move towards...
[fader setFromValue:[NSNumber numberWithFloat:1.0]];
// ... 0.0 where it finishes at t = 1.0
[fader setToValue:[NSNumber numberWithFloat:0.0]];
```

Notice how these properties take an **NSNumber** as an argument. Because animation objects need to be able to support different data types (an animation that changes the position of a layer would need values that are of type CGPoint, for example), the type of these properties is id — any Objective-C object.

However, you can't just pass any object you like; **CABasicAnimation** expects the appropriate object determined by the key path. For scalar values, like opacity, you can wrap a number in an **NSNumber** instance. For properties represented by structures, like position, you will wrap the structures in instances of **NSValue**.

```
CABasicAnimation *mover =
                [CABasicAnimation animationWithKeyPath:@"position"];
[mover setDuration:1.0];
[mover setFromValue:[NSValue valueWithCGPoint:CGPointMake(0.0, 100.0)]];
[mover setToValue:[NSValue valueWithCGPoint:CGPointMake(100.0, 100.0)]];
```

The difference between **CABasicAnimation** and **CAKeyframeAnimation** is that basic animations only interpolate two values while keyframe animations can interpolate as many values as you want. For a **CAKeyframeAnimation**, the values are put into an **NSArray** in the order in which they are to occur. This array is then set as the values property of the **CAKeyframeAnimation** instance.

```
CAKeyframeAnimation *mover =
                     [CAKeyframeAnimation animationWithKeyPath:@'position"];
NSArray *vals = [NSMutableArray array];
[vals addObject:[NSValue valueWithCGPoint:CGPointMake(0.0, 100.0)]];
[vals addObject:[NSValue valueWithCGPoint:CGPointMake(100.0, 100.0)]];
[mover setValues:vals];
[mover setDuration:1.0];
```

Each value is called a *keyframe*. Keyframes are the values that the animation will interpolate through. The animation will take the property it is animating through each of these keyframes over its duration, interpolating between each one. A basic animation is actually the same thing as a keyframe animation except it is limited to two keyframes. Regardless of which type of animation object is used, the values are called keyframes. (**CAKeyframeAnimation** also adds the ability to change the timing of each of the keyframes, but that is getting a little too advanced for what we want to talk about right now.)

The other two **CAAnimation** subclasses are used less often. **CAAnimationGroup** instances hold an array of animation objects. When one is added to a layer, the animations will run concurrently.

```
CABasicAnimation *mover = [CABasicAnimation animationWithKeyPath:@"position"];
[mover setDuration:1.0];
[mover setFromValue:[NSValue valueWithCGPoint:CGPointMake(0.0, 100.0)]];
[mover setToValue:[NSValue valueWithCGPoint:CGPointMake(100.0, 100.0)]];

CABasicAnimation *fader = [CABasicAnimation animationWithKeyPath:@"opacity"];
[fader setDuration:1.0];
[fader setFromValue:[NSNumber numberWithFloat:1.0]];
[fader setToValue:[NSNumber numberWithFloat:1.0]];

CAAnimationGroup *group = [CAAnimationGroup animation];
[group setAnimations:[NSArray arrayWithObjects:fader, mover, nil]];
```

CATransition animates layers as they are transitioning on and off the screen. On Mac OS X, **CATransition** is made very powerful by Core Image Filters. On iPhone OS, it can only do a couple of simple transitions like fading and sliding. (**CATransition** is used by **UINavigationController** when pushing a view controller's view on to the screen.)

Spinning the Time with CABasicAnimation

As mentioned in Chapter 18, every view has an implicit layer. In this section, you are going to use an animation object to spin the implicit layer of the time field in HypnoTime's **CurrentTimeViewController** when it is updated (Figure 19.4). Quick update on what we mean by explicit and implicit animations and layers:

- explicit animation: an instance of a **CAAnimation** subclass

- implicit animation: an animation that occurs when setting an implicitly animatable property of a **CALayer**; happens automatically

- explicit layer: a layer created by calling **[[CALayer alloc] init]** or **[CALayer layer]**

- implicit layer: a layer created by a view when the view is instantiated; happens automatically

Figure 19.4   Current time mid-spin

Open HypnoTime.xcodeproj. Before you can write any Core Animation code, you need link to the framework that contains Core Animation: QuartzCore.

Add the QuartzCore framework to your project. The animation code you will write in this exercise will be in CurrentTimeViewController.m. So, at the top of this file, import the header from the QuartzCore framework.

```
#import <QuartzCore/QuartzCore.h>

@implementation CurrentTimeViewController
```

In order to spin the timeLabel, you need an animation object that will apply a 360 degree rotation over time to a layer. So we need to determine four things:

• What type of animation object suits this purpose?

• What key path handles rotation?

• How long should the animation take to complete?

• What values should the animation interpolate over?

To answer the first question, think about the number of keyframes an animation needs to make a complete revolution. It only needs two: a non-rotated value and a fully-rotated value. The animation will interpolate between these two points; therefore, **CABasicAnimation** can handle this task.

To determine the key path, we must find the property of **CALayer** that deals with rotation. This property is its transform, the transformation matrix that is applied to the layer when it draws. The transform of a layer can rotate, scale, translate, and skew its frame. This exercise only calls for rotating the layer, and, fortunately, you can isolate the rotation of the transform in a key path (Figure 19.5). Therefore, the key path of the basic animation will be transform.rotation.

Figure 19.5   Core Animation Extensions To Key-Value Coding Documentation

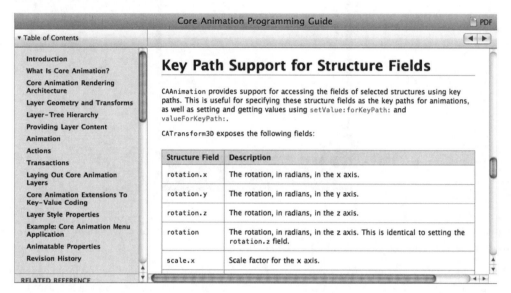

The duration of this animation should be one second: enough time for the user to see the spin but not too much time that they get bored watching it.

Lastly, we need the values of the two keyframes: the documentation says that the transform.rotation is in radians. The two values will then be 0 radians and 2 * PI radians for a full revolution. The default value of the transform property is the identity matrix — it has no rotation. When using a **CABasicAnimation**, if you do not supply a fromValue, the animation will assume that fromValue is the current value of that property. Therefore, you only have to supply the final keyframe to this animation object. Add the creation of the animation object to the method **showCurrentTime:** in CurrentTimeViewController.m.

```
- (IBAction)showCurrentTime:(id)sender
{
    NSDate *now = [NSDate date];
    static NSDateFormatter *formatter = nil;
    if (!formatter) {
        formatter = [[NSDateFormatter alloc] init];
        [formatter setDateStyle:NSDateFormatterShortStyle];
    }
    [timeLabel setText:[formatter stringFromDate:now]];

    // Create a basic animation
```

```
CABasicAnimation *spin =
            [CABasicAnimation animationWithKeyPath:@"transform.rotation"];

// fromValue is implied
[spin setToValue:[NSNumber numberWithFloat:M_PI * 2.0]];
[spin setDuration:1.0];
}
```

Now that you have an animation object, it needs to be applied to a layer for it to have any effect. **CALayer** instances implement the method **addAnimation:forKey:** for this purpose. This method takes two arguments: an animation object and a key. This key is *not* the key path; it is simply a human-readable name for this animation. Later on, you might want to reference an animation that a layer is performing. You will use this key to get that animation object. Add the following line of code to **showCurrentTime:**.

```
- (IBAction)showCurrentTime:(id)sender
{
    NSDate *now = [NSDate date];
    static NSDateFormatter *formatter = nil;
    if (!formatter) {
        formatter = [[NSDateFormatter alloc] init];
        [formatter setDateStyle:NSDateFormatterShortStyle];
    }
    [timeLabel setText:[formatter stringFromDate:now]];

    CABasicAnimation *spin =
                [CABasicAnimation animationWithKeyPath:@"transform.rotation"];

    [spin setToValue:[NSNumber numberWithFloat:M_PI * 2.0]];
    [spin setDuration:1.0];

    // Kick off the animation by adding it to the layer
    [[timeLabel layer] addAnimation:spin
                              forKey:@"spinAnimation"];
}
```

Build and run the application. The label field should spin 360 degrees when the user updates it — either by switching to the Time tab or tapping the button. Note how the animation object exists independently of the layer it is applied to. This animation object could be added to any layer and that layer would rotate 360 degrees. You can create animation objects and keep them around for later use; however, make sure you retain them if you plan to do this. (Because there is no **alloc** in **animationWithKeyPath:**, the animation object is autoreleased.)

Timing functions

You may notice that the label field's layer lurches into motion and stops suddenly. It would look nicer if it gradually accelerated and decelerated. This sort of behavior is controlled by the animation's timing function. By default, the timing function is linear — values are interpolated linearly. The timing functions will change how these animations are interpolated. They will not change the duration or the keyframes, though. Change the timing function of the animation:

```
- (IBAction)showCurrentTime:(id)sender
{
    NSDate *now = [NSDate date];
    static NSDateFormatter *formatter = nil;
    if (!formatter) {
        formatter = [[NSDateFormatter alloc] init];
        [formatter setDateStyle:NSDateFormatterShortStyle];
    }
    [timeLabel setText:[formatter stringFromDate:now]];

    // Create a basic animation
    CABasicAnimation *spin =
                [CABasicAnimation animationWithKeyPath:@"transform.rotation"];

    [spin setToValue:[NSNumber numberWithFloat:M_PI * 2.0]];
    [spin setDuration:1.0];

    // Set the timing function
    CAMediaTimingFunction *tf = [CAMediaTimingFunction
                        functionWithName:kCAMediaTimingFunctionEaseInEaseOut];
    [spin setTimingFunction:tf];

     // Make the animation move the layer
    [[timeLabel layer] addAnimation:spin
                            forKey:@"spinAnimation"];
}
```

Build and run the application. Note the difference.

There are four timing functions, you have seen linear and ease-in-ease-out. There is also kCAMediaTimingFunctionEaseIn (accelerates gradually, stops suddenly) and kCAMediaTimingFunctionEaseOut (accelerates suddenly, stops slowly).

Animation completion

Sometimes you want to know when an animation is finished. How would you know when the animation is complete? Every animation object can have a delegate, and it sends the message **animationDidStop:finished:** to its delegate when an animation stops. Edit CurrentTimeViewController.m so that it logs a message to the console when the animation stops.

```
- (void)animationDidStop:(CAAnimation *)anim finished:(BOOL)flag
{
    NSLog(@"%@ finished: %d", anim, flag);
}

- (IBAction)showCurrentTime:(id)sender
{
    NSDate *now = [NSDate date];
    static NSDateFormatter *formatter = nil;
    if (!formatter) {
        formatter = [[NSDateFormatter alloc] init];
        [formatter setDateStyle:NSDateFormatterShortStyle];
    }
    [timeLabel setText:[formatter stringFromDate:now]];
```

```
    // Create a basic animation
    CABasicAnimation *spin =
                [CABasicAnimation animationWithKeyPath:@"transform.rotation"];
    [spin setToValue:[NSNumber numberWithFloat:M_PI * 2.0]];
    [spin setDuration:1.0];

    // Set the timing function
    CAMediaTimingFunction *tf = [CAMediaTimingFunction
                        functionWithName:kCAMediaTimingFunctionEaseInEaseOut];
    [spin setTimingFunction:tf];

    [spin setDelegate:self];

    // Make the animation move the layer
    [[timeLabel layer] addAnimation:spin
                            forKey:@"spinAnimation"];
}
```

Build and run the application. Notice the log statements when the animation is complete. If you press the button several times quickly, the animation in progress will be interrupted by a new one. The interrupted animation will still send the message **animationDidStop:finished:** to its delegate; however, the finished flag will be NO. You will typically use this delegate method to either chain animations or update another object when an animation completes.

Bouncing the Time with a CAKeyframeAnimation

As an example of **CAKeyframeAnimation**, you are going to make the label field grow and shrink (Figure 19.6).

Figure 19.6   Current time mid-bounce

Comment out the spin animation and replace it with a nice bounce. The method **showCurrentTime:** should look like this:

```
- (IBAction)showCurrentTime:(id)sender
{
    NSDate *now = [NSDate date];
    static NSDateFormatter *formatter = nil;
    if (!formatter) {
        formatter = [[NSDateFormatter alloc] init];
        [formatter setDateStyle:NSDateFormatterShortStyle];
    }
    [timeLabel setText:[formatter stringFromDate:now]];

    // Create a key frame animation
    CAKeyframeAnimation *bounce =
                    [CAKeyframeAnimation animationWithKeyPath:@"transform"];

    // Create the values it will pass through
    CATransform3D forward = CATransform3DMakeScale(1.3, 1.3, 1);
    CATransform3D back = CATransform3DMakeScale(0.7, 0.7, 1);
    CATransform3D forward2 = CATransform3DMakeScale(1.2, 1.2, 1);
    CATransform3D back2 = CATransform3DMakeScale(0.9, 0.9, 1);
    [bounce setValues:[NSArray arrayWithObjects:
                        [NSValue valueWithCATransform3D:CATransform3DIdentity],
                        [NSValue valueWithCATransform3D:forward],
                        [NSValue valueWithCATransform3D:back],
                        [NSValue valueWithCATransform3D:forward2],
                        [NSValue valueWithCATransform3D:back2],
                        [NSValue valueWithCATransform3D:CATransform3DIdentity],
                        nil]];
    // Set the duration
    [bounce setDuration:0.6];

    // Animate the layer
    [[timeLabel layer] addAnimation:bounce
                                forKey:@"bounceAnimation"];
}
```

Build and run the application. The time field should now scale up and down and up and down when it is updated. The constant CATransform3DIdentity is the *identity matrix*. When the transform of a layer is the identity matrix, no scaling, rotation, or translation is applied to the layer: it sits squarely within its bounding box at its position. So, this animation starts at no transformation, scales it a few times, and then reverts back to no transformation.

Once you understand layers and the basics of animation, there isn't a whole lot to it — other than finding the appropriate key path and getting the timing of things right. (There might also be some linear algebra in there... but we don't want to scare you.) Core Animation is one of those things you can play around with and see results immediately. So play with it!

Challenge: More Animation

When the time label bounces, it should also change its opacity. Try and match the fading of the opacity with the shrinking and growing of the label. As another challenge, after the

CurrentTimeViewController's view slides onto the screen, have the What time is it? button slide in from the other direction.

For the More Curious: Presentation and Model Layers

What would happen if you were to omit the final CATransform3DIdentity from the bounce animation? You can see for yourself that the bounce "snaps" back into its original position as the animation ends. Why doesn't the layer just stop at the final position when the animation ends? A layer has properties like any other object. When an animation is added to a layer, it temporarily modifies the layer but does not change the actual property it is modifying. Therefore, if you are animating a layer to a new value at which it should remain after the animation is finished, you must set the property you are animating to the final value.

Let's use an example to make this easier to understand: you want a layer to move from point A to B and then stay at point B using **CABasicAnimation** with key path position. To do this, you must add the animation to the layer to perform the animation and then set the layer's position property to point B so it remains there after the animation completes. When would you set the position property? Crazily enough, you can do it before or after you apply the animation.

```
CABasicAnimation *move = [CABasicAnimation animationWithKeyPath:@"position"];
[move setFromValue:[NSValue valueWithCGPoint:[layer position]];
[move setToValue:[NSValue valueWithCGPoint:pointB]];

// You could set the destination position here...
[layer setPosition:pointB];

[layer addAnimation:move forKey:@"move"];

// Or you could set the destination position here
[layer setPosition:pointB];
```

Okay, so why does setting the final position work in either of those spots? Redrawing doesn't happen while the thread of execution is in your method. The run loop has to regain control, and only then will it begin animating and drawing. Since the layer is animating the next time it is supposed to be drawn, it doesn't matter what its position property is set to, the animated version of the layer is being drawn instead.

Core Animation makes a distinction between the values of the properties of a layer and the values of the properties of a layer *while animating*. When a layer is not animating, you can, of course, determine the values of its properties by sending the appropriate messages to the layer instance. When a layer is animating, you can get the current value of its properties that are being displayed on the screen by accessing a layer's **presentationLayer**. Sending the message presentationLayer to a layer will return a copy of the layer object, and the copy will have the current values for each property while animating.

```
CGPoint whereIsItWhenAnimationStops = [layer position];
CGPoint whereIsItNow = [[layer presentationLayer] position];
```

This is useful if you need to change a layer's animation while another animation is already occurring. If a layer is moving from point A to point B, and the user's input forces the layer to move to point C during the animation, you would have to know where the layer currently is to make a smooth transition to point C. Querying the presentation layer is also useful if you are using a layer for timing in your application. Imagine a game that has animating objects on the screen, and if the user taps one of the objects, it blows up. Only the presentation layer knows where the object currently is on the screen.

There is one "gotcha" to this process: if you do not specify a `fromValue` when using **CABasicAnimation** and set the property to the ending point of the animation, no animation occurs. Why? Without a `fromValue`, the animation assumes that the starting point of the animation is the current value of the layer for that key path. If the starting value is the same as the final value, there is no change and therefore no animation. (If the `fromValue` is not set, it is computed when the run loop starts the animation, not when you add the animation to a layer.)

20

Media Playback and Background Execution

Many applications on a mobile device have a need for audio and video playback. The iPhone SDK offers a few options for audio and video playback routines, and, in this chapter, you will learn how to use the most common ones.

Figure 20.1   MediaPlayer

Creating the MediaPlayer Application

Create a Window-Based Application in Xcode. Name this project MediaPlayer.

This application will have a very simple interface so that you can concentrate on the guts of media playback. The application will display two buttons that will initiate different types of audio playback, and it will also display a movie. The object diagram for this application is shown in Figure 20.1.

Figure 20.2   MediaPlayer object diagram

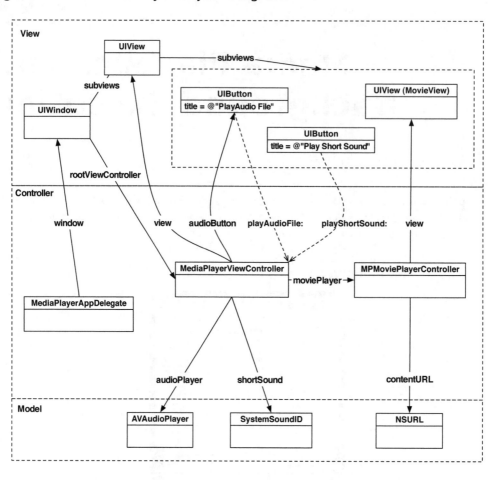

Create a new **UIViewController** subclass with a XIB file. Name this subclass
MediaPlayerViewController.m. In MediaPlayerAppDelegate.m, import the header file
for **MediaPlayerViewController**, create an instance of it and set it to be the window's
rootViewController.

```
#import "MediaPlayerAppDelegate.h"
#import "MediaPlayerViewController.h"

@implementation MediaPlayerAppDelegate
@synthesize window;

- (BOOL)application:(UIApplication *)application
    didFinishLaunchingWithOptions:(NSDictionary *)launchOptions
{
    MediaPlayerViewController *vc = [[MediaPlayerViewController alloc] init];
    [window setRootViewController:vc];
    [vc release];
```

```
    [window makeKeyAndVisible];

    return YES;
}
```

The buttons for playing audio need action methods. Declare these methods (and an instance variable for one of the buttons whose title will change during runtime) in MediaPlayerViewController.h.

```
@interface MediaPlayerViewController : UIViewController
{
    IBOutlet UIButton *audioButton;
}
- (IBAction)playAudioFile:(id)sender;
- (IBAction)playShortSound:(id)sender;
@end
```

Save this file. Open the MediaPlayerViewController.xib file in Interface Builder to configure the interface.

In Interface Builder, double-click the View object in the doc window to open it. Drag two **UIButton** objects onto it and title them as shown in Figure 20.3. Then, make the action connections from each of the buttons back to the **MediaPlayerViewController**. Finally, connect the audioButton outlet to the button labeled Play Audio File.

Figure 20.3   Interface Builder connections

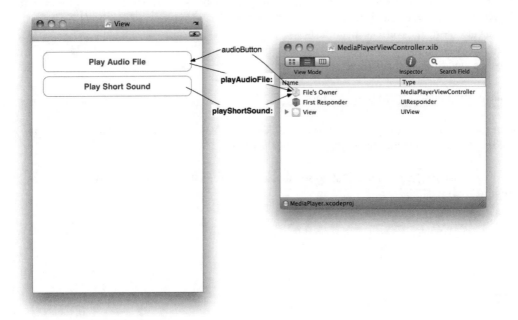

Save MediaPlayerViewController.xib and quit Interface Builder.

In order to build and run the application without warnings, you will need a stub method for each of the IBActions you declared. In MediaPlayerViewController.m, implement them as follows.

```
- (IBAction)playAudioFile:(id)sender
{
    NSLog(@"playAudioFile!");
}
- (IBAction)playShortSound:(id)sender
{
    NSLog(@"playSound!");
}
```

If you want to check your connections, you can build and run the application. The log messages should show up on the console.

Playing System Sounds

Audio files come in many different formats. The format describes the organization of the audio data within the file. Some files, like MP3 and M4A, have been compressed and require a decoder for playback. Compressed files are much smaller in size but require more work by the processor to play. For short sound effects, compression doesn't save much disk space, and the extra work it takes to decode a compressed file may affect an application's performance. (Short sound effects are typically used as an interface element. They are not critical to an application but add to the atmosphere you are trying to create.)

The AudioToolbox framework gives you the ability to register short sound effects on the system sound server. We call sounds registered with the system sound server *system sounds*. System sounds are short sound effects that must

• be a sound file less than 30 seconds in length

• have data in linear PCM or IMA4 format

• be packaged as one of the following three types: Core Audio Format (.caf), Waveform audio format (.wav), or Audio Interchange File Format (.aiff)

To start registering and playing system sounds, add the AudioToolbox framework to your project (Figure 20.4).

Figure 20.4   Adding the AudioToolbox framework

After a system sound is registered, you are given a new **SystemSoundID** that references that sound. A **SystemSoundID** is really just an integer that you can think of as a ticket. When you want to play a registered sound effect, you tell the sound server the number on your ticket. Declare a **SystemSoundID** instance variable in MediaPlayerViewController.h. Because this type is declared in AudioToolbox framework, you will also need to import AudioToolbox's top-level header file.

```
#import <AudioToolbox/AudioToolbox.h>
@interface MediaPlayerViewController : UIViewController
{
    IBOutlet UIButton *audioButton;
    SystemSoundID shortSound;
}
```

The audio data for a system sound must be contained in a file located on the device. In this chapter, you will bundle a short audio clip file with the application. Locate the file Sound12.aif and add it to the Resources group of the project. (This file and other resources can be downloaded from http://www.bignerdranch.com/solutions/iPhoneProgramming.zip.)

You will grab the full path to the Sound12.aif file and register its contents with the system sound server when the application launches using **NSBundle**'s **pathForResource:ofType:** method. The object returned from this method is of type **NSString**, but, to register a system sound, you need to call the function **AudioServicesCreateSystemSoundID** and pass the path as a **CFURLRef** object.

You will use **NSURL**'s **fileURLWithPath:** to create an **NSURL** instance and cast that to its toll-free bridged counterpart: **CFURLRef**. In **MediaPlayerViewController**'s **init** method, get a path to the Sound12.aif file and register its contents as a system sound. Add the following code to MediaPlayerViewController.m.

```
- (id)init
{
    self = [super initWithNibName:@"MediaPlayerViewController" bundle:nil];

    // Get the full path of Sound12.aif
    NSString *soundPath = [[NSBundle mainBundle] pathForResource:@"Sound12"
                                                          ofType:@"aif"];
    // If this file is actually in the bundle...
    if (soundPath) {
        // Create a file URL with this path
        NSURL *soundURL = [NSURL fileURLWithPath:soundPath];

        // Register sound file located at that URL as a system sound
        OSStatus err = AudioServicesCreateSystemSoundID((CFURLRef)soundURL,
                                                        &shortSound);
        if (err != kAudioServicesNoError)
            NSLog(@"Could not load %@, error code: %d", soundURL, err);
    }
    return self;
}
- (id)initWithNibName:(NSString *)nibNameOrNil bundle:(NSBundle *)nibBundleOrNil
{
    return [self init];
}
```

AudioServicesCreateSystemSoundID has a return value — an error code. Only one value can be returned from a function; therefore, the **SystemSoundID** cannot be returned to the caller. To get that value back from the function, you pass the address of a **SystemSoundID** variable to the function. This function then writes the value of the **SystemSoundID** to that location in memory. This is called *passing by reference* and allows the function to change the value of a variable.

```
void passByReference(int *intPointer)
{
    *intPointer = 5;
}
void passByValue(int intValue)
{
    intValue = 10;
}
void function()
{
    int value = 0;
    passByValue(value); // value still equal 0 here
    passByReference(&value); // value now equals 5
}
```

You will now implement code to play this sound when the appropriate button is tapped. Back in the MediaPlayerViewController.m, implement the method **playShortSound:**.

```
- (IBAction)playShortSound:(id)sender
{
    AudioServicesPlaySystemSound(shortSound);
}
```

Build and run your application. You should hear a pleasant noise every time you tap the Play Short Sound button. (Make sure your volume is turned up.) Most of the time, you will keep a system sound available the entire time an application is running. However, if you want to dispose of a short sound to free up memory while an application is running, you can call the C function **AudioServicesDisposeSystemSoundID**.

```
    AudioServicesDisposeSystemSoundID(aSystemSound);
```

On the iPhone (but not the iPad or iPod touch), you can use system sounds to vibrate the device. Add the following line of code to MediaPlayerViewController.m to trigger vibration.

```
- (IBAction)playShortSound:(id)sender
{
    AudioServicesPlaySystemSound(shortSound);
    AudioServicesPlaySystemSound(kSystemSoundID_Vibrate);
}
```

Build and run the application on an iPhone and tap the short sound button. It will play the sound and vibrate in your hand.

Playing Audio Files

Playing a compressed audio file is as simple as playing a short sound. To play a compressed audio format or a file that is longer than 30 seconds, you will use the class **AVAudioPlayer**. In addition to playing longer, compressed audio, this class also gives you much more control over audio playback. You will use an instance of this class to play an MP3 file. Locate the file Music.mp3 and add it to your Resources group. (This file and other resources can be downloaded from http://www.bignerdranch.com/solutions/iPhoneProgramming.zip.)

This class is defined in the AVFoundation framework. Add the AVFoundation framework to your project and import its header file into MediaPlayerViewController.h. Declare an instance variable of type **AVAudioPlayer**.

```
#import <AVFoundation/AVFoundation.h>

@interface MediaPlayerViewController : UIViewController <AVAudioPlayerDelegate>
{
    IBOutlet UIButton *audioButton;
    SystemSoundID shortSound;

    AVAudioPlayer *audioPlayer;
```

Once again, you will implement the set up for this form of media playing in
MediaPlayerViewController.m. Add the following code to the top of **init**.

```
- (id)init
{
    self = [super initWithNibName:@"MediaPlayerViewController" bundle:nil];

    NSString *musicPath = [[NSBundle mainBundle] pathForResource:@"Music"
                                                          ofType:@"mp3"];
    if (musicPath) {
        NSURL *musicURL = [NSURL fileURLWithPath:musicPath];
        audioPlayer = [[AVAudioPlayer alloc] initWithContentsOfURL:musicURL
                                                             error:nil];
        [audioPlayer setDelegate:self];
    }
```

And as before with the short sound, you will have the associated button begin
playback of the audioPlayer. Replace the implementation of the following method in
MediaPlayerViewController.m.

```
- (IBAction)playAudioFile:(id)sender
{
    if ([audioPlayer isPlaying]) {
        // Stop playing audio and change text of button
        [audioPlayer stop];
        [sender setTitle:@"Play Audio File"
                forState:UIControlStateNormal];
    }
    else {
        // Start playing audio and change text of button so
        // user can tap to stop playback
        [audioPlayer play];
        [sender setTitle:@"Stop Audio File"
                forState:UIControlStateNormal];
    }
}
```

Build and run the application. Tap the Play Audio File and listen for the sound.

With **AVAudioPlayer**, you have more control over the audio playback, and you can halt its
playback whenever you choose. You can also implement delegate methods for an **AVAudioPlayer**
that will allow you to control what happens when the audio player finishes playing or when it gets
interrupted.

When the audio player finishes, you will want to revert the title of the button that plays the audio file back to Play Audio File. Implement the delegate method for this in MediaPlayerViewController.m.

```
- (void)audioPlayerDidFinishPlaying:(AVAudioPlayer *)player
                    successfully:(BOOL)flag
{
    [audioButton setTitle:@"Play Audio File"
            forState:UIControlStateNormal];
}
```

Build and run the application. Let the audio file finish on its own and watch the playback button return to its original state when the file ends.

Audio playback will be interrupted when a phone call occurs. When the iPhone interrupts an **AVAudioPlayer** instance from playing, it pauses the music for you. You can also perform additional tasks with the delegate method **audioPlayerDidBeginInterruption:**, such as updating your user interface. Another delegate method, **audioPlayerEndInterruption:**, is sent to the **AVAudioPlayer**'s delegate when the phone call ends. Implement this method in MediaPlayerViewController.m.

```
- (void)audioPlayerEndInterruption:(AVAudioPlayer *)player
{
    [audioPlayer play];
}
```

Playing Movie Files

MPMoviePlayerController is responsible for playing movies on the iPhone. The YouTube application uses the same class to play its movies, so you've probably seen the interface before (Figure 20.5).

Figure 20.5   MPMoviePlayerController in action

Playing a movie file on the iPhone is fairly restricted. You are limited to two formats:

- H.264 Baseline Profile Level 3.0, up to 640 x 480 resolution at 30 frames per second

- MPEG-4 Part 2 video, Simple Profile

(Fortunately, iTunes has an option to convert video files into these formats. In iTunes, select a movie file and choose Create iPod or iPhone Version from the Advanced menu.)

Instances of **MPMoviePlayerController** can also play streaming video from a URL somewhere off in internet land. However, you should seriously consider the problems of this approach on a mobile device. If you have the choice, either bundle a movie file with the application or have your application download the video to the application sandbox after a user launches it. If you do not have the choice, be aware that Apple can reject your application if a video file is too large to be transported over the network in an appropriate amount of time. For example, your application can be rejected if it claims to support the original iPhone (using the Edge network) and streams video at more than 1MB per second.

In order to use **MPMoviePlayerController**, you must add yet another framework to your project. Add the MediaPlayer framework to your project and import the appropriate header file at the top of MediaPlayerViewController.h. Create an instance variable in **MediaPlayerViewController** for the movie player, as well.

```
#import <MediaPlayer/MediaPlayer.h>

@interface MediaPlayerViewController : UIViewController <AVAudioPlayerDelegate>
{
    MPMoviePlayerController *moviePlayer;
```

In this exercise, you will bundle the Layer.m4v movie with the application. Locate this file and add it to your project's Resources group. (This file and other resources can be downloaded from http://www.bignerdranch.com/solutions/iPhoneProgramming.zip.)

To load the movie, add the following code to the top of **init** in MediaPlayerViewController.m.

```
- (id)init
{
    self = [super initWithNibName:@"MediaPlayerViewController" bundle:nil];

    NSString *moviePath = [[NSBundle mainBundle] pathForResource:@"Layers"
                                                          ofType:@"m4v"];
    if (moviePath) {
        NSURL *movieURL = [NSURL fileURLWithPath:moviePath];
        moviePlayer = [[MPMoviePlayerController alloc]
                            initWithContentURL:movieURL];
    }
}
```

A **MPMoviePlayerController** has a view property. This view contains the movie and controls for playing that movie. When **MediaPlayerViewController**'s view finishes loading, you will add the moviePlayer's view to it. Override **viewDidLoad** in MediaPlayerViewController.m.

```
- (void)viewDidLoad
{
    [[self view] addSubview:[moviePlayer view]];
    float halfHeight = [[self view] bounds].size.height / 2.0;
    float width = [[self view] bounds].size.width;
    [[moviePlayer view] setFrame:CGRectMake(0, halfHeight, width, halfHeight)];
}
```

Build and run the application. The movie player will appear in the bottom half of the screen. You can tap the Play button within that view to begin playback. You can also tap the Fullscreen button to present that video in full-screen mode. Note that only one instance of **MPMoviePlayerController** can operate within an application. Therefore, you should not create multiple instances of **MPMoviePlayerController**. If your application intends to present a movie in multiple places, you should either reuse a single movie player controller or destroy movie player controllers that aren't being used and recreate them later.

If you wish to present a full-screen only video, you can use the class **MPMoviePlayerViewController** (notice the addition of *View* in the class name). This class inherits from **UIViewController** and manages a view that presents a movie. Instantiating a **MPMoviePlayerViewController** is just like instantiating a **MPMoviePlayerController**:

```
MPMoviePlayerViewController *playerViewController =
    [[MPMoviePlayerViewController alloc] initWithContentURL:movieURL];
```

To present the full-screen video on top of an existing view controller, you send the message **presentMoviePlayerViewControllerAnimated:** to a view controller that is currently on the screen.

```
[viewController presentMoviePlayerViewControllerAnimated:playerViewController];
```

Alternatively, you can add a **MPMoviePlayerViewController** to a tab bar or navigation controller.

Note that, internally, a **MPMoviePlayerViewController** uses a **MPMoviePlayerController**. Therefore, creating an instance of **MPMoviePlayerViewController** will invalidate any existing movie player controllers as you can only have one movie player at a time.

When you instantiate an **MPMoviePlayerController**, it immediately begins loading the video you ask it to. This loading happens on another thread so that your application does not halt while the video loads. A video loaded from disk will most likely be ready to play immediately, but one being streamed from the internet may take some time to load. You may not want to display an unloaded video right away. Therefore, you can register for a load state notifications to determine when you present a movie player's view on the screen. The loadState property of a movie player tells you whether or not the movie is playable, stalled or has enough data to not only play but the movie player can continue playing without interruption.

```
[[NSNotificationCenter defaultCenter]
    addObserver:self
        selector:@selector(displayPreloadedVideo:)
            name:MPMoviePlayerLoadStateDidChangeNotification
          object:moviePlayer];

- (void)displayPreloadedVideo:(NSNotification *)note
{
    MPMoviePlayerController *mp = [note object;
    if([mp loadState] == MPMovieLoadStatePlaythroughOK)
        [[self view] addSubview:[mp view]];
}
```

An instance of **MPMoviePlayerController** posts notifications for other events, too. Check out the documentation for the class to see all available notification names.

Now you can play any sort of media you like! Remember that audio and video files are relatively large compared to other resources you might have in an application. Gratuitous use of these types of resources may increase an application bundle's size and the amount of time it takes to download the application.

Background Processes

On iOS 4.0, applications can play audio even when they are not the active application. You will modify the MediaPlayer application so that it continues playing audio even when its interface is not on the screen.

By default, when the user presses the Home button, an application is put into the background state and then transitioned to the suspended state shortly thereafter. Audio playback cannot continue in the suspended state because no code can be executed. Your application can request to stay in the background state instead of transitioning to the suspended state by adding a key-value pair to the Info property list.

Open MediaPlayer-Info.plist. Add a new row to this file by selecting the last row and clicking the plus button (+) next to it. In the Key column of the new row, enter UIBackgroundModes. The

Key column will automatically update to display Required background modes and its value will become an array that has a single item.

Figure 20.6 Info property list with background audio mode

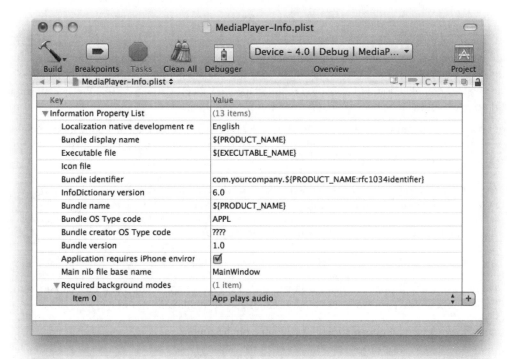

Click the disclosure tab next to the text Required background modes, and the items in the array will appear beneath it. There is currently one empty item. Enter the text audio in the value column and it will automatically update to display App plays audio.

An application registered for background audio will only continue playing audio of a certain *audio category*. Every application has a single instance of **AVAudioSession** that manages the category of audio it plays. This category determines whether an application silences other sounds on the device so it can record audio without noise, or play and record audio at the same time or, in this case, an continue playing audio in the background.

To change the audio session's category, you send it the message **setCategory:error:** with one of the defined constants. The category that allows an application to continue playing audio in the background is AVAudioSessionCategoryPlayback. Update the code in the **init** method of MediaPlayerViewController.m.

```
if(musicPath) {
    NSURL *musicURL = [NSURL fileURLWithPath:musicPath];
    [[AVAudioSession sharedInstance]
                setCategory:AVAudioSessionCategoryPlayback error:nil];
    audioPlayer = [[AVAudioPlayer alloc] initWithContentsOfURL:musicURL
                                                    error:nil];
    [audioPlayer setDelegate:self];
}
```

Build and run the application. Tap the button titled Play Audio File and then press the Home button. Notice how the track keeps playing even while you are in other applications. When the track ends, the application will transition to the suspended state. Also notice that the system sound will not play while in the background # that's just the way it is.

An application operating in the background is under more strict rules than an application in the foreground. Here are some general guidelines an application should follow when it is operating in the background:

- *Do not* use OpenGL ES or shared system resources (like the address book). The operating system will terminate your application if it notices you do either of these two things.

- *Do not* update your views, the user can't see them anyway.

- *Do* release unneeded memory, similar to when responding to a low-memory warning.

- *Do* throttle back the application's workload. For example, an application that plays audio in the background should perform just enough tasks to play the audio and nothing else.

- *Do* hide any personal information that is visible on the screen.

An application that runs in the background is still subject to termination by the operating system when memory gets low. The operating system will first issue a low memory warning to all applications in the active or background state. If there is still not enough memory available, the OS will start purging suspended applications. If a memory deficit still exists after suspended applications are purged, background applications are then terminated.

When an application that is running in the background is terminated, its delegate is gracefully sent the message **applicationWillTerminate:** and given a moment to perform any final tasks. However, you should still save any state information for a background application in the method **applicationDidEnterBackground:** to be sure.

Other forms of background execution

In addition to audio playback, there are two types of standard background execution: voice over internet protocol (VOIP) and location updates. You may add the location or voip to the **setCategory:error:** array in the info property list to configure your application to support these modes. VOIP is its own, very complicated process that is well outside the scope of this book. However, location updates (and the various possibilities for them) are worth discussion.

An application that is in the background (for any reason) will continue to receive location updates. As the location is updated, the delegate of the **CLLocationManager** is sent **locationManager:didUpdateToLocation:fromLocation:** as normal. You can specify that an application wants to remain in the background specifically for location updates by adding the location key to its UIBackgroundModes. An application that registers location as a background mode will remain in background mode as long as a **CLLocationManager** is actively updating its location.

However, continually updating the location while running in the background is a big drain on the battery. If your application doesn't require precise updates at frequent intervals, you can instead monitor for signification location changes. A significant location happens when the device switches to a new cell phone tower. (Cell phone towers in metropolitan areas are typically a quarter- to half-mile apart and two miles apart in more rural areas.)

The added benefit of monitoring for significant location changes is that even if your application is suspended, the operating system will briefly wake your application up in the background. When it is woken up, the location manager's delegate is sent the appropriate message so your application can handle the change in location. To enable significant location changes, send the message **startMonitoringSignificantLocationChanges** to an instance of **CLLocationManager** when it is instantiated.

```
CLLocationManager *manager = [[CLLocationManager alloc] init];
[manager startMonitoringSignificantLocationChanges];
```

While VOIP, audio playback and location updates are the standard fare for executing background tasks indefinitely, you may also have reason to temporarily stay in the background for longer. For example, an application downloading a file from the internet may want to finish downloading that file before it becomes suspended. You can ask the operating system for additional time to complete a background task with the **UIApplication**'s method **beginBackgroundTaskWithExpirationHandler:**.

The operating system may or may not give you additional time to complete the task depending on system constraints. The amount of time is never guaranteed. You should also never use this method to attempt to keep your application in the background just for the sake of keeping it in the background. It is rare that an application would need to use this method of background execution, therefore, we won't cover it extensively. If you are absolutely sure your application needs this functionality, consult the Executing Code in the Background section of the iPhone Application Programming Guide.

Low-level APIs

In this section, you have been exposed to the simplest, highest-level API for sound and video. If you plan to do a lot of audio work (either recording or playing), you should go deeper and learn about the audio queues, which are part of the AudioToolbox framework. You may also want to study Core Audio, the framework upon which all of this is built. In addition, in iOS 4.0 or later, you can use the Core Video framework for low-level video management.

Challenge: Audio Recording

You can also record audio with the iPhone SDK. Using the class **AVAudioRecorder**, record audio data and then play it back with a new button. (Remember, you can't write data to the application bundle.)

21

Web Services

A web service is an application that runs on a web server. An iPhone application can ask a web service to execute methods that the web service implements. Typically, a web service's methods will collect data from the iPhone application and store it in a database or return information from that database to the iPhone application (or both). The data transferred between a web service and a client application is typically formatted into XML or JSON format.

To work with a web service, an iPhone application must make a connection to a web server, transfer properly formatted data between the two, and parse any data returned.

Figure 21.1   TopSongs application

Break On Through - The Doors
Brown Eyed Girl - Van Morri...
Come On Eileen - Dexys Mid...
Hotel California - Eagles
Break On Through - The Doors
Jump Around - House of Pain
Layla - Eric Clapton
Dock of the Bay - Otis Redding

Creating the TopSongs Application

In this chapter, you will use the Cocoa Touch web service classes to pull data from a RSS feed. Apple publishes a number of RSS feeds that can be consumed. (You can see them all at `http://`

www.apple.com/rss/.) One of them keeps track of the top 10 downloaded songs from iTunes. The application you will write in this chapter will present a list of these songs.

Figure 21.2   TopSongs object diagram

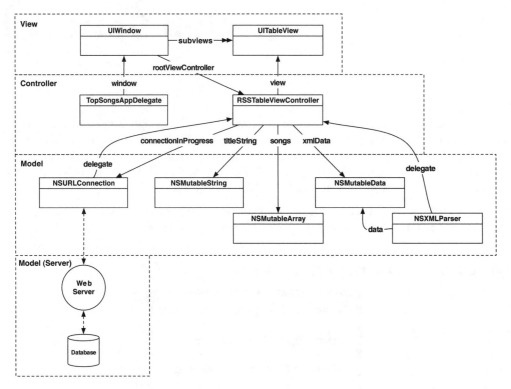

Create a new Window-Based Applicaton application and name it TopSongs. TopSongs will have a **UITableView** that shows the artist and title of each song.

Create a new **UIViewController** subclass and name it **RSSTableViewController**. (Remember: New File... from the File menu, select Cocoa Touch Class, then UIViewController subclass.)

RSSTableViewController will be responsible for fetching the song list, storing the song titles in an **NSMutableArray**, and presenting those titles in its tableView. In RSSTableViewController.h, add an instance variable for the array. (Also, change the superclass to **UITableViewController**.)

```
@interface RSSTableViewController : UITableViewController
{
    NSMutableArray *songs;
}
@end
```

Setting up the interface

Let's get the interface details out of the way before the fun stuff. In RSSTableViewController.m, override the designated initializer **initWithStyle:** to instantiate songs.

```
- (id)initWithStyle:(UITableViewStyle)style
{
    if (self = [super initWithStyle:style]) {
        songs = [[NSMutableArray alloc] init];
    }
    return self;
}
```

Implement the data source methods to return cells that have the textLabel displaying the NSString instances that will be held in songs.

```
- (NSInteger)tableView:(UITableView *)tableView
 numberOfRowsInSection:(NSInteger)section
{
    return [songs count];
}
- (UITableViewCell *)tableView:(UITableView *)tableView
        cellForRowAtIndexPath:(NSIndexPath *)indexPath
{
    UITableViewCell *cell =
            [tableView dequeueReusableCellWithIdentifier:@"UITableViewCell"];
    if (cell == nil) {
        cell = [[[UITableViewCell alloc]
                    initWithStyle:UITableViewCellStyleDefault
                  reuseIdentifier:@"UITableViewCell"] autorelease];
    }

    [[cell textLabel] setText:[songs objectAtIndex:[indexPath row]]];

    return cell;
}
```

In TopSongsAppDelegate.m, instantiate an **RSSTableViewController** and set it as the root view controller of the window. (Don't forget to import RSSTableViewController.h.)

```
#import "TopSongsAppDelegate.h"
#import "RSSTableViewController.h"

@implementation TopSongsAppDelegate

@synthesize window;
- (BOOL)application:(UIApplication *)application
    didFinishLaunchingWithOptions:(NSDictionary *)launchOptions
{
    RSSTableViewController *tvc = [[[RSSTableViewController alloc]
                        initWithStyle:UITableViewStylePlain] autorelease];
    [window setRootViewController:tvc];

    [window makeKeyAndVisible];
    return YES;
}
```

Build and run the application. You should see an empty table view on the screen.

Also, note that, in this application, we don't keep a pointer to the instance of **RSSTableViewController** anywhere. Some of the other applications in this book do the same thing: we instantiate a view controller in the application delegate, and then the application delegate forgets that the view controller ever existed. (There is no instance variable for the view controller in the application delegate.)

Some programmers keep pointers to their view controller objects in the application delegate. Other objects then access these view controllers by doing something like this:

```
TopSongsAppDelegate *del = [[UIApplication sharedApplication] delegate];
RSSTableViewController *tvc = [del rssTableViewController];
```

This is bad. In a well-designed application, the application delegate is not responsible for passing around controller objects. If you find yourself needing to ask the application delegate for a reference to a view controller, you may need to re-think the design of your application. Page through this book and study the object diagrams for each exercise for an example of how to architect an application.

The only reason you would keep a pointer to a view controller in the application delegate is if a view controller needs to be sent messages when an application event occurs. For example, if a view controller has model objects that need to be written to disk when the application terminates, the application delegate will have an instance variable that points to the view controller. Then, you can send messages to that view controller in the method **applicationWillTerminate:**.

Fetching Data From a URL

Now you are going to fetch some data from a web server. To help with this process, there are three classes: **NSURL**, **NSURLRequest**, and **NSURLConnection** (Figure 21.3).

Figure 21.3   Relationship of web service classes

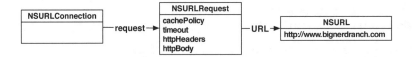

Each of these classes has an important role in communicating with a web server:

- **NSURL** instances contain the location of the web application in URL format. For simple web services, the URL will be composed of the base address, the web application you are communicating with, and any arguments that are being passed.

- **NSURLRequest** instances hold all the data necessary to communicate with a web server. This includes an **NSURL** object, as well as a caching policy, a limit on how long you will give the web server to respond, and additional data passed through the HTTP protocol. (**NSMutableURLRequest** is the mutable subclass of **NSURLRequest**.)

- **NSURLConnection** instances are responsible for actually making the connection to a web server, sending the information in its **NSURLRequest**, and gathering the response from the server.

Open RSSTableViewController.h and add two instance variables and a method declaration:

```
#import <UIKit/UIKit.h>

@interface RSSTableViewController : UITableViewController
{
    NSMutableArray *songs;
    NSMutableData *xmlData;
    NSURLConnection *connectionInProgress;
}
- (void)loadSongs;
@end
```

Working with NSURLConnection

NSURLConnection instances can communicate with a web server in two ways: synchronously or asynchronously. Because passing data back and forth between a remote server can take some time, synchronous connections are generally frowned upon as they will stall your application until the connection completes.

Therefore, this chapter will teach you how to perform an asynchronous connection with **NSURLConnection**. When an instance of **NSURLConnection** is created, it needs to know the location of the web application and the data it is passing to that web server. It also needs a delegate. When told to start communicating with the web server, **NSURLConnection** will initiate a connection to the location, begin passing it data, and possibly receive data back. Its delegate will be updated along the way with information you can use.

In RSSTableViewController.m, implement the **loadSongs** method to create an **NSURLRequest** and a connection to the web server in that request. The **NSURLRequest** will ask the http://ax.itunes.apple.com website for the top 10 songs in XML format, and the **NSURLConnection** instance makes the connection.

```
- (void)loadSongs
{
    // In case the view will appear multiple times,
    // clear the song list (In case you add this to an application
    // that has multiple view controllers... )
    [songs removeAllObjects];
    [[self tableView] reloadData];

    // Construct the web service URL
    NSURL *url = [NSURL URLWithString:@"http://ax.itunes.apple.com/"
                @"WebObjects/MZStoreServices.woa/ws/RSS/topsongs/"
                @"limit=10/xml"];

    // Create a request object with that URL
    NSURLRequest *request =
            [NSURLRequest requestWithURL:url
                            cachePolicy:NSURLRequestReloadIgnoringCacheData
                        timeoutInterval:30];
```

```
    // Clear out the existing connection if there is one
    if (connectionInProgress) {
        [connectionInProgress cancel];
        [connectionInProgress release];
    }

    // Instantiate the object to hold all incoming data
    [xmlData release];
    xmlData = [[NSMutableData alloc] init];

    // Create and initiate the connection - non-blocking
    connectionInProgress = [[NSURLConnection alloc] initWithRequest:request
                                                           delegate:self
                                                    startImmediately:YES];
}
```

Kick off the loading whenever **RSSTableViewController**'s table view appears on the screen by overriding **viewWillAppear:** in RSSTableViewController.m.

```
- (void)viewWillAppear:(BOOL)animated
{
    [super viewWillAppear:animated];
    [self loadSongs];
}
```

Build the application to make sure there are no syntax errors. This code, as it stands, will make the connection to the web service and retrieve the top 10 songs. However, there is one problem: you don't see those songs anywhere. You need to implement some of the delegate methods for **NSURLConnection** to collect the XML document returned from this request.

The delegate of an **NSURLConnection** is responsible for overseeing the connection and collecting the data returned from the request. (This data is typically an XML or JSON document; for this specific web service, it is XML.) However, the data returned usually comes back in pieces. The delegate needs to collect the pieces and put them together. Implement the following method in RSSTableViewController.m to put all of the data received by the connection into the instance variable xmlData.

```
// This method will be called several times as the data arrives
- (void)connection:(NSURLConnection *)connection didReceiveData:(NSData *)data
{
    [xmlData appendData:data];
}
```

When a connection has finished retrieving all of the data from a web service, it then sends the message **connectionDidFinishLoading:** to its delegate. In this method, you are guaranteed to have the complete response from the web service request and can start working with that data. For now, just print out the string representation of that data to the console to make sure good stuff is coming back. Implement this method in RSSTableViewController.m.

```
- (void)connectionDidFinishLoading:(NSURLConnection *)connection
{
    // We are just checking to make sure we are getting the XML
    NSString *xmlCheck = [[[NSString alloc] initWithData:xmlData
                                         encoding:NSUTF8StringEncoding]
                                         autorelease];
    NSLog(@"xmlCheck = %@", xmlCheck);
}
```

There is a possibility that a connection will fail. If an instance of **NSURLConnection** cannot make a connection to a web service, it will tell its delegate through the message **connection:didFailWithError:**. Note that this message gets sent for a *connection* failure, like having no internet connectivity or a server that doesn't exist. For other types of errors, like the data sent to a web service is in the wrong format, information will be returned in **connection:didReceiveData:**. Implement the following delegate method to inform your application of a connection failure in RSSTableViewController.m.

```
- (void)connection:(NSURLConnection *)connection
  didFailWithError:(NSError *)error
{
    [connectionInProgress release];
    connectionInProgress = nil;

    [xmlData release];
    xmlData = nil;

    NSString *errorString = [NSString stringWithFormat:@"Fetch failed: %@",
                            [error localizedDescription]];
    UIActionSheet *actionSheet =
          [[UIActionSheet alloc] initWithTitle:errorString
                                      delegate:nil
                             cancelButtonTitle:@"OK"
                        destructiveButtonTitle:nil
                             otherButtonTitles:nil];
    [actionSheet showInView:[[self view] window]];
    [actionSheet autorelease];
}
```

Try building and running your application. You should see the XML results in the console. If you put your device in Airplane Mode (or it is not connected to a network), you should see a friendly error message when you try to fetch again.

Parsing XML

Now you're going to parse the XML that has come back using the class **NSXMLParser**. You're going to create the parser, give it a delegate, and tell it to start. As the parser reads through the data, it will send messages to its delegate like "Hey, I just started a new element!" and "Hey, I just read some text!"

In **connectionDidFinishLoading:**, delete the code you wrote to log the XML and replace it with code to kick off the parsing and set its delegate to point at the instance of **RSSTableViewController**.

```
- (void)connectionDidFinishLoading:(NSURLConnection *)connection
{
    // Create the parser object with the data received from the web service
    NSXMLParser *parser = [[NSXMLParser alloc] initWithData:xmlData];

    // Give it a delegate
    [parser setDelegate:self];

    // Tell it to start parsing - the document will be parsed and
    // the delegate of NSXMLParser will get all of its delegate messages
    // sent to it before this line finishes execution - it is blocking
    [parser parse];

    // The parser is done (it blocks until done), you can release it immediately
    [parser release];
    [[self tableView] reloadData];
}
```

In RSSTableViewController.h, add the NSXMLParserDelegate protocol to the class declaration.

```
@interface RSSTableViewController : UITableViewController
    <NSXMLParserDelegate>
```

As the text within an XML tag is read, you may get many delegate methods that contain pieces of the text in that element. You will, however, want all the chunks of useful data gathered into one string. So, declare a mutable string instance variable in RSSTableViewController.h:

```
@interface RSSTableViewController : UITableViewController
    <NSXMLParserDelegate>
{
    NSMutableString *titleString;
    NSMutableArray *songs;
    NSMutableData *xmlData;
    NSURLConnection *connectionInProgress;
}
- (void)loadSongs;
@end
```

Now implement the delegate methods in RSSTableViewController.m. The XML data contains a number of entry elements. Each entry refers to one song and within that element are more elements that hold information about the song: its title, the iTunes Store link to it, an image representing it, and more. This application will grab the title of each song entry and put it in the array songs. Therefore, when the delegate is informed of a new element, check to see if it is a title element and prepare an **NSMutableString** to collect the text within it. Implement the following delegate method in RSSTableViewController.m.

```
- (void)parser:(NSXMLParser *)parser
didStartElement:(NSString *)elementName
   namespaceURI:(NSString *)namespaceURI
  qualifiedName:(NSString *)qName
     attributes:(NSDictionary *)attributeDict
```

```
{
    if ([elementName isEqual:@"title"]) {
        NSLog(@"found title!");
        titleString = [[NSMutableString alloc] init];
    }
}
```

This method has a lot of arguments. For this application, only elementName is of any use. However, if you are interested in the other elements in this XML document, you can check the values of these parameters to further qualify the element.

Once inside an element, the parser will read the string data and pass it to its delegate through the message **parser:foundCharacters:**. This method may get called multiple times for a single title. Implement this method to append the newly found characters to the titleString.

```
- (void)parser:(NSXMLParser *)parser
    foundCharacters:(NSString *)string
{
    [titleString appendString:string];
}
```

Notice that in this method there is no parameter for the name of the element that the characters appeared in. It is up to you to set any needed state in the method that informs the delegate of the start of a tag (the method you implemented before this one). In this application, titleString is nil unless a title tag was found. Therefore, when **parser:foundCharacters:** is sent to the instance of **RSSTableViewController**, the characters in a title element are stored while others are ignored. (Messages to nil do nothing.)

When an element is finished, the delegate is informed with the following message. Implement this method so that it takes the text found in the title element and adds the final string to songs.

```
- (void)parser:(NSXMLParser *)parser
 didEndElement:(NSString *)elementName
  namespaceURI:(NSString *)namespaceURI
 qualifiedName:(NSString *)qName
{
    if ([elementName isEqual:@"title"]) {
        NSLog(@"ended title: %@", titleString);
        [songs addObject:titleString];

        // Release and nil titleString so that the next time characters
        // are found and not within a title tag, they are ignored
        [titleString release];
        titleString = nil;
    }
}
```

Build and run the application. After a moment of running, the top 10 downloaded songs will appear on the screen. Now you can conform to popular culture in iPhone style.

There is one little issue left to resolve. The first "song" that appears on the list is actually not a song at all: it is the title of the RSS feed. All entry elements contain a title element, but the top-level element, feed, also has a title element. You will check to make sure that title elements are only read from entry elements. In RSSTableViewController.h, add an instance variable to keep track of whether the parser is reading an entry element.

```
@interface RSSTableViewController : UITableViewController
    <NSXMLParserDelegate>
{
    BOOL waitingForEntryTitle;
```

Right now, when a title element begins, you instantiate an **NSMutableString** so that any characters found in this element are added to it. When the element ends, that string is added to the list of songs. Instead of doing this for every title element, you will make sure that you are currently inside an entry element. Add the following code to **parser:didStartElement:namespaceURI:qualifiedName:attributes:** in RSSTableViewController.m.

```
- (void)parser:(NSXMLParser *)parser
didStartElement:(NSString *)elementName
  namespaceURI:(NSString *)namespaceURI
 qualifiedName:(NSString *)qName
    attributes:(NSDictionary *)attributeDict
{
    if([elementName isEqual:@"entry"]) {
        NSLog(@"Found a song entry");
        waitingForEntryTitle = YES;
    }
    if ([elementName isEqual:@"title"] && waitingForEntryTitle) {
        NSLog(@"found title!");
        titleString = [[NSMutableString alloc] init];
    }
}
```

Now, when an entry element begins, waitingForEntryTitle is set to YES and a subsequent title element will be collected. Therefore, when a entry element ends, you will revoke permission for **RSSTableViewController** to create a new titleString. Add the following code in RSSTableViewController.m.

```
- (void)parser:(NSXMLParser *)parser
 didEndElement:(NSString *)elementName
  namespaceURI:(NSString *)namespaceURI
 qualifiedName:(NSString *)qName
{
    if ([elementName isEqual:@"title"] && waitingForEntryTitle) {
        NSLog(@"ended title: %@", titleString);
        [songs addObject:titleString];
        [titleString release];
        titleString = nil;
    }
    if ([elementName isEqual:@"entry"]) {
        NSLog(@"ended a song entry");
        waitingForEntryTitle = NO;
    }
}
```

Build and run the application again. You will see the top 10 songs and nothing more.

There are a few more things worth mentioning about web services and parsing XML:

- There is no one generic solution for communicating with web servers. In the real world, a web service will have specific requirements for parameter submission. It is up to you, the developer, to read the documentation for any web service you plan on using and to provide the expected format.

- You have implemented only three of the XML parser delegate methods; there are seventeen others. Not all XML is this simple, so remember to check the documentation for the **NSXMLParser** class if you need to handle more intricate areas of XML parsing.

- In this chapter, you made a simple request and cherry-picked the resulting XML for the data you wanted. Some applications, however, will need to do more with the returned XML. This can require building up a class hierarchy to be used later. (Note that there is no tree-based XML parser in the iPhone SDK, and you will have to implement your own if you need that type of object hierarchy.)

For the More Curious: The Request Body

Sometimes, especially when dealing with SOAP web services, you will need to pack data (usually XML) into the body of the URL request. To do this, you'll need to use **NSMutableURLRequest**, a subclass of **NSURLRequest**.

```
NSURL *someURL = ...;
NSString *xmlString = ...;
NSData *data = [xmlString dataUsingEncoding:NSUTF8StringEncoding];
NSMutableURLRequest *req =
    [NSMutableURLRequest requestWithURL:someURL
                            cachePolicy:NSURLRequestReloadIgnoringCacheData
                        timeoutInterval:90];
[req setHTTPBody:data];
[req setHTTPMethod:@"POST"];
```

Creating a general-purpose solution to all SOAP-based web services is difficult, but solving the problem for a *specific* SOAP-based web service is not too tricky. Just get the person who wrote the web service to send you an example of the XML in a request and the resulting response XML.

Challenge: More Data

Create another **UIViewController** subclass that will display more of the data for each song entry. When one of the songs is selected, push that view controller onto the screen.

For the More Curious: Credentials

When you try to access a web service, sometimes it will respond with a "Who the heck are you?" This is known as an *authentication challenge*. You then need to send a username and password (a *credential*) before the challenge sender will send its genuine response.

There are objects to represent these ideas. When the challenge is received, your connection delegate is sent a message that includes an instance of **NSURLAuthenticationChallenge**. The sender of that challenge conforms to the NSURLAuthenticationChallengeSender protocol. If you want the data, you give the challenge sender an instance of **NSURLCredential**. It typically looks something like this:

```
- (void)connection:(NSURLConnection *)conn
 didReceiveAuthenticationChallenge:(NSURLAuthenticationChallenge *)challenge
{
    // Have I already failed at least once?
    if ([challenge previousFailureCount] > 0) {

        // Why did I fail?
        NSError *failure = [challenge error];
        NSLog(@"Can't authenticate: %@", [error localizedDescription]);

        // Give up
        [[challenge sender] cancelAuthenticationChallenge:challenge];
        return;
    }

    // Create a credential
    NSURLCredential *newCred =
            [NSURLCredential credentialWithUser:@"sid"
                                       password:@"MomIsCool"
                             persistence:NSURLCredentialPersistenceNone];

    // Supply the credential to the sender of the challenge
    [[challenge sender] useCredential:newCred
            forAuthenticationChallenge:challenge];
}
```

If you are dealing with a more secure and sophisticated web service, it may want a certificate (or certificates) to confirm your identity. Most, however, just want a username and a password.

Credentials can have persistence. There are three possibilities:

- When you supply NSURLCredentialPersistenceNone, you are saying to the URL loading system, "Forget this credential as soon as you use it."

- When you supply NSURLCredentialPersistenceForSession, you are saying to the URL loading system, "Forget this credential when this application terminates."

- When you supply NSURLCredentialPersistencePermanent, you are saying to the URL loading system, "Put this credential in my keychain so that other applications can use it."

22

Address Book

Any application can access the iPhone's contact database. You can read from and write to that database, and you also have access to the interface elements of the Address Book. In this chapter, you will add Address Book support to your Homepwner application. In particular, you will specify which contact in your address book will inherit a possession in the case of your death.

Figure 22.1 Homepwner with Address Book

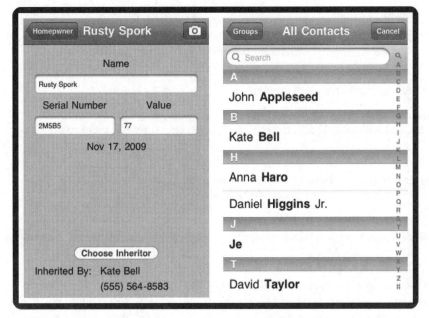

The People Picker

To get a person-picking interface like the Contacts application, you will use
ABPeoplePickerNavigationController.

Open Homepwner.xcodeproj, and add both AddressBook.framework and
AddressBookUI.framework, as shown in Figure 22.2. The first framework is for low-level Address Book operations that manipulate the data that is stored in the Address Book. The AddressBookUI framework is the code for the interface elements of the Address Book.

Figure 22.2   Framework list

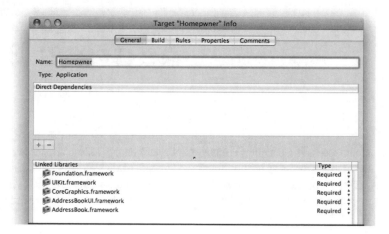

Shortly, you will add a button and three labels to the **ItemDetailViewController**'s view. Because the view is being created in a XIB file, you will need outlets for two of the labels and an action for the button. Add the following declarations the ItemDetailViewController.h.

```
#import <AddressBookUI/AddressBookUI.h>

@interface ItemDetailViewController : UIViewController
    <UINavigationControllerDelegate, UIImagePickerControllerDelegate>
{
    ...

    IBOutlet UILabel *inheritorNameField;
    IBOutlet UILabel *inheritorNumberField;
}
- (IBAction)chooseInheritor:(id)sender;
...
@end
```

Save this file and open ItemDetailViewController.xib in Interface Builder. You will start to run out of room on this **UIView** as you add the necessary subviews. It is difficult to position the objects when you know that a **UINavigationBar** is going to shift them all down during runtime. To simulate the interface as it will appear with a navigation bar, select the View in the doc window. In the Attributes tab of the Inspector, change the Top Bar popup button in the Simulated User Interface Elements section. Set this to Navigation Bar instead of None, as shown in Figure 22.3. (By default, the simulated Status Bar will be set to Gray — the default for an application.)

Figure 22.3 Simulating the Navigation Bar

This won't change the view itself, but it will show you how much space you have to work with if there is a **UINavigationBar** on screen the same time as this view.

Drag three **UILabel** instances and a **UIButton** onto the View and position them as shown in Figure 22.4. Then connect the outlets from File's Owner to the labels and set the **UIButton**'s target-action pair to File's Owner's **chooseInheritor:** method.

Figure 22.4 Additions to ItemDetailViewController

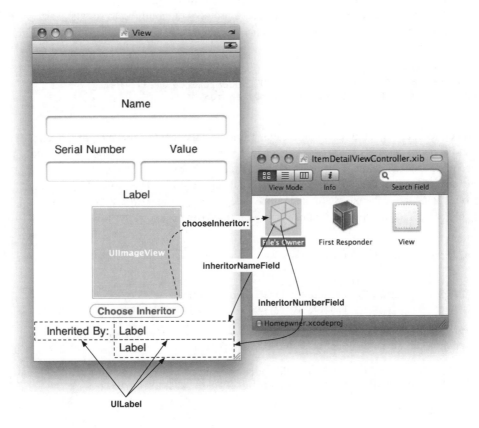

Save the XIB file and return to Xcode. You will implement the method **chooseInheritor:** to lazily create an instance of **ABPeoplePickerNavigationController** and present it modally on the screen. This is the same technique you used to show the camera interface in an earlier exercise. Enter the action method for the button in ItemDetailViewController.m.

```
- (void)chooseInheritor:(id)sender
{
    // Allocate a people picker object
    ABPeoplePickerNavigationController *peoplePicker
                = [[ABPeoplePickerNavigationController alloc] init];

    // Put that people picker on the screen
    [self presentModalViewController:peoplePicker animated:YES];

    [peoplePicker release];
}
```

Build and run the application. Tap the Choose Inheritor button. A list of all the contacts stored on the device will slide onto the screen. It's stuck on this screen, though, because you have yet to implement the delegate methods for **ABPeoplePickerNavigationController**. This class, from the AddressBookUI framework, will show the user's contacts database.

First, declare that that **ItemDetailViewController** conforms to the ABPeoplePickerNavigationControllerDelegate protocol (a mouthful, to say the least). Add the following declaration to ItemDetailViewController.h.

```
@interface ItemDetailViewController : UIViewController
    <UINavigationControllerDelegate, UIImagePickerControllerDelegate,
    ABPeoplePickerNavigationControllerDelegate>
```

When you want an object to receive messages from the **ABPeoplePickerNavigationController**, you set the people picker's peoplePickerDelegate property. Why call it peoplePickerDelegate instead of delegate? **ABPeoplePickerNavigationController** is a subclass of **UINavigationController**, which can also have a delegate object. Therefore, the navigation controller behavior of the people picker can be delegated to another object. Set the people picker's peoplePickerDelegate to the **ItemDetailViewController** instance after it is created.

```
- (void)chooseInheritor:(id)sender
{
    // Allocate a people picker object
    ABPeoplePickerNavigationController *peoplePicker
                = [[ABPeoplePickerNavigationController alloc] init];

    // Give our people picker a delegate so we can respond to messages
    [peoplePicker setPeoplePickerDelegate:self];

    // Put that people picker on the screen
    [self presentModalViewController:peoplePicker animated:YES];

    [peoplePicker release];
}
```

The ABPeoplePickerNavigationControllerDelegate protocol has three methods, and all three are required. The first method is **peoplePickerNavigationControllerDidCancel:**. This message is sent to the peoplePickerDelegate when the Cancel button is tapped on the people picker's view. You will just dismiss the people picker from the screen when this message is sent. Implement the method in ItemDetailViewController.m.

```
- (void)peoplePickerNavigationControllerDidCancel:
    (ABPeoplePickerNavigationController *)aPeoplePicker
{
    // Take people picker off the screen
    [self dismissModalViewControllerAnimated:YES];
}
```

Build and run the application. You'll get two warnings that say you haven't fully implemented the ABPeoplePickerNavigationControllerDelegate, but ignore them for now. Tap the Choose Inheritor button and then tap the Cancel button on top of **ABPeoplePickerNavigationController**. It will slide off the screen now. Easy enough, right?

Additions to Possession Class

In order for this application to work properly, the **Possession** class must have variables for the name and phone number of the inheritor. It also needs to know how to encode and decode these two variables. In Possession.h, add these instance variables and the properties for them.

```
@interface Possession : NSObject <NSCoding>
{
    ...

    NSString *inheritorName, *inheritorNumber;
}
@property (nonatomic, copy) NSString *inheritorName;
@property (nonatomic, copy) NSString *inheritorNumber;
```

In Possession.m, handle the lifetime of each of these instance variables. First, synthesize them.

```
@implementation Possession
@synthesize inheritorName, inheritorNumber;
```

Then allow them to be unarchived by decoding them in **initWithCoder:**.

```
- (id)initWithCoder:(NSCoder *)decoder
{
    self = [super init];

    [self setPossessionName:[decoder decodeObjectForKey:@"possessionName"]];
    [self setSerialNumber:[decoder decodeObjectForKey:@"serialNumber"]];
    [self setValueInDollars:[decoder decodeIntForKey:@"valueInDollars"]];
    [self setImageKey:[decoder decodeObjectForKey:@"imageKey"]];
    dateCreated = [[decoder decodeObjectForKey:@"dateCreated"] retain];
```

```
    thumbnailData = [[decoder decodeObjectForKey:@"thumbnailData"] retain];

    [self setInheritorName:[decoder decodeObjectForKey:@"inheritorName"]];
    [self setInheritorNumber:[decoder decodeObjectForKey:@"inheritorNumber"]];

    return self;
}
```

For them to be decoded, you need to encode them in the first place. Add these lines to
encodeWithCoder:.

```
- (void)encodeWithCoder:(NSCoder *)encoder
{
    // For each instance variable, archive it under its variable name
    [encoder encodeObject:possessionName forKey:@"possessionName"];
    [encoder encodeObject:serialNumber forKey:@"serialNumber"];
    [encoder encodeInt:valueInDollars forKey:@"valueInDollars"];
    [encoder encodeObject:dateCreated forKey:@"dateCreated"];
    [encoder encodeObject:imageKey forKey:@"imageKey"];
    [encoder encodeObject:thumbnailData forKey:@"thumbnailData"];

    // Put new inheritor data in to an archive
    [encoder encodeObject:inheritorName forKey:@"inheritorName"];
    [encoder encodeObject:inheritorNumber forKey:@"inheritorNumber"];
}
```

And finally, release the new instance variables in the **dealloc** method.

```
- (void)dealloc
{
    [thumbnail release];
    [thumbnailData release];
    [possessionName release];
    [serialNumber release];
    [dateCreated release];
    [imageKey release];
    [inheritorName release];
    [inheritorNumber release];
    [super dealloc];
}
```

Address Book Functions

Now that **Possession** instances have a place for the inheritor's name and number, you can retrieve
that information from the **ABPeoplePickerNavigationController** and add them to a possession.

When the people picker first appears on the screen, it lists all of the contacts in
the Address Book by name. When one of these contacts is selected, the message
peoplePickerNavigationController:shouldContinueAfterSelectingPerson: is sent to its
peoplePickerDelegate. This message's parameters contains an **ABRecordRef**. An **ABRecordRef**
stores all of the information for one contact.

You're going to use the C functions in the AddressBook framework to access the properties of an **ABRecordRef**. To get a property from a record, you will copy the value for one of its pre-defined properties. A property, in the context of the Address Book, is a constant. For example, the name of the property for the first name of a record is kABPersonFirstNameProperty. There are many different properties that an **ABRecordRef** can store a value for. (You can also create your own properties.)

You can think of an **ABRecordRef** as an **NSDictionary**. The properties are the keys, and the values are, well, the values. When you want a value, you will copy it to a variable by using the function **ABRecordCopyValue**. Because the AddressBook is a collection of C functions, the objects returned by this method are not Objective-C objects.

You can get the name and phone number out of the **ABRecordRef** passed to this delegate method. Implement the following method in ItemDetailViewController.m.

```
- (BOOL)peoplePickerNavigationController:(ABPeoplePickerNavigationController *)p
    shouldContinueAfterSelectingPerson:(ABRecordRef)person
{
    // Get the first and last name from the selected person
    NSString *firstName = (NSString *)ABRecordCopyValue(person,
                                          kABPersonFirstNameProperty);
    NSString *lastName = (NSString *)ABRecordCopyValue(person,
                                          kABPersonLastNameProperty);

    // Get all of the phone numbers for this selected person
    ABMultiValueRef numbers = ABRecordCopyValue(person, kABPersonPhoneProperty);

    // Make sure we have at least one phone number for this person
    if (ABMultiValueGetCount(numbers) > 0) {
        // Grab the first phone number we see
        CFStringRef number = ABMultiValueCopyValueAtIndex(numbers, 0);
        // Add that phone number to the possession object we are editing
        [editingPossession setInheritorNumber:(NSString *)number];
        // Set the on screen UILabel to this phone number
        [inheritorNumberField setText:(NSString *)number];

        // We used "Copy" to get this value, we need to manually release it
        CFRelease(number);
    }

    // Create a string with first and last name together - full name
    // Ignore last or first name if it is null
    NSString *name = [NSString stringWithFormat:@"%@ %@",
            (firstName ? firstName : @""),
            (lastName ? lastName : @"")];
    [editingPossession setInheritorName:name];

    // Manually release all copied objects
    [firstName release];
    [lastName release];
    CFRelease(numbers);

    // Update onscreen UILabel
    [inheritorNameField setText:name];
```

```
// Get people picker object off the screen
[self dismissModalViewControllerAnimated:YES];

// Do not perform default functionality (which is go to detailed page)
return NO;
}
```

If you remember that **CFStringRef** is toll-free bridged with **NSString**, most of this code becomes self-explanatory. Just note that the word **Copy** in the C functions for getting values from an **ABRecordRef** means you are responsible for releasing these variables using **CFRelease**. (Or, if you cast them to an **NSString**, you can send them the message **release**. If you leave them as **CFStringRef**, it's important to know that, just as with any Core Foundation object, you can't call **CFRelease** on NULL.)

Some values of an **ABRecordRef** are *multi-values*. The kABPersonPhoneProperty is a multi-value, which works a lot like an array. An **ABMultiValueRef** contains an ordered list of items. Each one of these items has a value and a label (Figure 22.5). For the kABPersonPhoneProperty, the value of an item is the phone number itself (as a string), and the label is the location of that number (home, mobile, office, etc., also as a string). In this code, you made sure there is at least one number for this contact before accessing the first number in the multi-value.

Figure 22.5   ABMultiValue

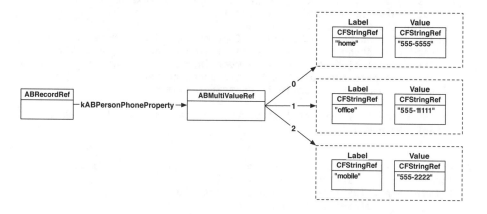

Many properties of an **ABRecordRef** are multi-values, and they aren't always strings. The documentation will give you all the information you need for each standard Address Book property.

Build and run the application. Tap the Choose Inheritor button and then one of the contacts from the list. The name and phone number of that person will now appear on the **ItemDetailViewController** page, as shown in Figure 22.6. When you exit the application, this information will get archived. Your possessions now have a home if bad things happen to you.

Figure 22.6 ItemDetailViewController with Inheritor

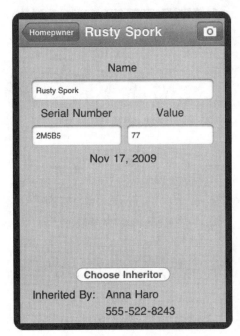

To update the two new inheritor labels when **ItemDetailViewController**'s view appears on the screen, place these two lines at the end of **viewWillAppear:** in ItemDetailViewController.m.

```
    [inheritorNameField setText:[editingPossession inheritorName]];
    [inheritorNumberField setText:[editingPossession inheritorNumber]];
}
```

Build and run the application. You can now set, view, and archive the beneficiary of a **Possession** instance.

For the More Curious: That Other Delegate Method

The compiler still has a complaint about not implementing the last method in ABPeoplePickerNavigationControllerDelegate, **peoplePickerNavigationController: shouldContinueAfterSelectingPerson:property:identifier:**. While you don't need this method in this application, we will talk about it anyway. When the people picker is on the screen, the user can tap a contact, and the delegate is sent the message **peoplePickerNavigationController:shouldContinueAfterSelectingPerson:**. That method returns a boolean value for whether the people picker should continue. If you returned YES (and didn't dismiss the modal view controller), a detailed page for the selected contact will appear (Figure 22.7).

Figure 22.7   Address Book detail page

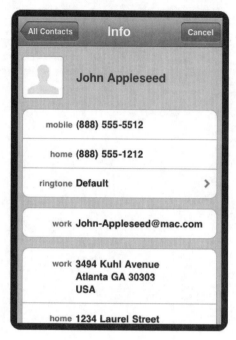

When that detailed page is on the screen and the user selects one of the fields (like a phone number), a message is sent to the people picker delegate:

```
- (BOOL)peoplePickerNavigationController:(ABPeoplePickerNavigationController *)p
     shouldContinueAfterSelectingPerson:(ABRecordRef)person
                               property:(ABPropertyID)property
                             identifier:(ABMultiValueIdentifier)identifier
{
    // Perform default functionality (like dial phone number, send email)
    return YES;
}
```

When this method returns YES, the action for the selected field takes place. With a phone number, the Phone application takes over and dials it. For an e-mail address, the Mail application opens a new message to that address. The last two parameters sent with this message are the property that was selected (the phone property, for example) and the identifier if the selected field is part of an **ABMultiValueRef** (the identifier would be something like "mobile" or "home" for the phone property).

You can implement this method as above in ItemDetailViewController.m to get rid of the final warning about not implementing the people picker protocol.

23

Localization

The appeal of the iPhone is global — iPhone users live in many different countries and speak many different languages. You can ensure that your application is ready for this global audience through the processes of internationalization and localization. Internationalization is making sure your native cultural information is not hard-coded into your application. (By cultural information, we mean language, currency, date formats, number formats, and more.) Localization, on the other hand, is providing the appropriate data in your application based on the user's Language and Region Format settings. You can find these settings in the Settings application by selecting the General row and then the International row.

Figure 23.1   International Settings

Incredibly, Apple makes these processes simple. An application that takes advantage of the localization APIs does not even need to be recompiled to be distributed in other languages or regions. (By the way, internationalization and localization are big words. Commonly, they are abbreviated to i18n and L10n, respectively. In order to prevent confusion, I will type out the full words. But you owe me a beer at the next WWDC.)

Internationalization using NSLocale

In this chapter, you're going to to localize the possession detail view of Homepwner. In this first section, you will use the class **NSLocale** to internationalize the currency symbol for a value of a possession and the format of the date on which it was created.

NSLocale knows how different regions display symbols, dates, and decimals and whether they use the metric system. **NSLocale** instances represent one region's settings for these variables. In the Settings application, the user can choose a region like United States or United Kingdom. (Why does Apple use "region" instead of "country"? Some countries have more than one region with different settings. Scroll through the options in Region Format to see for yourself.)

When you send the message **currentLocale** to **NSLocale**, the instance of **NSLocale** that represents the user's region choice is returned. Once you have a pointer to that instance of **NSLocale**, you can start asking it questions like, "What's the currency symbol for this region?" or "Does this region use the metric system?" To ask a question, you send the **NSLocale** instance the message **objectForKey:** with one of the **NSLocale** constants as an argument. (You can find all of these constants in the **NSLocale** documentation page.)

First, let's internationalize the currency symbol displayed in each **HomepwnerItemCell**. Open Homepwner.xcodeproj and, in HomepwnerItemCell.m, locate the method **setPossession:**. When the text of the valueLabel is set in this method, the string "$%d" is used, which makes the currency symbol always a dollar sign. Replacing that code with the following will get and display the appropriate currency symbol for the user's region.

```
- (void)setPossession:(Possession *)possession
{
    NSString *currencySymbol = [[NSLocale currentLocale]
                            objectForKey:NSLocaleCurrencySymbol];
    [valueLabel setText:[NSString stringWithFormat:@"%@%d",
                currencySymbol,
                [possession valueInDollars]]];

    [nameLabel setText:[possession possessionName]];
    [imageView setImage:[possession thumbnail]];
}
```

Build and run the application. If the currency symbol is the dollar sign in your region, you'll need to change your region format in order to test this code. Exit the Homepwner application in the simulator by clicking the Home button and change your region format to United Kingdom in the Settings application.

Run your application again. This time, you will see values displayed in pounds (£). (Note that this is not a currency conversion from dollars to pounds; you're replacing the symbol, but the numbers stay the same.)

NSDateFormatter has a **locale** property, which is automatically set to the device's current locale. Run the application again. Select a possession, and (if your region is still set to United Kingdom) the date will appear in the British format: day/month/year.

Localizing Resources

Now that you've internationalized the currency symbol and date, let's turn to localization. Localization is the process by which substitutions for a region or a language setting are created. This usually means one of two things:

- generating multiple copies of resources like images, sounds, and interfaces for different regions and languages

- creating and accessing "strings tables" to translate text into different languages

Any resource, whether an image or a XIB file, can be localized with very little work. In this section, you're going to localize one of Homepwner's interfaces: the ItemDetailViewController.xib file. Right-click (or Control-click) ItemDetailViewController.xib in the project window and select Get Info from the contextual menu. In the General tab of the window that appears, click the button labeled Make File Localizable, as shown in Figure 23.2.

Figure 23.2 Resource before localization

This window will change, and a list of all of the localizations for ItemDetailViewController.xib will appear. As of now, there's only English. Click the Add Localization button at the bottom of the window and enter *Spanish* in the drop-down box that appears. Then click Add. Now the window should match the one shown in Figure 23.3.

Figure 23.3   Localized resource

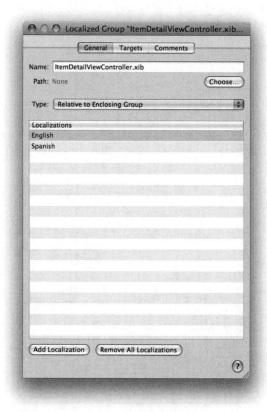

When you add a localization, two things happen: a copy of the resource file is made and the existing copies are separated into distinct .lproj directories named after the localizations. In this case, look in the Finder where ItemDetailViewController.xib was, and you will see two directories: English.lproj and Spanish.lproj. There is a copy of ItemDetailViewController.xib in each.

Figure 23.4 Localized XIB in the project window

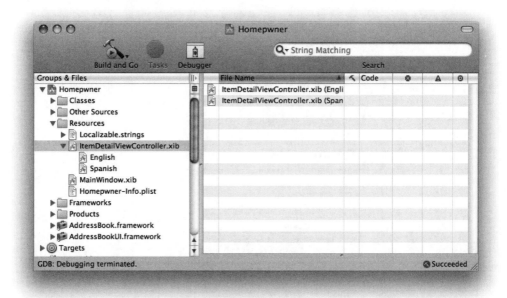

Now, back in Xcode, look under Homepwner's Resources. Click the disclosure button next to ItemDetailViewController.xib in the project window, as shown in Figure 23.4, and then open the Spanish file. This is the ItemDetailViewController.xib that is in the Spanish.lproj folder.

When the Spanish XIB file opens, the text is unfortunately still in English. You do have to translate it yourself; that part isn't automatic. Use Figure 23.5 as a guide to change the labels and button titles to Spanish.

Figure 23.5   Spanish ItemDetailViewController.xib

Remember that there's nothing special about localizing a XIB file as opposed to another resource like an image file. You follow the same procedure.

Once you have finished localizing this XIB file, you will want to test it. There is a little Xcode glitch to be aware of: sometimes Xcode just ignores a resource file's changes when you build an application. To ensure that the application gets the updated resources when it is built, select Clean from the Build menu. Cleaning a project simply trashes the application bundle and forces it to be rebuilt from scratch. Now build and run the application.

Homepwner's detail view will not appear in Spanish until you change the language settings on the device. Exit the application and change the language settings to Español in Settings. Once you have changed the device's language to Spanish, run your application again. Select a possession row, you will see the interface in Spanish.

NSLocalizedString and Strings Tables

In many places in your applications, you create **NSString** instances dynamically or use string literals that are displayed to the user. To display translated versions of these strings, you must create a strings table. A strings table is a file containing a list of key-value pairs for all of the strings your application uses and their associated translations. It's a resource file that you add to your application, but you don't need to do a lot of work to get data from it.

Whenever you have a string in your code, it appears like this:

```
@"Add New Item..."
```

To internationalize a string in your code, you replace literal strings with the macro **NSLocalizedString()**.

```
NSString *translatedString =
    NSLocalizedString(@"Hello!", @"The greeting for the user");
```

This function takes two arguments: a key (which is required) and a comment (which is not). The key is the lookup value in a strings table. At runtime, **NSLocalizedString()** will look through the strings tables bundled with your application for a table that matches the user's language settings. Then, in that table, the function gets a translation that matches the key. (The second argument is unused by the function; you will see why it matters in a moment.)

Now you're going to internationalize the string "Add New Item...". In ItemsViewController.m, locate the method **tableView:cellForRowAtIndexPath:** and change the line of code that sets the text of the basicCell.

```
- (UITableViewCell *)tableView:(UITableView *)tableView
        cellForRowAtIndexPath:(NSIndexPath *)indexPath
{
    if ([indexPath row] >= [possessions count]) {
        UITableViewCell *basicCell = [tableView
                dequeueReusableCellWithIdentifier:@"UITableViewCell"];

        if (!basicCell)
            basicCell = [[[UITableViewCell alloc]
                            initWithStyle:UITableViewCellStyleDefault
                            reuseIdentifier:@"UITableViewCell"] autorelease];

        // Set the textLabel of the basic cell from a strings table lookup
        [[basicCell textLabel] setText:NSLocalizedString(@"AddNewItem",
                                @"textLabel for add cell: Add New Item...")];

        return basicCell;
    }
    ...
```

Once you have a file that has been internationalized with **NSLocalizedString()**, you can generate strings tables with a command-line application.

Open Terminal.app in the /Applications/Utilities directory. Once Terminal launches, you'll need to navigate to the location of ItemsViewController.m. If you are familiar with Unix, have at it. If not, you're about to learn a cool trick. In Terminal, type the following:

```
cd
```

followed by a space.

Use Finder to find the Classes directory of your project, which contains ItemsViewController.m. Drag the Classes folder icon from the file system onto the Terminal window. Terminal will fill out the path for you. Hit return. The current working directory of Terminal is now the Classes directory. For example, my terminal command looks like this:

```
cd /iphone/Solutions/Homepwner/Classes/
```

To generate the strings table, enter the following into Terminal and hit return:

```
genstrings ItemsViewController.m
```

A file named Localizable.strings will be created in your Classes directory. Drag this file into the Resources group of your project window. When the application is compiled, this resource will be copied into the main bundle.

Oddly enough, Xcode sometimes has a problem with strings tables. Open the Localizable.strings file in your project window. If you see a bunch of upside-down question marks, you need to reinterpret this file as Unicode (UTF-16). Right-click to Get Info on the file and select Unicode (UTF-16) from the pop-up menu next to File Encoding. It will ask if you if you want reinterpret or convert. Choose Reinterpret.

Figure 23.6   Localized Strings Tables in the project window

The file should look like this:

```
/* textLabel for add cell: Add New Item... */
"AddNewItem" = "AddNewItem";
```

Change it to this:

```
/* textLabel for add cell: Add New Item... */
"AddNewItem" = "Add New Item...";
```

Notice that the comments in your strings table are the ones you supplied to `NSLocalizedString()`.

Now that you've created `Localizable.strings`, localize it the same way you did the XIB file. (Strings tables are resources, too!) Select Get Info from the contextual menu and click Make File Localizable. Add the Spanish localization and then return to the Resources directory and open the Spanish version of `Localizable.strings` (Figure 23.6). The text on the lefthand side is the *key* that is passed to `NSLocalizedString()`, and the string on the righthand side is what is returned. Change the text on the righthand side to the Spanish translation shown below.

```
/* textLabel for add cell: Add New Item... */
"AddNewItem" = "Agregue el nuevo artículo...";
```

Build and run the application again. Tap the Edit button, and the bottom row will appear in Spanish. If it does not, you might need to clean your project and rebuild. (Or check your user language setting.)

Challenge: Another Localization

Practice makes perfect. Localize Homepwner for another language.

For the More Curious: NSBundle's Role in Internationalization

The real work of adding a localization is done for you by the class `NSBundle`. When a `UIViewController` is initialized, it is given two arguments: the name of a XIB file and an `NSBundle` object. The bundle argument is typically `nil`, which is interpreted as the application's *main bundle*. (The main bundle is another name for the application bundle — all of the resources and the executable for the application. When an application is built, all of the `lproj` directories are copied into this bundle.)

When the view controller loads its view, it asks the bundle for the XIB file. The bundle, being very smart, checks the current language settings of the device and looks in the appropriate `lproj` directory. The path for the XIB file in the `lproj` directory is returned to the view controller and loaded.

`NSBundle` knows how to search through localization directories for every type of resource using the instance method `pathForResource:ofType:`. When you want a path to a resource bundled with your application, you send this message to the main bundle. Here's an example using the resource file myImage.png:

```
NSString *path = [[NSBundle mainBundle] pathForResource:@"myImage"
                                          ofType:@"png"];
```

The bundle first checks to see if there is a myImage.png file in the top level of the application bundle. If so, it returns the full path to that file. If not, the bundle gets the device's language settings and looks in the appropriate lproj directory to construct the path. If no file is found, it returns nil.

24

Bonjour

Bonjour is Apple's implementation of the ZeroConf standard, which allows services to advertise themselves on a network. It also allows clients to search for services. In this chapter, you are going to create an application that advertises its presence on the local network. It will also search for other devices on the network that advertise the same Bonjour service. The application will display a table view that lists every device running the Bonjour service on the network and a message that the application includes in its advertisement.

Figure 24.1   Two users have published messages

Publishing a Service

Create a new Window-based Application called Nayberz. The first step is to advertise a Bonjour service. This is done by creating an instance of **NSNetService** and publishing it. In NayberzAppDelegate.h, add an instance variable for the net service you are publishing:

```
#import <UIKit/UIKit.h>

@interface NayberzAppDelegate : NSObject <UIApplicationDelegate> {
    UIWindow *window;
    NSNetService *netService;
}

@property (nonatomic, retain) IBOutlet UIWindow *window;

@end
```

Then, in NayberzAppDelegate.m, create and publish the service:

```
- (BOOL)application:(UIApplication *)application
    didFinishLaunchingWithOptions:(NSDictionary *)launchOptions
{
    // Create an instance of NSNetService
    netService = [[NSNetService alloc]
                       initWithDomain:@""
                                 type:@"_nayberz._tcp."
                                 name:[[UIDevice currentDevice] name]
                                 port:9090];

    // As the delegate, you will know if the publish is successful
    [netService setDelegate:self];

    // Try to publish it
    [netService publish];

    [window makeKeyAndVisible];
    return YES;
}
```

In that same file, add two net service delegate methods:

```
- (void)netServiceDidPublish:(NSNetService *)sender
{
    NSLog(@"published: %@", sender);
}

- (void)netService:(NSNetService *)sender didNotPublish:(NSDictionary *)errorDict
{
    NSLog(@"not published: %@ -> %@", sender, errorDict);
}
```

Back in NayberzAppDelegate.h, add the following protocol to the class declaration:

```
@interface NayberzAppDelegate : NSObject
    <UIApplicationDelegate, NSNetServiceDelegate>
```

When the user exits an application that uses Bonjour, you should shut down the advertisement of services and restart the advertisement when the application launches again. Add two more application delegate methods to NayberzAppDelegate.m to do this:

```
- (void)applicationDidEnterBackground:(UIApplication *)application
{
    [netService stop];
}
- (void)applicationWillEnterForeground:(UIApplication *)application
{
    [netService publish];
}
```

Build and run the application. You will see on the console that the service was successfully published.

Browsing for Services

Now you're going to create a **UITableViewController** that displays the Bonjour services that the application discovers in its table view. It will have an instance of **NSNetServiceBrowser** and an array of **NSNetService** objects that it finds. In Xcode, create a new UIViewController subclass (without a XIB) and name it **TableController**.

Open TableController.h and change the superclass to **UITableViewController**.

```
@interface TableController : UITableViewController
```

Now create an instance of this view controller and put it on the window. In **application:didFinishLaunchingWithOptions:**, create the instance and put its view on the window. Also, import the header file for **TableController** at the top of NayberzAppDelegate.m:

```
#import "TableController.h"
@implementation NayberzAppDelegate
- (BOOL)application:(UIApplication *)application
    didFinishLaunchingWithOptions:(NSDictionary *)launchOptions
{
    netService = [[NSNetService alloc]
                        initWithDomain:@""
                                  type:@"_nayberz._tcp."
                                  name:[[UIDevice currentDevice] name]
                                  port:9090];
    [netService setDelegate:self];

    [netService publish];

    TableController *tableController = [[[TableController alloc] init] autorelease];
    [window setRootViewController:tableController];
    [application setStatusBarHidden:YES];

    [application setStatusBarHidden:YES];

    [window makeKeyAndVisible];
    return YES;
}
```

Build and run the application. The table view will appear, but it will be empty. Next you are going to fill it with data.

Open TableController.h and add two instance variables:

```
#import <UIKit/UIKit.h>

@interface TableController : UITableViewController
{
    NSMutableArray *netServices;
    NSNetServiceBrowser *serviceBrowser;
}

@end
```

In TableController.m, create an **init** method that specifies the style of the table view and creates an empty mutable array. Then, create an instance of **NSNetServiceBrowser** and start it searching:

```
- (id)init
{
    [super initWithStyle:UITableViewStylePlain];

    // Create an empty array
    netServices = [[NSMutableArray alloc] init];

    // Create a net service browser
    serviceBrowser = [[NSNetServiceBrowser alloc] init];

    // As the delegate, you will be told when services are found
    [serviceBrowser setDelegate:self];

    // Start it up
    [serviceBrowser searchForServicesOfType:@"_nayberz._tcp."
                                   inDomain:@""];

    return self;
}
- (id)initWithStyle:(UITableViewStyle)style
{
    return [self init];
}
```

Add the **NSNetServiceBrowserDelegate** and **NSNetServiceDelegate** protocols to the class declaration:

```
@interface TableController : UITableViewController
    <NSNetServiceDelegate, NSNetServiceBrowserDelegate>
```

Also, override the required data source methods:

```
- (NSInteger)tableView:(UITableView *)table
 numberOfRowsInSection:(NSInteger)section
{
    return [netServices count];
}
```

```objc
- (UITableViewCell *)tableView:(UITableView *)tv
        cellForRowAtIndexPath:(NSIndexPath *)indexPath
{
    NSNetService *ns = [netServices objectAtIndex:[indexPath row]];

    UITableViewCell *cell = [[self tableView]
                dequeueReusableCellWithIdentifier:@"UITableViewCell"];
    if (!cell) {
        cell = [[UITableViewCell alloc] initWithStyle:UITableViewCellStyleValue2
                                      reuseIdentifier:@"UITableViewCell"];
        [cell autorelease];
    }
    [[cell textLabel] setText:[ns name]];
    return cell;
}
```

Now implement the net service browser delegate methods:

```objc
// Called when services are found
- (void)netServiceBrowser:(NSNetServiceBrowser *)browser
          didFindService:(NSNetService *)aNetService
              moreComing:(BOOL)moreComing
{
    NSLog(@"adding %@", aNetService);

    // Add it to the array
    [netServices addObject:aNetService];

    // Update the interface
    NSIndexPath *ip = [NSIndexPath indexPathForRow:[netServices count] - 1
                                         inSection:0];
    [[self tableView] insertRowsAtIndexPaths:[NSArray arrayWithObject:ip]
                            withRowAnimation:UITableViewRowAnimationRight];

}

// Called when services are lost
- (void)netServiceBrowser:(NSNetServiceBrowser *)browser
        didRemoveService:(NSNetService *)aNetService
              moreComing:(BOOL)moreComing
{
    NSLog(@"removing %@", aNetService);

    // Take it out of the array
    NSUInteger row = [netServices indexOfObject:aNetService];
    if (row == NSNotFound) {
        NSLog(@"unable to find the service in %@", netServices);
        return;
    }
    [netServices removeObjectAtIndex:row];

    // Update the interface
    NSIndexPath *ip = [NSIndexPath indexPathForRow:row inSection:0];
    [[self tableView] deleteRowsAtIndexPaths:[NSArray arrayWithObject:ip]
                            withRowAnimation:UITableViewRowAnimationRight];
}
```

Build and run the application on more than one device on the local network. (One of these devices can be the simulator.) In the table view, you will see the device names of all the phones on the local network.

TXT Record

Sometimes it is convenient for a service to include additional useful information that can be read by clients. For example, a printer may tell clients it is in the third-floor library, or a workstation might display the rules for using it. Every **NSNetService** has a *TXT Record* for this purpose. In NayberzAppDelegate.h, declare a method that will create a TXT record for the netService.

```
}
@property (nonatomic, retain) IBOutlet UIWindow *window;

- (void)setMessage:(NSString *)str forNetService:(NSNetService *)service;

@end
```

Define this method in NayberzAppDelegate.m.

```
- (void)setMessage:(NSString *)str forNetService:(NSNetService *)service
{
    // Pack the string into an NSData
    NSData *d = [str dataUsingEncoding:NSUTF8StringEncoding];
    // Put the data in a dictionary
    NSDictionary *txtDict = [NSDictionary dictionaryWithObject:d forKey:@"message"];
    // Pack the dictionary into an NSData
    NSData *txtData = [NSNetService dataFromTXTRecordDictionary:txtDict];
    // Put that data into the net service
    [service setTXTRecordData:txtData];
}
```

In NayberzAppDelegate.m, update **application:didFinishLaunchingWithOptions:** so that it gives the netService an initial message.

```
- (BOOL)application:(UIApplication *)application
    didFinishLaunchingWithOptions:(NSDictionary *)launchOptions
{
    netService = [[NSNetService alloc]
                          initWithDomain:@""
                                    type:@"_nayberz._tcp."
                                    name:[[UIDevice currentDevice] name]
                                    port:9090];
    [netService setDelegate:self];

    NSString *messageString = @"You all kinda smell";
    [self setMessage:messageString forNetService:netService];


    [netService publish];
```

```
    TableController *tableController = [[[TableController alloc] init] autorelease];
    [window setRootViewController:tableController];
    [application setStatusBarHidden:YES];

    [window makeKeyAndVisible];
    return YES;
}
```

The TXT record is not in the initial contact from the published service; the client must first *resolve* it. You can think of the initial contact (when the **NSNetServiceBrowser** finds the service) as the first meeting between two people. Resolving, then, is their first date, where the client finds out a bunch of additional information about the service it has found. In TableController.m, send these services on a nice date.

```
- (void)netServiceBrowser:(NSNetServiceBrowser *)browser
           didFindService:(NSNetService *)aNetService
              moreComing:(BOOL)moreComing
{
    NSLog(@"adding %@", aNetService);

    // Add it to the array
    [netServices addObject:aNetService];

    // Update the interface
    NSIndexPath *ip = [NSIndexPath indexPathForRow:[netServices count] - 1
                                        inSection:0];
    [[self tableView] insertRowsAtIndexPaths:[NSArray arrayWithObject:ip]
                            withRowAnimation:UITableViewRowAnimationRight];

    // Start resolution to get TXT record
    // The success or failure of the resolution will be sent to the delegate.
    [aNetService setDelegate:self];
    // Give 30 seconds to figure out additonal info, else fail.
    [aNetService resolveWithTimeout:30];
}
```

When the net service succeeds in resolving, it sends the message **netServiceDidResolveAddress:** to its delegate. When this message is sent, the TXT record for the net service will be valid. Implement this method in TableController.m.

```
- (void)netServiceDidResolveAddress:(NSNetService *)sender
{
    // What row just resolved?
    int row = [netServices indexOfObjectIdenticalTo:sender];
    NSIndexPath *ip = [NSIndexPath indexPathForRow:row inSection:0];
    NSArray *ips = [NSArray arrayWithObject:ip];

    // Reload that row - the data source will pull the TXT record out
    [[self tableView] reloadRowsAtIndexPaths:ips
                            withRowAnimation:UITableViewRowAnimationRight];
}
```

Display the message in the table view cell:

```
- (UITableViewCell *)tableView:(UITableView *)tv
        cellForRowAtIndexPath:(NSIndexPath *)indexPath
{
    NSNetService *ns = [netServices objectAtIndex:[indexPath row]];

    NSString *message = nil;

    // Try to get the TXT Record
    NSData *data = [ns TXTRecordData];

    // Is there TXT data? (no TXT data in unresolved services)
    if (data) {

        // Convert it into a dictionary
        NSDictionary *txtDict = [NSNetService dictionaryFromTXTRecordData:data];

        // Get the data that the publisher put in under the message key
        NSData *mData = [txtDict objectForKey:@"message"];

        // Is there data?
        if (mData) {

            // Make a string
            message = [[NSString alloc] initWithData:mData
                                            encoding:NSUTF8StringEncoding];
            [message autorelease];
        }
    }

    // Did I fail to get a string?
    if (!message) {
        // Use a default message
        message = @"<No message>";
    }


    UITableViewCell *cell = [[self tableView]
                dequeueReusableCellWithIdentifier:@"UITableViewCell"];
    if (!cell) {
        cell = [[UITableViewCell alloc] initWithStyle:UITableViewCellStyleValue2
                                      reuseIdentifier:@"UITableViewCell"];
        [cell autorelease];
    }

    // Name on the left
    [[cell textLabel] setText:[ns name]];

    // Message on the right
    [[cell detailTextLabel] setText:message];
    return cell;
}
```

Build and run the application.

Socket Connections

A lot of people may read this chapter and think to themselves, "Well, I guess Bonjour is cool. But I don't see the point — all I can do is advertise a single chunk of text." Oh, but there is so much more!

When an **NSNetService** is resolved, you can send it the message **addresses**. This method returns an **NSArray** of NSData instances. Each **NSData** instance actually contains a sockaddr_in. A sockaddr_in is a TCP/IP structure that can be used for low-level TCP/IP communication. (There is typically only one address for a server, but there could be more.)

What's that mean? You can make socket connections to a server advertising an **NSNetService**, and, once you have a socket connection, you can communicate back and forth. Unfortunately, making a socket connection and passing data back and forth on it are beyond the scope of this book. Network programming is a huge topic, and there are plenty of resources out there. The best one is *Beej's Guide to Network Programming* (http://beej.us/guide/bgnet/).

To get you started, here's how to extract the sockaddr_in structure from an **NSNetService**. At the top of TableController.m, import two header files from the standard C library.

```
#import <netinet/in.h>
#import <arpa/inet.h>
```

When a Bonjour service is resolved, you will print out its IP address and port number. Add the following code to **netServiceDidResolveAddress:** in TableController.m.

```
- (void)netServiceDidResolveAddress:(NSNetService *)sender
{
    int row = [netServices indexOfObjectIdenticalTo:sender];
    NSIndexPath *ip = [NSIndexPath indexPathForRow:row inSection:0];
    NSArray *ips = [NSArray arrayWithObject:ip];
    [[self tableView] reloadRowsAtIndexPaths:ips
                        withRowAnimation:UITableViewRowAnimationRight];

    // Get all addresses for this server
    NSArray *addrs = [sender addresses];
    if([addrs count] > 0) {
        // Just grab the first address that it advertises
        NSData *firstAddress = [addrs objectAtIndex:0];

        // Point a sockaddr_in structure at the data wrapped
        // by firstAddress
        const struct sockaddr_in *addy = [firstAddress bytes];

        // Get a string that shows the IP address in x.x.x.x format
        // from the sockaddr_in structure
        char *str = inet_ntoa(addy->sin_addr);

        // Print that IP address as well as the port
        NSLog(@"%s:%d", str, ntohs(addy->sin_port));
    }
}
```

Build and run the application. When a net service resolves, check the console. You will see the IP address and port of the Bonjour server you found. Notice that the port printed to the console is the same port number you advertise the Bonjour service on.

If you wish to dive deeper into network programming, definitely read Beej's guide. Whether you program using standard C networking code or using Core Foundation or Foundation's streaming APIs, the concepts discussed in the guide are very important.

25

Settings

Many applications include preferences that users can customize. Whether users are picking the size of the text or storing passwords, there is a standard way of enabling iPhone application preferences. In this chapter, you will use the **NSUserDefaults** class to add a preference to your Nayberz application. This preference will specify the message that you publish in your net service (Figure 25.1).

Figure 25.1   Nayberz Settings pane

Settings Bundle

In the top-level directory of an iPhone application bundle, the filename Settings.bundle is reserved for a directory to contain the application's preference settings. To add preferences to your application, you add a Settings.bundle directory to your application. This directory must contain a file, Root.plist, where you set key-value pairs to define the application preferences. Once you've done this, your application will have its own pane in the Settings application where the user can set these preferences.

XCode makes it very easy to add a `Settings.bundle` to an application. Reopen `Nayberz.xcodeproj`. From the File menu, select New File.... In the table on the left side, under the iPhone OS group, select Resource. Then in the table on the right side, select Settings Bundle and click Next. The next screen will let you change the File Name and Location, but don't change them. Just be sure that the Add to Project: field is set to Nayberz and Targets: Nayberz is checked before you click Finish.

The `Settings.bundle` will now appear in your project's Groups & Files table. Use the disclosure buttons to reveal its contents, `Root.plist` and `en.lproj`. The `en.lproj` directory contains a strings table called `Root.strings`. The file `en.lproj/Root.strings` contains the English version of the text that will appear in the Nayberz pane of Settings. This means you can localize `Root.strings`.

Double-click on `Root.plist` to open it in the Property List Editor. You will see that it contains two keys at the root level: `StringsTable` and `PreferenceSpecifiers`. The value of the `StringsTable` key (Root) gives the name of the strings table file (`Root.strings`) that will be found in each localization directory. A value for this key is not required, but your application's settings will not be localized without one.

Right now, you are interested in the other key, `PreferenceSpecifiers`. The value of this key is an array of dictionaries. Each of these dictionaries defines a preference specifier. If you expand the `PreferenceSpecifiers` key in the Property List Editor, you will see the preference specifier dictionaries. These "sample" preferences were added by XCode when it created the `Settings.bundle` for you. If you expand these dictionaries, you will see the key-value pairs that define each of the preferences. Build and run Nayberz with these sample preferences. After your application starts, exit it. Then open Settings and scroll down to see Nayberz in the list. Select it and compare the key-value pairs in the dictionaries to the appearance of the properties in Settings. Pretty cool, huh?

Each preference specifier defines an attribute in Settings using key-value pairs. Here we'll discuss three of those keys: `Type`, `Key`, and `DefaultValue`. (Yeah, I know. One of the keys is actually named `Key`.)

The value for `Type` is one of seven constants that specifies the widget type used for this preference in Settings:

`PSTextFieldSpecifier`	a text field preference (a string)
`PSTitleValueSpecifier`	a read-only string preference (used to display preference values as formatted strings)
`PSToggleSwitchSpecifier`	a toggle switch preference (one of two values)
`PSSliderSpecifier`	a slider preference (a range of real number values)
`PSMultiValueSpecifier`	a multi-value preference (a set of mutually exclusive values)
`PSGroupSpecifier`	a group item preference (used to organize groups of preferences on a single page)
`PSChildPaneSpecifier`	a child pane preference (used to link to a new page of preferences)

Note that `PSGroupSpecifier` and `PSChildPaneSpecifier` do not specify actual preferences; they control the grouping and paging of preferences in Settings.

The value for `Key` is a string to be associated with the preference. Each of these strings must be unique within your `PreferenceSpecifiers`. Your application code will use this key to reference that preference.

The value for `DefaultValue` is the "factory setting" — the value of the preference when the user first downloads the application. This value must be of the type that the preference specifier expects (e.g., `string` for `PSTextFieldSpecifier`).

Depending on the type of the preference specifier, there may be other keys available to configure the appearance of the associated widget. Some of these keys are required, some are not. The documentation of the preference types and the available keys for each of those types is in the "Settings Application Schema Reference" in the documentation.

Now you are going to delete the sample preferences and replace them with a single new preference. This preference will have the key `BNRMessagePrefKey`, and it will specify the user's preference for the message broadcast by Nayberz. The factory setting will be "I love you all." If you double-click on `Root.plist`, it will open in the Property List Editor (and the XML will be hidden). In this editor, you could add and remove items and edit their values. In this case, however, you're going to edit the XML file directly. Right-click on `Root.plist`. Select Open As from the pop-up menu and then select Source Code File. Remove the existing preferences and replace them with the single preference shown below.

```xml
<?xml version="1.0" encoding="UTF-8"?>
<!DOCTYPE plist PUBLIC "-//Apple//DTD PLIST 1.0//EN"
    "http://www.apple.com/DTDs/PropertyList-1.0.dtd">
<plist version="1.0">
<dict>
    <key>StringsTable</key>
    <string>Root</string>
    <key>PreferenceSpecifiers</key>
    <array>

        <dict>
            <key>Type</key>
            <string>PSTextFieldSpecifier</string>
            <key>Title</key>
            <string>Message</string>
            <key>Key</key>
            <string>BNRMessagePrefKey</string>
            <key>DefaultValue</key>
            <string>I love you all.</string>
        </dict>

    </array>
</dict>
</plist>
```

Save the file. You have just created a text field in the Nayberz pane of Settings where the user can set a personal value for the `BNRMessagePrefKey` preference. Here you only created a single preference, but there could be many in a complex application. Remember that each preference needs a unique key, and it is best to be verbose with these key names. Here you have a prefix

("BNR" for Big Nerd Ranch), a name ("Message"), and the suffix "PrefKey." This way, no one will get confused about what the keys in your code mean.

Save Root.plist and build and run your application. After your application starts up, exit it. Open Settings and scroll down to find Nayberz. Select it and set your preference for the Nayberz message.

NSUserDefaults

Now the user can set the preference for BNRMessagePrefKey. But you still need to write a little code to respect the user's preference in your application. The **NSUserDefaults** class makes this very simple. It has a class method **standardUserDefaults** that returns the singular instance of **NSUserDefaults** for your application. **NSUserDefaults** is essentially an **NSMutableDictionary** with keys and values. Its keys are the keys for your preference specifiers in Root.plist, and its values are the user's settings for those preferences.

Registering defaults

Every time the application launches, you will need to remind it what the factory defaults are by "registering" your factory defaults using the DefaultValues from your Settings.bundle. To register your defaults, you build an **NSDictionary** containing a key-value pair for each preference. Each key will be a preference key, and its value will be the corresponding DefaultValue for the preference. Then you send this dictionary to the instance of **NSUserDefaults** using the **registerDefaults:** message.

The priority of the various defaults settings is as follows:

1. preferences set by the user in Settings (highest)

2. default values set in Root.plist in the Settings.bundle

3. default values set with **registerDefaults:** (lowest)

So if the user has already set a preference, it will override the other default values.

Your application needs to register its defaults *before* using the instance of **NSUserDefaults** to get the user defaults. So you're going to register them in the **initialize** method. In **initialize** in NayberzAppDelegate.m, load the Root.plist in the settings bundle and pull out the default values for every key. Note that **initialize** is a class method (denoted with a "+"):

```
+ (void)initialize
{
    NSString *path = [[NSBundle mainBundle] bundlePath];
    NSString *pListPath = [path
                stringByAppendingPathComponent:@"Settings.bundle/Root.plist"];

    NSDictionary *pList = [NSDictionary dictionaryWithContentsOfFile:pListPath];

    NSMutableArray *prefsArray = [pList objectForKey:@"PreferenceSpecifiers"];
    NSMutableDictionary *regDictionary = [NSMutableDictionary dictionary];
    for (NSDictionary *dict in prefsArray) {
        NSString *key = [dict objectForKey:@"Key"];
```

```
    if (key) {
        id value = [dict objectForKey:@"DefaultValue"];
        [regDictionary setObject:value forKey:key];
    }
}
[[NSUserDefaults standardUserDefaults] registerDefaults:regDictionary];
}
```

This generic implementation is a bit of overkill for our single preference, but you will definitely want this snippet of code when you write an application that has multiple preferences.

Using the defaults

Now you are ready to use **NSUserDefaults** to get the user's recorded preference for the message. Open NayberzAppDelegate.m and edit the **application:didFinishLaunchingWithOptions:** method:

```
- (BOOL)application:(UIApplication *)application
    didFinishLaunchingWithOptions:(NSDictionary *)launchOptions
{
    netService = [[NSNetService alloc]
                            initWithDomain:@""
                                    type:@"_nayberz._tcp."
                                    name:[[UIDevice currentDevice] name]
                                    port:9090];
    [netService setDelegate:self];

    // Get the shared instance of NSUserDefaults
    NSUserDefaults *ud = [NSUserDefaults standardUserDefaults];

    // Ask for the message string
    NSString *messageString = [ud stringForKey:@"BNRMessagePrefKey"];

    [self setMessage:messageString forNetService:netService];


    [netService publish];

    TableController *tableController = [[[TableController alloc] init] autorelease];
    [window setRootViewController:tableController];
    [application setStatusBarHidden:YES];

    [window makeKeyAndVisible];
    return YES;
}
```

Respecting changes in suspended applications

Now, in order to change this message, a user must quit the application, open the Settings application, change the value and re-launch Nayberz. However, we know that, as of iOS 4.0, when an application quits, it really just gets suspended. A suspended application does not get sent the message **application:didFinishLaunchingWithOptions:** when it is transitioned back to the active state, and that is where the TXT record of the net service is configured.

Therefore, Nayberz must somehow find out that its settings were changed externally when it is transitioned out of the suspended state. When an application is suspended, the operating system queues up any information the application may want to know about when it is activated. This information includes things like the battery level, device orientation, proximity state, current locale and preferences. If one of these items changes while an application is suspended, the application is informed when it becomes active through the notification center.

In order to catch these events, you must register observers in the notification center for any changes you are interested in. In this case, you are interested in the preferences changing. Add the following code near the end of **application:didFinishLaunchingWithOptions:** in NayberzAppDelegate.m.

```
[[NSNotificationCenter defaultCenter]
    addObserverForName:NSUserDefaultsDidChangeNotification
              object:nil
               queue:nil
          usingBlock:^(NSNotification *note) {
                  NSString *msgString = [ud stringForKey:@"BNRMessagePrefKey"];
                  NSLog(@"Resetting message: %@", msgString);
                  [self setMessage:msgString forNetService:netService];
              }];

[window makeKeyAndVisible];
return YES;
```

Now, when the user temporarily exits the application to change the BNRMessagePrefKey, Nayberz's notification center will post the NSUserDefaultsDidChangeNotification when re-launched. The block implemented for this notification will immediately update the netService with its new TXT record.

Note that the changes the operating system keeps track of for a suspended application are coalesced into a single message for each type of event. Therefore, if the user defaults change more than once while an application is suspended, the application is only notified once when activated again. For notifications like orientation changes, a single notification is posted to the notification center containing the net result of all orientation changes since the application was last active. A device that rotates from portrait, to landscape, back to portrait and then back to landscape again is only sent one UIDeviceOrientationChangedNotification notification, containing the current orientation of the device: landscape.

Users can now set their own messages, and Nayberz is complete. You don't have to do it this way, though. You could write your own settings interface within your application and not register preference specifiers in a settings bundle. Then, only your application could change the preferences. Or you could do both: write an interface *and* set up a Settings.bundle. The two ways will respect each other as long as you use **NSUserDefaults**.

26

SQLite

Once upon a time, SQL was created to access data in relational databases. While powerful, SQL required a database infrastructure. One day, Richard Hipp decided to create a library that would store data in tables and store those tables in a file instead of a relational database. With this library, you could use SQL commands to fetch data from the tables without requiring a database server process. You could also use SQL commands to insert, update, and delete rows of data. Dr. Hipp released the code for this library into the public domain and called it SQLite. The SQLite libraries are part of the iPhone OS.

SQLite is a nifty C library. It has great performance and reliability. Both the source for the library and the data files it creates are portable to a large number of platforms.

In the Homepwner application, you stored your data using an archive. Archives are very easy to use and support arbitrary object models. The downside of an archive is that it is read and written in its entirety. With SQLite, you can fetch only the data you need. You can also update individual rows of data. Thus, if you are dealing with a lot of data, using SQLite can radically improve the speed and memory footprint of your application. If you are dealing with a small amount of data, say, less than a thousand rows, archiving is all you need.

Creating the Nayshunz Application

This chapter will show you how to open a SQLite file and fetch data from it. It is done using a C API, so you will also spend some time converting C strings into **NSString** objects and back again. You will create an application that displays the names of nations stored in a SQLite database, as shown in Figure 26.1.

Figure 26.1   Nayshunz

The first step is to create a SQLite database file on the desktop and copy it into the resources of the application. The first time the application runs, it will copy that starting database to the Documents directory. In this chapter, you are only reading from a database, so making a copy of the database is not strictly necessary. However, this step is crucial if you want to edit a database.

The second step is to create a table view with sections using a common data structure: a tree of dictionaries and arrays. The tree for Nayshunz is shown in Figure 26.2.

Figure 26.2   Tree

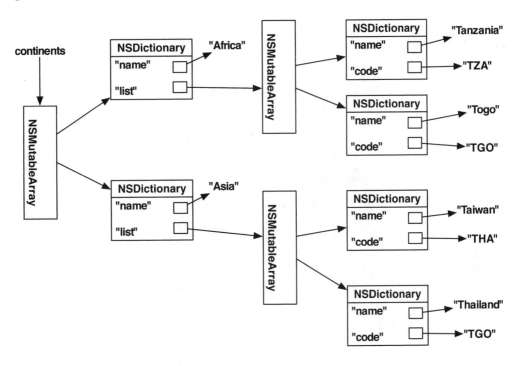

In Xcode, create a new Window-based Application called Nayshunz. Open NayshunzAppDelegate.h and add the following:

```
#import <UIKit/UIKit.h>
#import <sqlite3.h>

@interface NayshunzAppDelegate : NSObject
    <UIApplicationDelegate, UISearchBarDelegate, UITableViewDataSource>
{
    // Outlets
    IBOutlet UIWindow *window;
    IBOutlet UITableView *countryTable;
    IBOutlet UISearchBar *searchBar;

    // Model
    NSMutableArray *continents;

    // Database stuff
    sqlite3 *database;
    sqlite3_stmt *statement;
}

@property (nonatomic, retain) IBOutlet UIWindow *window;

@end
```

Open MainWindow.xib. Drop a search bar and a table view onto the window. Leave room under the table view for the keyboard, as shown in Figure 26.3.

Figure 26.3   Layout

Make the connections shown in Figure 26.4. Your instance of **NayshunzAppDelegate** will be the delegate of the **UISearchBar**. It will also be the dataSource of the **UITableView**. Set the pointers searchBar and countryTable to point to the **UISearchBar** and the **UITableView**, respectively.

Figure 26.4   Connections

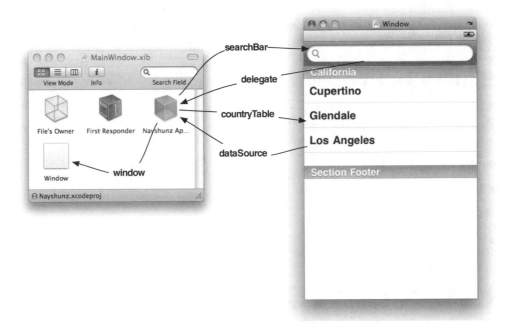

Creating the Database

Put the countries.sql file (downloaded from http://www.bignerdranch.com/solutions/ iPhoneProgramming.zip) on your desktop. (Take a look at the file in a text editor; it is a collection of SQL commands.) Start up Terminal. To create the new SQLite database file, issue these commands:

```
$ cd ~/Desktop
$ sqlite3 countries.db < countries.sql
```

If you are familiar with SQL, you can now use the sqlite3 command line to access the database from Terminal. Here's an example:

```
$ sqlite3 countries.db
SQLite version 3.4.0
Enter ".help" for instructions
sqlite> SELECT name, population FROM country
    WHERE name like 'z%' ORDER BY population;
Zambia|9169000
Zimbabwe|11669000
sqlite> .q
$
```

(If you'd like more help with SQL, check out Joe Celko's *SQL for Smarties*.)

From Finder, drag `countries.db` into your project under the Resources group. When the sheet appears, check the box that says Copy items into destination group's folder.

You will also need `libsqlite3.0.dylib` added to your project. Add it the same way you add a framework — from the Targets menu item in the project window.

Fetching Data

Now you are going fetch the rows, but the results will not appear in the table view yet. Open `NayshunzAppDelegate.m` and make it look like this:

```objc
#import "NayshunzAppDelegate.h"

@implementation NayshunzAppDelegate

@synthesize window;

- (id)init
{
    [super init];

    // Create the root of the tree
    continents = [[NSMutableArray alloc] init];

    // Where do the documents go?
    NSArray *paths =
        NSSearchPathForDirectoriesInDomains(NSDocumentDirectory,
                                            NSUserDomainMask, YES);
    NSString *path = [paths objectAtIndex:0];

    // What would be the name of my database file?
    NSString *fullPath = [path stringByAppendingPathComponent:@"countries.db"];

    // Get a file manager for file operations
    NSFileManager *fm = [NSFileManager defaultManager];

    // Does the file already exist?
    BOOL exists = [fm fileExistsAtPath:fullPath];

    // Does it already exist?
    if (exists) {
        NSLog(@"%@ exists - just opening", fullPath);
    } else {
        NSLog(@"%@ does not exist - copying and opening", fullPath);

        // Where is the starting database in the application wrapper?
        NSString *pathForStartingDB =
                [[NSBundle mainBundle] pathForResource:@"countries"
                                                ofType:@"db"];

        // Copy it to the documents directory
        BOOL success = [fm copyItemAtPath:pathForStartingDB
                                   toPath:fullPath
                                    error:NULL];
        if (!success) {
```

```
            NSLog(@"database copy failed");
        }
    }

    // Open the database file
    const char *cFullPath = [fullPath cStringUsingEncoding:NSUTF8StringEncoding];
    if (sqlite3_open(cFullPath, &database)
     != SQLITE_OK) {
        NSLog(@"unable to open database at %@", fullPath);
    }

    return self;
}

- (void)searchBar:(UISearchBar *)searchBar textDidChange:(NSString *)searchText
{
    // Only search if the user has typed something in
    if ([searchText length] != 0) {

        // Does the statement need to be prepared?
        if (!statement) {

            // '?' is a placeholder for parameters
            char *cQuery = "SELECT Continent, Name, Code FROM Country "
                           "WHERE Name LIKE ? ORDER BY Continent, Name";

            // Prepare the query
            if (sqlite3_prepare_v2(database, cQuery, -1, &statement, NULL)
            != SQLITE_OK)
            {
                NSLog(@"query error: %s", statement);
            }
        }

        // Add % to the end of the search text
        searchText = [searchText stringByAppendingString:@"%"];

        NSLog(@"searching for %@", searchText);

        // This C string will get cleaned up automatically
        const char *cSearchText =
                [searchText cStringUsingEncoding:NSUTF8StringEncoding];

        // Replace the first (and only) parameter with the search text
        sqlite3_bind_text(statement, 1, cSearchText, -1, SQLITE_TRANSIENT);


        // Loop to get all the rows
        while (sqlite3_step(statement) == SQLITE_ROW) {

            // Get the string in the first column
            const char *cContinentName =
                        (const char *)sqlite3_column_text(statement, 0);

            // Convert C string into an NSString
            NSString *continentName = [[[NSString alloc]
                        initWithUTF8String:cContinentName] autorelease];

            // Get the string in the second column
            const char *cCountryName =
```

```
                              (const char *)sqlite3_column_text(statement, 1);

            // Convert C string into an NSString
            NSString *countryName = [[[NSString alloc]
                        initWithUTF8String:cCountryName] autorelease];

            // Get the string in the third column
            const char *cCountryCode =
                        (const char *)sqlite3_column_text(statement, 2);


            // Convert C string into an NSString
            NSString *countryCode = [[[NSString alloc]
                        initWithUTF8String:cCountryCode] autorelease];

            NSLog(@"%@: %@ of %@", countryCode, countryName, continentName);

        }
        // Clear the query results
        sqlite3_reset(statement);
    }

    // Load the table with the new data
    [countryTable reloadData];
}

#pragma mark Table View Data Source Methods

- (NSInteger)tableView:(UITableView *)table
 numberOfRowsInSection:(NSInteger)section
{
    return 0;
}

- (UITableViewCell *)tableView:(UITableView *)tableView
        cellForRowAtIndexPath:(NSIndexPath *)ip
{
    return nil;
}

#pragma mark application Delegate Methods

- (BOOL)application:(UIApplication *)application
    didFinishLaunchingWithOptions:(NSDictionary *)launchOptions
{
    [window makeKeyAndVisible];

    // Bring up the keyboard immediately
    [searchBar becomeFirstResponder];
    return YES;
}

- (void)applicationWillTerminate:(UIApplication *)application
{
    sqlite3_close(database);
}


@end
```

Build and run the application. Watch the log. You will see a list of countries when the user types characters into the search bar.

Making and Using the Tree

Now that you are successfully getting the data, you need to put it into a tree so that you can access it with the table view data source methods.

In NayshunzAppDelegate.m, extend the **searchBar:textDidChange:** delegate method:

```
- (void)searchBar:(UISearchBar *)searchBar textDidChange:(NSString *)searchText
{
    // Clear the data structures
    [continents removeAllObjects];

    if ([searchText length] != 0) {

        if (!statement) {

            char *cQuery = "SELECT Continent, Name, Code FROM Country "
                          "WHERE Name LIKE ? ORDER BY Continent, Name";

            if (sqlite3_prepare_v2(database,cQuery, -1, &statement, NULL)
            != SQLITE_OK)
            {
                NSLog(@"query error: %s", statement);
            }
        }

        searchText = [searchText stringByAppendingString:@"%"];

        const char *cSearchText =
                [searchText cStringUsingEncoding:NSUTF8StringEncoding];

        sqlite3_bind_text(statement, 1, cSearchText, -1, SQLITE_TRANSIENT);

        NSString *lastContinentName = nil;
        NSMutableArray *currentNationList;

        while (sqlite3_step(statement) == SQLITE_ROW) {

            const char *cContinentName =
                    (const char *)sqlite3_column_text(statement, 0);

            NSString *continentName = [[[NSString alloc]
                    initWithUTF8String:cContinentName] autorelease];

            // Is this a new continent?
            if (!lastContinentName || ![lastContinentName isEqual:continentName])
            {

                // Create an array for the nations of this new continent
                currentNationList = [[NSMutableArray alloc] init];

                // Put the name and the array in a dictionary
                NSDictionary *continentalDict =
                        [[NSDictionary alloc] initWithObjectsAndKeys:
```

```
                            continentName, @"name",
                            currentNationList, @"list", nil];

            // Release array retained by the dictionary
            [currentNationList release];

            // Add the new continent to the array of continents
            [continents addObject:continentalDict];

            // Release the dictionary being retained by the array
            [continentalDict release];
        }

        // Note the continent name so that we know if we need to make a
        // new continent dictionary next time through the loop
        lastContinentName = continentName;

        const char *cCountryName =
                    (const char *)sqlite3_column_text(statement, 1);
        NSString *countryName = [[[NSString alloc]
                initWithUTF8String:cCountryName] autorelease];

        const char *cCountryCode =
                    (const char *)sqlite3_column_text(statement, 2);
        NSString *countryCode = [[[NSString alloc]
                initWithUTF8String:cCountryCode] autorelease];

        // Create a dictionary for this nation
        NSMutableDictionary *countryDict = [[NSMutableDictionary alloc] init];
        [countryDict setObject:countryName forKey:@"name"];
        [countryDict setObject:countryCode forKey:@"code"];

        // Put the nation's dictionary in the list for the current continent
        [currentNationList addObject:countryDict];

        // Release the dictionary retained by the array
        [countryDict release];

        }
        sqlite3_reset(statement);
    }

    // Load the table with the new data
    [countryTable reloadData];
}
```

Now the table view data source methods must use the tree. Add (or replace) these methods in
NayshunzAppDelegate.m:

```
#pragma mark Table View Data Source Methods

- (NSInteger)numberOfSectionsInTableView:(UITableView *)tableView
{
    // Return the number of continents
    return [continents count];
}
```

```objc
- (NSString *)tableView:(UITableView *)tableView
titleForHeaderInSection:(NSInteger)section
{
    // Get the dictionary for the continent for this section
    NSDictionary *continentDict = [continents objectAtIndex:section];

    // Return the name of the continent
    return [continentDict objectForKey:@"name"];
}


- (NSInteger)tableView:(UITableView *)table
 numberOfRowsInSection:(NSInteger)section
{
    // Get the dictionary for the continent for this section
    NSDictionary *continentDict = [continents objectAtIndex:section];

    // Get the array of nations for this continent
    NSArray *nations = [continentDict objectForKey:@"list"];

    // Return the number of nations on this continent
    return [nations count];
}

- (UITableViewCell *)tableView:(UITableView *)tableView
        cellForRowAtIndexPath:(NSIndexPath *)ip
{
    // Get the dictionary for the continent for this section
    NSDictionary *continentDict = [continents objectAtIndex:[ip section]];

    // Get the array of nations for this continent
    NSArray *nations = [continentDict objectForKey:@"list"];

    // Which nation is at the required row?
    NSDictionary *nationDict = [nations objectAtIndex:[ip row]];

    // What is its name?
    NSString *nationName = [nationDict objectForKey:@"name"];

    // Try to reuse an existing cell
    UITableViewCell *cell =
            [tableView dequeueReusableCellWithIdentifier:@"UITableViewCell"];

    // None available?
    if (!cell) {

        // Make a new cell
        cell = [[UITableViewCell alloc] initWithStyle:UITableViewCellStyleDefault
                                      reuseIdentifier:@"UITableViewCell"];
        [cell autorelease];
    }

    // Put the name of the country on the cell
    [[cell textLabel] setText:nationName];

    return cell;
}
```

Build and run the application.

Challenge: Fetching More Data

There is lots more data in the database. When someone selects a country, bring up another view with details about the selected country.

Challenge: Custom Objects

In this chapter, the information retrieved from the database was stored in the collection objects **NSArray** and **NSDictionary**. Try storing the data as an array of custom objects. The type of these objects will be called **Nation**, and you will write the implementation for it. It should have, at the very least, an **NSString** instance variable that stores the name of the nation.

27

Core Data

Using the C API for SQLite is one way to store and access data on the iPhone. The Core Data framework simplifies this process by providing an ORM for Objective-C and SQLite. ORM stands for *Object-Relational Mapping*. If you think of a table in a relational database as a class, then each row represents one instance of the class, and each column represents an instance variable. Core Data fetches rows from the table and turns them into objects (Figure 27.1). When these objects are edited, Core Data updates the row in the table accordingly. It also takes care of inserting and deleting rows as objects are created and destroyed.

Figure 27.1 Role of Core Data

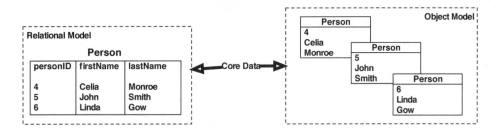

The class/table is known as an *entity* in Core Data. The column/instance variable is an *attribute* of that entity. In this diagram, there is one entity called **Person**. It has three attributes: personID, firstName, and lastName.

It gets a little more complicated if you have more than one table and relationships between them. In a relational database, these relationships are handled using primary keys and foreign keys. Each row in a table gets a unique ID number, which is the *primary key* of that table. If another table has a column that references that ID number, the column is a *foreign key*. The relationship from the table with the foreign key is "to-one"; after all, that unique ID can only refer to one row. The relationship going the other way is typically "to-many". (If you'd like more help understanding relational data, we suggest reading Joe Celko's *SQL for Smarties*.)

Thus, Core Data uses two distinct types of properties: *attributes* and *relationships*. Attributes can be expressed as simple data types: **NSNumber**, **NSString**, **NSDate**, **NSData**, etc. Relationships refer to other entities and are represented by pointers (for to-one relationships) and instances of **NSSet** (for to-many relationships), as shown in Figure 27.2.

Figure 27.2   Relationships

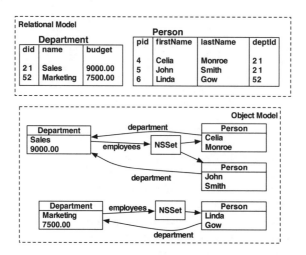

To use Core Data, you must first describe your entities and their attributes and relationships in a model file. (Some programmers refer to this as "the model," but since we are already using "model" to mean classes that are not views or controllers, we will specifically refer to "the model file.") The model file is created in Xcode.

Objects that hold data are instances of **NSManagedObject**. You can subclass **NSManagedObject** to add custom behavior to your managed object. For example, consider the Person objects in Figure 27.1. You might create a subclass of **NSManagedObject** called **Person** so that you could give it a **fullName** method.

Core Data also needs to know when these objects are edited so that the changes can be written to the SQLite database. An instance of the class **NSManagedObjectContext** monitors the managed objects to provide this information. You fetch managed objects into a managed object context. When you want to save the changes, you ask the context to save them for you.

Figure 27.3   NSManagedObjectContext

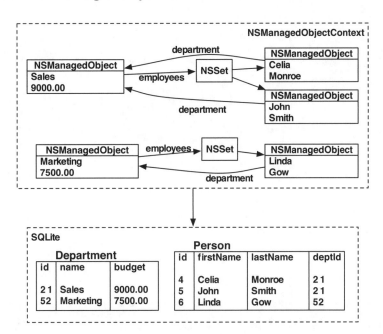

Creating the Inventory Application

To get a feel for Core Data, you need an object model of some complexity. (For simple object models, using SQLite directly is just as easy.) So, in this chapter, you are going to write a real application called Inventory with several screens and a complex object model.

Big Nerd Ranch keeps an inventory of stuff like T-shirts and coffee mugs ("schwag"). The inventory, however, is kept in several locations. We need to write a simple application to keep track of our inventory using Core Data. We will have a table of locations (like "Jaye's Basement") and a table of assets (like "Coffee Mug"). There will be a third table with a count, a date, and references to the other two tables. ("There were 12 Coffee Mugs in Jaye's Basement on March 12, 2010"). We will refer to the rows of that table as "inventories." The data model is shown in Figure 27.4.

Figure 27.4   Data model

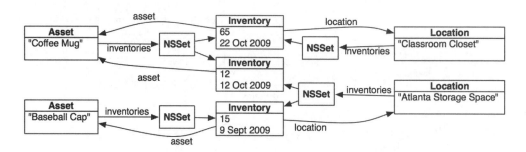

In Inventory, you will keep the interface as simple as possible: the user will be able to create new assets and locations but not edit or delete them (Figure 27.5).

Figure 27.5   Screens for Inventory

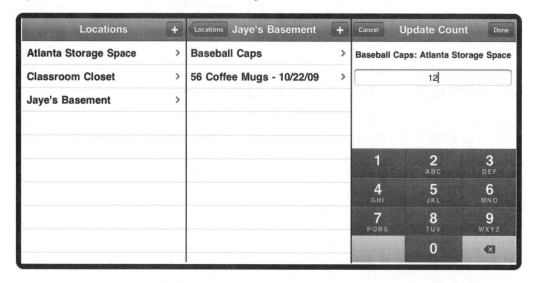

In Xcode, create a new project of type Window-based Application and check the box labeled Use Core Data for storage. Name the project Inventory. When the project window appears, open the Resources group and open the Inventory.xcdatamodel.

Editing the model file

Create three new entities in the model: **Asset**, **Inventory**, and **Location** by clicking on the + button at the bottom of the Entity table. In each case, leave the class **NSManagedObject** as shown in Figure 27.6. These are concrete entities, not abstract. And they have no parent entity.

Figure 27.6   Create three entities

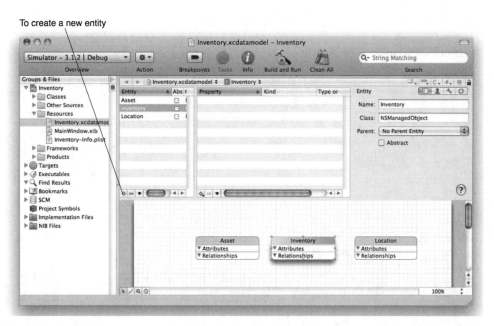

Now add the properties for each entity starting with **Asset**. **Asset** has one attribute and one relationship. The attribute is named label, and it is a String. The relationship is named inventories, and it is a to-many relationship with the **Inventory** entity (Figure 27.7).

Figure 27.7   Properties of Asset entity

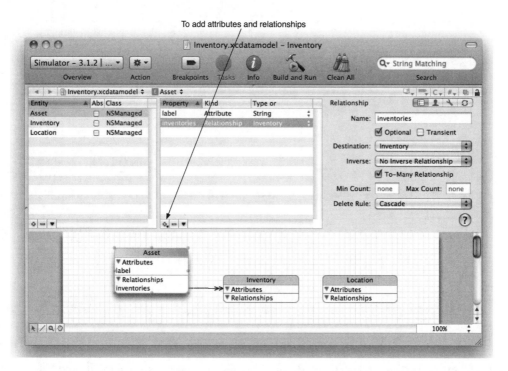

You must select a delete rule for the inventories relationship. The delete rule is the answer to the question "What happens to the **Inventory** objects associated with an asset when that asset is deleted?" There are four possible answers:

Cascade   When an asset is deleted, the inventories for that asset are also deleted automatically.

Nullify   When an asset is deleted, the inventories for that asset have their asset pointer set to nil.

Deny   You can't delete an asset if inventories for that asset exist.

No Action   This says, "Core Data, don't worry about it. I'll take care of it." (This option is rarely used.)

Set the delete rule for the inventories relationship to be Cascade.

The **Location** entity is similar to **Asset**. It needs an attribute named label of type String and a to-many relationship to **Inventory** called inventories. Set the delete rule for the relationship to Cascade (Figure 27.8).

Figure 27.8   Properties of Location entity

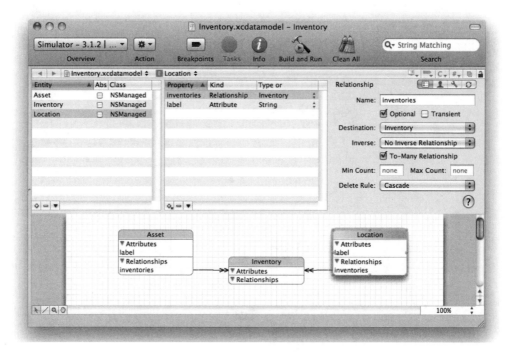

The **Inventory** entity is a little different from the others. It has two attributes: count (a 16-bit integer) and date (a date). Inventory also has relationships to the **Asset** and **Location** entities.

Add a to-one relationship named asset to the **Inventory** entity. The destination is the **Asset** entity. This relationship is the inverse to **Asset**'s inventories relationship. Set the delete rule to Nullify (Figure 27.9).

Figure 27.9   Inventory's asset relationship

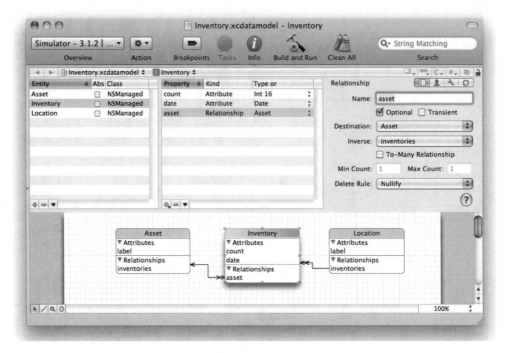

Add a second to-one relationship named location to the **Inventory** entity. The destination is the **Location** entity. This relationship is the inverse to **Location**'s inventories relationship. Set the delete rule to Nullify (Figure 27.10).

Figure 27.10   Inventory's location relationship

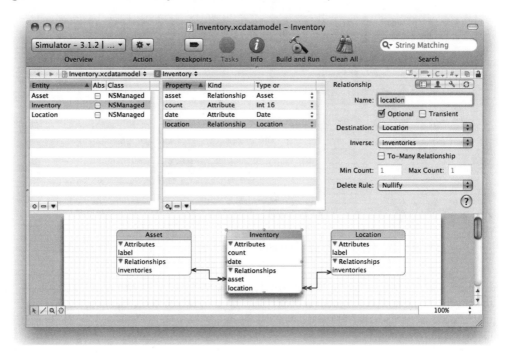

Your model file is complete. Save it.

In this exercise, you are using generic instances of **NSManagedObject**, which are very much like dictionaries. If you wanted to, you *could* subclass **NSManagedObject** and create the classes **Inventory**, **Asset**, and **Location**.

AppController

The name **InventoryAppDelegate** is weak; this object is much more than just a delegate. So, let's rename it **AppController** using the refactoring tool. Select the text InventoryAppDelegate after @interface in InventoryAppDelegate.h. In the Edit menu, select Refactor. In the panel, rename **InventoryAppDelegate AppController**:

Figure 27.11 Renaming InventoryAppDelegate

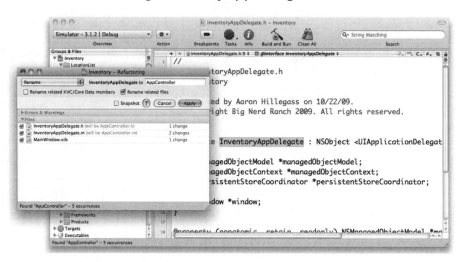

Take a minute before we go any further to browse AppController.m. Notice how it lazily loads the model, creates an **NSPersistentStoreCoordinator**, and puts an **NSManagedObjectContext** atop the coordinator. Also, notice that it saves the changes you have made to the objects when the application is terminating.

In AppController.h, add an instance variable to hold on to the navigation controller that you will be using later. Also add a class method for getting hold of the **AppController** (there will be only one). Finally, declare a method for fetching arrays of objects from the **NSManagedObjectContext**:

```
@interface AppController : NSObject <UIApplicationDelegate>
{
    NSManagedObjectModel *managedObjectModel;
    NSManagedObjectContext *managedObjectContext;
    NSPersistentStoreCoordinator *persistentStoreCoordinator;
    UIWindow *window;

    UINavigationController *navigationController;
}

// Class method for convenience
+ (AppController *)sharedAppController;

- (NSArray *)allInstancesOf:(NSString *)entityName
               orderedBy:(NSString *)attName;

// In later versions of Xcode, these property declarations may appear in a
// category in AppController.m. If that is the case, move them here.
@property (nonatomic, retain, readonly) NSManagedObjectModel
                                              *managedObjectModel;
@property (nonatomic, retain, readonly) NSManagedObjectContext
                                              *managedObjectContext;
```

```
@property (nonatomic, retain, readonly) NSPersistentStoreCoordinator
                                        *persistentStoreCoordinator;
@property (nonatomic, retain) IBOutlet UIWindow *window;

- (NSString *)applicationDocumentsDirectory;
@end
```

Open AppController.m. At the beginning of the class, add the static variable and methods that you will need:

```
#import "AppController.h"

static AppController *sharedInstance;

@implementation AppController

@synthesize window;

- (id)init
{
    if (sharedInstance) {
        NSLog(@"Error: You are creating a second AppController");
    }
    [super init];
    sharedInstance = self;
    return self;
}

+ (AppController *)sharedAppController
{
    return sharedInstance;
}

- (NSArray *)allInstancesOf:(NSString *)entityName
                  orderedBy:(NSString *)attName
{
    // Get the managed object context
    NSManagedObjectContext *moc =
            [[AppController sharedAppController] managedObjectContext];

    // Create a fetch request that fetches from 'entityName'
    NSFetchRequest *fetch = [[NSFetchRequest alloc] init];
    NSEntityDescription *entity = [NSEntityDescription entityForName:entityName
                                           inManagedObjectContext:moc];
    [fetch setEntity:entity];

    // If 'attName' is not nil, have the results sorted
    if (attName) {
        NSSortDescriptor *sd = [[NSSortDescriptor alloc] initWithKey:attName
                                                        ascending:YES];

        NSArray *sortDescriptors = [NSArray arrayWithObject:sd];
        [sd release];

        [fetch setSortDescriptors:sortDescriptors];
    }
```

```
// Try to do the fetch
NSError *error;
NSArray *result = [moc executeFetchRequest:fetch
                                     error:&error];
[fetch release];

// Did the fetch fail?
if (!result) {

    // Display an alert view
    UIAlertView *alertView = [[UIAlertView alloc]
                      initWithTitle:@"Fetch Failed"
                            message:[error localizedDescription]
                           delegate:nil
                  cancelButtonTitle:@"OK"
                  otherButtonTitles:nil];
    [alertView autorelease];
    [alertView show];
    return nil;
}

// Return the array of instances of NSManagedObject
return result;
}
```

LabelSettingViewController

Now you're going to create two subclasses of **UITableViewController** (no XIB file):

- **LocationListViewController**

- **AssetListViewController**

and two subclasses of UIViewController (with XIB file):

- **LabelSettingViewController**

- **CountViewController**

If you feel particularly stylish, you can create a group in your project for each view controller, as shown in Figure 27.12.

Figure 27.12 New view controllers

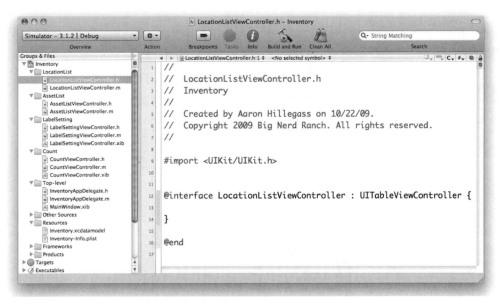

Depending on your version of Xcode, you may have boilerplate code that will not compile in LocationListViewController.m and AssetListViewController.m. It would look like this:

```
- (NSInteger)numberOfSectionsInTableView:(UITableView *)tableView {
    // Return the number of sections.
    return <#number of sections#>;
}

- (NSInteger)tableView:(UITableView *)tableView
 numberOfRowsInSection:(NSInteger)section {
    // Return the number of rows in the section.
    return <#number of rows in section#>;
}
```

If this is the case, delete **numberOfSectionsInTableView:** and make the other method return 0:

```
- (NSInteger)tableView:(UITableView *)tableView
 numberOfRowsInSection:(NSInteger)section {
    // Return the number of rows in the section.
    return 0;
}
```

In earlier chapters, we had you create subclasses of **UITableViewController** by creating a subclass of **UIViewController** and then changing the superclass in the header file to **UITableViewController**. We did this specifically to avoid the problem this template code might create. Now you are familiar enough with Xcode and **UITableViewController** that it doesn't hurt to create your subclasses with this potentially problematic template.

The least interesting view controller is **LabelSettingViewController**. Its only job is to give the user a text field to name new assets and locations (Figure 27.13).

Figure 27.13   LabelSettingViewController

Open LabelSettingViewController.h and add an outlet, two actions, and a property called value:

```
#import <UIKit/UIKit.h>

@interface LabelSettingViewController : UIViewController
{
    IBOutlet UITextField *textField;
    NSString *value;
}
- (IBAction)cancel:(id)sender;
- (IBAction)create:(id)sender;
@property (nonatomic, copy) NSString *value;

@end
```

Now open LabelSettingViewController.xib. Drop a label and a text field on the window. Set File's Owner's textField outlet to point to the text field, as shown in Figure 27.14.

Figure 27.14 LabelSettingViewController.xib

In LabelSettingViewController.m, keep the variable value and the text field in sync:

```
@synthesize value;

- (id)init
{
    [super initWithNibName:nil bundle:nil];

    [self setTitle:@"New Record"];

    // Set up navigation items
    UIBarButtonItem *bbi;

    // Done item
    bbi = [[UIBarButtonItem alloc]
            initWithBarButtonSystemItem:UIBarButtonSystemItemDone
                                 target:self
                                 action:@selector(create:)];
    [[self navigationItem] setRightBarButtonItem:bbi];
    [bbi release];

    // Cancel item
    bbi = [[UIBarButtonItem alloc]
            initWithBarButtonSystemItem:UIBarButtonSystemItemCancel
                                 target:self
                                 action:@selector(cancel:)];
    [[self navigationItem] setLeftBarButtonItem:bbi];
    [bbi release];

    return self;
}

// Override the superclass's designated initializer
- (id)initWithNibName:(NSString *)n bundle:(NSBundle *)b
```

```
{
    return [self init];
}

- (void)dealloc
{
    [textField release];
    [value release];
    [super dealloc];
}

#pragma mark View Controller Lifecycle

- (void)viewDidLoad
{
    [super viewDidLoad];
    [textField setAutocorrectionType:UITextAutocorrectionTypeNo];
}

- (void)viewDidUnload
{
    [super viewDidUnload];
    [textField release];
    textField = nil;
}

- (void)viewDidAppear:(BOOL)animated
{
    [super viewDidAppear:animated];

    // Make the keyboard appear
    [textField becomeFirstResponder];
}

#pragma mark Actions

- (IBAction)cancel:(id)sender
{
    // Clear the value
    [self setValue:nil];

    // Slide back to the previous view controller
    [[self navigationController] popViewControllerAnimated:YES];
}

- (IBAction)create:(id)sender
{
    // Set the value
    [self setValue:[textField text]];

    // Slide back to the previous view controller
    [[self navigationController] popViewControllerAnimated:YES];
}
```

LocationListViewController

LocationListViewController will fetch the Location objects into the NSManagedObjectContext and display them in a table view (Figure 27.15).

Figure 27.15 LocationListViewController

You're also going to add a navigation item that the user can click to get to the
LabelSettingViewController. In LocationListViewController.h, declare an instance
variable to hold the fetched **Location** objects. Also, declare a variable to hold on to the
LabelSettingViewController:

```
#import <UIKit/UIKit.h>
@class LabelSettingViewController;

@interface LocationListViewController : UITableViewController
{
    NSMutableArray *locationList;
    LabelSettingViewController *labelSettingViewController;
}
@end
```

Now in LocationListViewController.m, add these methods:

```
#import "LocationListViewController.h"
#import "AppController.h"
#import "LabelSettingViewController.h"

@implementation LocationListViewController

- (id)init
{
    [super initWithStyle:UITableViewStylePlain];

    // Fetch the location list
```

```
    AppController *ac = [AppController sharedAppController];
    NSArray *list = [ac allInstancesOf:@"Location" orderedBy:@"label"];
    locationList = [list mutableCopy];

    [self setTitle:@"Locations"];

    // Create the Add navigation item
    UIBarButtonItem *item = [[UIBarButtonItem alloc]
            initWithBarButtonSystemItem:UIBarButtonSystemItemAdd
                                 target:self
                                 action:@selector(createNewLocation:)];
    [[self navigationItem] setRightBarButtonItem:item];
    [item release];

    return self;
}

// Override the superclass's designated initializer
- (id)initWithStyle:(UITableViewStyle)style
{
    return [self init];
}

- (void)dealloc
{
    [locationList release];
    [super dealloc];
}


#pragma mark Action methods

- (void)createNewLocation:(id)sender
{
    labelSettingViewController = [[LabelSettingViewController alloc] init];
    [[self navigationController] pushViewController:labelSettingViewController
                                          animated:YES];
}

#pragma View Controller Lifecycle

- (void)viewWillAppear:(BOOL)animated
{
    [super viewWillAppear:animated];

    // Am I coming back from the LabelSettingViewController?
    if (labelSettingViewController) {
        NSString *value = [labelSettingViewController value];

        // Did the user give a value for the label?
        if ([value length] > 0) {

            AppController *ac = [AppController sharedAppController];
            NSManagedObjectContext *moc = [ac managedObjectContext];

            // Create a new object and insert it into the managed object context
            NSManagedObject *newLoc =
                [NSEntityDescription insertNewObjectForEntityForName:@"Location"
                                             inManagedObjectContext:moc];
            [newLoc setValue:value forKey:@"label"];
```

```
        [locationList addObject:newLoc];

        // Resort the array
        NSSortDescriptor *sd = [[NSSortDescriptor alloc] initWithKey:@"label"
                                                        ascending:YES];
        NSArray *sds = [NSArray arrayWithObject:sd];
        [sd release];
        [locationList sortUsingDescriptors:sds];

        // Redisplay the table view
        [[self tableView] reloadData];
    }
    [labelSettingViewController release];
    labelSettingViewController = nil;
    }

    // Clear the selection
    NSIndexPath *selectedPath = [[self tableView] indexPathForSelectedRow];
    if (selectedPath) {
        [[self tableView] deselectRowAtIndexPath:selectedPath animated:NO];
    }
}


#pragma mark Table view methods
// These methods are replacing methods that were generated automatically
// when the class was generated.

- (NSInteger)tableView:(UITableView *)tableView
 numberOfRowsInSection:(NSInteger)section
{
    return [locationList count];
}


- (UITableViewCell *)tableView:(UITableView *)tableView
        cellForRowAtIndexPath:(NSIndexPath *)ip
{

    static NSString *CellIdentifier = @"LocationCell";

    UITableViewCell *cell =
            [tableView dequeueReusableCellWithIdentifier:CellIdentifier];
    if (cell == nil) {
        cell = [[UITableViewCell alloc] initWithStyle:UITableViewCellStyleDefault
                                      reuseIdentifier:CellIdentifier];
        [cell autorelease];
    }

    NSManagedObject *location = [locationList objectAtIndex:[ip row]];
    [[cell textLabel] setText:[location valueForKey:@"label"]];
    [cell setAccessoryType:UITableViewCellAccessoryDisclosureIndicator];
    return cell;
}
```

Now put this view controller in a navigation controller and onto the screen. Go back to AppController.m and import the header at the top:

```
#import "LocationListViewController.h"
```

Then, in **application:didFinishLaunchingWithOptions:**, create the **UINavigationController** and the **LocationListViewController**:

```
- (BOOL)application:(UIApplication *)application
    didFinishLaunchingWithOptions:(NSDictionary *)launchOptions
{
    LocationListViewController *rvc = [[LocationListViewController alloc] init];

    navigationController =
        [[UINavigationController alloc] initWithRootViewController:rvc];
    [rvc release];

    [window setRootViewController:navigationController];
    [window makeKeyAndVisible];
    return YES;
}
```

Build and run the application. You can add new locations, but selecting an existing location in the table view won't do anything yet.

AssetListViewController

The **AssetListViewController** is a lot like the **LocationListViewController**. For a given location, it will display a list of all the assets. If there is an inventory for that asset at that location, it will display the inventory data (Figure 27.16).

Figure 27.16   AssetListViewController

Open `AssetListViewController.h`. Add variables to hold the selected location, the list of all assets, and the **LabelSettingViewController**:

```
#import <UIKit/UIKit.h>
@class LabelSettingViewController;

@interface AssetListViewController : UITableViewController {
    NSManagedObject *location;
    NSMutableArray *assetList;
    LabelSettingViewController *labelSettingViewController;
}
- (NSManagedObject *)inventoryForAsset:(NSManagedObject *)asset;
- (void)setLocation:(NSManagedObject *)loc;

@end
```

Open `AssetListViewController.m`.

```
#import "AssetListViewController.h"
#import "AppController.h"
#import "LabelSettingViewController.h"

// All instances of AssetListViewController will share a single
// instance of NSDateFormatter
static NSDateFormatter *dateFormatter;

@implementation AssetListViewController

- (id)init
{
    [super initWithStyle:UITableViewStylePlain];

    AppController *ac = [AppController sharedAppController];

    // Fetch all the assets
    NSArray *list = [ac allInstancesOf:@"Asset" orderedBy:@"label"];
    assetList = [list mutableCopy];

    // Set the navigation items
    UIBarButtonItem *item = [[UIBarButtonItem alloc]
                initWithBarButtonSystemItem:UIBarButtonSystemItemAdd
                                     target:self
                                     action:@selector(createNewAsset:)];

    [[self navigationItem] setRightBarButtonItem:item];
    [item release];

    // Is the dateFormatter nil?
    if (!dateFormatter) {

        // Create a date formatter
        dateFormatter = [[NSDateFormatter alloc] init];
        [dateFormatter setDateStyle:NSDateFormatterShortStyle];
    }

    return self;
}
```

```objc
- (id)initWithStyle:(UITableViewStyle)style
{
    return [self init];
}


- (void)dealloc
{
    [location release];
    [assetList release];
    [super dealloc];
}


- (NSManagedObject *)inventoryForAsset:(NSManagedObject *)asset
{
    NSArray *inventoriesForLocation = [location valueForKey:@"inventories"];
    for (NSManagedObject *mo in inventoriesForLocation) {
        if ([mo valueForKey:@"asset"] == asset) {
            return mo;
        }
    }
    return nil;
}

- (void)setLocation:(NSManagedObject *)loc
{
    [loc retain];
    [location release];
    location = loc;

    [self setTitle:[location valueForKey:@"label"]];
}

#pragma mark Action methods

- (void)createNewAsset:(id)sender
{
    labelSettingViewController = [[LabelSettingViewController alloc] init];
    [[self navigationController] pushViewController:labelSettingViewController
                                          animated:YES];
}

- (void)viewWillAppear:(BOOL)animated
{
    [super viewWillAppear:animated];

    // Am I coming back from the LabelSettingViewController?
    if (labelSettingViewController) {

        NSString *value = [labelSettingViewController value];
        if ([value length] > 0) {

            AppController *ac = [AppController sharedAppController];
            NSManagedObjectContext *moc = [ac managedObjectContext];

            NSManagedObject *newAsset =
                [NSEntityDescription insertNewObjectForEntityForName:@"Asset"
                                            inManagedObjectContext:moc];
```

```
            [newAsset setValue:value forKey:@"label"];
            [assetList addObject:newAsset];

            NSSortDescriptor *sd =
                [[NSSortDescriptor alloc] initWithKey:@"label" ascending:YES];
            NSArray *sds = [NSArray arrayWithObject:sd];
            [sd release];
            [assetList sortUsingDescriptors:sds];
            [[self tableView] reloadData];
        }
        [labelSettingViewController release];
        labelSettingViewController = nil;
    }

    NSIndexPath *selectedPath = [[self tableView] indexPathForSelectedRow];
    if (selectedPath) {
        [[self tableView] deselectRowAtIndexPath:selectedPath animated:NO];
    }
}

#pragma mark Table view methods

// Customize the number of rows in the table view
- (NSInteger)tableView:(UITableView *)tableView
 numberOfRowsInSection:(NSInteger)section
{
    return [assetList count];
}

// Customize the appearance of table view cells
- (UITableViewCell *)tableView:(UITableView *)tableView
         cellForRowAtIndexPath:(NSIndexPath *)ip
{

    static NSString *CellIdentifier = @"InventoryCell";

    UITableViewCell *cell =
        [tableView dequeueReusableCellWithIdentifier:CellIdentifier];
    if (cell == nil) {
        cell = [[UITableViewCell alloc] initWithStyle:UITableViewCellStyleDefault
                                      reuseIdentifier:CellIdentifier];
        [cell autorelease];
    }

    NSManagedObject *asset = [assetList objectAtIndex:[ip row]];

    NSManagedObject *inventory = [self inventoryForAsset:asset];

    NSString *assetName = [asset valueForKey:@"label"];

    if (inventory) {
        NSDate *date = [inventory valueForKey:@"date"];
        NSString *inventorySummary = [NSString stringWithFormat:@"%@ %@ - %@",
                                     [inventory valueForKey:@"count"],
                                     assetName,
                                     [dateFormatter stringFromDate:date]];
        [[cell textLabel] setText:inventorySummary];
    } else {
        [[cell textLabel] setText:assetName];
    }
```

```
    [cell setAccessoryType:UITableViewCellAccessoryDisclosureIndicator];
    return cell;
}
```

@end

A view controller is no good if you can't get to it. Go back to LocationListViewController.m and push the new view controller onto the navigation controller when the location is selected:

```
- (void)tableView:(UITableView *)tableView
    didSelectRowAtIndexPath:(NSIndexPath *)ip
{
    AssetListViewController *anotherViewController =
                [[AssetListViewController alloc] init];
    [anotherViewController setLocation:[locationList objectAtIndex:[ip row]]];
    [[self navigationController] pushViewController:anotherViewController
                                          animated:YES];
    [anotherViewController release];
}
```

You also need to import AssetListViewController.h at the top of LocationListViewController.m.

Build and run the application. Now you can create new assets. Note, however, that a new asset appears at all locations.

CountViewController

The last view controller that you are going to create enables the user to enter counts for assets at particular locations (Figure 27.17).

Figure 27.17   CountViewController

Open CountViewController.h and declare some instance variables and methods:

```
#import <UIKit/UIKit.h>

@interface CountViewController : UIViewController {
    IBOutlet UITextField *numberField;
    IBOutlet UILabel *promptField;
    NSManagedObject *asset;
    NSManagedObject *location;
    NSNumber *count;
}
- (IBAction)update:(id)sender;
- (IBAction)cancel:(id)sender;

@property (nonatomic, retain) NSManagedObject *asset;
@property (nonatomic, retain) NSManagedObject *location;
@property (nonatomic, retain) NSNumber *count;

@end
```

Save the file.

Open CountViewController.xib and drop a label and a text field on the view. Connect the outlet numberField to the text field. Connect the outlet promptField to the label. Set the text field to take number input, as shown in Figure 27.18.

Figure 27.18   CountViewController.xib

Open CountViewController.m:

```objc
#import "CountViewController.h"

@implementation CountViewController

@synthesize asset, location, count;

- (id)init
{
    [super initWithNibName:nil bundle:nil];

    UIBarButtonItem *bbi;
    bbi = [[UIBarButtonItem alloc]
            initWithBarButtonSystemItem:UIBarButtonSystemItemDone
                             target:self
                             action:@selector(update:)];
    [[self navigationItem] setRightBarButtonItem:bbi];
    [bbi release];

    bbi = [[UIBarButtonItem alloc]
            initWithBarButtonSystemItem:UIBarButtonSystemItemCancel
                             target:self
                             action:@selector(cancel:)];
    [[self navigationItem] setLeftBarButtonItem:bbi];
    [bbi release];

    [self setTitle:@"Update Count"];

    return self;
}
```

```objc
- (id)initWithNibName:(NSString *)n bundle:(NSBundle *)b
{
    return [self init];
}


- (void)dealloc
{
    [numberField release];
    [promptField release];
    [count release];
    [asset release];
    [location release];
    [super dealloc];
}


- (void)updateInteface
{
    NSString *prompt = [NSString stringWithFormat:@"%@: %@",
                                    [asset valueForKey:@"label"],
                                    [location valueForKey:@"label"]];

    [promptField setText:prompt];
    [numberField setText:[count stringValue]];
}

#pragma mark View Controller Lifecycle

- (void)viewDidLoad
{
    [super viewDidLoad];
    [self updateInteface];
    [numberField becomeFirstResponder];
}

- (void)viewDidUnload
{
    [super viewDidUnload];
    [numberField release];
    numberField = nil;
    [promptField release];
    promptField = nil;
}

#pragma mark Actions

- (IBAction)update:(id)sender
{
    NSString *countString = [numberField text];
    int countInt = [countString intValue];
    [self setCount:[NSNumber numberWithInt:countInt]];
    [[self navigationController] popViewControllerAnimated:YES];
}
```

```
- (IBAction)cancel:(id)sender
{
    [self setCount:nil];
    [[self navigationController] popViewControllerAnimated:YES];
}
```

```
@end
```

Once again, the new view controller is unreachable. Go back to `AssetListViewController.h` and declare an instance variable to hold a reference to the **CountViewController**:

```
CountViewController *countViewController;
```

Near the top of `AssetListViewController.h`, let the compiler know about the class:

```
@class CountViewController;
```

In `AssetListViewController.m`, display the view controller if the user selects a row:

```
- (void)tableView:(UITableView *)tableView
    didSelectRowAtIndexPath:(NSIndexPath *)ip
{
    countViewController = [[CountViewController alloc] init];
    [countViewController setLocation:location];
    NSManagedObject *asset = [assetList objectAtIndex:[ip row]];
    [countViewController setAsset:asset];

    [[self navigationController] pushViewController:countViewController
                                          animated:YES];
    // Will release countViewController in viewWillAppear: when it is popped
}
```

You will also need to import the header file at the top of `AssetListViewController.m`:

```
#import "CountViewController.h"
```

If the user returns from a **CountViewController**, take the input:

```
- (void)viewWillAppear:(BOOL)animated
{
    [super viewWillAppear:animated];

    // Am I coming back from the LabelSettingViewController?
    if (labelSettingViewController) {
        NSString *value = [labelSettingViewController value];
        if ([value length] > 0) {

            AppController *ac = [AppController sharedAppController];
            NSManagedObjectContext *moc = [ac managedObjectContext];
```

```
        NSManagedObject *newAsset =
                [NSEntityDescription insertNewObjectForEntityForName:@"Asset"
                                        inManagedObjectContext:moc];
        [newAsset setValue:value forKey:@"label"];
        [assetList addObject:newAsset];

        NSSortDescriptor *sd = [[NSSortDescriptor alloc] initWithKey:@"label"
                                                     ascending:YES];
        NSArray *sds = [NSArray arrayWithObject:sd];
        [sd release];
        [assetList sortUsingDescriptors:sds];
        [[self tableView] reloadData];
    }
    [labelSettingViewController release];
    labelSettingViewController = nil;
}

// Am I coming back from the CountViewController?
if (countViewController) {
    NSNumber *count = [countViewController count];
    if (count) {
        NSManagedObject *asset = [countViewController asset];
        NSManagedObject *inventory = [self inventoryForAsset:asset];

        if (!inventory) {
            AppController *ac = [AppController sharedAppController];
            NSManagedObjectContext *moc = [ac managedObjectContext];

            inventory = [NSEntityDescription
                            insertNewObjectForEntityForName:@"Inventory"
                                inManagedObjectContext:moc];

            [[asset mutableSetValueForKey:@"inventories"]
                                    addObject:inventory];
            // The inverse relationship is set automatically, thus this line:
            // [inventory setValue:asset forKey:@"asset"];
            // is unnecessary

            [[location mutableSetValueForKey:@"inventories"]
                                    addObject:inventory];
        }
        [inventory setValue:count forKey:@"count"];
        NSDate *now = [NSDate date];
        [inventory setValue:now forKey:@"date"];

        [[self tableView] reloadData];
    }
    [countViewController release];
    countViewController = nil;
}
NSIndexPath *selectedPath = [[self tableView] indexPathForSelectedRow];
if (selectedPath) {
    [[self tableView] deselectRowAtIndexPath:selectedPath animated:NO];
}
}
```

Be sure to import CountViewController.h at the top of the file!

Build and run the application. Nice, huh?

How It All Works

In the last chapter, you worked with SQLite directly. In this chapter, you used SQLite via Core Data. You might wonder what SQL commands Core Data is executing. Using private API, you can get Core Data to log its activities to the console. (While the SQL commands are interesting to see, the use of private API may cause this code to break one day. So do not ship an application that uses it.) Add to the **init** method in AppController.m:

```
- (id)init
{
    if (sharedInstance) {
        NSLog(@"Error: You are creating a second AppController");
    }
    [super init];
    sharedInstance = self;

        Class privateClass = NSClassFromString(@"NSSQLCore");
    // You will get a compiler warning here, ignore it
    [privateClass setDebugDefault:YES];

    return self;
}
```

Build and run the application again. Make sure the Debugger Console is visible so you can see the SQL logging. Add a few locations and inventory items; then navigate around the app looking at various items. Notice that managed objects are fetched in a lazy manner. This is done with *faults*.

A managed object can have a relationship to another entity, either to-one or to-many (recall that you created relationships for *your* managed objects earlier in this chapter in your Inventory.xcdatamodel file). If a managed object has such a relationship, when it is fetched, the objects at the other end of the relationship are *not* fetched. Instead fault objects are created. There are to-many faults (which stand in for sets) and to-one faults (which stand in for managed objects). So, for example, when the locations are fetched into your application, the instances of **Inventory** and **Asset** are not. The relationship inventories is represented by a to-many fault that is pretending to be a set (Figure 27.19).

Figure 27.19   Faults

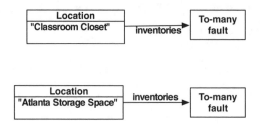

When you send a message to a set, it might actually be a fault, but luckily your code doesn't need to know or care about that. If the set is a fault, Core Data will fetch the objects for that relationship, as shown in Figure 27.20. (In practice, the message **count** usually triggers the to-many fault.)

Figure 27.20   Faults, part 2

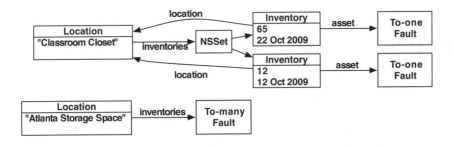

This lazy fetching makes Core Data not only easy to use, but also quite efficient.

Watch the SQL in the console and notice that the data is only saved to the SQLite file when you quit the application.

Trade-offs of Persistence Mechanisms

At this point, you have seen all the common ways that iPhone applications can store their data: archiving, web services, direct SQLite, and Core Data. Which is best for your application? Use Table 27.1 to help you decide.

Table 27.1. Data storage pros and cons

Technique	Pros	Cons
Archiving	Allows ordered relationships (arrays, not sets). Easy to deal with versioning.	Reads all the objects in (no faulting). No incremental updates.
Web Service	Makes it easy to share data with other devices and applications.	Requires a server and a connection to the internet.
SQLite	Can fetch lazily. Incremental updates. Full power of SQL.	Requires more code than archiving or Core Data. No real ordered relationships.
Core Data	Lazy fetches by default. Incremental updates.	Versioning is awkward (but can certainly be done using an **NSModelMapping**). No real ordered relationships. Much of the power of SQL is inaccessible.

Challenge 1: Deleting

Add deletion of assets or locations to the application. You will need to tell the managed object context to delete the object:

```
AppController *ac = [AppController sharedAppController];
NSManagedObjectContext *moc = [ac managedObjectContext];
[moc deleteObject:someObject];
```

Challenge 2: Custom NSManagedObject Subclasses

You may have noticed that you used the method **valueForKey:** many times. This can become awkward and error-prone in a large application. You can simplify this code by subclassing **NSManagedObject** to represent each of the entities you defined in your model. These subclasses will have @property declarations corresponding to the properties you created in the model editor, and you will replace code like this:

```
NSManagedObject *newAsset =
        [NSEntityDescription insertNewObjectForEntityForName:@"Asset"
                                    inManagedObjectContext:moc];
[newAsset setValue:value forKey:@"label"];
```

with direct accessor calls:

```
MyAsset *newAsset = [NSEntityDescription insertNewObjectForEntityForName:@"Asset"
                                                inManagedObjectContext:moc];
[newAsset setLabel:value];
```

Hint: Xcode will generate the .h and .m files for you.

28

Developing for the iPad

After revolutionizing personal computing and the mobile device, Apple has taken its game to tablet computing with the introduction of the iPad. Fortunately for you, the iPad runs iPhone OS. Writing an iPad application is nearly identical to writing an iPhone application — you will use the same classes and design patterns. However, there are a few minor differences that you should be aware of. This chapter will discuss those differences.

Throughout this chapter, we will refer to the iPad, iPhone, and iPhone OS. To clarify those terms: iPhone OS is the operating system that runs on the iPad, iPhone, and iPod touch; iPhone refers to both the iPhone and the iPod touch devices.

Universal Applications

When writing an application for iPhone OS, you can create two separate applications for the two devices (the iPad and the iPhone) or a single *universal application*. While you have the option of creating two applications and submitting them to the App Store independently, Apple recommends creating a universal application. A universal application runs on both the iPhone and iPad and is a single entry on the App Store, but it takes a bit more work to get it to run cleanly.

Porting existing projects to the iPad

An application built for the iPhone can be run on the iPad without any changes. However, it will run in an iPhone-sized window. If you wish for users to experience your application in all its glory on the iPad or take advantage of iPad-only features, you will need to upgrade your application to support the iPad. In this chapter, you will create a universal Wherewasi application. Open the Whereami.xcodeproj project that you created in Chapter 4. (Remember, we changed the name of the application to Wherewasi, but the project is still named Whereami.xcodeproj.)

In Whereami's project window, locate the Whereami target in the Targets group. Right- or Control-click the Whereami target and select Upgrade Current Target for iPad from the contextual menu that appears. (Figure 28.1). You will be prompted with a sheet that asks if you want a universal application or device-specific applications. Choose One Universal application and hit OK (Figure 28.2).

Figure 28.1   Upgrading to a universal application 1

Figure 28.2   Upgrading to a universal application 2

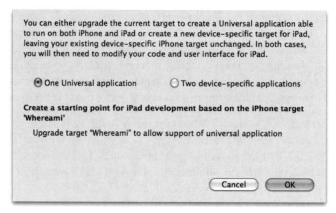

Two noticeable things will happen after upgrading the target: a Resources-iPad group
will appear in the project window and the Whereami-Info.plist will be updated. Open

Whereami-Info.plist (found in the Resources group of the project window). A new key has been added to the property list: Main nib file base name (iPad), and it has been set to MainWindow-iPad. Now, when this application is executed, the operating system will determine the device it is being run on and choose the correct NIB file to load.

In addition to these two changes, some of the build settings for your project will have changed. These changes are taken care of by Apple; you shouldn't try and set them manually.

Wherewasi now technically runs natively on the iPad, so build and run the application. Oh, gross! The interface is a disaster. Let's fix that.

Re-designing Wherewasi's interface

Check out the Resources-iPad group in the project window. Inside this group is a MainWindow-iPad.xib file, matching the name of the value for the Main nib file base name (iPad) key in the info property list. This is the NIB file that will get loaded when Wherewasi is launched on an iPad. Open this file in Interface Builder.

Double-click on the Window object to view it. This window is much larger than the window in the iPhone's MainWindow.xib, and your interface is scattered about the window. Resize the **MKMapView** so it spans the entire window. Reposition the **UITextField** and **UIActivityIndicator** near the top and in the center of the window, as shown in Figure 28.3.

Figure 28.3   Updated Wherewasi Interface

Save MainWindow-iPad.xib and exit Interface Builder. Yes, it was that simple. Build and run the application again to see your updated interface.

Want to make sure your iPhone interface still looks good? Select Set Active Executable from the Project menu and choose the iPhone option from the sub-menu that appears next to it. Build and run your application again to see the original iPhone application.

More considerations: universal view controllers

The previous section outlined the basic steps you must take to prepare a universal application. However, more complicated applications will require more changes. For instance, if your application has view controllers, you must load the correct view for the device your application is running on.

If your view controller is loading its view from a NIB file, you must create another NIB file that has a view configured for the larger window size. Stick with Apple's convention and suffix your iPad NIB files with -iPad. (MainWindow.xib and MainWindow-iPad.xib, for example.)

Also, within your view controller's **init** method, you will need to perform a run-time check to see which NIB file to load. Here is the point where you get excited that we taught you to override the designated initializer for your **UIViewController**s to **init** and determine the NIB file to load from within that method. A view controller in a universal application will take advantage of the **userInterfaceIdiom** property of **UIDevice** to determine which NIB file to load in its **init** method. Here is an example:

```
@implementation MyUniversalViewController
- (id)init
{
    NSString *nibFileToLoad = @"MyUniversalViewController";
    // If the device is an iPad, suffix the nibFileToLoad with "-iPad"
    UIDevice *device = [UIDevice currentDevice];
    if([device userInterfaceIdiom] == UIUserInterfaceIdiomPad)
        nibFileToLoad = [nibFileToLoad stringByAppendingString:@"-iPad"];

    // Extra initialization goes here

    return [super initWithNibName:nibFileToLoad bundle:nil];
}
@end
```

New iPad Stuff

iPad applications have a few more classes to work with than their itty-bitty predecessors. As of this writing, these classes are only available on the iPad. Time will tell if these new classes will become available on the iPhone. Some of the more important classes are:

- **NSAttributedString**: Strings can now have different attributes that change their look. Attributes are things like bold, italic, colors, alignment, and other things that make up rich text.

- **UISplitViewController**: This class is a replacement or supplement for navigation controllers. In a way, it is a navigation controller that fits multiple views on the screen at once.

- **UIGestureRecognizer** (and subclasses): These classes will perform gesture recognition (like pinch-pull or rotate) for you so you won't have to implement your own technique in the various **UIResponder** methods.

- Core Text: The text editing APIs from the desktop have made their way to the iPad. You can write your very own text editor!

All of the concepts and classes you have learned in this book leave you more than prepared to use these new features. Check out the documentation to add these new classes to your toolkit. And always remember, just because a feature is new doesn't mean you have to use it.

For more information about developing for the iPad, check out the iPad Programming Guide in the developer documentation.

Index

Symbols

Index